116/94

THE NEW URBAN SOCIOLOGY

Mark Gottdiener

Consulting Editor:
Craig Calhoun
The University of North Carolina, Chapel Hill

McGraw-Hill, Inc.
New York   St. Louis   San Francisco   Auckland   Bogotá
Caracas   Lisbon   London   Madrid   Mexico City   Milan
Montreal   New Delhi   San Juan   Singapore   Sydney
Tokyo   Toronto

THE NEW URBAN SOCIOLOGY

Acknowledgments appear on pages 357–358 and on this page by reference.

 This book is printed on recycled, acid-free paper containing
10% postconsumer waste.

2 3 4 5 6 7 8 9 0 DOC   DOC 9 0 9 8 7 6 5 4

ISBN 0-07-023912-6

This book was set in Times Roman by Monotype Composition Company.
The editors were Phillip A. Butcher and Bob Greiner;
the production supervisor was Paula Keller.
The cover was designed by A Good Thing, Inc.
The photo editor was Elyse Rieder.
R. R. Donnelley & Sons Company was printer and binder.

Library of Congress Cataloging-in-Publication Data

Gottdiener, Mark.
     The new urban sociology / Mark Gottdiener.
          p.   cm.
     Includes bibliographical references and index.
     ISBN 0-07-023912-6
          1. Metropolitan areas—United States   2. Suburbs—United States.
     3. Suburban life—United States.   4. Urbanization—United States—
     History.   5. Sociology, Urban—United States.   I. Title.
     HT334.U5G657   1994
     307.76'0973—dc20   93-23576

ABOUT THE AUTHOR

Mark Gottdiener is Professor of Sociology at the University of California, Riverside. He is the author/editor of eight books, including *The Social Production of Urban Space* and *Planned Sprawl: Private and Public Interest in Suburbia.* Translations of his work are used in several countries. His main interests are urban sociology, contemporary social theory, and the semiotics of culture.

For Jennifer, Felix, and Zev

CONTENTS

Preface   xiii

Chapter 1: The New Urban Sociology   1

Defining the Metropolitan Region   7
Megacities around the World   8
A New Approach to Urban Sociology   11

    Global Capitalism and the Metropolis   11
    Pull Factors and the Political Economy of Real Estate 13
    The Importance of Culture in Metropolitan Life   14

Summary: The Socio-Spatial Approach   16
The Plan of the Book   17

Chapter 2: The Origins of Urbanization and the Characteristics of Cities   19

Classical Cities: Athens, Rome, and Beijing   22
Ancient Urbanization   26
Urbanization after A.D. 1000   28
Capitalism and the Rise of the Industrial City   31

• Box 2.1   Some Classical Writings about Conquered Cities   21
• Box 2.2   Two Poets View the City   35

Chapter 3: Urbanization in the United States   37

The Stages of Urban Growth   37

    The Colonial Period: 1630 to 1812   38
    The Era of Expansion: 1812 to 1920   44

• Box 3.1   Case Study of Colonial Philadelphia   45
• Box 3.2   The Tenement Circa 1860s   49
• Box 3.3   A Case Study: Chicago in the Nineteenth Century   51

Chapter 4: The Metropolitan Period in the United States: 1920 to 1960

57

Spatial, Functional and Demographic Differentiation of the City	58
Changes in Spatial Differentiation	59
Changes in Functional Differentiation	61
Changes in Demographic Differentiation	64
Suburbanization and Regional Maturation	65
The Pattern of U.S. Urbanization: A Summary	73
• Box 4.1 New York City in the Metropolitan Period	63
• Box 4.2 Profile of 1950s Levittown, Long Island	70

Chapter 5: The Restructuring of Settlement Space: 1960 to 1990

75

How Cities Have Changed: Deindustrialization and Deconcentration	76
Economic and Social Restructuring	77
How Suburbs Have Changed	82
Push and Pull Factors in Suburbanization	83
Suburban Social Characteristics	84
Economic Deconcentration	86
Beyond Suburbia: The Multinucleated Region	89
The Shift to the Sunbelt	90
Push and Pull Factors in Sunbelt Development	96
Recent Sunbelt Trends	97
• Box 5.1 Plant Closures at Youngstown, Ohio	78

Chapter 6: The Rise of Urban Sociology

101

Simmel on the City	103
The Chicago School: Park, Burgess, and McKenzie	105
The Chicago School: Louis Wirth	110
The Chicago School: Other Considerations	113
Contemporary Urban Ecology	115
An Example: The Timing of Suburbanization	118
• Box 6.1 Wirth's Propositions	113
• Box 6.2 Case Study: Gangland Chicago, 1927	116

Chapter 7: Contemporary Urban Sociology: The Sociospatial Approach

121

Political Economy and the City	122
Marx, Weber, and Engels	122
Uneven Development	124

The Revival of Urban Political Economy: Henri Lefebvre   125
Class Conflict Theories: Gordon, Storper and Walker, and Castells   128
Class Accumulation Theories: Harvey and Scott   132

Recent Sociological Approaches   138

The Growth Machine   138
The Sociospatial Perspective: Real Estate and Government Intervention   139
The Global Economy   144

Summary   145

• Box 7.1   David Harvey's Case Study of Baltimore   133

Chapter 8: People, Lifestyles, and the Metropolis 147

Class Differences and Spatial Location   147

Class Stratification in the United States   147
The Wealthy   148
Yuppies, Dinks, and the Suburban Middle Class   152
The Working Class, the Working Poor, and the Underclass   154

Women, Gender Roles, and Space   156

Women and the Urban Political Economy   158
Women and the Environment   163

Ethnicity and Immigration   164

First Wave   165
Second Wave   165
Theories of Immigrant Adjustment   166
Third Wave   170

Summary   174

• Box 8.1   The Philadelphia Gentlemen   150
• Box 8.2   The Urban Upscale Lifestyle   155
• Box 8.3   The Middle Class Suburban Lifestyle   157
• Box 8.4   The Working Class at Home in Cities and Suburbs   158
• Box 8.5   The Ghettoized Poor   161
• Box 8.6   Spatial Segregation and Ethnicity   167
• Box 8.7   Ethnic Suburbs   172

Chapter 9: Neighborhoods, the Public Environment, and Theories of Urban Life 175

Does Space Affect Behavior? The Search for Community   177

Field Research on Community   178
Network Analysis: Does Location Matter?   180

Does Space Affect Behavior? A New Theory of Urbanism   182

The Sociospatial Approach to Metropolitan Culture   182
Mental Maps and the Semiotics of Place   184

Behavior in Public Space   188
Neighboring and Community   191

Types of Neighborhoods and Community Interaction   194
Summary   197

• Box 9.1   Field Work Methodology   179
• Box 9.2   Network Analysis   181
• Box 9.3   Questionnaire and Interview Method   185
• Box 9.4   The Method of Mental Maps   186
• Box 9.5   Swaddling Shoppers: A Mall's Cocoon Effect   189

Chapter 10: Metropolitan Problems: Poverty, Racism, Crime, Housing, and Fiscal Crisis   199

The Antiurban Bias   200
Theories of Urban Problems   200

Wirthian Theory   201
Compositional Approach   201
Subcultural View   201
The Sociospatial Perspective   201

Racism and Poverty   203

Racism   203
Poverty   207
Economic Restructuring and the Problems of the Poor   208
Poverty and Race   208

Crime and Drugs   211

Crime   211
Why Crime Is an Urban Problem: Its Costs   215
Crime and Drugs   215
Suburban Crime   217

The Fiscal Crisis and Public Service Problems   217

Fiscal Crisis   218
Social Service Cutbacks: Education, Infrastructure   219

Housing   222

Suburban Inequities   222
Homelessness   223

Summary   225

Chapter 11: Local Politics: City and Suburban Governments   227

The Machine   228
Progressive Reforms   230

Theories of Local Politics   231

Pluralist Theory   232
Elite Theory   232
State Managerialism   233
Which View Is Correct?   234

The Drama of Local Politics   235

Empowerment: Ethnic and Racial Changes   235
Social Movements   236
Suburban Social Movements   237

The Declining Power of Local Politics   244
Summary   246

• Box 11.1   The Struggle for Black Empowerment: The Case of
New York City   238
• Box 11.2   The Campaign for Welfare Rights   240

Chapter 12: Third World Urbanization   249

Changing Perspectives on Third World Urbanization   249
Demography and Third World Urbanization   253
Primate City Development Patterns   255
Shantytown Development   256
The Informal Economy and Coping Strategies   257
Urban Social Movements and Politics   259
Patterns of Third World Urbanization   261

Latin America   261
Asia   263
Africa and the Arab Countries   268

Summary   269

• Box 12.1   Lagos, Nigeria   251
• Box 12.2   Singapore   267

Chapter 13: Urbanization in the Industrialized World: Western and Eastern Europe and Japan   271

Western Europe   271

Great Britain   273
Italy   275
France   276
Germany   278
Spain   280

Eastern Europe   281
   Central City Decline   282
   The Demographic Pattern of Land Use   282
   Housing Shortage   283
   The Emergence of Free Markets   284
Japan   284
Summary   288
• Box 13.1   Paris and Culture   277
• Box 13.2   Tokyo   287

Chapter 14: Environmental Issues and Metropolitan Planning   291

Environmental Quality   293
Metropolitan Planning   296
Planning in the United States   297
The Sociology of Land Use Planning   298
   Physicalist Fallacy   299
   Elitist/Populist Dilemma   299
Utopian Schemes: Howard, Le Corbusier, and Wright   301
Planning Critics: Jacobs, Krier, and the Goodmans   307
Trends in Planning Today   309
Summary   311
• Box 14.1   The Case of Bellevue, Washington   300

Chapter 15: Metropolitan Social Policy and the Future of Urban Sociology   315

The Tragedy of the Commons and Uneven Development   315
   The Tragedy of the Commons   316
   Uneven Development and Policy: Redistributive Programs 317
Urban and Metropolitan Policy   319
   Support for: Slum Removal   320
   Support for: Economic Development   324
   Support for: Global Competition   325
Privatism and Issues of Social Justice   327
   Lack of Community Benefits from Public Investment 328
   Lack of Economic Return on Public Investment   329
   Fostering of Cutthroat Competition   329
   The Decline of Democracy in Local Politics   330
Urban Policy: The Political Debate   331
   Liberal Positions on Urban Problems   331
   Conservative Approaches to Urban Problems   331
   Overcoming the Liberal/Conservative Impasse   332

Future Prospects 334

 Future Prospects of the Metropolis 334
 The Future of the Urban Inquiry 338

- Box 15.1 The Case of Public Housing 322
- Box 15.2 The World Trade Towers 326

Bibliography 341

Acknowledgments 357

Index 359

PREFACE

When I was in graduate school I was introduced to urban sociology by a well-known field researcher, David Street, and became passionately committed to the discipline. It seemed to me that urban sociology offered everything that was attractive about sociology. It required an interdisciplinary understanding of economics, politics, and culture. It was concerned with the reality of everyday life and how people lived. It possessed great themes of immigrant adjustment, neighborhood relations, the nurturing of friendships, the raising of families, community ties, active and exciting politics, economic changes, the making and losing of fortunes, the burden and benefits of work, the dependency of daily life on the environment, the shadow of crime, murder, muggings, and the dark side of human existence. As a graduate student I was eager to learn about it all. From my experience I came to an understanding that remains at the core of my work: Urbanists should be interested in actual reality. We should be inspired by daily life and be able to explain it in its full complexity even if abstraction and theory are also important concerns.

When I was in graduate school I also learned about the theory of urban ecology, because that was the only explanatory paradigm taught at U.S. universities. My dissertation work, a comprehensive study of the development of Long Island (a suburban region adjacent to New York City), later became my first book (1977). While revising this material, it became increasingly clear to me that the urban ecological paradigm was inadequate as an explanatory framework for the changes occurring in the United States since 1950. My great dissatisfaction with mainstream urban sociology and my passionate interest in explaining the patterns of development I had observed led me to reconceptualize the field.

Over the last decade I have devoted myself to introducing new ideas about the role of economics (1985), politics (1986), and culture (1986) in urban analysis. This effort culminated in a new kind of urban theory (1985) and a new paradigm for the discipline (Gottdiener and Feagin, 1988). My work joined the efforts of others (Lefebvre, 1974; Castells, 1977; Harvey, 1973; Pickvance, 1977) in what has come to be called The New Urban Sociology.

Over the last decade I have also devoted myself to the teaching of urban sociology. The discontent that plagued my research also limited my ability to instruct my students in the understanding of contemporary life. Slowly and laboriously I began to frame specific concepts and arguments that I felt improved the approach of urban sociology. This text represents the culmination of my long effort over several decades.

The central organizing concepts of this text were devised in response to the limitations of other textbooks in the field. Without exception, urban sociologists, for example, focus principally on the large central city as an object of analysis. Suburban considerations may be treated, but they usually are reserved for a chapter buried somewhere in the discourse. This bias distorts reality. In the United States the majority of people live in suburbs, not in large, central cities. This text, therefore, presents a balanced account of metropolitan life and focuses on the entire metropolitan region, including cities, suburbs, recreational areas, small towns, industrial parks, malls, and highways. Each chapter presents as much about what I call the *multicentered* metropolitan region as about the large, central city.

A second feature of this book also grew out of my response to the limitations of other texts. Often discussions about the nature of urban development are biased in favor of economic accounts. I believe all environments function because they are *meaningful* spaces and that cultural considerations play a significant role in metropolitan life. This text seeks to demonstrate these relationships without bias toward a single factor. I have aimed for a balanced view of economic, political, and cultural considerations in the study of metropolitan development.

Often, texts are written as a series of disconnected chapters reporting facts about one topic after another without providing an overarching vision. This book is an exception. While it is perhaps impossible to escape the need to survey many topics that seem to possess little connection, the new urban sociology is an integrated paradigm of thinking about metropolitan life. My version of this approach, the *sociospatial* perspective, pervades each chapter. Its basic premise is that spatial or environmental and locational considerations are always part and parcel of social relations. We cannot talk about one without also talking about the latter. The sociospatial perspective is not urban ecology, although it also stresses the role of location in social relations. Unlike ecology, explanation does not follow biological principles and the drama of development cannot be reduced to the effects of technological change alone. In contrast, the socio-spatial perspective is a synthesis of environmental considerations and the factors of class, race, gender, lifestyle, economics, culture, and politics in the development of metropolitan regions. Each chapter borrows from this thematic perspective to present discussions of specific topics ranging from crime to third-world development and, when possible, makes comparative distinctions.

The goal of this text is not just to be innovative but to be up-to-date. Its chapter topics are the same as those found in other urban texts. The fruits of discontent with the outdated mainstream perspective are realized in the execution of the material. When discussing the development of ancient cities, for example, cultural and political considerations are considered as important as economic ones. In addition, the urban history of the United States is presented as high drama involving fortunes made through real estate speculation as much as through industry. It is as important to know the nature of suburban as well as city crime, just as social problems are best understood as metropolitan and regional concerns rather than being the exclusive product of city living. The diversity of daily life requires the full spectrum of race, class, and gender considerations for its discussion. And, lastly, when we turn our attention to metropolitan policy and the environment, we want to know *why* programs fail, *what* ideologies govern metropolitan growth, and *how* we can improve metropolitan life.

There are some chapters, however, that are contained in this text that depart somewhat from the typical fare of other presentations. I consider the metropolitan changes occurring in the United States since 1960 so unique that I have devoted a separate chapter to their discussion. Furthermore, in the chapters on urban history and contemporary development, it is necessary to take a global perspective and provide comparative material. In addition to a chapter on the third world, which is now standard in urban texts, I have added a new discussion of changes in Europe and Japan. Finally, unlike most urban sociology texts, this book has a separate chapter on metropolitan politics and another one on metropolitan policy and the environment. Both are important for an understanding of how people manage and how to make better the space of everyday life.

The writing of this text was an extended project stretching over many years. It could not have been done without the crucial help provided by a number of people. I wish to thank friends in academia for their support—Joe Feagin, Bob Antonio, Ray Hutchison, Nestor Rodriguez, Bob Parker, David Diaz, Eric Monkkonen, Leonard Wallock, and Peter Muller in the United States; Phil Gunn, Lena Lavinas, Sandra Lincioni, and Sueli Schiffer in Brazil; Alexandros Lagopoulos and Nikos Komninos in Greece; Chris Pickvance and Desmond King in England; Dorel Abraham in Romania; and Jens Tonboe in Denmark.

I was most fortunate to have McGraw-Hill as a publisher because of the pleasant and supportive relationship it nurtures with the authors. The writing of this text would not have been possible without the extensive help of Sylvia Shepard and the support of Phil Butcher as editors. Melissa Mashburn and Bob Greiner also provided invaluable guidance in production, and Safra Nimrod and Elyse Reider supplied the photos. Here at the University of California, Riverside, Yvette Samson worked on the testbank.

Thanks are also due to the reviewers of this text: Brian Aldrich, Winona State University; Craig Calhoun, University of North Carolina, Chapel Hill; Robert L. Carroll, University of Cincinnati; George Kephart, Pennsylvania State University; Jerry Lembcke, College of the Holy Cross; Nestor Rodriguez, University of Houston; Thomas Shannon, Radford University; Steven L. Vassar, Mankato State University; and J. Talmadge Wright, Loyola University.

Finally, as any writer of texts quickly learns, the long working hours and need for concentration can interfere with family life. I am very fortunate to have an understanding and supportive family. My wife Jennifer and my two boys, Felix and Zev, have been very patient with me. It is to them that I dedicate this book.

Mark Gottdiener

1

THE NEW URBAN SOCIOLOGY

It is morning across the United States, and people have brushed off sleep and prepared themselves for the day. While most Americans live within metropolitan regions, they meet their circumstances in different ways. Using composite types constructed from case studies, newspaper or magazine stories, and personal observations, here are several examples of everyday life:

Larry Worthington lives in Costa Mesa, a section of Orange County, California, adjacent to Los Angeles. He is a lawyer and works for the county in another town, Santa Ana. Larry is married and has two children and a pet dog. Both he and his wife work. They own a house, two cars, and a small boat which they occasionally take sailing on weekends. The Worthingtons' combined income is over $100,000 a year, yet they are not affluent. Their housing costs alone amount to $30,000 a year, because housing in Orange County is very expensive. Car payments and maintenance add several more thousand in bills, but life would not be possible without an automobile in Southern California. Because both of the Worthingtons work, they must pay for after-school day care for their children—another expense of several thousand a year. When all costs are added up, this family cannot meet every obligation and so the Worthingtons end each year in debt.

On this typical morning Larry is stuck in the expected, everyday lineup of cars on the freeway. His twenty-mile commute to work takes him an average of 1½ hours each way. He has plenty of time to consider his looming debts as well as the daily needs of his job while waiting for the stop-and-go traffic to advance a few more inches along the road. He tries to focus on music from the car stereo.

Or:

Esther Hernandez wakes up every morning around five o'clock with the first sounds of advancing traffic. She can't help it. She lives outdoors on a subway grate located on the corner of 40th Street and Lexington Avenue in Manhattan. Esther is homeless. When she first came to New York from the Dominican Republic she found work in the garment center as a sewing machine operator. With the opportunity for piecework (a kind of overtime) she was able to afford an apartment in the South Bronx.

Several years ago she lost her job when the company she worked for declared bankruptcy. Due to the decline in garment manufacturing within New York City, she has been unable to find another job since that time. For a while she collected unemployment insurance and when that ran out, she thought about going on welfare. Last March her building in the South Bronx burned down. She lives now on the street with all her possessions piled into a shopping cart. She has already been raped twice. As winter sets in she thinks about going back to the Dominican Republic, but then she remembers that her family sent her to New York because there were no jobs at home. "Maybe things are better there now," she wonders.

Or:

Dave, Sean, Felix, and Hakim are playing free video games at the Nintendo booth in a mall located in Gwinnett County outside of Atlanta. It's a half hour after high school began, but few people notice that the boys should be elsewhere. They've already spent well over one hour playing games at the video arcade. Few adults bother to look in there, and the arcade itself is tucked away on one of the more isolated arms of the giant mall. It's a perfect place to hang out while the school day is still on.

Dave, Sean, Felix, and Hakim are good friends. They were born and brought up in the affluent suburban area outside the city of Atlanta. Children of privilege, they still have their complaints. Above all else they are terribly bored. They do not have enough exciting things to do. Every Friday, in the early evening, they pile into one of their cars and drive to Peachtree Plaza in downtown Atlanta. It's very much like their own mall at home, only bigger and constructed underground. There is more crime to worry about at Peachtree. The girls that hang out there are cuter and more sophisticated, too, say the quartet. The boys don't always know what to expect, and that makes it exciting.

Or:

Nancy Wright and her husband, Irv, live in Chicago. They've been married for less than a year. Nancy and Irv met in college at Northwestern and, having dated for three years, were married after graduation. Nancy has a job she likes at a branch of the public library. She majored in library science and considers herself lucky to have found a permanent position so soon after graduating. Irv also likes what he does. He's a manager for a well-known department store in town. He majored in business administration and also considers himself fortunate to have a job. Irv and Nancy have more money than they spend. In fact, they are saving up to buy a house. Right now they rent. As part of their budget plan, they've decided not to purchase a car. Irv takes the elevated train to work. He worries about being mugged. Usually he wears a beat-up trench coat over a nice suit and he abandons the coat as soon as he gets to work.

He also carries his good pair of shoes in a bag and wears sneakers for the train ride. It gives him a sense of security to know he can run when he needs to. His wife, Nancy, was mugged once on her way home from work. One winter evening when it was already quite dark, a young man grabbed her less than a block from her apartment and held a knife to her throat. She gave him her purse, but then he started to drag her into the bushes next to an apartment building. Nancy thinks he was going to rape her. Luckily, two men from the next building came out and saw what was happening. The mugger fled and she was saved.

On this particular morning both Nancy and Irv leave for work with a similar knot inside their stomachs—hoping that no violent incident will mar the day. They think about the future and the need to leave the city, especially because they want to start a family soon. Lately, housing prices in the good suburbs have become quite high, and it will take them longer to save than they had once hoped. But they feel confident they'll get there. As they settle into their respective commutes, they think about what their suburban home might look like and the kind of furniture that they will need.

The suburb, the city, the affluent and the poor, young and old, male and female, black and white—our metropolitan regions are the scene of many contrasts, of complex lives being lived in intricate social and physical surroundings. Not everything is obvious. Thoughts betray the difficult choices and contending forces that structure what we see. Daily routines encompass an incredible variety of jobs, housing choices, leisure activities, hopes, dreams, nightmares. This profile and the characteristic stories we have just read are merely suggestive of what we all must experience within the urbanized regions in the United States and in an increasing number of countries around the globe. It's a street-level view and a highly personalized one. What does the metropolis, which is made up of countless people like the Worthingtons, Esther Hernandez, and the Wrights, look like from the air? How do the lives of so many other people mesh together as an urban mosaic visible to some bird's eye?

If we flew over our metropolitan regions, we would be struck most strongly by the immensity of scale. Urbanized development characteristically extends for 100 miles around our largest cities. The built-up region contains a mix of cities, suburbs, vacant space, intensely farmed agricultural land, malls, and recreational areas—all of which are interconnected and bridged by communication and commuter networks including highways, rail, telecommunications, and satellite or cellular based links. Figure 1.1 shows the regional extent of development.

The population of these areas characteristically ranks in the millions. Interestingly enough, most of the people residing in metropolitan regions live *outside* the large central cities and in the suburbs. They have lived that way in the United States since at least the 1970s when this change was brought to our attention by census figures. At present 86 percent of all Americans live in metropolitan regions. This pattern of urban growth was not characteristic of cities in the past.

Cities used to be highly compact spatial forms with a distinct center that dominated in both an emotional and economic sense the urbanized area surrounding it. Once inhabitants went outside the city, they would be surrounded by countryside. As the famous urban historian, Lewis Mumford (1961), once observed, cities served as both

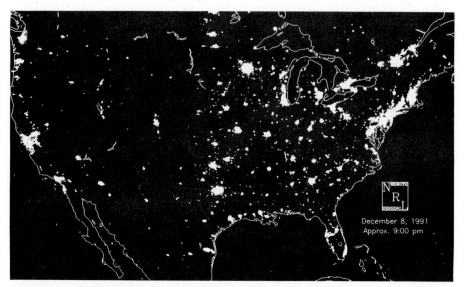

Figure 1.1   Satellite image of United States at night. Note the difference in settlement density between the west and the rest of the country.

The sprawling metropolitan region of the city of San Francisco with Marin County to the north.

TABLE 1.1
Ten Most Populated U.S. Cities, 1980–1990

City	Population 1990	Population 1980	Percentage of change 1980–1990
New York City, NY	7,322,564	7,071,639	3.5
Los Angeles, CA	3,485,398	2,966,850	17.5
Chicago, IL	2,783,726	3,005,072	−7.4
Houston, TX	1,630,553	1,595,138	2.2
Philadelphia, PA	1,585,577	1,688,210	−6.1
San Diego, CA	1,110,549	875,538	26.8
Detroit, MI	1,027,974	1,203,339	−14.6
Dallas, TX	1,006,877	904,078	11.4
Phoenix, AZ	983,403	789,704	24.5
San Antonio, TX	935,933	785,880	19.1

Source: *Census of Population and Housing, 1990.* U.S. Department of Commerce, Bureau of the Census, Summary Tape, File 1C (CD-Rom); *Census of Population, Characteristics of the Population, Number of Inhabitants, U.S.* U.S. Department of Commerce, Bureau of the Census, Summary, Table 27.

huge magnets and containers which concentrated people and economic activities or wealth within well-defined, bounded spaces. Table 1.1 lists the ten most populated cities in the United States. While some of the figures are impressive, such as a total of over 7 million or 3½ million for New York City and Los Angeles, respectively, they do not illustrate the massive regional growth of metropolitan areas and their population concentration in the United States. Compare this table with Table 1.2, which indicates the metropolitan regions associated with these large cities. The New York metro region, for example, contains almost 18 million people, while the area around Los Angeles is home to 14.5 million residents.

Today the city has exploded. There is no one focus or "downtown," as there was in the past. People live and work in widely separated realms. Most of the population is urban, so most live in or near some city. But, progressively fewer people each year live within the large central cities that were the population foci of the past. Instead, we now call home the expanding regions of urbanization that are associated with a mix of cities, towns, suburbs, and exurban areas. This new form of settlement space is called the *multinucleated metropolitan region,* and it is the first really new way people have organized their living and working arrangements in 10,000 years. In contrast to the characteristics of the bounded city, the new form of space can be typified by two features: it extends over a large region and it contains many separate centers, each with its own abilities to draw workers, shoppers, and residents (see Table 1.2).

Some geographers, for example, have also begun to speak of multinucleated metropolitan regions. According to Peter Muller (1981), these areas can be understood best as composed of different *realms.* Realms are differentiated according to four factors: physical terrain, physical size, the level and kinds of physical activity within the realm (most particularly the kinds of minicenters), and the character of the regional transportation network. Commuting flows are particularly critical to multinucleation on a regional scale.

For example, Los Angeles contains six distinct realms within a region of approxi-

TABLE 1.2
Twenty Most Populated Metropolitan Areas

Area	1990	1980	1970	1960	Percentage of change, 1980–1990	Percentage of change, 1970–1980	Percentage of change, 1960–1970
New York-No. New Jersey-Long Island, NY-So. Conn., NY-NJ-CT CMSA/NECMA	17,953,372	17,412,203	18,071,522	16,174,478	3.1	-3.6	11.7
Los Angeles-Anaheim-Riverside, CA CMSA	14,531,529	11,497,549	9,980,850	7,751,616	26.4	15.2	28.8
Chicago-Gary-Lake County, IL-IN-WI CMSA	8,065,633	7,973,290	7,778,948	6,934,966	1.6	2.0	12.2
San Francisco-Oakland-San Jose, CA CMSA	6,253,311	5,367,900	4,754,366	3,723,158	16.5	12.9	27.7
Philadelphia-Wilmington-Trenton, PA-NJ-DE-MD CMSA	5,899,345	5,680,509	5,749,093	5,130,704	3.9	-1.2	12.1
Detroit-Ann Arbor, MI CMSA	4,665,236	4,762,764	4,788,369	4,223,280	-1.8	-.7	13.4
Washington, DC-MD-VA MSA	3,923,574	3,250,921	3,040,307	2,213,814	20.7	6.9	37.3
Dallas-Fort Worth, TX CMSA	3,885,415	2,930,568	2,351,568	1,715,505	32.6	24.6	37.1
Boston-Lawrence-Salem-Lowell-Brockton, MA NECMA	3,783,817	3,662,888	3,709,642	3,357,607	3.3	-1.3	10.5
Houston-Galveston-Brazoria, TX NECMA	3,711,043	3,099,942	2,169,128	1,570,758	19.7	42.9	38.1
Miami-Ft. Lauderdale, FL CMSA	3,192,582	2,643,766	1,887,892	1,268,993	20.8	40.0	48.8
Atlanta, GA MSA	2,833,511	2,138,136	1,684,200	1,247,829	32.5	27.0	35.0
Cleveland-Akron-Lorain, OH CMSA	2,759,823	2,834,062	2,999,811	2,732,350	-2.6	-5.5	9.8
Seattle-Tacoma, WA CMSA	2,559,164	2,093,285	1,836,949	1,428,803	22.3	14.0	28.6
San Diego, CA MSA	2,498,016	1,861,846	1,357,854	1,033,011	34.2	37.4	31.4
Minneapolis-St. Paul, MN-WI MSA	2,464,124	2,137,133	1,981,951	1,611,345	15.3	7.8	23.0
St. Louis, MO-IL MSA	2,444,099	2,376,968	2,429,376	2,161,228	2.8	-2.2	12.4
Baltimore, MD MSA	2,382,172	2,199,497	2,089,438	1,820,314	8.3	5.3	14.8
Pittsburgh-Beaver Valley, PA CMSA	2,242,798	2,423,311	2,556,029	2,574,775	-8.0	-5.4	-.7
Phoenix, AZ MSA	2,122,101	1,509,175	971,228	663,510	40.6	55.4	46.4

Note: MSAs are metropolitan statistical areas; CMSAs are consolidated metropolitan statistical areas; NECMAs are New England consolidated metropolitan areas, which are based on townships and require a separate way of aggregating areas in the metropolitan region.
Source: State and Metropolitan Area Data Book 1991. U.S. Department of Commerce, Economics and Statistics Administration, Bureau of the Census, Table 2; *State and Metropolitan Area Data Book 1986.* U.S. Department of Commerce, Economics and Statistics Administration, Bureau of the Census, Table A.

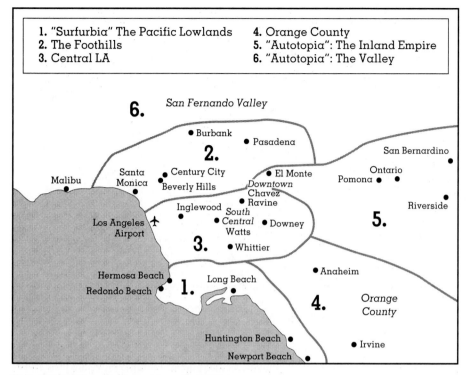

1. "Surfurbia" The Pacific Lowlands   4. Orange County
2. The Foothills   5. "Autotopia": The Inland Empire
3. Central LA   6. "Autotopia": The Valley

Figure 1.2   The realms of Los Angeles.

mately fifty square miles and a metro population in 1990 of 14,531,529. Development
is sandwiched between several mountain ranges, especially the long escarpment created
by the San Gabriel and San Bernardino mountains to the north which runs all the way
east over 100 miles into the desert. On the west coast is the Pacific Ocean, another
barrier. The six realms are central Los Angeles (the old city center), the San Fernando
Valley (the "valley"), Pacific foothills (Santa Monica to Pasadena), Pacific lowlands
(beach cities—Hermosa, Redondo Beach), eastern Orange County (a separate metropolitan region that is exclusively suburban), and finally, the San Gabriel and Pomona
Valleys (extending eastward and including Pomona, Ontario, and San Bernardino)—
see Figure 1.2.

Defining the Metropolitan Region

As early as the 1940s, census takers attempted to capture regional and multicentered
growth. They devised the term *Standard Metropolitan Area* (SMA), which included a
city of at least 50,000 and its surrounding suburbs within the county. This concept
was changed again in 1959 to the current one, the *Standard Metropolitan Statistical
Area* (SMSA), when it was recognized that regional growth had spread across counties.
By the 1980s this concept was shortened to the term *Metropolitan Statistical Area*

(MSA). The MSA is composed of at least one large city of 50,000, along with its county and all surrounding counties that are linked economically with it. The latter link is determined by measuring the extent to which people in outlying counties travel to work to the designated MSA. If enough people commute to work from outside city boundaries, the county they reside in becomes part of the MSA. While the number of MSAs in the United States continues to grow (as of the 1990 census there were 254), there are still two states, Wyoming and Vermont, which do not contain any (see Table 1.2 on page 6).

In the 1970s it was recognized that regional growth and the sociospatial integration of cities was more extensive than the links captured by the MSA concept. A new term was devised, the *Standard Metropolitan Consolidated Area* (SMCA). The SMCA was used for the first time in the 1980 census and does not do away with the MSA. It represents a higher order of integration for metropolitan areas that contain *several* MSAs, such as the Los Angeles/Orange County/Riverside/San Bernardino complex in Southern California or the New York/New Jersey/Connecticut complex on the east coast. Both of these regions contain more people than the entire country of Canada. At present there are seventeen SMCAs in the United States (see Table 1.2). They are prime illustrations of the concept of *metropolitan region* which is so important to this text.

Table 1.2 reveals some interesting aspects of metropolitan growth. First, there are a significant number of areas that have large populations, rather than only one or two (see Chapter 12 on primate cities). Second, when compared with Table 1.1 we can see that while some cities have large populations, their metropolitan regions are proportionately more populated. Philadelphia had a population in 1990 of over 1.5 million, but its metro region was more than three times that size, or 5.9 million; Phoenix's 1990 population was less than one million, but its metro region contained over 2 million people. Third, many regions of the northeast or midwest either grew slowly or lost population since the 1970s, while regions of the south and southwest grew rapidly. This illustrates the Sunbelt shift discussed in chapters 5 and 7. For example, the Detroit region declined by 1.8 percent and Cleveland by 2.6 percent, while the Los Angeles region grew by 26.4 percent and Phoenix by 40.6 percent between 1980 and 1990.

Megacities Around the World

Not every country of the world is experiencing the new form of space, that is, multicentered metropolitan growth, but all countries seem to be subject to a process of urban development which produces gigantic cities and regional urbanization. According to Dogan and Kasarda (1988) only 78 metropolises across the globe had populations of 1 million or more in 1950. By 1985 there were 258. Among these, 42 had more than 4 million population, 56 had between 2 and 4 million, 158 had between 1 and 2 million and 300 had between 1/2 and 1 million. By the year 2010 it is estimated that there will be 511 metropolises across the globe with populations exceeding 1 million. By the year 2005 we will already experience a world urbanization of half the entire population. Growth of these regions is also expected to accelerate. By the year 2025

Note similarity in skyscraper construction between New York City (above) and Hong Kong (below).

it is estimated that there will be 135 giant urbanized regions with populations of over
4 million. They alone will contain over 1.26 billion people by the year 2025, as
compared with a population of just 88 million in 1950. Table 1.3 indicates the twenty
largest *megacities* in the world with their projected populations to the year 2000.

According to Table 1.3 it is expected that the megametropolises of the United
States and Western Europe will lose population or grow slowly, while megaregions
elsewhere will experience explosive growth. Thus, the population estimates for the
year 2000 for London and Essen project declines from 1990 levels, while New York
City, Los Angeles, and Paris are expected to experience slow growth. In contrast,
however, Mexico City, São Paulo, Seoul, Bombay, Cairo, and Manila, among others,
are projected to grow substantially.

In the developed countries of the world, those located principally in Western
Europe and the United States, the number of metropolises with a population over
1 million was 110 in 1985 and is expected to increase to 128 in the year 2000 and
153 by the year 2025. In contrast, from 1950 to 2025, or seventy-five years' time, the
number of metropolises with a population of over 4 million in the developing countries
will increase from 31 to 486, or a multiple of sixteen times. This explosive growth
implies, as we shall see in Chapter 12, an immense social crisis for the developing
countries. But the growing multinucleated metropolitan regions in the advanced countries also represent serious challenges.

TABLE 1.3
The World's Twenty Largest Cities by Location and Population
Population in millions

City and country	Rank	1990	2000 (projection)	Density (sq. miles)
Tokyo-Yokohama, Japan	1	26,952	29,971	24,463
Mexico City, Mexico	2	20,207	27,872	37,314
São Paulo, Brazil	3	18,052	25,354	38,528
Seoul, South Korea	4	16,268	21,976	45,953
New York City, U.S.*	5	14,622	14,648	11,473
Osaka-Kobe-Kyoto, Japan	6	13,826	14,287	27,833
Bombay, India	7	11,777	15,357	120,299
Calcutta, India	8	11,663	14,088	54,607
Buenos Aires, Argentina	9	11,518	12,911	21,233
Rio de Janeiro, Brazil	10	11,428	14,169	42,894
Moscow, Russia	11	10,367	11,121	27,117
Los Angeles, U.S.*	12	10,060	10,714	8,985
Manila, Philippines	13	9,880	12,846	50,978
Cairo, Egypt	14	9,851	12,512	92,168
Jakarta, Indonesia	15	9,588	12,804	122,033
Tehran, Iran	16	9,354	14,251	79,594
London, U.K.	17	9,170	8,574	10,551
Paris, France	18	8,709	8,803	20,123
Delhi, India	19	8,475	11,849	59,102
Essen, Germany	20	7,474	7,239	10,653

*Includes partial metro area population.
Source: *Statistical Abstract of the U.S., 1991.* U.S. Department of Commerce, Economics and Statistics
Administration, Bureau of the Census, Table 1437, p. 835.

A New Approach to Urban Sociology

How did these changes come about? What is daily life like in the multinucleated metropolitan region? How does life there differ from that in the past? How has the city construction process, or *urbanization*, given way to the regional process of concentrated central city development, dispersed minicentered districts, and sprawling suburbanization? What is metropolitan culture like in the new regional spaces, and how does it differ from city life of the past? The answers to these and other questions will be the subject of this book. Our discussion is about urban sociology, but it is not about the city alone. On the pages that follow we take an integrated perspective according to the regional focus of multinucleation. Both city and suburban life have to be considered. But there is much more.

There are three additional dimensions to the new urban sociology: the shift to a global perspective, attention to the political economy of pull factors in urban and suburban development, and appreciation for the role of culture in metropolitan life and in the construction of the built environment.

Global Capitalism and the Metropolis

Cities are the children of economic, political, and cultural forces. In recent years urbanists have come to appreciate just how important the link is between cities or suburbs and changes in the economy. Prior to the 1970s, discussions about urban political economy assumed that the most critical influences emerged from the behavior of local businesspeople. A resident of a town might open up a store or factory. The owner would be known by others in the area. Jobs would be created and local residents would apply and fill them. Products of factories might be sold nationally, but locals would take pride in homegrown commodities and support the businesses of neighbors by their patronage, often because there was no place else to go.

This state of affairs no longer exists today. Since the 1970s, economic activity has become increasingly controlled from the global level. Businesses are owned and managed by people from distant locations. The local TV repair place, for example, may represent a manufacturer, such as Sony, whose headquarters are in another country, say Japan. The TV sets themselves might be assembled in yet another country, say Korea or Malaysia. Finally, foreign representatives of the manufacturer may live in this country and supervise the selling and repairing of their company's product. Reversing this example, there are also many U.S. companies, such as Ford Motors, that themselves are engaged in such manufacturing, marketing, and administrative activities overseas. In short, economies today are linked across the globe, and the small, local factory with ties to the adjacent community has given way to the multinational corporation and to the global flow of investment as the dominant economic forces.

There are important implications for the study of metropolitan regions arising from the global perspective. Prior to the 1970s, urbanists saw changes in the city as emerging from the interplay of many local interests interacting together in a shared and common space. According to the sociologist Gerald Suttles (1972:8), this *ecological* approach, as it is called, meant that the organization of the city was not caused by "the planned or artificial contrivance of anyone." Rather, it emerged out of the "many independent personal decisions based on moral, political, ecological, and economic considerations." Today we possess a different understanding of urban organization as being caused by the actions of powerful interests, many of which have their home bases in places far removed from local areas. Their decisions, for example, to open a plant somewhere, close one down someplace else, buy up farms to build houses, or sell homes to put up minimalls or apartment buildings are all so important that they affect the well-being of the entire community.

The perspective that is adopted in this text, however, does not suggest that all important influences on metropolitan development derive from the global level. There are also important economic and political forces that arise from within community territory that can account for change. In the following chapters, therefore, we shall be considering the contribution to metropolitan development of all sociospatial levels: the global, the national, and the local. It is the interplay of the forces from the different levels within the local space that is the most interesting.

An additional change in perspective on urban sociology brought about by appreciating the global bases of economic activity involves a renewed emphasis on the study of capitalism as a socioeconomic system (Chase-Dunn, 1985). Our society is a capitalist one. In the recent past our main ideological rival was the communist bloc in Eastern Europe and China which advocated an alternative economic system. During the last four years communism has been dismantled in most countries that practiced it, and a far greater number of countries than before now embrace capitalism. As a consequence, we can say with a great deal of confidence that the world today represents a global *capitalist* system.

The capitalist system is based on limited government regulation of business. Goods and services are bought and sold by private individuals or corporations in markets. People and corporations with money are free to invest it wherever they choose. Workers have limited job security and must sell their labor for a wage by bargaining with capitalist owners or their management representatives. The purpose of economic activity in capitalism is the pursuit of profit. Since the 1960s capital investment has ranged the globe in an ever more fluid fashion, searching out the best combinations of costs and benefits for profit. Businesses compete with each other for the largest share of profit, and losers may go out of business or be bought up by winners. Job gains and job losses from mobile capital investment can occur in any country. Aspects of social needs (such as environmental quality or support for the community quality of life) that are in conflict with the profit motive are usually not considered by capitalism unless the local citizens or their government requires it.

Since the 1970s urbanists have paid increasing attention to the relationship between capitalism and the metropolis (see Chapter 7). Competition among businesses which may not have a direct effect on space has been overshadowed by the competition between different places for their share of global investment (see chapters 5, 12, and 13). Local populations and community well-being are also affected by changes in job needs, the level of economic activity, and growing lifestyle disparities between low-skilled or semiskilled workers and professionals living in the metropolis (see Chapter 10). All of these aspects constitute a new dimension to the study of urban sociology.

Pull Factors and the Political Economy of Real Estate

Prior to the 1970s, urban analysts looked at city and suburban growth as an expression of individual desires. For example, people moved from the city to the suburbs, it was believed, because they preferred the latter's lifestyle. Or, in another case, investors picked a particular plot of land to develop because they liked its size and location. Individual actions based on individually held beliefs or needs might be termed the *demand-side* or push factor view of market activity, because they express the ways in which people and business act on their own desires. Urban sociology prior to the 1970s viewed growth almost exclusively in this manner.

At present we are aware of several factors that operate to promote development in specific ways and thereby mold individual desires through incentives. These causes represent the *supply-side* or pull factor view of individual choice. Powerful social forces can create opportunities that persuade people to follow courses of action that they might otherwise not. Two supply-side sources of incentives in the development of metropolitan regions are government and the real estate industry.

The Role of Government in Development. The abstract model of capitalism represents this economic system as involving limited government intervention. This is not the case for modern economies. The United States, like other industrialized nations, has an economy that is influenced greatly not only by government regulations but also by the direct spending of government tax dollars on particular public projects. The combined action of laws or regulations and direct investment provides incentives for both businesses and individual consumers to behave in certain ways.

When city dwellers, who may be renters, announce that they want to move to the suburbs, they are expressing their own personal preference. This decision may be occasioned by push factors (demand-side) such as increasing crime and high rents. But, when pressed for reasons, movers may also remark that the suburb they have chosen contains single-family homes that are affordable. Furthermore, due to government tax incentives on mortgage payments, it pays to own your home rather than rent. Government programs provide an enticement that pulls people in the direction of home ownership.

So the decision to move to the suburbs is a complex one that is prompted by both demand- and supply-side factors. For years it was the latter dimension that was neglected by urbanists. Today we have a greater appreciation, in particular, for the way government has operated to create opportunities and incentives that channel behavior in specific ways. In subsequent chapters we shall see how this "political economy," the linked actions of business and government in the development of metropolitan regions, promotes growth.

The Role of Real Estate as a Special Factor in Growth. With some notable exceptions (Hoyt, 1933; Hughes, 1928; Form, 1954), early urban sociologists have neglected the critical role that the real estate industry plays in metropolitan development. Recall from the discussion above that, at one time, urban organization was not viewed as the product of any particular interest but as the interplay of many separate ones (the ecological approach). Presently, we understand that the opposite is often the case.

Special interests such as global corporations can make or break a town depending on where they decide to invest new capital, as we have seen. But the single most important source of special interests in the development of the metropolis is the real estate industry.

Real estate includes all those corporations and banks that invest in the development of land use and housing including the land and the built environment themselves. The construction of new spaces proceeds through the actions of all those individuals, financial conduits, and corporations that make money from the change (turnover) in land use. Because a great deal of money can often be made through this type of activity, real estate interests are powerful special actors in the development of the metropolis, and their influence is greatly felt.

At any given time and on any piece of land, real estate forces can converge to turn over the existing use and engage in development that changes the utilization of local space. All of this is done in the pursuit of profit which comes as a consequence of development for different uses of land. Thus, in addition to understanding the political economy of production, it is also important to understand the political economy of real estate. Consider, for example, an individual farm of say 100 acres lying outside but adjacent to a developing city. Suppose its value as farmland is $400 an acre for a total of $40,000 as a working farm. Suppose too that an interstate highway is being built which will run from the large city parallel to this plot of land and on toward some other town. This highway, of course, is constructed with tax dollars by the government. It will have the purpose of opening up the rural area to business and residential development.

Suppose now that a developer becomes interested in this tract of land. He/she could easily offer the farmer twice the value of what the farm is worth. Then, by dividing it up into streets and housing plots, he/she could develop a community. The 100 acres might, for example, contain 80 acres of housing plus a medium-sized commercial shopping mall. Or perhaps 60 acres of single-family homes would be built along with 20 acres of condominium apartments and the remainder of the land would be devoted to light manufacturing or minimalls. In any event, by some variation of land turnover into new uses the developer could typically make several hundred percent in profit by building up and selling off developed land. In this way, not only has the environment changed, but turnover in this tract sets the stage for development of the land around it, thereby adding to the pressure to build up the entire region of what was once rural farmland around the city.

Perhaps, for example, one area of this same development is redeveloped for commercial use. Suddenly, structures in that section are also demolished to make room for a commercial building housing doctors' offices. The character of the community is altered again with the change in land use. And so on, as every few years new ways of utilizing land compel influential real estate investors to think up new ways of making money from the turnover in land use. In subsequent chapters we shall observe the important role real estate plays in the development of cities and the growth of metropolitan environments.

The Importance of Culture in Metropolitan Life

Many of the discussions of urban issues involve economic and political concerns. As we have seen above, some of the more important aspects of the new urban sociology

The famous Ginza district in Tokyo lights up at night—an example of urban signs.

emphasize a greater attention to political economy. But this is not all there is to the new approach. People live in a symbolic world that is *meaningful* to them. They possess sentiments and ideas and attempt to communicate with others using common concepts.

Much of this interaction is organized through the direct use of spoken or written language. A significant part, however, employs expressive symbols that are objects used to convey meanings. One of the principal sources of symbolic life involves aspects of the built environment. For example, cities and suburbs are the sites of many subcultures—ethnic, religious, racial, gender-specific, and age-related. Neighborhoods within the metropolis composed of concentrations of these subcultures can readily be identified by objects that are signs of subcultural status. For example, ethnic areas of the city advertise themselves by the signs in front of restaurants, bakeries, specialty shops, and religious institutions (see Chapter 8). People use such signs to orient themselves in the act of engaging in metropolitan life.

The study of culture and the role of objects as signs constitutes a significant part of the new urban sociology. Sociologists have studied metropolitan life as culturally meaningful for some time. What is new and different is the way such meanings are associated with objects in addition to words. For example, cities often try to develop an image that boosts attention to them in order to attract investment and tourists. A variety of images has been used, such as signs of industry ("motor city"), signs of regional growth ("the twin cities"), signs of vision ("the city of tomorrow"), and signs of life's good quality ("the city of leisure"). Slogans such as these are often linked to images or objects, such as a skyline or graphic logo of some kind. In this way a particular symbolic identity is created for a place, which gives the impression that it is special. The study of culture which links symbols to objects is called *semiotics*, and the special subfield that studies the built environment in this manner is called *spatial semiotics.*

Spatial semiotics studies the metropolis as a *meaningful* environment. Each of the buildings in the city, for example, performs a function for society. People often associate the appearance of the building with that function. In this way, the built object, the building, becomes a sign of its use. Thus, a large bank building represents what a bank does and what customers do there when they enter. Often, banks are made of marble with brass fixtures and a kind of luxurious feel. We associate that atmosphere with banking. Government buildings, in contrast, represent political authority. Public buildings are usually constructed to convey the image of authority. Often they might incorporate a classic theme of Greek-style columns or convey political importance by the placement of auspicious statues at the entrance.

In the past, approaches to urban sociology have neglected the symbolic aspect of space, although some early exceptions are interesting (see Wohl and Strauss, 1958). The perspective which will be followed in this book integrates the symbolic nature of environments with more traditional factors that comprise social behavior, such as class, race, gender, age, and social status. Space, then, is another compositional factor in human behavior. We call this new perspective on metropolitan life the *sociospatial* approach.

Summary: The Sociospatial Approach

In the past, urbanists have regarded the space of habitation as only a container of social activities. But this view is limited. Space not only contains actions but also acts as a meaningful object to which we orient our actions. The factor of space constitutes a part of social relations and is intimately involved in our daily lives. It affects the way we feel about what we do. In turn, people alter space and construct new environments to fit their needs better. Hence, there is a *dual* relationship between people and space. On the one hand, human beings act according to social factors such as gender, class, race, age, and status within and in reaction to a given space. On the other hand, people also create and alter spaces for themselves that express their own needs and desires.

The sociospatial perspective adopted by this book links the dual relationship between people and space with the social factors that are the bases of individual behavior. The most basic concept of this approach is that of *settlement space*, which refers to the built environment in which people live. Settlement space is both constructed and organized. It is built by people who have followed some meaningful plan for the purposes of containing economic, political, and cultural activities. Within it people organize their daily actions according to the meaningful aspects of the constructed space. In subsequent chapters we shall discuss how sociospatial factors determine the construction and use of settlement space. Over time we shall also see how change has occurred and how constructed environments are, in turn, molded by sociospatial factors.

In summation, the sociospatial perspective consists of attention to the following dimensions of daily life:

1. We adopt a regional perspective that considers urban and suburban settlement space. We study the multinucleated metropolitan region and how it got that way over the course of time.
2. All settlement spaces are considered not only within their local and national contexts, but as linked to the global system of capitalism. We pay special attention to the powerful forces of economics and politics, whose decisions influence the well-being of local areas whether they derive from the metropolitan, the national, or international levels.
3. Settlement spaces are affected by government policies and by the actions of the real estate industry. These supply-side forces provide the incentives and opportunities which pull and mold individual behaviors and channel metropolitan development in certain specific ways.
4. Settlement spaces are always meaningful places. Everyday life is organized according to symbols which include social interaction but also the material objects that are part of the built environment. We adopt a sociospatial perspective to capture the interaction between space and society. Some of the factors that affect behavior are traditional concepts of sociology, such as gender, class, social status, age, and race. To these we add the element of space itself. Space operates in a dual way. It affects behavior as a built environment which contains action and as a meaningful object. In turn, people alter and construct places as a way of expressing their needs and desires.

The Plan of the Book

In the following chapters we shall explore the traditional topics of urban sociology in new ways while covering the basic material of the field. Chapter 2 addresses the origins of urbanization in the ancient world. Several explanations are proposed for the process of modernization which rely on the central role of cities. This chapter considers early cities around the globe and ends with a discussion of city growth in Western Europe. Chapters 3, 4, and 5 deal with the history of urbanization in the United States. The colonial, metropolitan, and contemporary features of urban development are discussed in each of these three chapters.

Chapters 6 and 7 devote themselves to the field of urban sociology itself. The former considers classical urban theories, while the latter devotes itself to the *new urban sociology* and its relation to the *sociospatial perspective* of this text. The lessons of the first five chapters are also examined in light of the new perspective. In chapters 8 and 9 we turn our attention to the "lived" aspects of the city or the people that make up urban life. The former chapter takes a detailed look at the people themselves and their ways of life, while the latter discusses theories of urban life and the methodologies that sociologists have used to study people in cities and suburbs.

Chapter 10 deals with the important problems and issues facing urban communities at present. Aspects of contemporary sociospatial patterns of urbanization are highlighted in this discussion. Chapter 11 considers local politics and covers both urban and suburban political activities. In chapters 12 and 13 we turn our attention to the globe and examine urban life in a variety of settings. The former chapter focuses on urbanization in the third world countries stressing the features that are held in common as well as interesting differences. Chapter 13 discusses the patterns of restructuring that are lately characteristic of the industrialized world and stresses common features with the U.S. case as discussed in Chapter 5.

The final sections of the book look at ways of governing and administering urban and suburban areas. Chapter 14 considers the important issue of the environment. Special attention is paid to the sociospatial aspects of environmental costs. This chapter also considers the case of metropolitan planning in the United States and seeks to understand its limited success. Chapter 15 evaluates the changes that have occurred in the nature of government intervention within cities. Policy is seen to be closely related to ideological positions taken with regard to the limits of government intervention. This final chapter then looks at the prospects of metropolitan life and the relative well-being of urban sociology as a field of inquiry. It is suggested that the uniquely "urban" emphasis of urban sociology be dropped in favor of the regional perspective of the sociospatial approach.

CHAPTER

2

THE ORIGINS OF URBANIZATION AND THE CHARACTERISTICS OF CITIES

Historians estimate that urbanization, or the building of and living in compact, densely populated places, appeared as early as 10,000 years ago. Continuously used, densely populated settlements can be found in the Middle East that date back over 6,000 years and in the Indus valley in India that date back over 4,000 years. Other centers of ancient urban life include the Minoan civilization of Crete (1800 B.C.) and the cities of China (circa 2000 B.C.). The new world of America was the last to develop cities. The first appeared only about 1,000 years ago in South America, while the cities of the United States and Canada are at most 350 years old.

The population of ancient cities tended to be small by our standards. Mohenjo-Daro in the Indus Valley had a population at its height of approximately 20,000 inhabitants. Until the late Middle Ages, no city could compare with ancient Rome, which housed over 1 million people in the first century A.D.

Several ancient cities possessed remarkable structural features that made urban living not only possible but also quite comfortable. Mohenjo-Daro had a grid street system making maximum use of space, and an open sewer system that allowed for the elimination of waste and rainwater. Jericho, in ancient Israel, possessed a system of canals that aided the irrigation of fields outside the city. The palace at Knossos, on Crete, which is over 3,000 years old, was several stories high, and was designed to allow light to enter from the roof as well as the sides. However, it is easy to overemphasize these special cases. Most ancient cities, such as Athens, were plagued by unsanitary housing conditions and streets.

According to the historian Fernand Braudel (1973: 373), life in the early towns captured, on the one hand, the stimulation of exposure to new ideas and the luxuries of worldly goods, and, on the other, the struggle to preserve resources against places in the surrounding area that threatened attack.

The citizens of the early towns lived an urban life that was fragile. Precariousness was, perhaps, an inevitable consequence of the growth of cities. According to Sjoberg (1960) cities were the sites of power. In order to be secure, it was necessary for early cities to exercise their strength and dominate the *hinterland,* that is, the relatively less developed area outside the boundaries of the large city. Then in order to prosper, it was necessary to expand the hinterland sphere of domination. As sites of wealth, ancient cities were protected by fortifications, and warfare between cities was quite common. Average town citizens lived under the constant threat of attack by roving bands of warriors or the armies of other towns. Often it was the case for victors simply to kill off or enslave defeated city populations, and then the city itself would be burned to the ground. The classic play by the Greek author Euripides, *The Trojan Women,* and the section of the Bible called Lamentations exemplify the ill-fortune that all cities faced from the threat of war (see Box 2.1). In the former work, Euripides wrote about

Ur in ancient Babylon. Note the grid street construction.

BOX 2.1 SOME CLASSICAL WRITINGS ABOUT CONQUERED CITIES
The Trojan Women by Euripides

Scene: The action takes place shortly after the capture of Troy. All Trojan men have been killed or have fled; all women and children are captives. The scene is an open space before the city, which is invisible in the background, partly demolished and smoldering (Fitts, 1966: 151). [Hecuba is the former Queen of Troy whose husband, King Priam, has been killed.]

Hecuba: Such a state I keep
to sit by the tents of Agamemnon.
I am led captive
from my house, an old, unhappy woman,
my head struck pitiful.
Come then, sad wives of the Trojans
whose spears were bronze,
their daughters, brides of disaster,
let us mourn the smoke of Ilion.
And I, as among winged birds
the mother, lead out
the clashing cry, the song; not the song
wherein once long ago
when I held the sceptre of Priam
my feet were queens of the choice and led
the proud dance to the gods of Phrygia.

D. Fitts. 1966. *Greek Plays in Modern Translation*. New York: Holt, Rinehart and Winston, p. 156.

Lamentations (the Bible)

Oh how doth she sit solitary—the city that was full of people is become like a widow! She that was so great among the nations, the princess among the provinces, is become tributary!

She weepeth sorely in the night, and her tears are on her cheeks; she hath none to comfort her among all her lovers; all her friends have dealt treacherously toward her, they are become her enemies.

Exiled is Judah because of affliction, and because of the greatness of servitude; she dwelleth indeed among the nations, she findeth no rest; all her pursuers have overtaken her between the narrow passes.

. . . Jerusalem remembereth in the days of her affliction and of her miseries all her magnificent things which have been in the days of old: when her people fell in to the hand of the adversary, with none to help her, the adversaries looked at her, they laughed at the cessation of her glory.

(Chapter 1, verses 1–7)

the ancient city of Troy in Asia Minor after it was defeated by the Greeks. The men were killed or taken into slavery and the women were parceled out to the victors. In the latter work, the ancient Hebrews lament the loss of their city, Jerusalem, from their exile in Babylonia.

Domination by successful rulers located in ancient cities led, in turn, to more trade and commerce but also to more war and the exercise of power over the countryside. Early urban existence constituted a drama involving such interwoven spheres of every-day life as agricultural production, regional and foreign trade, military conquest and rule, and the pursuit of arts and sciences based on the relative success of economic and political activities.

Most discussions of early cities focus on the apparent division of labor and economic activities around which the concentrated population was organized. In this way city life is discussed as a progression from limited to complex specialization of work and functional organization. But not only were cities the locus of social functions, they were and remain *meaningful* space. Cities did not simply appear because certain fundamental social activities matured at a certain time. Cities had to be produced or, rather, *constructed*. In ancient societies every settlement was built by a group using a distinctive set of symbols and a model of space that was inherently meaningful to that group (Lagopoulos, 1986). For example early cities, such as Ur in ancient Babylon, were often produced using cosmological codes which mandated geometrical relations between the city and the heavens, such as an east-west axis, and within the city through geometrical arrangements of the buildings.

Early religious codes distinguished between the sacred and the profane and also endowed structures with the protection of the gods. Around 500 B.C., the Etruscans, ancestors of the Romans, built cities first by plowing a "sacred furrow" as a large enclosure in a religious ceremony. The city could only be built within this space signifying the sacred domain and separated from the profane space of the rest of the world. Only later, in fourteenth- and fifteenth-century Europe, did cities first appear without religious or cosmological codes guiding the construction of space. At this time and continuing very much to the present day in Europe (and the United States), the meaning of buildings (such as a bank) corresponded to the function they performed in the society without any necessary connection to some overarching symbol. In the early settlements, by way of contrast, there was a strong identification between what was meant by buildings and how individuals living within the city conceived of the meanings of buildings.

In short, as the sociospatial perspective suggests, the ancient city was the combined product of political power, economic functions, and overarching symbolic meanings that expressed deeply held beliefs of the inhabitants. Let us consider three examples, classical Athens, Rome, and Beijing.

Classical Cities

Ancient Athens in Greece was constructed according to a cosmological code which was then overlaid by religious symbols linked to the pantheon of Greek gods, such as

Zeus represented by a statue. The entire city itself was built to honor the goddess Athena. The figure used to design Athens was the circle, and all buildings followed geometrical design principles such as "the golden mean." In the center of the circle was the *agora* which was not simply the marketplace, but in fact, the *public hearth* or *hestia koine,* the center of the community. The public hearth was considered to be the *omphalos* or the *center of the world* (see Figure 2.1).

As Athens developed, its trading function matured, allowing many Athenians to acquire great wealth. The agora grew in importance and became the economic center of the Athenian region. However, the meaning of the agora was not dominated by economic significance alone. Rather, the central organizing concept for Athenians became their political life, and the space of Athens became overlaid by a political code that supplanted the earlier cosmological/religious one. Thus, in ancient Athens the street network was a radial form emanating out from the center of the omphalos. This is to be distinguished from both the precocious grid planning of the Indus Valley cities and the haphazard growth of Mesopotamia.

The intent of radial development was not dictated by the economic concern of easy access to the market but by the political principle that all homes should be equidistant from the center because all Athenian citizens were equal. Within the center were placed the *citizen assembly hall,* the *city council hall,* and the *council chamber,* all structures linked to the institution of city politics.

In a second example, after 200 B.C., ancient Rome was constructed using a

Figure 2.1   Ancient Athens with the Acropolis mound and the Temple of Athena (the Parthenon). Below the Acropolis is the marketplace (Agora).

Figure 2.2   The Roman Forum.

different model—one that emanated from a royal or imperial code that stressed grandeur, domination, and excess. Roman space was based not on the political equality of its citizens, but on the military power of the state, even though it borrowed republican ideas from ancient Greece. In the case of Rome, as was also true of Athens, functional spaces serving principally an economic function were embedded in a larger, meaningful space governed by political and cultural symbols.

Initially the buildings of the Roman center or *forum* were built on a human scale. As the empire expanded and the Republic switched to an imperial monarchy, Rome was refashioned by the imperial code to gargantuan scale. The *circus maximus,* where chariot races took place, seated *over* 100,000 people, while the famous *Colosseum* accommodated over 80,000 (see Figure 2.2).

As the empire prospered the 1 million or more residents of Rome lived off of the great wealth that poured into the city. Eventually the center became known for its decadence and idleness. At one time a full 159 days out of the Roman year were declared public holidays! Of these, 93, or one-fourth of the entire year, were devoted to games at the empire's expense. Alongside this parasitic existence immense urban problems developed due to the deterioration of housing, the large number of poor people attracted to the city, and the dangerous lack of proper sanitation facilities or services for most of the residents.

Ancient Rome became a city of the rich and the poor, a society wedded to spectacle and consumption instead of commerce and trade. By the time the barbarians showed up at its walls (after A.D. 400), the city had long since become mired in its own insolvable crises of excess and dependence.

Our final example comes from Asia, which also gave birth to immense civilizations. The city of Beijing in China was a product of a form of society similar to that of ancient Rome, namely, the production of space based on slave labor, the dominance of the agricultural hinterland, and the ultimate control of all life by the royalty. Beijing, however, reached its height fully 1,500 years after Rome. At that time, during the European Middle Ages, it was the largest city in the world, with the enormous population of 2 million people.

Beijing was the capital city of the Manchu emperors. Much of the space was given over to the functional needs of the economy and its division of labor. Hence it was a practical city of business and commerce. At the same time, however, the Ming dynasty claimed for itself the center, which became sacred and restricted. This *Forbidden City* contained the emperor's palace, where the ruler, his family, his court, and all his functionaries lived. All others were restricted from entering under pain of death. And much like modern-day Tokyo (see Chapter 13) which has as its "empty center" the palace of the emperor (Barthes, 1973), all traffic in the city of Beijing was obliged to detour around the forbidden center (see Figure 2.3).

The Forbidden City was a product of the omnipotent power of the Ming dynasty, but it was also over-endowed at every turn with cosmological symbols such as indicators of celestial bodies. As Braudel (1973: 428–9) describes:

> The heart of the palace was behind the second wall. This was the forbidden city, the Yellow City, where the Emperor lived protected by his guards, by check points at the gates, protocol, ramparts, moats and the vast corner pavilions with twisted roofs, the *Kiaoleou.* Every building, every gate and every bridge had its own name and, as it were, its own

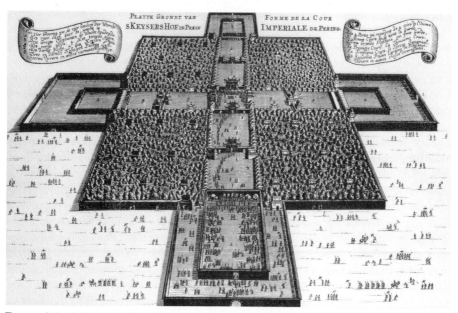

Figure 2.3   Palace of the Chinese emperor and the Forbidden City at the center.

customs and practices. The forbidden town measured 1 kilometer by 780 meters. "It could hold the Louvre comfortably."

In sum, most discussions of early urbanization focus on the importance of trade, commerce, and military domination. These are indeed the critical factors in the rise of cities. Our three examples, however, illustrate the way economic aspects of life are intertwined with political and cultural factors that are woven together to produce settlement space. In ancient times cities were centers of commerce but they were also meaningful spaces and were most often built as expressions of state power. Usually, and due to the high degree of integration present in early civilizations, some overarching ideas or a select combination of meanings or themes existed which organized the symbols of space. In the case of Greece, space was meaningful for cosmological and political reasons; Roman space was dedicated to the glory of the Caesar and the empire; while the Beijing of the Manchu dynasty possessed a sacred and forbidden center dedicated completely to the emperor. In short, without the wealth they generated and politically controlled, these cities could not have been the seats of great empires, but without their symbols they could not have given expression to the culture of civilization.

Ancient Urbanization

Social scientists are interested in the origin of cities because the process of early urbanization holds insights into the origins of social structure. In particular, studies of early cities provide clues for an understanding of how complex social relations arose and how strong bonds were maintained among residents who were often unrelated. The best known theory of the rise of cities was proposed by V. Gordon Childe (1950, 1954). According to Childe ancient cities developed a social organization that was different from rural society in many respects and which provided the social basis for modern life. In recent years, however, Childe's theory has been criticized. Let us consider what he proposed and how Childe's theory has been modified today.

Childe viewed the development of society in terms of distinct stages and considered the emergence of urban life as a critical evolutionary phase in the rise of modern civilization. City building was part of an "urban revolution" that also brought with it a set of special social relations that are characteristic of modern life. The first step toward an urban society occurred when hunting and gathering societies shifted to food production in relatively stable and sedentary groups. According to Childe, once the urban revolution began, civilization progressed and evolved to more complex forms of social life sustained by an urban economy based on trade and craft production. It is principally from Childe that we have received the idea that urbanization develops through specialization of work and the separation of different functions through increasing interdependence of societal tasks. These social relations were considered different from those found in rural society, and they provided the basis of modern civilization.

For Childe, the urban revolution possessed a number of distinct characteristics, including (1) a large population of several thousand inhabitants; (2) craft people, merchants, priests, and state functionaries that worked full time in these specialized occupations; (3) control of food production in the hinterland and the storage of the surplus; (4) a ruling class that possessed absolute control over the society; (5) numerical and alphabetical notational systems for information processing; (6) cultural forms of expression that were progressively refined, such as art and music; and finally, (7) the existence of trade with other centers, some of which were at a considerable distance. In short, the large ancient city was the "cradle of civilization."

Childe's theory of early urbanization was quite influential and may be accurate as a *descriptive* interpretation of ancient city life. However, it also asserted an evolutionary view of development according to which civilization passes first through the stage of hunting and gathering, then to agriculture, and finally to urban-based economies, with an ever more complex and interdependent form of social organization leading up to a contemporary, "modern" stage. Recent thought on the origin of cities based on new archeological evidence rejects Childe's evolutionary theory and instead favors a discontinuous process of development. According to Eisenstadt and Shachar (1987: 27), cities did *not* grow out of farming villages. In certain places they emerged in the earliest days of settlement as an independent phenomenon, when population pressures forced people to live on marginal lands. So in contrast to Childe's view it was (a) the availability of an agricultural surplus and, (b) population pressures that provided the impetus for the city building process or *urbanization.* These two factors were probably the ones most responsible for the appearance of cities in the ancient world. Because of the need to create a livelihood on marginal agricultural lands, early residents of towns innovated alternative economic activities including trade, full-time craft work, and even religion, whose products could then be exchanged for essentials, thereby providing the basis for an urban, city-based economy that could survive on trade.

Archeologists have known for some time that signs of civilization such as the production of pottery in quantity or the use of writing coexisted with the development of agriculture, rather than appearing at the later stages of agriculturally based societies as evolutionary theories maintain. For example, one of the oldest cities, Jericho (still existing today in modern Israel), already possessed a complex urban culture based on trade and crafts over 4,000 years ago, that is, *prior* to the domestication of grain in the surrounding region (Eisenstadt and Shachar, 1987: 27).

While the social division of labor and its growing complexity certainly contributed to urban development, economic factors alone did not produce the first cities. The market, by itself, can never provide adequate control or guidance, that is, *regulation,* for social organization. In fact, the classical sociologists Emile Durkheim, Karl Marx, and Max Weber all argued that everyday actions in a market society generate problems and conflict that call for regulation by political and cultural means. "The most important of such problems were the construction of trust or solidarity (stressed by Durkheim), the regulation of power (Marx and Weber) and the provision of both meaning and legitimation for social activities so prized by Weber" (Eisenstadt and Shachar, 1987: 50).

In sum, recent scholarship has critiqued Childe's theory on two counts. Urbanization was not an evolutionary process passing from one stage to another, more complex, one over time, and the increasing sophistication of the division of labor was not the main cause of development, but was a consequence of urban life. As the sociospatial perspective suggests, economic, political, and cultural institutions meshed together to promote growth. Consequently, the genius of ancient civilizations lies as much in their cultural mechanisms that justified rule by the few—either plutocracy (rule by the powerful) or theocracy (rule by the religious elite)—and in their political techniques of regulation or administration of social activities, as it does in their economic success.

The glory that was Rome, for example, depended in this sense not just on the market-based division of labor, but also on the innovation of Roman citizenship, on the way citizens were integrated meaningfully into political life, on the republican institution of the Senate, and, ultimately, on the power of central authority administered faithfully by all the functionaries in small towns throughout the empire.

The classical civilizations may have spawned great cities, but they could not overcome the precariousness of urban life. Consequently, they did not follow an evolutionary historical path as Childe suggested. When Rome fell (around A.D. 800), Europe reverted to small-town life and did not develop large cities for many centuries. Across the globe evidence exists of great urban places that grew and died, such as the Inca city of Cuzco in the Peruvian Andes, or the lost city of Angor Wat in Cambodia. Until quite recently, in most parts of the world, rural rather than urban relations dominated society despite the presence of cities. Hence, societies dominated by urban relations are a relatively recent phenomenon that emerged after the fall of Rome. Let us consider the conditions that created urban life in the period after A.D. 1000.

Urbanization after A.D. 1000

When the Roman empire fell, urban space in Europe was reclaimed by the countryside and its feudal relations. Towns needed to defend themselves in the absence of a central authority. They became small, fortified settlements like the medieval castle. Consequently, in Europe during the Middle Ages, the level of urbanization was low. Few places exceeded 10,000 in population. In contrast, the cities of Asia, the Near East, and what is now Latin America housed thriving, populated communities during this same period.

Most historians contend that the cities which emerged around the globe after A.D. 1000 were the products of powerful national rulers and the success of regional trade, rather than deriving from social relations that were uniquely urban in nature, as Childe's theory suggests. Hence, in most societies, city life remained precarious and dependent on social relations that emanated from state power. It was not until the seventeenth century with the rise of capitalism in Western Europe that urban life appeared to be propelled by forces emerging from within cities themselves. In China, for example, towns were organized by the state under the infallible rule of the emperor and for the principal purpose of administration. These were secular kingdoms united under a political hierarchy to harness the economic wealth of the countryside. Under the imperial capital were arrayed the provincial capitals dispersed throughout the kingdom, and under these were clustered the still smaller county capitals of the Chinese empire. In sum, commerce and trade combined with the power of the state to produce the towns of the Orient.

Much the same story characterized the Middle East, which also contained places with populations that eclipsed those in Europe after the year A.D. 1000. With the coming

While London (above) grew as a city in the Middle Ages, so did other, non-European places, such as Damascus (below).

Both cities contained a fortified wall for protection, religious buildings, and a palace or seat of government, as well as housing.

of Islamic hegemony, cities appeared that solidified the control of territory under the Muslim rulers or caliphs (see Chapter 12). Islam also took over older cities built by the Romans, such as Constantinople. To these it added two types of "new" towns across North Africa and the Near East: *Villes Crées* were fortress cities constructed by Islamic rulers as administration centers, and *Villes Spontanées* arose as trading centers constructed without preconceived plans but sanctioned by the caliph. Thus, Islamic society possessed a robust system of cities, but these were all products of state-directed territorial expansion and administration. As in the Chinese case, the rulers needed cities to control the territory and commerce of the hinterland.

The experience of India during this same period between the years 1000 and 1700 also replicates the combined role of royal administration on the one hand and the importance of local trade on the other in the sustenance of Oriental cities. As elsewhere in Asia and the Middle East, the size and well-being of Indian cities was a consequence of the power of central state authority rather than of social relations eminating from the urban community itself. Braudel (1973: 413) provides an interesting illustration of the dependency of the city on the power of the state in his examination of India during the seventeenth century:

> The example of India shows how much these official towns were bound up with the prince—to the point of absurdity. Political difficulties, even the prince's whim, uprooted and transplanted the capitals several times. . . . As soon as its prince abandoned it the town was jeopardized, deteriorated and occasionally died.

When a Mogul prince left Delhi . . .

> on a journey to Kashmir in 1663, the whole town followed him because they could not live without his favors and liberality. An improbable crowd formed, estimated at several hundred thousand people by a French doctor who took part in the expedition. Can we imagine Paris following Louis XV during his journey to Metz in 1744?

Finally, in Latin America the Aztec and Inca civilizations achieved impressive heights during this same period. As late as the 1600s Spanish explorers marveled at the awesome scale of New World urbanization. Yet, as the example of Aztec civilization in Mexico shows, these places were closely connected to the agricultural relations of the hinterland and could not be considered modern cities. According to Murray Bookchin (1974: 7–8),

> An illustration of the earliest cities can be drawn from descriptions of the Aztec "capital" of Tenochtitlán, encountered by Spanish *conquistadores* only three centuries ago. At first glance, the community is deceptively similar in appearance to a modern city. . . . The city's resemblance . . . rests on its lofty religious structures, its spacious plazas for ceremonies, its palaces and administrative buildings. Looking beyond these structures, the city in many respects was likely a grossly oversized pueblo community.

As Bookchin points out, in the case of Aztec cities, the horticulturally based activities of the family clans organized social relations within the city. These clan-based social orders reached into the very heart of city life. Integration around the agricultural economy was so complete that Aztec cities did not even develop money and retained a barter system. Just as for the case of the Orient, commercial and craft activities carried on within Tenochtitlán could not explain either its immense physical space or the size of its population. The principal role of the city was to serve as the center for the Aztec rulers and their administrative functions, much like the case of Beijing.

It was not until the late Middle Ages in Europe that towns acquired political independence from the state. The classical sociologist Max Weber (1966) considered this autonomy as necessary for the establishment of an urban community. For Weber the key to city life was the creation of an independent urban government that was elected by the citizens of the city itself. Classical Athens and early Rome were two examples. Weber believed that in the late Middle Ages, Europe also developed cities of this type. For Weber an urban community consisted of a fusion of the fortress and the marketplace where trade and commercial relations predominated; a legal court of its own that had the authority to settle local disputes; and partial political autonomy which allowed residents to elect authorities that could administer daily affairs.

If the cities of the later European Middle Ages enjoyed autonomy, it was relatively short-lived. By the eighteenth century nation-states had acquired control of territory, and the commercial-trading economy was global in scale, thereby making individual places dependent on each other. Weber's remarks about the city were meant to suggest that there may once have been uniquely *urban* social relations that characterized city life and which helped to transform society from a rural, agriculturally based system of social organization to one that is considered "modern." For example, urban life was sustained by a mode of social organization that, when compared to rural areas, consisted of greater emphasis on specialized jobs, the decline of family authority and the rise of contractual and political relations, and a replacement of the strong ties binding people together based on kinship with those based on the interdependence of sharing the same fate as the city. In addition to Weber, other classical sociologists also developed ways of studying the contrast between premodern and modern societies. Ferdinand Tonnies, for example, called this the shift from *gemeinschaft* to *gesellschaft,* or the change from a society based on intimate contacts to one based on contract, while Emile Durkheim considered modernization as a change from a society based on mechanical solidarity, or a low degree of specialization, to one based on organic solidarity, or a high degree of specialization and interdependence.

In retrospect, it seems clear that the force which propelled the development of cities in Europe did not involve some uniquely "urban" cause, but was a direct consequence of the rise of capitalism and industrialization. It is this change that defines the development from the relatively autonomous urban community in Europe of the seventeenth and eighteenth centuries to the large industrial and postindustrial cities that we know today.

Capitalism and the Rise of the Industrial City

Throughout the world, especially in North Africa, Asia, and the Near East, cities were the sites of vigorous trade and the economic activities associated with commerce. However, trade by itself did not sustain the rise of cities in Western Europe. Distinguishing the developing towns of the late Middle Ages from other such places was the emergence of capitalism based on a money economy.

The economy of the feudal manor, for example, was characterized by *simple commodity production.* That is, craft products were produced for exchange, but the owners remained the direct producers of the products themselves. Exchange itself could be facilitated using any object or service that was equivalent according to the cultural judgment of the society. This barter system prevailed for several hundred years in Europe after the fall of Rome and existed elsewhere in the Middle East and Asia.

In the later Middle Ages, beginning with the twelfth century, the general and accepted use of money and a fully developed commodity market within the city that was regulated by local government allowed the people with capital to hire both labor and resources in order to produce goods. The classical sociologist Karl Marx was the foremost student of the rise of capitalism. He called the type of economy made possible by capital and city regulation of markets *extended commodity production.* That is, unlike simple commodity production which ended in the exchange of goods or services, extended production began with money, or capital, and after production and exchange, ended with still more money which was then invested in a new cycle of accumulation.

In this manner commercial relations supported the accumulation of capital, and cities with such economies began to prosper beyond anything that had been known until that time. In addition, social and cultural relations also changed in the cities to sanction the pursuit of wealth through the accumulation of money. For example, the early Catholic Church prohibited the loaning of money, except within restricted guidelines, and limited the role of banks (see Vance, 1990). In the sixteenth century the Protestant Reformation swept away these cultural and social restrictions on the free flow of investment, providing a cultural basis for capitalist development (Weber, 1958). Once that point was reached, the accumulation process spilled out into the surrounding area as the new, money-based capitalist economy penetrated relations in the countryside. The history of the Occidental city, as Braudel, Weber, and Marx all agreed, became the history of capitalism.

Following these changes, eighteenth- and nineteenth-century cities in Western Europe experienced a population explosion of unprecedented proportions (McKeown, 1976). Table 2.1 illustrates some of this change. Between 1800 and 1900, for example, the population of London went from 861,000 to 6,480,000, while Berlin went from 172,000 to 2,424,000, although seaports, like Naples, grew much less.

Occupations became specialized, and the division of labor grew ever more complex as capitalism developed. Aided by emergent nation-states, the political and legal relations of capitalism began to dominate the countryside in Europe. Capitalism required the legal sanctification of private property, and this resulted in the "commodification" of many aspects of society. All this buying and selling meant that markets were formed and prospered, providing people with even more ways to make money.

Land, for example, which was once held only by the nobility and the church, became commodified and for purchase by anyone with money. A real estate market emerged that cut up and parceled out land for sale. A second market, this one for labor, emerged as the serfs, who were bound by feudal traditions to their masters, were freed only to become commodified wage laborers. As feudal relations of dependence and reciprocity were broken down by capitalism and the pursuit of monetary accumulation, immense numbers of people were forced out of the rural, farming areas and into the cities where they looked for work by selling their labor for a wage on the labor market.

TABLE 2.1
Growth of Cities in Europe, 1700 to 1990
Population in thousands

City	1700	1800	1900	1990
London, England	550	861	6,480	9,170
Paris, France	530	547	3,330	8,709
Naples, Italy	207	430	563	2,960
Lisbon, Portugal	188	237	363	2,396
Amsterdam, Holland	172	201	510	—*
Rome, Italy	149	153	487	3,021
Madrid, Spain	110	169	539	4,451
Vienna, Austria	105	231	1,662	2,313
Berlin (unified), Germany	—*	172	2,424	3,022

*Unavailable from comparable sources.
Source: Adapted from T. Chandler and G. Fox. 1974. *3000 Years of Urban History.* New York: Academic Press, pp. 321–341. *Statistical Abstract of the U.S., 1991.* U.S. Department of Commerce, Economics and Statistics Administration, Bureau of the Census, Table 1437, pp. 835–836.

With the coming of the industrial revolution, this "urban implosion" or shift of population from rural to urban places reached truly astounding proportions. According to Lewis Mumford (1961) the cities of the late eighteenth century contained relatively few people, numbering less than 600,000 (see Table 2.1). By the middle of the nineteenth century, capitalist industrialization created cities of a million or more all across the face of Western Europe. The most dramatic changes were experienced in England and Wales because it was there that the scale of industrialization and capitalist development was most advanced (see Table 2.2).

According to Geruson and McGrath (1977: 25), urban counties in Britain grew by 30 percent between 1780 and 1800 and again by approximately 300 percent between 1801 and 1831 (see Table 2.2). Commercial and industrial counties experienced a net population increase of 378,000 people between 1781 and 1800, and an additional 720,000 people between 1801 and 1831. At the very same time, agricultural counties *lost* 252,000 people during the first period and lost 379,000 between 1801 and 1831 (see Table 2.2).

Census figures at the time of the nineteenth century were not always accurate. Nevertheless Braudel (1973: 376) suggests that around the turn of the century several

TABLE 2.2
The Population Shift From Agricultural to Urban Counties, England and Wales, 1701 to 1831
Net migration in thousands

Year	Agricultural counties	Urban/Commercial counties
1701–1751	−232	548
1751–1781	−115	330
1781–1801	−252	378
1801–1831	−379	720

Source: Adapted from R. Geruson and D. McGrath. 1977. *Cities and Urbanization.* New York: Praeger, Table 2-2, p. 26.

The industrial city: view of the city of Lawrence, Massachusetts, in the 1800s, showing the site of the fallen Pemberton Mills as well as Washington Mills and Duck Mills in the immediate vicinity. (See also Chapter 3.)

regions in Europe tipped their population balance from rural to urban, especially in England and the Netherlands, a truly momentous occurrence. In short, for the first time in history, several nations changed from populations that were predominantly rural to ones that were dominated by urban location, and this is why the urbanization process in Western Europe after the 1700s was so significant.

By the middle 1800s, Western Europe possessed many industrialized cities. What was life like in them? The cities that emerged in the nineteenth century, unlike the ancient places, were not conceived according to some overarching symbolic meaning, such as religious or cosmological codes. Development was a haphazard affair. Individual capitalists did what they willed, and real estate interests operated unchecked by either legal code or cultural prescription. Land was traded like other goods. About the only clear pattern that emerged involved the spatial separation of the rich and the poor. The industrial city of Western Europe became the site of a clash of classes—the workers against the capitalists. Observing the excesses of the time and the utter devastation visited on working-class life by the factory regime of capitalism, Karl Marx (1967) recognized that class struggle would become the driving force of history. It was left for Friedrich Engels (1973), Marx's close friend, to document in graphic terms the pathological nature of uneven development characterizing urban growth under capitalism (Berman, 1985). In fact, several books were written in the nineteenth century which developed this theme, as Sharpe and Wallock note:

> Struck by the rapid growth and widespread poverty of England's urban centers, several contemporaries conducted what became classic surveys of the modern city: Friedrich Engels, *The Condition of the Working Class in England;* Henry Mayhew, *London*

BOX 2.2 TWO POETS VIEW THE CITY
Chicago (excerpt)
by Carl Sandburg

Hog Butcher for the World,
Tool Maker, Stacker of Wheat,
Player with Railroads
   and the Nation's Freight Handler;
Stormy, husky, brawling,
City of Big Shoulders . . .

Carl Sandburg. 1944. *Chicago Poems.* New York: Harcourt Brace Jovanovich.

London
by William Blake

I wander thro' each charter'd street,
Near where the charter'd Thames does flow,
And mark in every face I meet
Marks of weakness, marks of woe.
In every cry of every Man,
In every Infant's cry of fear,
In every voice, in every ban,
The mind-forg'd manacles I hear.
How the Chimney-sweeper's cry
Every black'ning Church appalls;
And the hapless soldier's cry,
Runs in blood down Palace walls.
But most thro' midnight streets I hear
How the youthful Harlot's curse
Blasts the new born Infant's tear,
And blights with plagues the Marriage hearse.

G. Keynes. 1977. *William Blake: Songs of Innocence and Experience.* New York: Oxford University Press.

Labour and the London Poor; and Charles Booth, *Life and Labour of the People in London.* In carrying out their detailed investigations of the Victorian underworld . . . each pointed out what Booth called "the problem of poverty in the midst of wealth" (1987: 3).

In chapters to follow we will see that many of the ideas associated with modern life have their origins in observations made about industrial cities. The same core problem of uneven development—the graphic contrast between the wealthy and the poor, for example, and the contradictions between progress and misery—remains very much at the center of the urban dynamic in cities around the globe. On the one hand, the city represented hope to all those laboring under meager conditions in the countryside. It was the site of industrialization and the great dream of modernization and progress. On the other hand, the powerful forces of urbanism dwarfed the individual and crushed the masses into dense, environmentally strained spaces. The city rhythm, unlike that of the country, was above nature, and life was worth only as much as the daily wage it could be exchanged for. These contrasting images of the city are captured by two poems—the promise of urban life in a poem by Carl Sandburg; the horror, by William Blake (see Box 2.2).

Were cities in the United States much like their European counterparts? There is some evidence that the early Native Americans of the Mississippi developed settlement spaces of considerable population concentration (Nash, 1974). The processes of urbanization and capitalism which created large cities in Europe during the nineteenth century also thrived in the United States at the same time. In many ways, U.S. cities were governed by the same dynamic as in Europe. In some important ways, however, the former cities represent unique cases in the history of urbanism. We will explore this record in the next chapters.

CHAPTER 3

URBANIZATION IN THE UNITED STATES

The United States is one of the most urbanized nations on the globe. Many of its people, however, dislike the large city. Thomas Jefferson (1977) suggested that cities were the source of evil and corruption that would threaten the young democracy's political system. Despite such sentiments, U.S. urban growth has been prolific and remains unabated after 300 years. For much of that history the everyday life of Americans was defined in urban terms.

In many respects development here mirrors the same trends and effects of social forces unleashed in Western Europe. We experienced, for example, the same industrial revolution as England did and even contributed significantly to its technological breakthroughs. Everyone has probably heard of McCormick's reaper or Thomas A. Edison's lightbulb. Such inventions helped the United States compete with industrial giants like England in the nineteenth century.

Yet, for all its close links to the Old World, the city building process in the United States exhibits several features that exaggerate aspects of urbanization found elsewhere. These include (a) the lack of walls or fortifications around cities; (b) real estate development as a major sector in the economy of capitalism; (c) the ideology of privatism which limits the role of the state and which places emphasis on individual accomplishments as the basis of community; (d) the effect of large-scale immigration and population churning on cities; and (e) the regional dispersal of the metropolis. In what follows I shall illustrate these features while discussing the larger context of U.S. urban history rather than focusing on them alone.

The Stages of Urban Growth

There is a variety of factors that contributed to urban expansion in the United States. The role of economic forces; transportation, construction, and communication technology;

TABLE 3.1
Stages of Capitalism and Stages of Urbanization in the United States

Stages of Capitalism	Stages of Urbanization
Mercantile-Colonial Period	Colonial Period: 1630 to 1812
Industrialization Period	Era of Expansion: 1812 to 1920
Monopoly Capitalism Period	Metropolitan Period: 1920 to 1960
Global Capitalism Period	Deconcentration Era: 1960 to today

political changes; immigration policy; and success at wars are but some of the major causes for the development of city building. The following discussion encapsulates the effects of these and other factors by applying the sociospatial perspective. In particular we recognize that *explanation for urban patterns is best when connection is made between the production of settlement space and the society's political economy.* According to the sociospatial perspective, this does not mean that the clearly defined stages of metropolitan growth are directly correlated to exact stages of economic development, only that important features of each period in economic development are associated in certain ways with important factors in the phases of metropolitan change (see Table 3.1).

Most analysts seem to agree with the historian Eric Monkkonen (1989) that three distinct stages characterize growth in the United States since the seventeenth century. We shall consider these as (1) the Colonial Period: 1630 to 1812; (2) the Era of Expansion: 1812 to 1920; and (3) the Metropolitan Period: 1920 to 1960. But I also find it necessary to modify the historical approach and add a fourth stage, the Deconcentration Era: 1960 to the present. The latter two periods will be studied in subsequent chapters after we have learned the lessons of our less immediate history as an urbanizing nation.

The stages of urban development correspond to the growth periods in the development of U.S. capitalism. These are (1) the Mercantile-Colonial Period; (2) the Industrialization Period; and (3) the Monopoly Capitalism Period. The fourth stage that I have added, the Deconcentration Era, corresponds to the fourth stage of capitalism, (4) Global Capitalism. These periods do not represent an evolutionary theory of development such as that of Childe in the last chapter. Although cities in the United States went through these periods, there is no reason why another society has to pass through exactly the same sequence as the United States, as indeed other countries' economic transformations also differ from ours. Furthermore, according to the sociospatial perspective, stages in metropolitan growth and in the political economy are only loosely coupled, as mentioned above. Nonetheless, discussion of separate phases of city building is an effective way of organizing our analysis of the connection between developments in the U.S. political economy and the forms of settlement space over time.

The Colonial Period: 1630 to 1812

The United States was colonized by European capitalist societies operating according to the political economy of *mercantilism* which was an early stage of global capitalism.

In this system the nation-states of Europe organized the expansion of their local economies at a time when manufacturing was *not* industrialized and with the aid of the political apparatus of the nation-state. The wealth of countries, it was believed, depended on the well-being of commerce or trade, while domestic manufacture was protected from foreign competition by government tariffs. Mercantilist theory called for the colonization of resource rich but undeveloped areas of the globe accomplished through the state's own military and naval power. Wealth would increase if raw materials could be plundered from the undeveloped colonies, while manufactured articles would be produced exclusively in the home countries. By these arrangements, the maximum amount of work would be given to the nation's own laborers and excess population could be drained off to the colonies.

In the 1700s the cities of the United States were little more than colonial outposts of England, France, and Spain located on the shores of a country with a foreboding and unsettled interior. The attention and the energies of the colonists were directed eastward across the Atlantic Ocean toward the colonial powers and events in Europe. The existence of these cities was guaranteed by the might of the colonial power's navy and military organization.

Colonial cities were port cities. The docks and warehouses, the shipping, insurance, and trading companies constituted the focus of urban development. Further back from the port facilities merchant and counting houses were located, while behind the port district the beginnings of residential quarters, principally for the colonial businessmen and their families, were located. Artisans of all kinds who engaged in handicraft manufacture of the simple implements required for daily life were also located in the

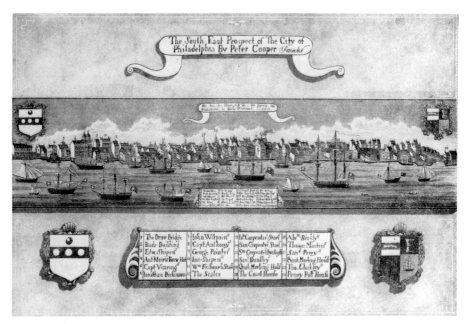

Colonial Philadelphia. (See Box 3.1, page 45.)

town. Their shops and residences were situated throughout the port district. Land use in early Boston, for example, is illustrated by Figure 3.1 below.

As mercantilism developed it also became a way of relieving population pressures by promoting immigration to the colonies. This, in turn, stimulated a nascent real estate industry in the port cities. Many U.S. cities, in fact, were laid out to accommodate both mercantile economic functions *and* residential real estate speculation. Often, single entrepreneurs in England were granted permission by the Crown to set up their own town as just such a speculative enterprise. The case of Philadelphia, founded in the late 1600s by the Quaker entrepreneur William Penn, is illustrative of the combined mercantile and real estate venture:

> Philadelphia was laid out in 1681 on a plan that was probably the original speculator's design for an American City, a plot that measured one by two miles and was easily divided into lots that might be sold at a distance (Vance, 1990: 265).

The colonial cities of the United States prospered because of the success of British mercantilism. Each of the largest towns filled an economic function connected with European trade. Boston was the center for colonial provisions; Newport specialized in shipbuilding and slavetrading; New York trading focused on flour and furs; Philadelphia, on meat, wheat, and lumber; and Charleston was known for the export of rice and indigo. Initially, Baltimore had few natural advantages, and it lagged behind the growth of these five, but in the later 1700s its businesses specialized in the flour exporting

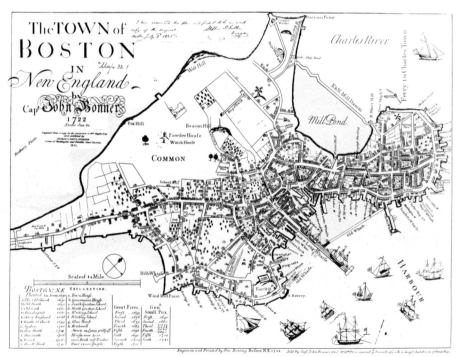

Figure 3.1   Colonial Boston, 1722. Note the spatial features of the port.

TABLE 3.2
Twenty Most Populated Colonial Cities, 1790

City	Total population	Rank
New York City, NY	32,305	1
Philadelphia, PA	28,522	2
Litchfield, CT	20,278	3
Boston, MA	18,038	4
Northern Libertiestown, PA	9,907	5
Rensselaerwick, NY	8,305	6
Watervliet, NY	7,422	7
Stephentown, NY	7,209	8
Newport, RI	6,744	9
Canaan, NY	6,670	10
Providence, RI	6,371	11
Canajoharie, NY	6,155	12
Fishkill, NY	5,941	13
Frederickstown, NY	5,932	14
Southwark, PA	5,663	15
Marblehead, MA	5,661	16
Gloucester, MA	5,317	17
Amwell, NJ	5,201	18
Washington, NY	5,190	19
Cambridge, NY	5,009	20

Source: *A Century of Population Growth in the United States, 1790–1900.* U.S. Department of Commerce and Labor, Bureau of the Census, Table 104, p. 1909.

trade and it prospered. However, towns like Williamsburg, Virginia, which were laid out solely as political centers, never grew. Colonial cities and their populations are illustrated in Table 3.2.

In Table 3.2, which lists all towns with populations of 5,000 or more in 1790, we see that New York City and towns in New York State dominated the colonies. Some cities, like Philadelphia and Boston, remain important population centers today. Others, such as Stephentown, New York, or Southwark, Pennsylvania, never became metropolises.

By the time of the Revolutionary War, U.S. cities played a crucial role due to their demographic and economic power. The first confrontations, such as the Boston Tea Party, took place in cities. The wealth concentrated in New York, Boston, Philadelphia, and Newport also financed the revolt. Colonial cities became centers of propaganda that disseminated antiloyalist views throughout the colonies. At the time of the revolution, for example, thirty-six newspapers actively operated in the colonies (not all of which opposed the Crown). Finally, a major role was played by cities because they nurtured paramilitary organizations. These organizations became part of the colonial militia when war finally broke out. One example was the Sons of Liberty in the New York Colony:

> Founded in the fall of 1765 as a secret organization, the Sons of Liberty became a public body with meetings announced in newspapers. . . . In addition to communicating with other groups in the New York colony, the Sons of Liberty also kept in touch with organi-

zations in such other colonial towns as Boston, Baltimore, and Newport. The Sons of Liberty armed themselves and became a paramilitary group ready to resist British encroachments. The group also provided an organizing function, marshalling two thousand people in October 1765 to prevent the landing of stamps to be used for tax purposes (Hoover, 1971: 92).

One legacy of colonial dependency was the absence of autonomous government and the concomitant lack of political responsibility among the citizens of the cities. As colonies they were administered by agents of the English king. Precisely this lack of political influence may have contributed to the revolutionary fervor, because the growing wealth and population of the colonies had no democratic recourse in the administration of port cities. In any event, the absence of autonomy, according to the historian Sam Bass Warner, Jr. (1962), fostered a "laissez-faire" economic and social milieu which developed into the culture of *privatism* that so characterizes U.S. cities even today (see chapters 11 and 15).

Privatism, a legacy of our colonial history, refers to the civic culture that eschews social interests in favor of the private pursuit of individual goals. From the very beginning of our urban experience, residents already believed their principal responsibility lay in the pursuit of self-interest. Unlike the citizens of ancient Athens, for example, who were obligated to pledge their indebtedness to the city that gave them birth, residents of the American colonies were not responsible to the city, only to the colonial power. Over the years this restrained greatly the development of a civic culture that fosters community values and social responsibility. Instead, the limited vision of privatism remains in place. According to Warner:

> To describe the American tradition of privatism is not to summarize the entire American cultural tradition. . . . The tradition of privatism is, however, the most important element of our culture for understanding the development of cities. The tradition of privatism has always meant that the cities of the United States depended for their wages, employment, and general prosperity upon the aggregate successes and failures of thousands of individual enterprises, not upon community action. It has also meant that the physical forms of American cities, their lots, houses, families, and streets have been the outcome of a real estate market of profit-seeking builders, land speculators, and large investors (Warner, 1968: 4).

A second legacy of colonial dependency was the absence of independent city economic rights. European cities of the late Middle Ages were powerful economic enterprises because they possessed independent charters of governance as well as the legal right to mint their own currency and conduct trade in their name. Colonial America granted no such privileges to its cities, and they did not possess chartered rights. There were no city trade monopolies, no special currency, and no city property-rights beyond city borders, unlike Western Europe. Trade was organized by the large European conglomerates such as the Hudson's Bay Company. Any individual or group of entrepreneurs could break away from a U.S. city and settle in the hinterland, forming a separate town. The varied reasons for such fragmentation could be religious, political, or economic. What mattered was only the relative ability to split off and settle elsewhere under the protective umbrella of the colonial powers. Laissez-faire, privatism, and the ease of settlement characterized city life during the colonial period. Its obverse was the absence of political autonomy characteristic of the urban community as described by Max Weber. Interestingly enough, even after the U.S. revolution, cities failed to acquire independent political rights except as far as these were granted to them by the states. Hence, the legacy of the colonial period remains very much with us today in the form of weak city government and limited city political power.

A third legacy of colonialism was the physical absence of city walls. Max Weber's ideal city of the Middle Ages possessed defensible fortifications or walls. Elsewhere, forts usually defined the old city center. Thus, the word *Kremlin* in Russia and *Casbah* in Morocco both mean the same thing, a fortress. U.S. cities built by colonial powers never exhibited this trait (although in some cases they did have temporary stockades) because the home country provided for the general defense of the region by sustaining a standing army (Monkkonen, 1989). It took the revolution to reverse this lack of autonomy. Consequently, unlike the walled cities of Europe in the late Middle Ages, U.S. places provided for immense locational freedom. Land could always be developed at the fringe. To the clean-cut speculators' grid of the colonial port city was added a surrounding fringe that could always grow by accretion and land speculation. This particular pattern remains very much with us today as growth occurs constantly at the fringe of development in a pattern of sprawl.

A final legacy of the colonial city was the role played by land development as a singular source of wealth in the economy. For the residents of the United States and unlike Europe, land was plentiful and cheap. Very early in the history of this country it became clear to enterprising Europeans with money to invest that land development was a principal way of acquiring greater wealth. But the very nature of exploiting this resource requires concomitant locational activities of a group of people and the ultimate attraction of residential and commercial users. It does little good to stake a land claim, no matter how large, in a wilderness with no friendly residents around, without an attendant scheme for the eventual development of the land including state protection for the influx of population. Hence, early in U.S. history land developers adopted the practice of working closely with politicians and colonial authorities to promote the development of select places. This pattern of *boosterism* involving speculators, developers, politicians, and state authorities, or a *growth network* (Gottdiener, 1985) composed of varied individuals that are like-minded developers of land, was repeated many times in our history and remains characteristic of development today (see Chapter 7). The sheer quantity of undeveloped land presented by the U.S. case represents a graphic contrast to the pattern of urbanization in Western Europe (which has always reined in the interests of developers for the good of the larger society and because of real estate's scarce supply), although it may have parallels in the recent history of countries like Australia and Brazil which also have abundant land masses.

It is often noted in elementary school lessons that George Washington, our first president, had the occupation of surveyor in his youth. In fact, George and his family were active real estate speculators. Surveying was just one aspect of this work. As one historian put it, land was "the real wealth" of the colonies. Perhaps his crowning achievement was his participation in the booster effort to develop Washington, D.C., as the nation's capital. In the 1780s the district was nothing more than an inhospitable swamp of worthless real estate. All that was to change through the efforts of newly achieved political power and economic investment in land. According to accounts of the time, "In 1793 George Washington led a procession with two brass bands and Masons in full costume across the Tiber to a barbecue and land auction at which he purchased the first lots of the new capital's undeveloped swampland. . . . Self-promotion, boosterism, and constant attention to the economic main chance soon came to character-ize the young nation's cities" (Monkkonen, 1989: 63). The experience of life in colonial cities is illustrated in Box 3.1 about colonial Philadelphia.

The Era of Expansion: 1812 to 1920

The settlement of the vast U.S. territory following the Revolutionary War constituted a magnificent drama involving individuals representing the very legends of our country itself. As Gary Nash (1974) has observed, this drama was colored in red, white, and black, because it involved a three-way clash between white former colonists, Native Americans, and black slaves. Frontiersmen like Davey Crockett shouldered hunting muskets and fought the Indian Wars. Native Americans such as the Apache chief Geronimo and his people were driven from their lands, killed in vast numbers, or resettled to make way for the white people's development of the interior.

Industrialists like J. P. Morgan or Jacob Astor accumulated vast sums of money in trade, banking, and real estate, only to lose power and wealth to other upstarts, such as Jay Gould, with equally ambitious schemes. Politicians like President Grover Cleveland mingled with the active boosters of growth during a time when corruption was a way of life in government. In the middle of it all the fate of the nation was decided in a civil war. Great spokespeople like Frederick Douglass articulated the pain of suppression under which black people were living as slaves. Eventually, slavery was defeated but so too was the rural way of Southern life in a society that shifted from plantation agriculture to industrialized farming and manufacture. Technology, industrialization, city government, and land development took over the stage of ur-ban growth.

It is helpful to think of American capitalism as acting like a large land development agency in addition to its role as an industrial enterprise. During the period of formative growth, entrepreneurs singled out choice locations in the advancing path of expansion and built cities. According to the historian Richard C. Wade (1959), city construction took place in many cases *before* population influx. That is, urbanization in the United States was often land speculation which proceeded with the aid of local governments. In a sense, the establishment of a town as a political entity harnessed land to the control of growth interests. As a consequence of political reforms during the presidency of Andrew Jackson, it was comparatively easy for groups of capitalist land developers to declare their projects incorporated cities. Hence, with the aid of home rule, the expansion westward during the century between 1812 and 1920 when the majority of the U.S. population became city residents was an urban expansion and simultaneously an explo-sion in the number of governments at the local level. By founding towns, developers also used local governments to provide a civic or community structure for people who came there to live.

BOX 3.1 CASE STUDY OF COLONIAL PHILADELPHIA

The case of colonial Philadelphia illustrates the way culture in the form of religious attitudes linked with economic interests in the development of land. In the 1680s William Penn organized a group of fellow Quakers and obtained permission from the king of England to establish a colony in the New World which he called Philadelphia, or "the city of brotherly love." It was located at the confluence of the Delaware and Schuylkill rivers, and in 1683 there were 357 houses of settlement containing merchants and businessmen involved in mercantile trade, as well as local artisans and farmers who serviced the growing population.

Plentiful resources of the region supported the colony. Houses were fashioned from lumber or built of red brick, the latter more costly and reserved for the more affluent. Game and fish were staples of diet, along with oysters from the river basin. The Native Americans of the region were friendly and showed the colonists how to raise corn and produce hominy.

In 1710 a visitor to the colony, Richard Castelman, was so impressed with its quality of life that he wrote about it to friends in England:

> A noble, large and populous city ... here all religions are tolerated, which is one means to increase the riches of the place; here a journeyman taylor has 12 shillings a week, besides his board; and here even the meanest single women marry well, and, being above want, are above work. If the distressed people of England knew the comforts of this colony, and the easy means there is of a livelihood, they would never stay where they are, in a continual scene of poverty and misery (Repplier, 1898: 29).

Letters like the one above sent back home to England served to promote the colonies and, because conditions were worse for many in England, prompted people to try their luck in the New World. By 1720 Philadelphia was the center for immigrant entry into the United States and the largest of the colonies, numbering 10,000 inhabitants. By 1775 its population was 23,700.

By the time of the revolution, Philadelphia had long since abandoned its role as a religious center of the Quakers and assumed its status as a money-making mecca. At this time the civic ideology of privatism was already dominant. Personal achievement was measured in the successful search for wealth, while community interests were defined in terms of like-minded, money-making families (Warner, 1968: 3).

These real estate projects which opened the American frontier did not proceed in isolation. Entrepreneurs were also merchants or industrialists. Money was invested in commercial enterprises as well as in land. In fact, capital often flowed back and forth between investments in industry and investment in land. This relation will be explained more fully in Chapter 7. Thus, Cyrus McCormick, the inventor of the reaper, made millions in the 1800s from his factory, but his real wealth came from investment of those profits in real estate (Longstreet, 1973).

Many of the West's present-day cities were founded by the Southern Pacific–Central Pacific railroad builders. The photo shows two woodburner locomotives in front of El Capitan Hotel, one of the first buildings erected in Merced, California.

In addition, the technology of transport became an explicit means through which investors of capital centered in cities competed with each other to build new cities on the frontier. Thus, railroad entrepreneurs like Leland Stanford were also city builders. Let us consider the era of urban expansion according to these interrelated links between forms of capital, government policies and politicians, and forms of technology.

Land Development and Technology. Prior to the 1820s the U.S. urban population remained relatively stable at around 10 percent of the total. After that time a sudden burst of urbanization surfaced that did not abate until the 1930s. By the 1920 census over half of all Americans were already living in cities. Hence, in the 100 years from 1820 the United States had been transformed into an urbanized nation.

After the War of 1812 hinterland development was consolidated in the Ohio Valley and the Midwest. At this stage economic interests located within the large east coast cities turned an about-face by ignoring the mercantilist needs of trade with Europe, and actively pursued the development of the interior. In all respects, early westward expansion was highly dependent both on the development of transportation technology and on the protection of white settlers by government from attacks by Native-American residents. Land was realized as a capital investment only after transportation and communication infrastructure could be put in place. Roads had to be built. Tracks had to be laid. Telegraph lines were installed. Additionally, the safety of work crews for all these efforts had to be assured. Land was being taken from Native Americans, an effort that required organized government activity and military intervention.

Hinterland development did not follow automatically after the application of transportation technology to growth. Local capital had to be organized to bring about development. Often, entrepreneurs competed with each other over investments in the interior of the country because at the time, the unity of capital under corporate interests that cut across space and united efforts in different cities had not yet fully matured. Consequently, westward expansion was a characteristic of competitive capital and was often marked by the schemes of single individuals who sought to build up business and build a city at the same time.

For example, the earliest urban rivalry involved local capitalists situated in the important east coast port cities. Their future fortunes depended on the continuing success of their respective trade routes to the interior, because the latter was the source of goods for export and raw materials needed by local manufacturers.

Just after the War of 1812 the shortest route to the west lay across either Pennsylvania or Maryland. There were two roads—the "national road" out of Baltimore and the "Pittsburgh Pike" out of Philadelphia—but these links were inadequate for handling the heavy agricultural products of the interior (Rubin, 1970: 128). Instead, produce was shipped south on the Mississippi River to New Orleans, making that city the most important export center.

New York entrepreneurs saw their city faced with decline as the frontier expanded west. In 1817 they began construction of a canal that linked the Hudson River at Albany 364 miles westward to Buffalo on Lake Erie. In a bold stroke they hoped to create the most efficient link to the hinterland, with Buffalo becoming an inland port for the Great Lakes region of the Midwest. The canal was completed in 1825 and was so successful that it inspired a craze of canal building across the United States. From its inception, New York City competed effectively with New Orleans as an export point for agricultural produce.

As a result of the successful Erie Canal venture, Philadelphia and Baltimore financial interests were faced with decline, if not extinction. As the historian J. Rubin (1970: 131) notes, they responded with their own schemes, aided greatly by government laws and subsidies. Initially, Philadelphia interests demanded that the state proceed with a canal to Ohio. However, construction failed in the Allegheny Mountains and a rail segment was required. This occurred several times, so that Philadelphia ended up with a mixed canal and rail portage system that required several transshipments. The route was hopelessly incapable of competing with New York's Erie Canal.

Baltimore interests viewed Philadelphia's problems with trepidation. They saw the difficulty of crossing the Appalachian Mountains via canal. By the 1830s the steam locomotive had just been perfected in England and, in a venture as bold as the New York effort, they opted for the construction of a railroad line that would connect Baltimore with the Ohio Valley over the mountains. The line was eventually called the Baltimore and Ohio Railroad, and it was remarkably successful. As a consequence of these improvements, New York and Baltimore prospered while Boston and Philadelphia declined. In addition, the links to the interior in the 1830s helped found the midwestern Great Lakes cities of Chicago, Detroit, and Cleveland, which also prospered because of successful rail and canal traffic to east coast ports.

In the period between 1830 and 1920 the most significant technological innovation was the joint development of the steel rail and steam locomotive that perfected the long haul for commerce, resources, and people. Of the 153 major U.S. cities existing today, 75 percent had been established after 1840 when the railroad matured as an established infrastructure, and only 9 percent of these same major cities were built after 1910 (Monkkonen, 1989: 75). It would be simple to suggest that transportation technology alone caused the explosion of urbanization. This would be misleading. Technology became the means of growth, but inception and execution were the result both of the quest for wealth among entrepreneurs and of the desires of politicians in government at all levels—local, state, and federal—that joined these ventures, aiding them with political resources. It is precisely this conjuncture of investors, political power mongers, and the dream of wealth that characterizes the second stage of urbanization in the United States. According to the historians Glaab and Brown, for example,

> Earlier rivalries had been limited by nature—by the location of rivers and lakes. But railroads were not bound by topography, by the paths of river commerce, or by natural trade patterns. Railroads could be built anywhere, creating cities where they chose. Since the building of railroads was dependent to a considerable extent on subsidies from local communities, railroad leaders were willing to bargain with competing towns to obtain the best possible deal in stock subscriptions, bond issues, and right-of-ways. . . . The "boosterism" associated with the midwest and areas further west is largely a legacy of the late nineteenth century era of urban rivalry (Glaab and Brown, 1967: 112).

As we shall see as well in our discussion of the last two stages of urban growth, this pattern of capital investment coupled with government subsidies and competition between separate places is repeated countless times and characterizes urban growth and change in the United States and possibly elsewhere. As the sociospatial approach suggests, development was a consequence of a combination of economic, political, and cultural factors—the frontier myth and the American Dream of wealth combined with cooperative government officials and venture capitalists to urbanize the nation.

What exactly were the proportions involved in the lure of wealth that accompanied town building? Consider the case of the Illinois Central Railroad. Its promoters were also prolific city builders. In 1850 there were ten existing towns in the vicinity of the railroad's route. After expansion ten years later there were forty-seven, and by 1870 there were eighty-one. When the Illinois Central entrepreneurs could not make subsidy agreements with the politicians of existing towns for their right of way, they just built their own towns nearby. Champaign, Illinois, for example, was constructed directly by the railroad adjacent to the existing town of Urbana.

Another example shows us the size of the profit realized from real estate alone. Kankakee, Illinois, was built by this same railroad in 1855 at a cost of $10,000, and after just one year the owners had already realized $50,000 in lot sales, or a profit of 500 percent, with more city land remaining. A similar pattern was repeated as expansion

BOX 3.2 THE TENEMENT CIRCA 1860s

Usually such a building contained a narrow hall opening from a street or court; on each floor, including the cellar, two suites of rooms opened into the hall. Front and rear rooms of the building contained windows, but the bedrooms and closets in the middle were dark. In most cases, there was another tenement in the backyard, frequently altogether enclosed and accessible only through an alley. Alongside these buildings and in the yards were many little, irregular frame structures, some in dilapidated condition, serving partly as sheds and partly as homes for the overflow of the tenements. Such haphazard conditions of front and rear buildings on the same lot created an intricate array of rear courts and alleys, notoriously dark, foul-smelling, and encumbered with accumulations of filth (Ernst, 1970: 114).

moved west involving a host of other promoters and their railroads. In San Francisco, which had developed as the premier city of the west coast during this period, town lots that could be bought for $1,500 in 1850 were worth from $8,000 to $27,000 just three years later in 1853 (Glaab and Brown, 1967: 113, 121).

Manufacturing. So far the impression has been fostered that city building involved exclusively land development schemes combining capital, government, and transport technology. During the period between 1812 and 1920, however, the United States became a world leader in manufacturing. Forces of industrialization unleashed with such effect in England during this time had similar results here. During the period between 1850 and 1900, for example, U.S. production of textiles multiplied seven times, iron and steel increased ten times, the processing of agricultural products expanded fourteen times, and the production of agricultural implements increased twenty-five times (Hoover, 1971: 180).

The very heart of industrialization was the factory, which was the engine that drove the industrial stage of capitalism. But workers and capitalists were not simply disembodied abstractions. They were people who required places to live, raise families, and spend whatever leisure time they had. Industrialization, therefore, produced the factory town or community which contained workers' families and houses, machinery, and energy sources, all within close proximity.

The first American manufacturing city was Lowell, Massachusetts, which was located on the Merrimack River at a site where the water dropped ninety feet and provided the original power source for its factories. Investors chose this place for a complex of cotton mills and struck on the idea of importing a labor force of young women from the neighboring cities, especially Boston, because they would be easy to control as a source of nonunion labor power. The geographer James Vance gives this account of the city:

> In 1845, thirty-three of the large mill buildings ranged along the canals and banks of the Merrimack, making Lowell the largest cotton town in America and one of its few great industrial cities, with a population of thirty thousand. A full third of the population was engaged as operatives in the mills or their workshops, though female employment remained disproportionate with 6,320 females and 2,915 males (Vance, 1990: 347).

49

Early industrialization in the United States is associated with the names of entrepreneurs who perfected specific products. Singer sewing machines, Yale locks, Armour hams, McCormick reapers, and Remington typewriters are but some of these innovations. Later on, in most cases, the descendants of the originators carried on the family name and its business. In the 1860s the leading industries reflected early development of manufacturing and the persisting importance of the United States as a supplier of natural resources. Cotton goods, lumber, boots and shoes, and flour dominated. By 1910, according to Geruson and McGrath (1977: 68), the major industries reflected the maturation of manufacturing and consisted of machinery, iron and steel, lumber, clothing, and railroad cars, among other products.

Population Churning and Immigration. We have covered several features of the U.S. case so far. One of the most distinctive is the phenomenon of population turnover or churning which, for a time, was quite exaggerated here compared to other countries. From the mid-1800s to 1900s, U.S. cities functioned as giant magnets that attracted immigrants from all over the world. Prior to the 1800s most people came from the British Isles, or as slaves captured from Africa. After 1830 many more arrived from Germany, Scandinavia, Central and Eastern Europe, and China. Between 1800 and 1925 over 40 million immigrants entered the United States. Seventeen million arrived during the period between 1846 and 1900 alone (Vance, 1990: 359).

These figures, however, do not capture the way cities functioned as entry points for people. In effect, cities such as New York, Chicago, Philadelphia, and Boston processed vast numbers of immigrants from Europe and elsewhere, orienting them to life in America before many made their way into the hinterland. At this time the internal demographic differentiation of cities took on the characteristics commonly associated with their residential patterns, namely, mosaics of little worlds comprising ethnic enclaves of immigrants. The robustness of cultural life found there inspired succeeding generations of urban sociologists in their studies.

During the period of urban expansion, population churned throughout the large cities. By one conservative estimate, half of the residents moved each decade only to be replaced by still more immigrants (Monkkonen, 1989). A study of Boston in the year 1890, for example, revealed that with a total population of approximately 450,000 people, at least 600,000 had moved in a decade before, while somewhat more than 500,000 had moved out. In short, the population size of cities during the formative period of expansion is a static figure that disguises the massive movement of people into and out of these cities.

In a subsequent chapter we shall take a closer look at the importance of immigration to American cities. One way of appreciating population churning is to consider the economic and political opportunities created by the phenomenon. Each new immigrant had to be processed by federal, state, and local officials, which meant more government jobs. Schoolteachers were in constant demand, as were settlement house workers, religious functionaries, and the many specialized businesses that catered to the needs of arrivals from foreign lands. City economies thrived not only because of the influx of population but also because it turned over so frequently, making the same services necessary to new people with similar needs as previous arrivals. Above all else the

BOX 3.3 A CASE STUDY: CHICAGO IN THE NINETEENTH CENTURY

Although some contest the fact, Chicago was founded in 1779 by a black man, Jean B. P. de Saible, the son of a slave woman and a French aristocrat. It was called "Checagou" or "bad stink" by the Native Americans because it was marshland. But the two rivers, the Chicago and the Calumet, intersecting with Lake Michigan gave the area possibilities. In the 1800s, with the mass migrations west and the opening up of the Erie Canal, Chicago became a boomtown. It received a city charter in 1837. At this time in our nation's history, the sheer amount of money that was available from east coast investors and the massive numbers of immigrants looking for work all came together in the new towns and propelled them into greatness with unparalleled energy. One account of the 1850s is illustrative of the entire era that we have just examined:

> Hotels and boarding houses were always full, and full meant three in a bed sometimes, with the floor covered besides. . . . All about the outskirts of the settlement was a cordon of prairie schooners, with tethered horses between, interspersed with camp fires at which the busy housewives were ever preparing meals. A fast-writing lawyer could make five hundred dollars a day writing land titles. Everyday millions of dollars in land values changed hands. Farm lots, city frontage sold added up to millions of dollars. Everyone who had wooden stakes, a hammer, and greedy ways could mark out lots, set up in business, make himself plats of towns and cities that existed only in the spinning minds of the promoters (Longstreet, 1973: 26).

In our case study of Philadelphia we noted that letters home to England about the high quality of life in the colonies contributed to the popularity of immigration. The historian S. Longstreet quotes another letter home from a Chicago visitor to friends back East during the 1830s land boom (1973: 27). Tracts bought in 1833 for $5,500 sold three years later for $100,000. "Gordon D. Hubbard, Indian trader, bought two lots on La Salle Street for $66.66, sold them for $80,000" (Longstreet, 1973: 24).

After the land boom, the commercial and industrial capitalists arrived. Marshall Field, a young and enterprising merchant, came to Chicago from New York and opened a large general store in 1872. Later, using the French innovation of the department store, he founded a chain that exists to this day. Marshall Field's department store in Chicago set the commercial trends for the city. Cyrus McCormick, another entrepreneur from the East, settled in Chicago and perfected his reaper there. In 1847 he opened his first factory and by 1858 he was earning a million dollars a year selling his famous reapers.

By the 1860s Chicago was a railroad hub counting nine different lines

(continued)

that ran into the city. The Civil War made its people wealthy. Two men in particular, Philip D. Armour and Gustavas F. Swift, made their fortunes selling meat to the Union Army. Both men had come west from New England. They helped build the union stockyards, a 345-acre tract on the South Side that became the great slaughterhouse of the nation. Pigs, sheep, and steers were killed and processed there by the hundreds of millions. Armour and Swift became rich, but at the turn of the century, the famous muckracker, Upton Sinclair, in his book *The Jungle*, exposed the horrors of the meat packing industry and its deplorable working conditions which the owners had tolerated for decades.

The historian Edward Wagenknecht (1964: 105) considers the reputation of all these men secondary to "the greatest Chicagoan of all," Jane Addams. She possessed a "genuis for goodness," and, although not the originator of the settlement house movement, was its driving force at the turn of the century. Hull House, which opened its doors in the fall of 1889, became a center of social intervention in the lives of the impoverished immigrant workers in the town:

> Jane Addams saw the worst sights of her generation; she was familiar with every phase of the sacrifice of human values that is exacted when a great city places a purely commercial valuation upon the impulses of youth. .... Yet she insisted uncompromisingly on "the very energy of existence, the craving for enjoyment, the pushing of vital forces, the very right of every citizen to be what he is without pretense or assumption of virtue" (Wagenknecht, 1964: 109).

Jane Addams was one of the pioneers of the social work movement in this country, which tried to temper the harshness of unfettered capitalism by aspiring to a better life for urban dwellers through proper education, health care, family values, and aesthetic pursuits.

Chicago was not without its spectacular failures and successes. On October 8, 1871, a fire was started on the West Side in the O'Leary barn— by some children playing with matches, *not* by the famous cow. It spread quickly through the densely packed tenements, jumping the Chicago River to the South Side. The city went up in flames and it took two days before the fire was put out. About 15,000 acres of prime urban property were destroyed and, tragically, several hundred lives. Nearly 14,000 buildings were burned to the ground. It took years for the city to recover. In fact, in the years to follow the first of many recessions afflicted the United States in general and Chicago in particular. Capital dried up and businesses went under. Unemployment rose in the 1870s and with it the popularity of communist and socialist ideas.

By the 1880s a depression was in force for most of the United States. The businessmen of Chicago hired a private detective, Allan Pinkerton, and his gang to break up worker meetings which were being held with greater frequency. Chicago's laborers had become organized, as had workers in other U.S. cities, and they formed the Workingman's Party of the United

States. On May 8, 1886, they called for a mass rally to protest the depression conditions. It was to be held at the Haymarket on Randolph Street. "Two hundred cops waited at the Desplaines Police Station a block from the meeting. They were all issued new revolvers, said a report, and hickory skull-cracking clubs 'extra long.' Scores of detectives dressed as workers, as always, moved out to mingle with the crowd" (Longstreet, 1973: 251). During the rally, as the police massed to break up the meeting, someone threw a bomb at the police. Seven were killed and sixty were injured. No one knew who threw the bomb, but later the leaders of the workers, including August Spies, the editor of the communist paper *Arbeiter Zeitung*, were rounded up and given a mock trial; most were then hanged.

By the 1890s Chicago had recovered. It aspired to be a great city again. The business and political leaders decided to organize an exposition to commemorate Columbus' discovery of the New World. It was meant to be a world's fair that would glorify the virtues of civic planning in Chicago. The World's Columbian Exposition opened on May 1, 1893, on 6,000 acres. Classic white buildings of plaster in Greek, Roman, and Gothic revival dominated. But the innovative transportation building designed by Louis Sullivan captured the scene and ushered in a new era of urban architecture using brick construction, intersecting arches, and decorated facades. Four hundred thousand people passed through the fair, including President Grover Cleveland. Little Egypt, a belly dancer, was the big hit. Chicago captured the focus of the nation.

Columbian Exposition, Chicago, 1893.

The Lower East Side of New York City at the turn of the century.

rapid increase in population provided U.S. industry not only with much needed labor power but also with the bodies of consumers that could use the products being churned out by the factories. Export trade during this period of U.S. history was not as important as was the growing domestic market of consumers.

Population influx had a dramatic effect on the internal configuration of cities. Owners of buildings soon discovered that the voracious demand for housing could be met by converting structures to rental units. Later, new buildings called tenements were constructed specifically for rental use. Housing was designed in these buildings to squeeze as many families together as possible. The increased density made public health crises common. It also increased the risks of fire. On October 18, 1871, for example, the city of Chicago was almost destroyed by a single fire. Other fires at the turn of the century devastated cities like Boston and San Francisco.

Yet the escalating demand for housing also afforded handsome profits to owners of tenements. According to one estimate, annual returns on rentals could be as high as 40 percent and by 1890 as much as 77 percent of all city dwellers were renters (Glaab and Brown, 1967: 160). A description of a typical tenement is found in Box 3.2.

The Role of Technology: Building Innovations and Urban Transport. During the 1800s the spatial organization of the city changed as new forms of building introduced a larger scale to the physical environment, aided greatly by several innovations in construction. The balloon-frame house replaced heavy timber construction in the 1830s and made it possible for building to proceed more rapidly and with greater quantity than in the past. In 1848 James Bogardus introduced the use of cast iron columns and weight-bearing walls supporting the structure of nonresidential buildings which eliminated the need for heavy masonry construction and which opened the internal space of buildings so that factories and warehouses could maximize their unimpeded use of floor space. Elisha Otis invented the elevator, and by 1880 its widespread use enabled taller buildings to work more efficiently. Finally, in 1884 William L. Jenny erected the first skyscraper, the ten-story Home Insurance Building in Chicago, which was also the "first building with a fully iron structure carrying the weight of the edifice" (Vance, 1990: 471). The city of skyscrapers was not far away after that.

Tall building construction, unimpeded floor space allowing for the efficient place-ment of machinery, and the remarkable innovation of the elevator transformed the city into an arena of concentrated industry during the last half of the nineteenth century. Mobility of the workforce became a paramount concern at this time. The need for mass transport was met by a series of innovations, starting with the horse-drawn omnibus which carried twelve to twenty passengers (Glaab and Brown, 1967: 147). By the 1850s these were replaced by the horse-drawn railway car which not only facilitated the movement of people into and out of the "downtown" districts, but also provided the means by which the middle class could suburbanize (Warner, 1962). In the 1870s the horse was finally replaced by the steam powered locomotive. By 1881 the elevated lines or "L"s of New York City were carrying 175,000 passengers a day!

Finally, surpassing all these advances, a major breakthrough occurred in the 1870s when Nikola Tesla's discoveries on alternating current were applied to the production of electrical power. The dynamo replaced the battery, and electric trains and trolleys were perfected. Electrification made possible the extensive, nonpolluting trolley system and also the underground subway train. This change was remarkable. As Glaab and Brown observe, "In 1890, 69.7 percent of the total trackage in cities was operated by horses; by 1902 this figure had declined to 1.1 percent, while electric power was used on 97 percent of the mileage" (1967: 148).

The result of all these transformations was the diurnal rhythm of city life—masses of workers converging on business districts in the morning, only to disperse at day's end with the same great spurt aided by efficient and safe mass transit. By the 1920s the United States had successfully integrated millions of immigrants from over 100 countries into an industrial labor force. Its large cities were all built and humming with activity. Industrialization and urbanization had not only settled the frontier but led the country itself to a place among the world's powers. Box 3.3 illustrates the experience of the city of Chicago during this time.

CHAPTER
4

THE METROPOLITAN PERIOD IN THE UNITED STATES: 1920 TO 1960

T he period of urban expansion was a time when economic interests located within cities competed with each other and when land development in the West made people wealthy. This stage would pass as smaller businesses began to be gobbled up by larger interests. The phase of competitive capitalism slowly gave way to a new era, that of monopoly capitalism. In turn, cities grew progressively larger.

City building and population churning slowed down considerably in the United States in the 1900s following a series of economic depressions. This unsettling downturn culminated in the Great Depression of the late 1920s which lasted to the early 1930s. Urban activity picked up again as government reforms aided economic recovery and as the United States mobilized for another world war in the 1940s. During the metropolitan period cities not only grew larger, they also spread out beyond the political boundaries of their local governments. New areas of development became, in turn, new cities, or in many cases, urbanization simply engulfed the smaller towns adjacent to the large cities through a region-wide process of suburbanization.

In the metropolitan period it was becoming necessary to think about the urban phenomenon less in terms of the large city and more in terms of a region consisting of a mix of residential, work, recreational, and shopping places. The U.S. Department of the Census introduced the term *Standard Metropolitan Statistical Area* (SMSA—see Chapter 1) to account for the regional nature of development. Large central cities such as New York or Detroit also assumed vast economic importance far beyond their borders because of the businesses that were centered there, in this case finance or cars, respectively. This conjunction of spatial reach and economic might gave the city a new name, the "metropolis," or "mother city." Visions of the immense city outgrowing its boundaries began to appear in many countries. The German film *Metropolis* is one

Park Avenue, New York City—the grand vision of metropolitan life.

such example. Cities such as Tokyo, London, Paris, Berlin, Rome, Rio de Janeiro, and Calcutta all reached an unprecedented scale of size and population.

Following the 1930s period of recovery, the metropolitan pattern of increasing size and geographical territory became characteristic of many cities in the United States. Urban scientists became interested in the phenomenon of the metropolitan region, and many studies were carried out to discover its social, political, spatial, and economic characteristics (McKenzie, 1933; Schnore, 1957; Bollens and Schmandt, 1965). Research revealed that there were two processes in particular which contributed most to regional growth: greater differentiation of the system of cities, expressed as changes in spatial, functional, and demographic differentiation; and the process of suburbanization.

Spatial, Functional, and Demographic Differentiation of the City

According to the sociospatial perspective, metropolitan development and change do not occur because of economic factors alone but are also dependent on political and cultural relations. Economic activities, for example, require a workforce and certain community services, such as adequate schooling and health care, in order for businesses and their labor pools to survive over time. When there is a proper mesh between the human tissue of family and community life, and associated economic activities requiring particular skill levels, then both business and neighborhoods prosper. In short, the relations between the economy, political structure, and culture are reciprocal.

Accommodations between the social fabric of community life and the needs of business produced the early factory towns, such as Burlington, Vermont, and Birmingham, Alabama, during the early period of family capitalism. One characteristic of this phase was that sources of employment and the labor pool were close together and they were both tied to the general fate of the city itself. As the structure of capitalism changed in the 1930s, this equilibrium was shattered, and upheavals in the community went along with those in business. Neighborhood relations changed when people were thrown out of work after plants closed or businesses altered their skill needs. New demands were placed on school systems, city budgets, and families to aid in the adjustment. In many cases whether or not new ways of doing business were successful depended on how well the community, local government, and families adapted to change. Thus, while economic alterations affect the social fabric, the latter, in turn, can also affect the well-being of the local economy.

Consequently, each time new economic priorities are put in place, they affect the composition of territory and alter community life. The social organization of a particular place—the way it is organized according to locational choices of business, the scale of community, the flows of commuters, definitions of city service districts, the pace and structure of family life, and so on—is affected by the reciprocal relation between the local economy and the social fabric. In this chapter we shall discuss the changes brought about by the depression restructuring of the 1930s. They involve a process of *horizontal integration* of business activity coupled with metropolitan regional expansion. In the next chapter, we shall consider equally important changes that have occurred since 1960.

Changes in Spatial Differentiation

Following the Great Depression, the economic system of the United States changed from a comparatively competitive form of industrial capitalism with a relatively large number of firms in each industry to a concentrated form called "monopoly capitalism" (Baran and Sweezy, 1966) where ownership was consolidated in a few hands. One distinguishing characteristic of the new form was the growth of monopolistic (one firm) or oligopolistic (a select few firms) control of major industries. For example, automobile production prior to the 1930s involved a host of firms such as Studebaker, Hudson, Tucker, and De Soto, along with Ford, Pontiac, and Chrysler. These companies were scattered across much of the United States and their fates were often intertwined with specific cities and communities. After the 1930s production of automobiles was essentially in the hands of the Big Four—General Motors, Ford, Chrysler, and American Motors (today it's down to the first three). While these companies also maintained branch plants across the country, their operations were national in scope and their headquarters were no longer tied to the places where they had their major factories. The Detroit area, in particular, became the headquarters center for much of the auto industry, and decisions made there affected towns across the country. This change in the horizontal integration of large businesses to a more dispersed pattern coupled with greater concentration of ownership was also repeated in other industries, including steel, the production of consumer durables (such as electrical appliances), and even the consolidation of retailing outlets by giant department stores following branch marketing schemes (such as Sears Roebuck and Montgomery Ward).

Ford Motor plant in Detroit, Michigan. Note the full barges and active factories (1950s).

The changes in the scale of economic organization had spatial effects, especially on local community life, and several classic sociological studies documented them (Vidich and Bensman, 1960; Lynd and Lynd, 1937). Concentration of wealth and ownership led to greater horizontal integration of business activities and changes in the spatial relations between community, work, and region. That is, prior to the Depression, most companies had all their functions located together and generally in the same city. These firms were replaced by companies with divisions in any number of locations, which used dispersal in space to advantage in order to cut costs, especially labor costs. For example, a large company that might be part of an oligopoly in one industry would have its headquarters in a center such as New York where it might be close to the headquarters of the other oligopolists in the same industry. It would also be close to banking and related services necessary to the command and control function of business administration. Its specialized needs would stimulate the local community to supply laborers with adequate training for the jobs that were created. This same firm might have a branch plant for production located in Newark, a central distribution facility in Philadelphia, and so on, each with its own impact on the local community and labor force. Such a pattern of related functional differentiation and spatial or horizontal integration was replicated in many industries.

Changes in Functional Differentiation

As a consequence, after 1930, a new, functionally differentiated system of urban places had emerged in the United States. That is, different cities were the homes of different aspects of industry or commerce. Instead of competing with each other, as was the case during the previous period of competitive capitalism discussed in Chapter 3, local capital was now organized and integrated by a national system of concentrated wealth. This pattern was not a product of the city itself, but was attributable to the powers of institutions and social actors whose activities were deployed *within* the cities that were linked to the national corporations producing most of the country's wealth. Thus, horizontal integration and functional differentiation were two related outcomes in the restructuring of social organization after the 1930s. We call this interlinked complex of functionally differentiated activities located within urban places a *system of cities* (McKenzie, 1933; Berry, 1972; Bourne and Simmons, 1978). In studying this system, it is always important to keep in mind that functional differentiation is a feature of the particular complex of economic activities that are located within a city, rather than a characteristic of the city itself. Furthermore, the diverse activities across the nation are horizontally integrated by large corporations that possess "command and control" headquarters. By way of example, Table 4.1 illustrates the pattern of functional special-ization for eleven of the largest U.S. cities in 1990.

In Table 4.1 we can see that in 1990 virtually all cities had substantial sectors of service employment. Not surprisingly, Washington, D.C., is functionally specialized

TABLE 4.1
Functional Differentiation of Eleven Major U.S. Cities, 1990*
*Percentage employment in major industries by sector***

City	Manufacturing	Trade	Service	Other
Baltimore, MD	12.3	17.6	58.0	12.1
Boston, MA	9.9	16.6	64.6	8.9
Jacksonville, FL	9.4	22.7	52.4	15.5
Los Angeles, CA	18.4	20.1	50.3	11.1
New Orleans, LA	6.8	20.8	59.8	12.5
New York City, NY	11.4	17.2	60.3	11.0
San Diego, CA	13.9	21.7	53.9	10.6
San Francisco, CA	9.2	20.9	58.3	10.7
San Jose, CA	31.3	19.3	38.6	10.8
Seattle, WA	13.3	20.3	55.9	10.5
Washington, DC	4.3	11.9	74.8	9.0

* Other major cities did not have complete data for 1990.
** Functional categories consist of the following census categories:
1. Manufacturing, nondurable goods; Manufacturing, durable goods.
2. Wholesale trade; Retail trade.
3. Communications and public utilities; Finance, insurance, and real estate; Business and repair services; Personal services; Entertainment and recreation services; Health services; Educational services; Other professional and related services; Public administration.
4. Agriculture, forestry, and fisheries; Mining; Construction; Transportation.
    Source: Census of Population and Housing, 1990. U.S. Department of Commerce, Bureau of the Census, Summary Tape, File 3A (CD-Rom).

in this type of activity. In contrast, San Jose, at the heart of the high tech industry located in Silicon Valley, retains a functional specialization in manufacturing. Some cities, such as Los Angeles, Baltimore, and Seattle, also have significant manufacturing sectors despite a large service sector. Table 4.1, which does not contain a comprehensive list of all large cities, does indicate considerable variation in the percentage of employment among the functional sectors of manufacturing, trade, and service. A more detailed study of these differences would require exploring the kinds of businesses that compose each sector within each city. Thus, while Boston seems functionally specialized in services, with 64.6 percent of its employment in that sector, we might also wish to know what *kinds* of services are provided and their respective shares of the total. In addition, we might also ask just how many headquarters are located in that city in order to place Boston within the hierarchy of command and control centers. In short, variation in the breakdown of employment among the sectors of the economy within cities provides a great deal of information on how local, national, and global business activities concentrate in particular places.

By the 1960s the U.S. urban system consisted of a select group of large cities with populations ranging from several hundred thousand to over 7 million (see Table 5.1). This pattern represents *balanced urbanization* that is characteristic of the older industrialized countries such as England (see Chapter 12 for a contrast with less developed countries). Several studies have documented the structure of the urban system in the United States (Pred, 1973; Chase-Dunn, 1985). It is arranged across two different dimensions. On the one hand, cities seem to be distinguished by concentration of business in either manufacturing or services, with the larger cities less specialized. On the other hand, there is specialization in finances or commerce. Furthermore, from 1950 to 1970 the functional specialization of the cities in the U.S. system remained relatively stable (South and Poston, 1982). Such cities as New York, San Francisco, Chicago, and Atlanta, for example, were diverse areas, while places like Baltimore, Detroit, and Los Angeles were more concentrated in manufacturing; and Portland, Kansas City, and Minneapolis were specialized in financial activities and commerce. These specializations and rankings are somewhat different today, as we shall see in the next chapter. However, until at least the 1970s they characterized an urban system that reflected the increasing functional integration of the emergent national economy. Until the 1970s they also showed that important business activity remained concentrated within central cities. That is no longer as true today.

The immense economic changes bringing about the concentration of capital in large cities are only one aspect of the metropolitan era. As central cities prospered, they attracted talented people from all over the nation. Metropolises became centers of culture and political power as well. They were the sites of important museums, universities, and symphony orchestras. They housed art movements and literary revivals. With their immense populations they also wielded great political power. In many cases, such as Chicago and New York City, carrying the state in a presidential election meant, in effect, carrying the city. Much of this confluence of economic, political, and cultural centrality was to change rapidly beginning with the 1960s (see next chapter). But perhaps the best example of the world class metropolis during the period prior to this is New York City (see Box. 4.1).

BOX 4.1 NEW YORK CITY IN THE METROPOLITAN PERIOD

By the time of the Civil War, New York City was already the country's most populous city and its banking capital. By the 1920s New York had replaced London as the financial center of the globe. Its great skyscrapers such as the Empire State and Chrysler buildings, its museums and cultural institutions including Tin Pan Alley (28th Street) and Broadway theaters, and its universities made New York the cultural and intellectual center of the United States as well. At this time, the New York Yankees were the best team in baseball and arguably the best team ever. Their home run hitter, Babe Ruth, was so popular that the owner, "beer baron" Jacob Rupert, decided to build a large stadium to showcase the team (Allen, 1990). Yankee Stadium or "the house that Ruth built," with over a 60,000 seating capacity, was constructed in the Bronx and instantly sold out for many of its games.

By 1930 New York already had over 7 million people, a figure that is slightly less than the population today. The Depression hit the city especially hard. Although many people suffered and manufacturing began its unimpeded decline, the city enjoyed a renaissance under the mayorship of Fiorello La Guardia. An outstanding progressive leader, La Guardia used government to get things done. Parks were cleaned up and renovated, new highways were constructed, the subway system was consolidated and improved, and new housing and commercial construction was promoted. La Guardia built the first international airport for New York (now named after him). His administration peaked with the spectacular New York World's Fair from 1939 to 1940, which was visited by almost 45 million people (Allen, 1990: 280).

During the 1950s New York City became the center for corporate headquarters, if not the monopoly capital center for the globe as a whole. Beginning in 1952 with the construction of Lever House on Park Avenue, the new, international-style office building took over the skyline with its glass facades and square, flat roof. Midtown became a mass of high rise corporate towers. At this time the New York School of Art, including Jackson Pollock, Mark Rothko, and William de Kooning, assumed the global standard for modern art and the city became the culture capital of the world (Walloch, 1988). Arturo Toscanini, one of the greatest orchestra conductors, came to live in the city. The NBC Symphony Orchestra was created just for him and he appeared on television. The new invention, by the way, had its programming centered in New York City where all the network headquarters resided. By 1960, when the metropolitan period began its decline, there was still no more dynamic, exciting, culturally stimulating, and prosperous place in the United States.

Changes in Demographic Differentiation

Between 1930 and 1960 the complexion of metropolitan demographics also changed. As the metropolitan, corporate economy kicked in following the Depression, and large cities fought for their functional niche in the world, corporations hired a growing number of white collar professionals. Many more trained workers found employment in the sophisticated service industries that aided the activities of business headquarters. A growing number of these new urbanites were highly educated and well paid relative to the times. In the 1950s and 1960s many of these corporate employees preferred to live in the city. A study by Leo F. Schnore (1963) in 1960 revealed that metropolitan regions with comparatively newer core cities (those reaching a population of 50,000 after 1920) had higher family incomes, levels of education, and percentages of white collar employees in the central city than in the suburban ring. This breakdown is no longer the rule today, as we shall see in Chapter 5 when we consider the contemporary changes.

In other respects, central cities began to assume the dimensions of ethnic and racial concentration that we find at present. That is, beginning with the 1950s, demographic differentiation of the metropolitan population began to take on the sharp racial distinctions that are characteristic today. Writing in the 1960s Bollens and Schmandt remark:

> Within the metropolitan area itself, the ethnic colonies are concentrated largely in the central city. . . . Chicago, an urban complex of many nationality groups, furnishes a typical example. The latest census shows that of the approximately 600,000 foreign born living in the SMSA, 73 percent reside in the central city (1965: 96).

Bollens and Schmandt add about African Americans at the time that,

> The geographical segregation or distribution of ethnic settlements is even more pronounced when the non-white migrants, predominantly Negroes, are considered. . . . As the non-whites have migrated to urban places, they have tended to gravitate into the central cities of metropolitan areas. By 1960 over one-half the non-white population lived in such communities, a gain of 63 percent over 1950. Among the whites, on the other hand, there has been a continual shift from the central cities to suburbs with the result that in 1960, 52 percent of the whites in the 212 SMSA's lived outside the central cities compared to 22 percent of the non-whites (1965: 97).

The migration of blacks from the South involved a mass exodus. Millions left in the 1950s and 1960s. By the time of the 1960 census, only half the black population still resided in the South. Several factors were responsible, including the extensive use by the 1940s of the mechanical cotton picker and the phasing out of the sharecropper system in the deep South. Many African Americans went north, west, and east, attracted by the possibility of jobs in the newly booming military industries. Most of these migrants settled in the central cities. Returning again to the example of Chicago above, Nicholas Lemann notes,

> During the 1940s, the black population of Chicago increased by 77 percent, from 278,000 to 492,000. In the 1950s, it grew by another 65 percent, to 813,000; at one point 2,200 black people were moving to Chicago every week. By 1960, Chicago had

more than half a million more black residents than it had had twenty years earlier, and black migrants from the South were still coming in tremendous numbers (1991b: 70).

The metropolitan period began to decline in the 1960s at the time of massive suburbanization—predominantly of the white population. Hence while central cities retained their economic power, prior to 1960, their populations were already undergoing a remarkable transformation. Cities were becoming more minority oriented and less white middle class in population. Before discussing the changes since 1960 (next chapter), let us consider the process of suburbanization which is also responsible for producing the regional growth of the metropolis.

Suburbanization and Regional Maturation

While the presence of suburbanization is not unusual for industrialized countries, the massive scale of this phenomenon in the United States is quite distinctive among most societies, except for places like Australia and Canada. To be sure, many societies have experienced growth beyond city borders, but in the United States this has assumed the form of single-family home construction for the middle class on an unprecedented scale. Suburbanization of the white middle class to single-family homes accelerated its pace after the 1930s and especially after World War II, but it was always an important aspect of settlement patterns. As we learned in a previous chapter, U.S. cities did not possess walls. Fringe area development happened as the city itself grew. In Europe, the walls were essentially torn down or overgrown so that these countries also experienced suburbanization, but at a slower pace and with a different, more working-class-oriented mix of population that was housed in multifamily or apartment buildings.

Growth beyond city borders was a common feature of industrialized societies as early as the nineteenth century. In fact, the desire to live *outside* the city despite commuting there for work seems to be as old as the city itself. Although we can point to numerous writers who extol the virtues of city living, there has always been an expressed "antiurban" bias in every urbanized civilization. The biblical prophets, for example, took to the deserts east of Jerusalem to escape the excesses of the city and cleanse themselves. Across the centuries those who could afford to do so always had a country home to balance against time spent at a city address. The historian Kenneth Jackson offers the following excerpt from a letter written over 2,500 years ago as evidence that suburbanization was a process coextensive with urbanization itself: "Our property seems to me the most beautiful in the world. It is so close to Babylon that we enjoy all the advantages of the city, and yet when we come home we are away from all the noise and dirt" (1985: 12).

But the presence of a yearning for the country among city dwellers or some antiurban bias cannot explain the immense scale of suburbanization that is characteristic of the United States. There is a demand-side view of suburbanization that is instructive. By "demand side" we mean the production of a settlement space pattern through the desires of consumers and businesspeople acting in the marketplace. Demand-side theories of urbanization make the assumption that settlement patterns are the result of a large number of individuals interacting competitively in the market to satisfy desires.

Often they are simply aided by innovations in transportation technology. Many geographers, such as John Borchert (1967), and urban sociologists, such as Amos Hawley (1981), suggest this approach as an explanation of urban spatial patterns.

To an extent, the demand-side view helps us understand aspects of suburbanization, especially the desire of U.S. residents for a home of their own. Home ownership is a potent cultural symbol in our society. It provides people with their most important social status. Owning a home also links with other aspects of consumerism that express basic values in U.S. culture (Veblen, 1899).

There is also, however, a "supply-side" view to urban patterns. In this approach what counts in development is less the desires of individuals than the quests of special interests, especially networks of business people aided by allies in government that promote development in order to acquire profits. Joe R. Feagin sums up the supply-side view:

> Traditionally most urban analysts and scholars have argued that everybody makes cities, that first and foremost the choices and decisions by large groups of consumers demanding housing and buildings lead to the distinctive ways cities are built. But this is not accurate. Ordinary people often play "second fiddle." In the first instance, capitalist developers, bankers, industrial executives, and their business and political allies build cities, although they often run into conflict with rank-and-file urbanites over their actions. Cities under capitalism are structured and built to maximize the profits of real estate capitalists and industrial corporations, not necessarily to provide decent and livable environments for all urban residents (1983: 8).

The history of suburbanization in the United States is a long, protracted story of bold quests to acquire wealth through the development of fringe area land and individual or group pursuits of a residential vision that would solve the problems of city living. That is, an account of this phenomenon must consider supply-side and demand-side factors as intertwined.

In the early 1800s, for example, industrialists who had recently acquired fortunes, such as Leland Stanford in railroads, Andrew Carnegie in steel, and James B. Duke in tobacco (the so-called "nouveaux riches"), sought symbols of their new-found wealth. One practice was to purchase a palatial home with substantial space for manicured lawns and at some distance from the city. According to Thorstein Veblen (1899), who introduced the term "conspicuous consumption," space in these suburban homes was used as a symbol of "excess" and the ability to afford it. The fronts of houses were given over to large, manicured lawns labored over by a team of hired gardeners, lawns that were not used for anything except the growing of grass. The mansions themselves had many more rooms than were needed to house family and servants. Guests could always be accommodated on the spot with their own individual bedroom; space was simply held vacant. The backyards were devoted to "suburban" leisure—genteel games such as croquet or badminton, lazing in lawn chairs or simply walking in the garden. Conspicuous consumption, pastoral delights, and the large, single-family house with generous living space became for many Americans the suburban ideal. This cultural value which glorified a particular space fed the economic aspects of demand for home ownership outside the city. In Chapter 9 we shall see that other metropolitan lifestyles are also dependent on their own particular spaces for cultural expression.

Traditional explanations for suburbanization stress the importance of transportation technology as its cause (see, for example, Jackson, 1985; Muller, 1981; Hawley, 1981), with each innovation, such as the switch from commuter rail to automobile, signaling a new pattern of land use. Transportation modes, however, served only as *the means* for residential suburban development; they are not the cause. Transport technology was always used to further real estate developer schemes. The demand-side view demonstrates that the desire for the suburban lifestyle may have been active in the minds of urbanites because people emulated the rich and they disliked the confines of the large city. But dreams alone do not produce concrete spatial patterns. Rather, suburbanization was generated by the supply-side activities of real estate entrepreneurs and government subsidies responding to and feeding demand-side desires.

Initially suburban development leapfrogged over the urban landscape. Suburban housing was built as a separate town removed by several miles from city boundaries. In the late 1800s Westchester and Tuxedo Park outside New York City, Lake Forest and Riverside outside of Chicago, Hillsborough adjacent to San Francisco, Palos Verdes near Los Angeles, Shaker Heights eight miles from Cleveland, and Roland Park outside of Baltimore were all private developments built as towns. Most of these places advertised themselves as extolling suburban virtues, which at the time meant racial, ethnic, and class exclusion in addition to low-density residential living. It was not until the late 1940s that suburban development occurred on a mass scale. Hence, the desire for racial, class, and religious exclusion also added to the complex of cultural factors contributing to the desire to suburbanize.

The early deconcentration of industry followed this same pattern. In the 1800s owners of large businesses often moved all their operations outside the city by developing a separate town. The classic study of such "satellite cities" was done by Graham Taylor in 1915. Gary, Indiana, for example, was built on sand dunes at the base of Lake Michigan by U.S. Steel in the 1880s. At about the same time Pullman pulled his railroad car business out of Chicago and built Pullman, Illinois, a few miles away. In 1873 Singer Sewing Machine relocated from Manhattan to an existing city, Elizabeth, New Jersey, but converted it through its presence into a company town where the factory remained until 1982 when it closed due to foreign competition.

Taylor (1915) gives two main explanations for the creation of satellite cities. First, the new ventures represented an important investment in real estate as well as an industrial relocation. More space was needed for industrialized plants, hence the need to move out of the congested central city. But the need for space was coupled with the acquisition of real estate. Pullman, for example, expected to make as much money from the development of land he owned in the new city as from the factory itself. Second, industrialists pulled their plants out of cities because the latter were hotbeds of union activity. Workers in any one plant were invariably in contact with workers in other plants and other industries. The city concentrated unions as well as people. During the sequential recessions in the United States, beginning with the 1870s, strikes and worker activism were especially frequent. The decentralization of industry was an important tool for minimizing union influence, according to Taylor (see Chapter 7).

To be sure, transportation technology eventually played a profound role in suburbanization. After the 1920s, in particular, the movement of people to the suburbs was aided greatly by the mass production and consumption of the automobile. Prior to that time, regional metropolitan space was organized in a star-shaped form with greatest development situated along the fingers of rail corridors (see Figure 4.1). The private automobile enabled developers to work laterally and fill in the spaces between the mainline tracks. In the 1920s there were 23 million cars registered in the United States and that figure increased to 33 million ten years later. "By 1940, the U.S. auto registration rate exceeded 200 per 1000 population and the average number of cars per capita (which was 13 in 1920) had fallen to less than 5" (Muller, 1981: 39).

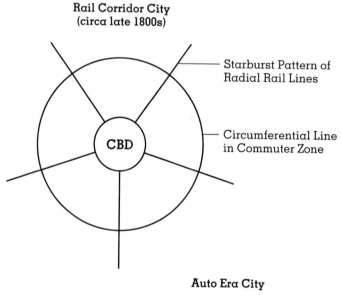

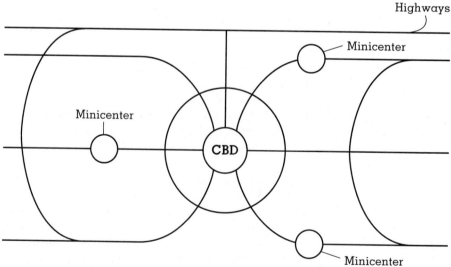

Figure 4.1   The rail corridor city versus the auto era city.

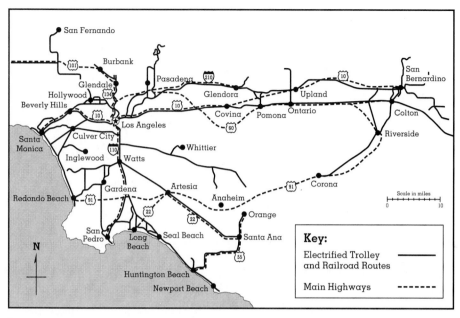

Figure 4.2   Trolley routes and auto highways in Los Angeles.

Turn of the century suburbanization played a great role in determining the patterns of growth that followed during the years between 1920 and 1960. Trolley lines and tract housing laid down in the previous period provided the material infrastructure, such as right of ways, sewers, and utility lines, for much of the urban growth that was to follow. It is often suggested, for example, that Los Angeles looks the way it does— spread out in a pattern of immense sprawl—because it was built during the age of the automobile. Actually, the formative period of development for Los Angeles took place *prior* to the invention of the auto. Los Angeles was a product of electrified trolley lines and very active, aggressive real estate speculation schemes that capitalized on the ease of home construction in the region (Crump, 1962). Today's freeways in Los Angeles simply follow the transit routes of the major trolley lines that once existed (see Figure 4.2). The fact that the latter were pollution free should not be lost on the present generation suffering from smog, nor should we forget Spencer Crump's (1962) case study which shows how automobile, oil, and highway construction companies colluded to sabotage the trolley car transit business.

The major thrust of suburbanization in the United States took place after 1920, with a profound acceleration of growth after World War II. Truly it can be said that present-day regional patterns of metropolitan development materialized during this time. Prior to the 1920s a suburban residence could only be afforded by the more affluent. After 1940 suburbanization became a mass phenomenon. So far in this chapter we have mentioned several supply-side factors contributing to decentralization. On the demand side we have indicated the profound cultural effect that the style of life associated with affluent suburbia had on the tastes of urban individuals and families.

BOX 4.2 PROFILE OF 1950s LEVITTOWN, LONG ISLAND

Prior to the 1940s, most homes were custom built or were renovated farm houses, and most of this suburban housing remained relatively expensive (Gottdiener, 1977). After the war voracious demand supported by federal government programs made it possible for housing to be built in large quantities, but construction techniques had not quite been perfected to build single-family homes that were affordable. Abraham Levitt and Sons was one of the nation's largest builders in the 1940s. Work on many military construction projects had provided the company with the experience necessary to build inexpensive housing on a mass basis. Levitt built the first large-scale, affordable suburban housing development on several thousand acres of converted potato farms in the town of Hempstead on Long Island adjacent to New York City:

> After bulldozing the land and removing the trees, trucks carefully dropped off building materials at precise 60-foot intervals. Each house was built on a concrete slab (no cellar); the floors were of asphalt and the walls of composition rock-board. . . . The construction process itself was divided into 27 distinct steps. . . . Crews were trained to do one job—one day the white-paint men, then the red-paint men, then the tile layers. Every possible part, and especially the most difficult ones, was preassembled in central shops, whereas most builders did it on site. Thus, the Levitts reduced the skilled component to 20–40 percent. . . . More than thirty houses went up each day at the peak of production (Jackson, 1985: 234).

Levitt was not at all sure that government subsidies and the GI Bill would prove effective in supporting homeownership on a mass basis, so the first houses were only offered for rent in 1947. Soon after, in 1949 and in response to overwhelming demand, they were sold outright. The two bedroom, Cape Cod boxes cost initially $6,990. The community, now called Levittown, eventually numbered over 17,000 houses and contained over 80,000 residents. Levitt's organization feared that if they let in blacks, they would run the risk of failing to sell their homes to the white majority. Consequently the developer carefully screened prospective customers for race. Hence the blue collar community, which became a symbol for the postwar American Dream, was not integrated.

While many Americans may have had the desire to leave the city, few had the means prior to World War II, especially because of the Great Depression. Here the federal government became crucially important in creating a mass housing market because its policies promoted single-family homes.

In the 1930s the Depression was devastating to the home construction industry. Because a principal asset of banks was (and still is) home mortgages, this economic downslide also had a devastating impact on the banking industry. In one estimate, housing values declined by 20 percent between 1926 and 1932, and by 1933 at least half of all home mortgages were in default (Jackson, 1985: 191). The Great Depression

Unlike large-scale developments of today (as we shall discuss in the next chapter), early suburban projects were marketed with a full complement of community amenities. Builders were obligated to supply a community quality of life, not just construct housing. Levittown came with nine swimming pools, sixty playgrounds, ten baseball diamonds, and seven "village greens" or minimall centers within the development (Jackson, 1985).

During the next few years Levitt and Sons built communities in Pennsylvania and in New Jersey. The modular construction process they innovated was duplicated by builders all over the United States and the mass construction of suburbia began.

After World War II, William J. Levitt built Levittown, ripping up 5,000 acres of Long Island, New York, and putting up 17,447 homes, all with the same floor plan, and all mass produced at a price well below the then-current market level.

altered the nature of U.S. capitalism because during this time the federal government changed from an indirect participant in the economy to a direct subsidizer of business. In the 1930s Washington, D.C., attempted a rescue of the housing industry and at the same time it hoped to save the banks.

In 1934 Congress passed the National Housing Act which established the Federal Housing Authority (FHA). Briefly put, for qualified houses, the federal government insured the buyer's mortgage. For banks, this took the risk out of private loans. It also pumped needed capital into the housing industry. Foreclosures went from 250,000 in 1932 to 18,000 by 1951 (Jackson, 1985: 203). The act also established the Federal

National Mortgage Association (Fannie Mae) which made the transfer of funds by banks across geographical and political boundaries easier in the United States. The Fannie Mae program and later Ginnie Mae, or the Government National Mortgage Association, helped restructure the banking community and subsidized mortgage lending on a mass scale.

Subsequent housing acts were passed in 1937 and 1941. Along with earlier initiatives, they established the homeowner's tax subsidy. Homeowners could now deduct the interest paid on mortgages from their taxes. This subsidy quite literally made it cheaper to own a home than to rent. Along with this tax subsidy, the Serviceman's Readjustment Act of 1944 perhaps had the most direct effects on housing. As the war was ending, Congress pledged to support returning servicemen with a package of welfare measures including subsidized education. One provision of this act established the Veterans Administration (VA) guaranteed loan program. Under the plan GIs could purchase homes with no money down. The mass exodus to suburbia was now guaranteed.

So we see that mass demand for housing was primed by government programs. Most new construction took place in the suburbs. Over 16 million returning servicemen were eligible for benefits under the 1944 act and a mass market was created. At this time, and due expressly to the war effort, the United States had perfected mass production assembly line techniques which could manufacture vast quantities of goods. All types of consumer durables including cars, washing machines, vacuum cleaners, toasters, dishwashers, refrigerators, and air conditioners were being produced on an immense scale after the 1940s. Suburban housing developments featured the new goods, and in the 1950s all aspects of mass production—housing, consumer durables, automobiles— combined to create the characteristic form of suburbia as the epitome of the consumer society. This political, economic, and cultural conjuncture which led to a society *domestically* producing and consuming mass quantities of goods with a large population engaged in assembly line factory work and active union membership is called *Fordism,* and it is a characteristic of Monopoly Capitalism. As we shall see in the next chapter, under Global Capitalism the structure of Fordism broke apart as manufacturing activity drained from the United States to countries elsewhere.

The beneficiaries of suburbanization were overwhelmingly white. From 1940 to 1960, in two decades, the majority of the white child-rearing middle class left the central cities for the suburbs. In the previous section we saw that this coincides with a period of mass black migration out of the South. This population transfer of whites and blacks is sometimes referred to as "white flight." Experts on the topic indicate that it is largely a product of the pull factors we have identified above (Frey, 1979). That is, whites did not leave large cities because blacks were moving in or the quality of life was declining. Rather, they left because the quality of life was much better in the suburbs and because government programs subsidized them. Racial factors, according to the demographer William Frey (1979), affected less the decision to move than the destination of choice. That is, whites preferred to move to exclusively white areas in the suburbs.

Racism played a more overt role in preventing African Americans from moving to the suburbs themselves. Few were able to make that change in status. Those blacks who did suburbanize could only find housing in other black areas outside the city. The color barrier was strictly enforced by suburban developers. Box 4.2, which contains a case study of Levittown, New York, illustrates both the mass phenomenon of suburbanization after World War II and the racial exclusion upon which it was based.

In sum, the following factors contributed to the decentralization of people to suburbs prior to the 1960s. On the demand side: city congestion, urban environmental concerns, the popularity of the suburban lifestyle, effective transportation choices. On the supply side: active real estate development and speculation at the urban fringe, decentralization of industry, government subsidized programs and tax incentives.

The Pattern of U.S. Urbanization: A Summary

The story of city growth in the United States is high drama. European settlers under the protection of global colonial powers confronted Native Americans and took their land away. Immense resources were harnessed by individual "robber barons" and later by corporate interests working collectively with state bureaucrats and politicians. Industry was propelled along by remarkable innovations, especially those that exploited new forms of energy and transformed the industrial process. In the span of a century, the United States became a major industrial power.

Many facets of U.S. urbanization exaggerated in scale of population and territory aspects of metropolitan growth found elsewhere. Cities were built without walls, and both suburbanization and regional expansion were present early in our history and have persisted as characteristics of the metropolitan pattern. Formation of city government and the role of the local state as a service supplier characterized the political economy. To this day municipal governments in the United States are much less involved in ameliorating the social conditions of existence than are their European counterparts. Alternatively, while other industrialized nations hem in development with extensive land use controls, local governments in the United States are often closely connected to real estate interests. By the 1970s the United States became the first nation of the globe with a majority of citizens living in suburbia, and life in this type of settlement space has influenced the culture of society to the present time.

CHAPTER

5

THE RESTRUCTURING OF SETTLEMENT SPACE: 1960 TO 1990

In the 1950s most people still lived in large cities with an economic base grounded in manufacturing. Although suburbanization had commenced decades earlier, this trend could not match the magnitude of central city growth. After 1960, processes of *deindustrialization,* that is, the loss of manufacturing, and of *deconcentration,* the movement of people and activities away from the large city, transformed the United States, and a new pattern of sociospatial organization emerged. The growth trends of the present are so powerful that they require special attention.

Since 1970, population growth has been greater for metropolitan areas outside city centers rather than inside them, which reverses the traditional urbanization process of population concentration. This process is known as population deconcentration. Commenting on the 1980 census when the trend was first recognized, a demographer noted, "For the first time in well over 100 years, there was virtually no major nationwide population trend in the direction of concentration" (Long, 1981: 1). For a brief time in the 1970s, even small incorporated cities lying outside the major metropolitan centers grew faster than the large cities, although by the 1980s that rapid growth had already subsided.

Other demographers are just as astounded by the changes of the last several decades. According to Frey and Speare (1988), most of the trends prior to the 1960s that characterized the U.S. population were altered and, in some cases, reversed during the last twenty years. First, there has always been a progressive drift of people from the East, Midwest, and South to the West. Between 1960 and 1990 this shift accelerated, producing rapid growth in the West. In addition, however, the South also grew remarkably between 1960 and 1990. Second, after the 1970s the South gained more than the West, for the first time, in net population growth. Together by the year 1980 the Sunbelt region of the West and South contained the *majority* of the nation's population—a historical shift, indeed!

Third, in the past large cities expanded faster than smaller ones. Since the 1970s this process has been reversed, with growth rates in smaller cities outstripping almost all larger ones. In 1970, for example, Phoenix was ranked eighteenth in the country with a population of just over 500,000. By 1990 it was ranked tenth, having grown by an incredible 58 percent. In contrast, with the exception of New York, all large Midwest and east coast cities *lost* population between 1970 and 1990. In the most extreme case, Detroit lost a staggering 31.5 percent of its people (see Table 5.1).

Finally, the shift of metropolitan residents to suburbia accelerated during this time. By 1970, in fact, more people lived in suburbia than in central cities. If, in 1920, we could say with truth that the United States had become an urbanized nation, today we can say with equal confidence that the United States is dominated by suburbanization. Summarizing, then, between 1960 and 1990 the United States went from a society dominated by large central cities in the Frostbelt to a nation with the bulk of its population living in the Sunbelt and in suburbia! Let us examine these changes according to the sociospatial perspective. Other approaches place too much emphasis on technological changes or the push factors of economic growth. In what follows we shall look at these considerations but also discuss the roles of government intervention, real estate activities, and the changed spatial arrangements of businesses and people.

How Cities Have Changed

In 1950 the proportion of total employment for manufacturing was 26 percent with the next largest sector, retailing and construction, accounting for 22.6 percent. By the 1980s the latter proportion was virtually unchanged but total employment in manufacturing dropped to 22 percent. The largest proportion of workers, or 24 percent, was employed in so-called *nodal services,* that is, transportation, finance, wholesaling, business repair, insurance, and real estate. In sum, cities shifted in thirty years from an economy dominated by manufacturing to one that specialized in services (Frey and Speare, 1988). For the largest cities, such as New York and Chicago, there is considerable evidence that the sector of capital involved in national and global processes of financial investing has taken over the downtown (Gottdiener, 1985; Sassen, 1991). Employment in the sector of finance capital alone has increased dramatically for the categories of investing services, management consulting, legal services, accounting services, and the like.

Observers like Bluestone and Harrison (1982) have referred to the drastic decline of manufacturing in the United States and other advanced countries as *deindustrialization,* or the closing of factories, the rise of manufacturing unemployment, and the relocation of manufacturing outside the country. Between 1970 and 1980 alone, the United States and Western Europe lost 8 million manufacturing jobs, while other countries around the globe, such as Japan and Korea, gained over 6 million (Yago, et al., 1984). We shall discuss the political economy of these changes more fully in Chapter 7.

A padlock on one of the main gates of the United States Steel plant in Youngstown, Ohio, tells the story. Steelworkers attempted, through the courts, to buy the plant and keep it going. A recent court decision was not in their favor and the plant is to be shut down and dismantled. (See Box 5.1, pages 78–79.)

Economic and Social Restructuring

In the 1950s the typical city was an industrial city. Factories filled the air with the smoke of manufacturing activity. Workers in plants lived nearby in so-called blue collar neighborhoods. Although predominantly white, this population was made up of many ethnic groups—Italian, Irish, Jewish, Polish, Hungarian, German, and Scandinavian. Everyday life was circumscribed by the factory routine for both women and men. A coordinated exodus of workers from their homes converged on the plants in the morning, while children ran off to neighborhood schools at about the same time. Schools provided vocational training for most boys and homemaker or secretarial skills for girls as a means of fitting them into a working-class world with limited aspirations that few thought would ever change. Several generations of working-class families grew to maturity within this type of milieu.

The Shift from Manufacturing to Service Industries. By the 1980s this pattern of everyday life had changed. Cities no longer were dominated by manufacturing, and working-class family life based on predictable employment opportunities in manufacturing had largely disappeared, producing attendant changes and crises in education and

BOX 5.1 PLANT CLOSURES AT YOUNGSTOWN, OHIO

The sheet steel and tube plant at Youngstown was founded by two local brothers in 1900. For several generations it provided families in the city with regular employment. In 1969 something happened to the company which is typical of other factories that eventually had to shut down (Bluestone and Harrison, 1982). It was bought out by a conglomerate located in another city, the Lykes Corporation, with interests in real estate, shipbuilding, banking, and ranching (Buss and Redburn, 1983: 15).

At the time of the purchase the steel industry was enjoying steady profits because of the war in Vietnam. In the early 1970s, however, it was hit with a crisis that involved many elements, including the rising importation of cheap steel from Europe and Asia. Between 1969 and 1978 the steel industry in the United States lost 95,000 jobs, or a drop of 17 percent. Between 1977 and 1980 alone U.S. Steel shut down more than six plants around the country, Bethlehem shut down two plants, and other, smaller companies folded their operations.

As the steel industry declined, owners of mills were faced with the dilemma of shutting down or modernizing. As a conglomerate, the Lykes Corporation was able to shift investment to other assets rather than continue to invest in the Youngstown company. In 1977 they shut down the major facilities at one of the plants, laying off 4,000 workers overnight. Eventually over 10,000 jobs in all were lost in the community as the entire operation shut down. According to the case study by Buss and Redburn,

> The Lykeses must bear responsibility for a good deal of the failure at Youngstown Sheet and Tube. From the beginning, they viewed the steel company primarily as an investment; it was never thought of as an operation that young Lykes men might wish to manage. Lykes Corporation decided to cut its losses at Youngstown Sheet and Tube by letting the steel-making operations flounder. . . . Second, Lykes began investing capital needed for renovating

job training. The city of Pittsburgh, for example, was once synonymous with steel. In 1930 over 32 percent of its workforce was engaged in manufacturing. By 1980 only 14 percent of the labor force was employed in manufacturing, and steel production engaged only 5.5 percent. In contrast, service employment had risen to 38 percent, thereby dominating the economy (Jezierski, 1988). Pittsburgh had been transformed from an industrial to a nodal service city. In the process, however, it lost 24 percent of its jobs and 37 percent of its population between 1940 and 1980. Between 1980 and 1990 it lost an additional 12.8 percent of its people. In sum, cities have shifted from an economy dominated by manufacturing to one that now specializes in services and retailing but with a smaller employed labor force and, in many cases, a smaller population than in the past (Frey and Speare, 1988: 4). The effects of deindustrialization on the community fabric of cities is discussed in Box 5.1.

A second and equally important change beginning with the 1960s was that most central cities experienced slow or no population growth. In effect, the child-rearing the steel mills into its nonsteel subsidiaries. This accelerated the decline of the antiquated mills (1983: 21).

As a global conglomerate, the Lykes Corporation was different from the family business which started the company in a period prior to monopoly capitalism. With the internationalization of capital, conglomerates can pick and choose among a variety of ways for making a profit. They can also take tax losses on investments that are not profitable. Considerations of community involvement and the responsibility of preserving employment sources for generations of local workers are not at issue. According to Buss and Redburn (1983: 22), the way the mills were shut down was outrageous. No advance warning was given. The company did not provide any transition programs for employees. "Workers simply had a job one day and no job the next." The company, which was located in New Orleans, refused to meet with local community leaders to discuss the closure. "Workers didn't just lose their jobs, they lost pension rights, status and other advantages of accrued seniority. All workers, after a brief period, lost their group health insurance coverage" (1983: 22).

Studies such as the one by Buss and Redburn have tried to document the effects of massive job loss on communities and individuals (Dooley and Catalano, 1980). The economy of the city will never be the same following the plant closures, although some light industry has returned to Youngstown. Job loss has profound emotional consequences for individuals and families. Buss and Redburn (1983) found that many families pulled together and helped each other out to cushion the effects. The initial period of a few years resulted in personal stress occurring only in a minority of cases, although the long-term effects have yet to be studied. Eventually some of the workers were able to find other jobs. Research discovered that despite the smaller salaries in alternative employment, workers went back to leading productive lives with a minimum of stress. What counts, it seems, for emotional security is simply to have steady employment, rather than a high salary. The case of Youngstown, Ohio, was repeated many times across the United States between 1970 and 1990.

middle class virtually abandoned the large city as a place to live. However, as with the other shifts, national figures mask the regional nature of this phenomenon, which occurred largely in the cities of the Northeast and Midwest. Between 1970 and 1980 New York City's population declined by 10.4 percent, although currently it is growing slowly again; Chicago declined 10.1 percent between 1970 and 1980 and an additional 7.4 percent between 1980 and 1990. Detroit lost 20.5 percent of its population between 1970 and 1980 and another 14.6 percent between 1980 and 1990 or almost 500,000 people in two decades. In contrast, the cities in the Sunbelt actually thrived during this same period. Los Angeles grew by 17.5 percent between 1980 and 1990 and became the second largest city in the country, while Houston gained 400,000 people between 1970 and 1990, becoming the fourth largest. Earlier cities like Jacksonville and San Jose grew by over 100 percent between 1960 and 1970. Table 5.1 shows the populations for twenty-four of the largest cities from 1960 and illustrates the regional differences in these population shifts.

TABLE 5.1
Twenty-four Most Populated U.S. Cities, 1960–1990

City	Population, 1990	Population, 1980	Population, 1970	Population, 1960	Percentage of change, 1980–1990	Percentage of change, 1970–1980	Percentage of change, 1960–1970
New York City, NY	7,322,564	7,071,639	7,894,862	7,781,984	3.5	−10.4	1.5
Los Angeles, CA	3,485,398	2,966,850	2,816,061	2,479,015	17.5	5.6	13.6
Chicago, IL	2,783,726	3,005,072	3,366,957	3,550,404	−7.4	−10.1	−5.2
Houston, TX	1,630,553	1,595,138	1,232,802	938,219	2.2	29.3	31.4
Philadelphia, PA	1,585,577	1,688,210	1,948,609	2,002,512	−6.1	−13.4	−2.7
San Diego, CA	1,110,549	875,538	696,769	573,224	26.8	25.7	21.6
Detroit, MI	1,027,974	1,203,339	1,511,482	1,670,144	−14.6	−20.5	−9.5
Dallas, TX	1,006,877	904,078	844,401	679,684	11.4	11.3	24.2
Phoenix, AZ	983,403	789,704	581,562	439,170	24.5	35.3	32.4
San Antonio, TX	935,933	785,880	654,153	587,718	19.1	20.2	11.3
San Jose, CA	782,248	629,442	445,779	204,196	24.3	36.7	118.3
Baltimore, MD	736,327	785,795	645,153	587,718	−6.3	−13.0	−3.5
Indianapolis, IN	731,327	700,807	744,624	476,258	4.4	−4.9	56.3
San Francisco, CA	723,959	678,974	715,674	740,316	6.6	−5.2	3.3
Jacksonville, FL	635,230	540,920	528,865	201,030	17.4	21.7	163.1
Columbus, OH	632,910	564,871	539,677	471,316	12.0	4.6	14.5
Milwaukee, WI	628,088	636,212	717,099	741,324	−1.3	−11.3	−3.3
Memphis, TN	610,337	646,356	623,350	497,524	−5.6	3.5	25.3
Washington, DC	606,900	638,333	756,510	763,956	−4.9	−15.7	−1.0
Boston, MA	574,283	562,944	641,071	697,197	2.0	−12.2	−8.1
Seattle, WA	516,259	493,846	530,831	557,087	4.5	−7.0	4.7
El Paso, TX	515,342	425,259	322,261	276,687	21.2	32.0	16.5
Cleveland, OH	505,616	573,822	750,903	876,050	−11.9	−23.6	−14.3
New Orleans, LA	496,938	557,515	593,471	627,525	−10.9	−5.9	−5.4

Source: Census of Population and Housing, 1990. U.S. Department of Commerce, Bureau of the Census, Summary Tape, File 1C (CD-Rom); *Census of Population, Characteristics of the Population, Number of Inhabitants,* U.S. U.S. Department of Commerce, Bureau of the Census, Summary, Table 27; *1970 Census of Population, Characteristics of Population, Number Inhabitants,* U.S. U.S. Department of Commerce, Bureau of the Census, Table 28.

Population declines in most cities were also matched by profound racial changes, with minority populations increasing. In New York City, for example, the black population increased from 21 percent in 1980 to 25 percent in 1988, and Detroit went from 43.7 percent to 63.1 percent. Along with the minority influx there was a white flight from the central cities, produced largely by the pull of suburbia (see Chapter 4). In many cities the combined black and Hispanic minorities became the majority, thereby changing the racial balance. The combined black and Hispanic population for our largest cities in 1988 was 45 percent for New York City (by 1990 it was over 50 percent); 44.5 percent for Los Angeles; 53.8 percent for Chicago; 45.2 percent for Houston; 41.6 percent for Philadelphia; 23.9 percent for San Diego; 65.5 percent for Detroit; 55.8 percent for Baltimore; and 25 percent for San Francisco. Over 300 minority mayors were elected in cities across the nation including Chicago, Detroit, Baltimore, El Paso (Hispanic), New Orleans, New York, Atlanta, and Washington, D.C. (see Chapter 11 for a discussion of minority empowerment).

Shifts in Ethnic Composition. Thirdly, our largest cities have experienced profound ethnic shifts. The waves of immigration from Western and Eastern Europe that gave U.S. cities much of their ethnic character ceased by the time of World War II. Beginning with the 1970s and accelerating in the 1980s new waves of immigration flowed through our largest cities, increasing the percentage of foreign-born living there. For example, in the Sunbelt cities such as San Diego, the population increase of 25.7 percent between 1970 and 1980 and additionally of 26.8 percent between 1980 and 1990 (see Table 5.1) reflected a large influx of Hispanic residents. In most other cities, however, the increasing proportion of new immigrants was from Asia, the Caribbean, and, in some cases such as New York, from Eastern Europe, where the foreign-born population rose from 5.4 percent of the total to 23.6 percent between 1970 and 1980 (see Chapter 9 for a more detailed discussion).

Uneven Development. The final change that took place in cities links economic shifts with changes in the composition of the population and uneven social development. As we have already discussed, employment growth was located principally in the service sector, especially in *nodal services* that were provided to corporations and banks— legal services, printing, business consulting, financial consulting, and related services in communication and transportation. Early observers of this trend toward specialization in nodal services suggested that they would provide the core industry for economic revitalization of cities following the profound decline in manufacturing (Noyelle and Stanback, 1984; Sassen-Koob, 1984). It is now clear that no real renaissance has taken place. What has occurred is that robust activity in advanced services has benefited a relatively small and select group of trained professionals that earn high salaries, while leading to modest employment in low paying service and clerical jobs in activities that aid the work of the highly paid core. The so-called service city actually consists of two layers—a core of nodal services forming the focus of internationally important economic growth that employs highly trained professionals, and a second segment of relatively low paid service workers who cater to the needs of the command and control industries and the relatively affluent professionals they employ.

In addition, manufacturing of a sort has returned to the city. In recent years non-unionized, low wage factory work has appeared, such as fashion industry sweatshops, which often rely on the use of undocumented workers (Davis, 1987). Such industry clashes with the glitz of the much touted "command and control" centers that large cities advertise as being their core economic function. This contrast between affluence and poverty, between "yuppie" professionals and the working poor or undocumented laborers, seems to characterize many cities today. This so-called "dual city" has recently been the subject of some debate (Mollenkopf and Castells, 1991). Social polarization has occurred in the city, but there are more divisions than the class distinctions between wealthy and poor, and this contrast has graphically increased within large cities in all areas of the world, not just the United States.

Additionally, immense numbers of less affluent, immigrant, and marginalized workers have created within the city a large, *informal* economy. The informal economy is defined as the combination of workers who are "off the books," goods produced in unregulated factories with non-unionized and undocumented laborers, goods and services produced and exchanged for barter (i.e., not cash but in kind), and goods and services sold without regulation on the streets. The informal economy in some countries often rivals the formal sector. Everywhere, this aspect of economic activity has emerged as an increasingly important way in which people within urban areas make a livelihood. One excellent example of the informal economy is the illegal drug industry, which runs into the billions of dollars in sales and is an international operation. And in cities like New York, there are illegal factories that manufacture "faux" designer fashion items, such as fake Rolex watches, and then use recent or undocumented immigrants to sell them on Manhattan street corners for only a fraction of the genuine article's price. Even discounting the major effect of drug dealing, the informal economy in large cities represents a formidable source of jobs and income (see Mingione, 1988). The informal economy is not usually discussed, and its presence clashes with the legitimated image of large cities as centers for multinational business leaders (Boer, 1990).

In sum, cities have changed remarkably since the 1960s. They have more minorities, due in part to a growing immigrant population. Except for these immigrants, population growth in the cities of the 1980s has been slow. Today's large cities possess a transformed economy that is more specialized in nodal services and low wage manufacturing, with a thriving informal economy of drug dealing and illegal factories that employ immigrants. All of these economic and social processes fuel a growing social disparity between the working poor, the underclass, new immigrants, and street vendors on the one hand, and affluent professionals on the other (see Chapter 9). Over the years the city has developed a less balanced, more risky, more precarious way of life. The illegal drug industry alone is responsible for an atmosphere of violent crime and threat that, in some areas such as Detroit or Washington, D.C., pervades the entire urban fabric.

How Suburbs Have Changed

In the 1950s and 1960s suburbs were considered places where urban professionals who worked in the city bought homes to live and raise a family. They were called "bedroom communities" for this reason (Jackson, 1985). We now know that this image merely represented an early view of such places. Since the 1960s suburbs have matured (Schnore, 1963). In many ways they have become diverse culturally, economically, and politically, much like medium-sized urban areas (Muller, 1981). Places like Tysons Corner, Virginia, outside of Washington, D.C.; Costa Mesa, California, beyond the boundaries of Los Angeles; and Dunwoody, Georgia, outside of Atlanta, are all important and developed suburbs.

Researchers have defined suburbs for study purposes as the "outside central cities" portion of the MSA. But this definition *under*estimates the expansion that has created new suburbs and regional development outside the MSA since 1970 (Muller, 1981). A compromise definition counts all the "outer rings" of the MSA as suburban, keeping in mind that this definition still underestimates the extent of deconcentration. In addition, the census has come to recognize that some areas of the country are now fully urbanized despite lying outside the MSA and lacking major city centers. Consequently, in the 1970s the census designated the suburban regions of Nassau-Suffolk Counties on the east coast (outside the New York City MSA) and Orange County on the west coast (outside the Los Angeles–Long Beach MSA) as all-suburban, independent MSAs. In the future it is very likely that other counties, such as those outside the cities of Chicago, San Francisco, and perhaps Houston, will also achieve independent MSA status. Therefore, we now recognize that many suburban regions contain as complex a social organization as do cities.

In 1970 the U.S. census noted for the first time that more people were living in suburbs than in other settlement spaces. At that time 37.1 percent of the population was suburban, compared with 31.5 percent that lived in the central city or 31.4 percent in rural areas. By 1990 even more rural areas had been absorbed by suburban growth and the plurality of that population increased further. According to the figures, 46 percent of the 1990 population lived in suburbia, 40 percent in central cities, and 14 percent in rural areas (U.S. Bureau of the Census, 1990). While virtually all cities suffered from no or slow growth over the past decades, suburban regions remain the most rapidly growing areas of the country.

The change to suburban dominance in population is reflected in comprehensive statistics on economic activity. In many cases suburbs have outpaced their adjacent central cities in economic importance since the 1970s. Muller cites, in particular, the example of Philadelphia and its surrounding suburbs (1981: 19). In the 1980s the suburbs outside Philadelphia contained 63 percent of the entire region's employment (i.e., including the central city itself), 67 percent of all manufacturing jobs, 68 percent and 70 percent of all wholesaling and retailing, respectively, and over 50 percent of all regional employment in financial, insurance, and business service sectors.

Push and Pull Factors in Suburbanization

Massive suburbanization since 1960 has occurred due to a combination of push and pull factors. Government intervention played a significant role in the development of the immense tracts of land outside large cities after World War II. Most instrumental were the tax laws allowing for the deduction of mortgage interest from income taxes.

In effect, this subsidized middle-class housing needs, and because most affordable single-family housing was and still is located in the suburbs, this program also subsidized suburbanization. Since the 1940s it has literally paid to own your own home.

The home mortgage subsidy is equal to or greater than all other government spending on housing (Feagin, 1983). Subsidization of suburbanization, however, did not stop at housing. During the 1950s pressure was placed on the federal government to construct a national system of highways. The result was the 1956 interstate highway program which acted in the name of national defense to subsidize the construction of over 40,000 miles of roads. A gasoline tax was imposed to pay for this construction, and at its height the highway fund amounted to $50 billion (Muller, 1981). This system of interstates carved up the countryside adjacent to cities, opening up the vast U.S. hinterland to suburbanization.

The combined efforts in promoting single-family housing and automobile transportation accomplished a form of suburbanization in the United States which differs from that of other advanced industrialized countries, such as Britain and Sweden. In the latter places ambitious mass transportation schemes were harnessed to aggressive town planning in order to produce suburban housing that was accessible and affordable.

In the United States, by contrast, mass transportation systems that had been in place prior to World War II were abandoned and replaced by highways that were the result of the cooperative efforts of automobile companies, highway construction firms, and local politicians (Crump, 1962; Whitt, 1982). The result is a suburban landscape consisting of immense regions of single-family home developments and the hegemony of the automobile culture (Weiss, 1988; Davis, 1986).

One of the most important observations about suburbia from the demand-side point of view is that it is quite a popular place to live. Despite the many criticisms, such as its boring lack of choices and homogeneity, most residents are happy with the suburbs and few miss living in or even visiting the city (Muller, 1981: 14). There is some evidence that suburbs are hard on adolescents and the elderly poor, but these groups are not powerful enough to alter either planning priorities of development or federal policies that subsidize suburban growth.

In the suburbs we seem to have found a happy marriage between middle class demand-side preferences for housing and living arrangements and supply-side subsidies providing the incentive structure for growth patterns. The landscape that such development has created, however, is very much a product of specific transportation and housing policies. These have sanctified the expensive, single-family home and surrendered regional space to the automobile culture. Without alternatives, the increasing social costs of this pattern of suburbanization become more evident each year.

Suburban Social Characteristics

There is no typical suburb, and just as understandably there is no unique suburban lifestyle, although there is a typical suburban everyday life which is associated with single-home ownership, automobile commutation, and low density neighborhoods which differs from life in the central city. The early work of Leo Schnore (1963) provided us with a quick means of judging the nature of suburbs on the basis of their relative independence as employing centers. Schnore suggested creating a ratio of the number of persons over 16 years employed within the suburb divided by the total number of persons over 16 years who work and are residents of the suburb. This employment/residence ratio gives an indication of whether a suburb is a net employing center (E/R over 1) and, therefore, independent of the large central city; a mixed employment and residential area (E/R less than .9 but more than .3) with a balanced growth much like an urban center; or essentially a bedroom community (E/R less than .3) that is much like the early dependent view of the suburb. As illustrated in Table 5.2, using hypothetical cases and the measure of E/R ratios, the variation among suburban types can be classified.

In the main, lower income whites as well as the more affluent have found places in the suburban region to live. Blacks, however, have over the years found it difficult to suburbanize even to this day. They represent around 5 percent of the total suburban population despite being 12 percent of the general population. Typically, black people suburbanize by moving to areas outside the central city that are directly adjacent to their city neighborhoods (Muller, 1981). As we have seen, therefore, blacks are considerably *over*represented in the central city and *under*represented in the suburbs relative to their total population. In other countries, such as Brazil, that also have a racially mixed society, large cities such as Rio de Janeiro have the opposite pattern. There, the blacks and the poor live in shantytown suburbs, with the affluent ensconced in the city center (see Chapter 12).

While whites have found suburbs open to them, the uniformity of housing price within each subdivision has resulted in graphic income segregation within suburban regions. Wealthier suburbs in particular have been successful in keeping blacks and the less affluent out of their areas through the home rule device of *exclusionary zoning*. That is, local control over land use and building codes enables individual communities to prohibit the building of low or moderately priced housing. This perpetuates the value of higher priced homes, thereby maintaining exclusivity. Years of such practices have made suburban housing increasingly more expensive, thus creating a housing shortage in suburbia for first-time buyers.

In sum, suburban regions have taken on diverse socioeconomic characteristics. For the white population there is considerable diversity of community type, although there are increasing class differences and a housing shortage due to the decreasing affordability of moderately priced units. African Americans remain relatively excluded

TABLE 5.2
A Comparison of Suburban Community Types Using Employment-to-Residence Ratios*

Suburban Type	Employment-to-Residence Ratio
Bedroom Community	Range: .1–.29
Residential/Service Area	.3–.6
Mixed Residential/Employment Area	.7–.9
Net Employment Region	1.0 or greater

*The employment-to-residence ratio is the total number of people employed within a community area divided by the total number of eligible workers living in that area.

from suburban living except in designated places. Hence, the vast suburban regions are increasingly segregated by class and race. In its own way this replicates the division of race and class within the central city. Thus, city problems of residential segregation have been duplicated in the suburbs and are now regionwide.

Economic Deconcentration

For the suburbs, economic deconcentration has meant a combined process of capturing both new job growth and decentralizing economic activities from the large central city, as well as the process of their recentralization in minicenters within the suburban region. Let us consider the separate economic dimensions of deconcentration.

Retailing. The total amount of all retailing in the United States, for example, is now dominated by malls located in suburban realms of the metropolis. By the time of the 1970 census, the suburban share of MSA sales passed the 50 percent mark for the fifteen largest MSAs. According to Muller,

> Steadily rising real incomes, fueled by the booming aerospace-led economy of the middle and late sixties, created a virtually insatiable suburban demand for durable consumer goods. With almost no pre-existing retail facilities in the burgeoning outer suburbs, huge capital investments were easily attracted from life insurance companies and other major financial institutions. Not surprisingly, regional shopping centers quickly sprang up at the most accessible highway junction locations as their builders strived to make them the focus of all local development (1981: 123).

Suburban shopping malls were so successful that their numbers increased more than tenfold from approximately 2,000 in 1960 to over 20,000 in 1980. Over time this success threatened central city shopping areas and bypassed them as the important places to consume. Sizes of suburban retailing centers increased over time to malls and supermalls. Houston's "Galleria" complex, for example, is modeled after the Galeria of Milan, Italy. It is several stories high and is built around an olympic-size skating rink which is open year-round, a feat of some proportions if you consider the warm, humid climate of Houston. The Galleria has 3 large department stores, over 200 smaller shops, 4 office towers, 2 hotels, over 15 restaurants and cinemas, nightclubs, and even a healthclub. Its seven-level parking facility has room for over 10,000 cars. Lately the name *Galleria* has become popular for malls in many other places in the United States, and it usually connotes a large and expansive upscale mall.

This type of spectacular, fully enclosed space for shopping has begun to replace the downtown streets of the central city department store district. As the success of malls has advanced, the scale of their construction has increased. Recently the phenomenon of "megamalls" has emerged as the new suburban focus of retailing. In the summer of 1992 a new, fully enclosed complex was constructed outside the city of Minneapolis that is so large it has room at its center for a seven-acre miniversion of a famous California theme park, Knotts Berry Farm. This "Mall of America," as it is called, contains 2 million square feet of space and enough parking for thousands of cars. Central cities cannot compete with such family attractions in immense suburban spaces.

Lenox Square Shopping Center outside of Atlanta is one of the largest in the South, covering 74 acres. Malls are one cornerstone of regional growth.

Manufacturing. We have noted the progressive decline of manufacturing in the United States and its devastating impact on central cities. Over the years suburban areas have changed their bedroom image in part by being the recipients of many new manufacturing industries that have remained active. By the 1980s the percentage share of manufacturing for the suburban rings of most metropolitan areas nationwide was over 50 percent. Boston and Pittsburgh, far example, have over 70 percent of their manufacturing located in the suburbs; Los Angeles, Detroit, San Francisco, St. Louis, and Baltimore have over 60 percent located in the suburbs.

Suburban developers innovated a form of space called the "industrial park" which is zoned entirely for business, especially manufacturing. Usually, local towns or county governments provide significant tax incentives, infrastructure, and other subsidies to attract manufacturing. The presence of such attractive and inexpensive locations in suburbia is one factor in the progressive deconcentration of manufacturing.

Most recently suburbs have innovated a new form of local space known as a high tech growth pole or "science park." These are more specialized research and development centers that are often linked with manufacturing and which are located near university facilities. The most spectacular example is Silicon Valley, which is adjacent to Stanford University in California. A corridor stretching from the city of San Jose to Palo Alto makes up the spine of Silicon Valley and contains over 800 factories that produce state-of-the-art electronics and computer products. This complex is intimately connected to the research resources of Stanford University, where the transistor was invented and where the largest electrical engineering department is located.

While Silicon Valley remains the best known of the new spaces created by high

Aerial view of industrial buildings. Silicon Valley, California.

tech industries, other examples of growth are Route 128 outside of Boston, the San Diego–LaJolla complex associated with electronic medical technology innovators, the Research Triangle complex located near the Duke and University North Carolina campuses, and the Iowa-to-Minnesota corridor of high tech medical firms anchored at the Mayo Clinic in Rochester, Minnesota. The area around Irvine, California, is very typical of the new spaces created by high technology industries. It is anchored by the University of California at Irvine campus and stretches for miles across what was once ranching and farming land. This region has been the subject of a study (Kling, Olin, and Poster, 1991) which argues that a new social order has developed here that surpasses the stereotype of suburban life and is based on consumerism, suburbia, professional occupations, and an economic base of knowledge or information processing industries. In Chapter 13 we shall discuss the emergence of similar spaces located in advanced industrial societies around the globe.

The significance of these high tech growth poles is that they foster industrial development that is completely independent of the central city. Because of their economic success, they often become the principal places in the society that earn money on the global market, thereby leading the country's growth (see Storper and Walker, 1991). In the past, models of industrial development have placed the city in a dominant role by referring to it as "the core," with the suburbs described as "the periphery." Development of society meant nurturing city-based industry. In this model that better describes urban growth in the '60s and '70s, manufacturing was believed to originate in the city and then migrate out to the suburbs. All evidence now rejects this concept. The city is no longer privileged as the incubator of most industries, although some new manufacturing, such as textiles and light manufacturing, may still start up there. Development begins just as frequently in the suburbs as the cities, and ". . . suburbia is quickly identified as a major zone of industrial expansion in its own right, in which *self-generated* growth has been primarily responsible for its current eminence" (Muller, 1981: 143). Hence, the new patterns challenge the way people once thought about economic development.

In sum, then, the central city has lost its role as the dominating node of a regional economy. Important businesses are likely to locate in the suburbs for many industries, and economic development is now a metropolitan regional affair.

Office and Administrative Headquarters. Perhaps the most significant example of the increasing importance of mature suburbs and, conversely, the decline of the central city is the progressive relocation of corporate headquarters to fringe areas. In the past such headquarters were almost exclusively located in the central city. Today this is much less the case, although many headquarters remain in city centers. During the 1960s New York City, for example, was host to over 130 of the Fortune 500 companies. By the 1980s the number was down to 73, and it is now at 59, or a loss of over 71 corporate headquarters in thirty years.

According to some recent books, large cities have emerged as the "command and control" centers for the global economy (Sassen, 1991; Noyelle and Stanback, 1984). This overstates the case for the economy in general and ignores decentralization to areas outside the city but within the metropolitan region (see Kephart, 1991). As indicated above, the largest cities have become the centers for finance capital activities, while other aspects of capitalism, such as producer services, marketing, and manufacturing, have decentralized. One indicator of this more complex spatial differentiation of functions is the phenomenal thirty-year decline in the number of corporate headquarters located in New York City.

We have seen that the city can no longer be regarded as the dominant location choice for manufacturing or corporate headquarters. But the maturation of suburban areas with regard to administrative employment is even more significant. Despite some predictions that, as metropolitan regions grew, central cities would retain their command and control functions (Hawley, 1981), this has not proven to be the case.

In a study of the twenty-one largest MSAs, Ruth Armstrong (1972, 1979) found that, leaving the special case of New York City aside, administrative functions were evenly distributed between large cities and their suburbs in 1960. During the decades following her study administrative and headquarter employment decentralized in favor of the suburbs, as companies such as Pepsico and General Electric abandoned centers like Manhattan for the adjacent suburban towns of Purchase, New York, and Fairfield, Connecticut, respectively. Several other studies have verified that this trend is continuing and that command and control centers are growing in the surburbs (Quante, 1976; Pye, 1977). In short, administrative functions, like all other economic activities, have been deconcentrating since the 1960s.

Over the years, then, suburbs have matured, becoming more and more like the diversified urban space of the past. They are autonomous employing regions with diverse populations (except for minority representation). As such we can no longer talk of some city-suburb hierarchy with a privileged city as the dominating center. In fact, for many metropolitan regions such as the St. Louis or Philadelphia area the power of the suburbs outweighs the central city itself.

Beyond Suburbia: The Multinucleated Region

By the 1990s suburban regions in many areas of the United States had so matured that development was occurring in peripheral areas independent of major urban centers.

This special and independent mode of regional, multinucleated growth was manifested as the *fully urbanized county,* such as Orange County, California, which is a net employing region with a labor force of over 1 million (Kling, Olin, and Poster, 1991). The most important characteristic of the fully urbanized county is that it does not contain any large cities, yet it functions much like a city by providing jobs as well as housing for its residents.

First studied by Gottdiener and Kephart (1991), the fully urbanized counties appeared in number during the 1980s, although two regions, Orange County in California and Nassau-Suffolk Counties in New York, had already achieved independent MSA status by 1980. Other multinucleated counties lie outside of MSAs. Oakland County in Michigan is typical, for example. It lies adjacent to but outside the Detroit MSA, had a 1980 population of *over* 1 million people, but its largest city contained only 76,715. It employed virtually all of the people that lived there with an E/R ratio of .93 in 1980, and grew by 11 percent between 1970 and 1980 (a rapid rate considering, especially, that Detroit itself declined in population). Oakland County's labor force was composed of 26 percent in manufacturing, 30 percent in retailing and wholesaling, and 25 percent in services, as well as other industries, that is, it possessed a balanced, diversified economy. Finally, in 1980 Oakland County had a median family income of $28,407—above the national average—and was 93 percent white.

Oakland County in Michigan was very much like at least twenty other multinucleated metropolitan regions located around the country which were identified as a new form of space because of their urban character and their deconcentrated form (Gottdiener and Kephart, 1991). In short, today our notion of suburbia has been transformed completely from the early pictures of the "bedroom community" to the fully urbanized but multicentered region. Results from the 1990 census suggest that this maturation process is continuing along the lines we have described.

The Shift to the Sunbelt

Without question the population and activity shift to the Sunbelt is the most important historical event of the last half of this century for the United States. The scale of change is immense and quite spectacular. Although variations exist, most analysts define the Sunbelt as thirteen southern states—Alabama, Arizona, Arkansas, Florida, Georgia, Louisiana, Mississippi, New Mexico, North Carolina, Oklahoma, South Carolina, Tennessee, and Texas—plus parts of two western states: California (southern counties below San Luis Obispo) and southern Nevada (Las Vegas, SMSA) (see Bernard and Rice, 1983). Between 1945 and 1975 the Sunbelt region doubled its population. In the decade between 1960 and 1970 Sunbelt MSAs received 63.8 percent of the total population increase for *all* MSAs (Berry and Kasarda, 1977: 168). Between 1970 and 1980 the Northeast lost 1.5 percent of its population, the Midwest gained only 2.6 percent, but the South grew by 21.5 percent and the West by 22.6 percent, including natural increase for all regions (Frey and Speare, 1988: 50).

Sunbelt cities such as El Paso, Texas, almost doubled their populations between 1970 and 1990, growing from 322,261 to 515,342. Phoenix, Arizona, went from 581,562

Phoenix, Arizona, one of the rapidly growing sunbelt metropolises.

in 1970 to 933,403 in 1990, and San Diego grew from 696,769 to 1,110,549 during the same period. All of this growth took place while Frostbelt cities stagnated with population decline or limited growth. See Table 5.3.

The phenomenal growth of the Sunbelt region is better illustrated by the metropolitan perspective of Table 5.4. It shows that between 1980 and 1990 the Los Angeles metro area grew by 26.4 percent, Dallas by 32.6, Houston by 19.7, Miami by 20.8, Atlanta by 32.5, San Diego by 34.2, and the Phoenix metro area by 40.6 percent, respectively. Similar increases were experienced during the 1970 to 1980 decade.

Rapid demographic growth was matched by rapid employment growth in the Sunbelt. Between 1970 and 1980 manufacturing expanded by 12 percent in the North, but more than double that, or 24.4 percent, in the South. While service employment grew by 11.5 percent in the North, it increased by 44 percent in the South and 47 percent in the West (Frey and Speare, 1988: 92). According to one observer, ". . . never in the history of the world has a region of such size developed at such a rate for so long a time" (Sale, 1975: 166).

The movement west and southward has been around for some time. Sunbelt states have been receiving a greater share of MSA population than the Frostbelt since the 1920s (Berry and Kasarda, 1977: 168). Indeed, the movement of people westward has been a trend in the United States since the 1800s. The shift to the Sunbelt, however, displaces the economic center of gravity in the United States toward the West from the east coast, and also obliterates what was once a core-periphery relation between a formerly agrarian South and West and an industrialized North and Midwest. Today, the Sunbelt is more formidable economically than other areas of the country. Between

TABLE 5.3
Population Growth for Sunbelt Cities, 1960–1990

City	Population, 1990	Population, 1980	Population, 1970	Population, 1960	Percentage of change, 1980–1990	Percentage of change, 1970–1980	Percentage of change, 1960–1970
Los Angeles, CA	3,485,398	2,966,850	2,816,061	2,479,015	17.5	5.6	13.6
Houston, TX	1,630,553	1,595,138	1,232,802	938,219	2.2	29.3	31.4
San Diego, CA	1,110,549	875,538	696,769	573,224	26.8	25.7	21.6
Dallas, TX	1,006,877	904,078	844,401	679,684	11.4	11.3	24.2
Phoenix, AZ	983,403	789,704	581,562	439,170	24.5	35.3	32.4
San Antonio, TX	935,933	785,880	654,153	587,718	19.1	20.2	11.3
San Jose, CA	782,248	629,442	445,779	204,196	24.3	36.7	118.3
Jacksonville, FL	635,230	540,920	528,865	201,030	17.4	21.7	163.1
Memphis, TN	610,337	646,356	623,350	497,524	-5.6	3.5	25.3
El Paso, TX	515,342	425,259	322,261	276,687	21.2	32.0	16.5
New Orleans, LA	496,938	557,515	593,471	627,525	-10.9	-5.9	-5.4

Source: Census of Population and Housing, 1990. U.S. Department of Commerce, Bureau of the Census, Summary Tape, File 1C (CD-Rom); Census of Population, Characteristics of the Population, Number of Inhabitants, U.S. U.S. Department of Commerce, Bureau of the Census, Summary, Table 27; 1970 Census of Population, Characteristics of Population, Number of Inhabitants, U.S. U.S. Department of Commerce, Bureau of the Census, Table 28.

TABLE 5.4
Metropolitan Regional Growth for the Sunbelt, 1960–1990

Area	1990	1980	1970	1960	Percentage of change, 1980–1990	Percentage of change, 1970–1980	Percentage of change, 1960–1970
Los Angeles-Anaheim-Riverside, CA CMSA	14,531,529	11,497,549	9,980,850	7,751,616	26.4	15.2	28.8
San Francisco-Oakland-San Jose, CA CMSA	6,253,311	5,367,900	4,754,366	3,723,158	16.5	12.9	27.7
Dallas-Fort Worth, TX CMSA	3,885,415	2,930,568	2,351,568	1,715,505	32.6	24.6	37.1
Houston-Galveston-Brazoria, TX NECMA	3,711,043	3,099,942	2,169,128	1,570,758	19.7	42.9	38.1
Miami-Ft. Lauderdale, FL CMSA	3,192,582	2,643,766	1,887,892	1,268,993	20.8	40.0	48.8
Atlanta, GA MSA	2,833,511	2,138,136	1,684,200	1,247,829	32.5	27.0	35.0
San Diego, CA MSA	2,498,016	1,861,846	1,357,854	1,033,011	34.2	37.4	31.4
Phoenix, AZ MSA	2,122,101	1,509,175	971,228	663,510	40.6	55.4	46.4

Source: State and Metropolitan Area Data Book 1991. U.S. Department of Commerce, Economics and Statistics Administration, Bureau of the Census, Table 2; *State and Metropolitan Area Data Book 1986.* U.S. Department of Commerce, Economics and Statistics Administration, Bureau of the Census, Table A.

1970 and 1980 almost three-fourths of all job growth took place in the Sunbelt. By the 1990s, however, the economic recession hit Sunbelt areas especially hard. California, for example, has suffered major job losses, as has Texas. Hence, current patterns of Sunbelt growth reflect a cycle of boom and bust.

Texas serves as an example of the Sunbelt shift. In 1950 its largest city, Houston, was ranked fourteenth in the country. Now Houston is our fourth largest city, just behind Chicago. The latter lost its longtime "second city" designation in 1980 when Los Angeles became more populous and was second in size to the largest city in the United States, New York. Texas, however, not only has one large metropolis, it has several. In fact, in 1990 it had more cities in the top ten than any other state: Houston, Dallas, and San Antonio. Between 1970 and 1980 the Texas economy grew two and one-half times faster than the nation's economy, and its manufacturing growth from 1975 to 1980 alone was the fastest in the nation (Feagin, 1988).

More recently, explosive Sunbelt growth has turned to bust. Texas in particular was hit hard by the recession beginning in the 1980s. For this reason the best way to describe Sunbelt development is in terms of boom and bust cycles rather than the once touted vision of unending growth. The case of Houston is illustrative of this pattern. Between 1970 and 1980 the city rode the crest of an unprecedented oil industry boom. Millions of people were drawn to the area and its job creation in manufacturing-related industries. After 1980, however, the boom in oil prices went bust as the price of a barrel plummeted from $30 to $11 (it's now recovered to around $18). Consequently, Houston entered a period of economic depression that was severe in the 1980s. The downturn lasted until 1987, during which time the city lost one in eight jobs and unemployment skyrocketed to well over 11 percent.

At present the economy has improved and a more stable pattern exists. The turnaround has been fueled by a shift from manufacturing dominance to service industries, in particular business, medical, and professional services including law and engineering. Unemployment went back down to 6 percent in 1992, although it remains unclear whether the local economy will continue to improve as long as the country remains in recession.

Push and Pull Factors in Sunbelt Development

As we have seen, the Sunbelt had an advantage over other parts of the United States because of its comparative economic potential. This represents a potent pull factor. The region has other advantages as well. Energy and tourism are also exploitable industries. Cheap energy, in particular, and the warmth of the Sunbelt climate cut home maintenance costs drastically compared to the Frostbelt. Low energy costs are a major locational incentive for business, both now and in the future. Lower home maintenance costs and comparatively lower home-owner tax rates also provide considerable incentives for people to move to the region.

A comparison between Frostbelt and Sunbelt locations reveals advantages for the latter regarding labor costs. Sunbelt places do not have a past history of union organizing, and wages there are comparatively lower for manufacturing industries (although higher for many professional services). Sunbelt cities flaunt what they call a "good business climate." This usually means the absence of unions, tax breaks to business, and a general "hands off" policy of minimal government regulation.

As in the case of suburbanization, one of the most potent supply-side forces that has developed the Sunbelt as a place to live and work is the operation of government intervention. To the extent that government subsidization of real estate development aided growth, it was instrumental in the population shift to the Sunbelt where real estate is a major industry. But government involvement goes way beyond this obvious observation. Most of the heavily subsidized government industries in the United States, including agribusiness, energy, and military spending, are pillars of the Sunbelt economy.

Over the years, for example, the heavily subsidized agriculture industry has witnessed an immense shift of population out of farm residence, from over 30 percent in 1920 to around 3 percent today. At the same time, the family farm involved in agriculture has given way to the large land holdings of corporations engaged in agribusiness. Farm production has become more specialized and part of a total conglomerate structure involving the growing, processing, and marketing of food by giant corporations linked to the multinational system of capital (Shover, 1976; Hightower, 1975; Berry, 1972).

An important consequence of the rise to hegemony of agribusiness has been the shift of food production away from the Northeast and Midwest and to the Sunbelt (Sale, 1975; Coughlin, 1979) where large, open tracts of land are being used. According to Sale (1975), the shift to agribusiness in the Sunbelt has made the family farm uneconomical, causing many small farmers to sell their land to suburban developers. Finally, it should be pointed out that agribusiness remains subsidized on a grand scale by the federal government, whose Department of Agriculture is the second largest bureaucracy after the Department of Defense (Shover, 1976).

A second pillar of Sunbelt growth is the energy industry, which is also subsidized by the government. The Atomic Energy Commission and its government affiliates is one of the largest employers in the state of New Mexico. In a case study of Houston, Texas, Joe R. Feagin (1988) shows how state supports underpin the energy industry while, at the same time, business leaders espouse the virtues of "free enterprise." Feagin observes that when discussing government involvement a distinction is made between state forms of regulation, which are opposed by business, and state promotion of economic activity, which is supported wholeheartedly.

In the case of the alleged "free enterprise" city of Houston, development was aided over the years by active government promotion of projects, while regulation was kept at a minimum (Feagin, 1988: 47). In addition, Feagin also shows that, contrary to the prevailing view of Sunbelt cities as economically backward until recent times, Houston was already a major agricultural center for the Texas cotton industry prior to the growth of the petroleum business. As the latter became the new focus of the local economy, government subsidization went hand in hand with the development of the city through private ventures. For example, the federal government provided funds for the dredging of the Houston ship channel and periodically cleared the important port facility for ship traffic. In addition, oil refining and new petrochemical industries during the 1940s were supported directly by the feds, ranking sixth in receipt of national government plant investment (Feagin, 1988: 68). Local businesses were the beneficiaries of these subsidies. As a consequence, Houston developed into the energy capital of the United States, only to be hit by a downturn and restructuring in the 1980s.

Finally, the third and last government subsidized pillar of Sunbelt growth is military spending. Since the 1950s, that is, after peace was declared in Europe, the major portion of the tax dollar has gone to military spending. During World War II, 60 percent of the total $74 billion spending effort went to the fifteen states of the Sunbelt (Sale, 1975: 170). Major industries in Sunbelt states were established during this time. Los Angeles became an aircraft and shipbuilding center. Kaiser Steel was formed in Southern California, importing many workers from the East. Petrochemical and energy related efforts were also subsidized, as we have already seen. Armaments industries and arsenals were expanded in the South and West. Huge military bases were constructed in California, Texas, Georgia, Florida, Alabama, and the Carolinas, among other Sunbelt states.

By the 1970s the fifteen Sunbelt states were receiving 44 percent of all military spending, including over 50 percent of the Defense Department payroll; had the majority of all military installations (60 percent); were employing more scientists and technicians than all the rest of the United States; and received 49 percent of "Pentagon research and development funds—the seed money that creates new technologies and industries" (Sale, 1975: 171). All of this effort and money has created a new industrial core in the Sunbelt that is supported by government spending. Because taxes are collected across the United States but differentially spent on military related activities, the federal government has for decades transferred wealth from all other regions of the United States to the Sunbelt.

Military spending in the Sunbelt region continued to grow throughout the 1980s on an immense scale. In 1975 military spending was approximately $90 billion. By 1987 it had increased to $390 billion, or a fourfold change taking place after the Vietnam War (Gottdiener, 1990). Arms sales in particular became a key U.S. industry in the 1980s, prompting one observer to suggest that the nation had switched to a permanent war economy (Mandel, 1975; see also Melman, 1983; Stubbing and Mendel, 1986).

With Sunbelt prosperity so closely linked to the well-being of arms sales, cuts in the military budget have had profound effects, leading to a downturn in the economic fortunes of states such as California. For example, in July of 1991 the McDonnell Douglas Corporation announced that it was laying off about 1,000 workers from its Southern California plant and shifting another 1,600 to its facilities in St. Louis, Missouri. The company cited "defense cutbacks and budget woes" (*Press Enterprise,* July 8, 1991: D-2) for its decision, which benefited the Midwest at the expense of the Sunbelt.

The loss of such military related jobs has turned the once recession-proof economy of California into another case of Sunbelt boom and bust. Since 1989 California has had economic woes so severe that they are eclipsed only by the days of the Great Depression. In 1991, for example, the state lost more jobs than any other, twice as many as the second-worst state, New York. And there is still no sign of an economic reversal. In that same year and for the first time in California's history, more people canceled their driver's licenses because they had moved to another state than applied for one. In short, the population boom in California related to its economic expansion may be over, although low-wage, illegal aliens continue to flock to the state.

Finally, it is important to note that government military spending is a key support of many suburban regions, even in the Frostbelt, and is not simply a Sunbelt phenomenon. Thus, between 1975 and 1980, for example, Suffolk County in New York and suburban Monmouth County in New Jersey, respectively, had 20 percent and 16 percent of their labor force growth in military related industries. By 1980 only Santa Clara County (i.e., Silicon Valley) had more military related expansion—31 percent total employment growth.

Recent Sunbelt Trends

The shift to the Sunbelt is a spectacular example of regional realignment experienced by an advanced industrial country. As we shall see in Chapter 13, there are parallels to the U.S. case in such countries as England, France and, particularly, Germany, which have also undergone regional shifts as a consequence of high technology industrial restructuring. Yet, despite these changes, it is possible to overstate the case of Sunbelt prominence. There are at least three reasons to temper the notion that this region is gaining in autonomy and power at the expense of areas elsewhere: the need to place Sunbelt economic activities within a national and global context, the boom and bust cycle of development, and the enormous environmental costs of growth.

Economic Differentiation and the Global Economy. Because the U.S. economy has become more functionally specialized, many of the rapidly growing Sunbelt industries

Aerial view of Disneyland in Anaheim, California. Theme parks and even theme malls are important to sunbelt growth.

are tied administratively and economically to Frostbelt centers. The latter still retain the majority of corporate headquarters, for example. Banking and finance are still controlled by Frostbelt interests (Gottdiener, 1985). In addition, since the 1970s many U.S. firms have been either bought out or heavily invested in by multinational corporations that have headquarters in other countries. Sunbelt factories, no matter how stable in employment, may be only a part of some larger operation that also includes Frostbelt command and control centers or worldwide organizations. Hence, splits between the regions are *not* autonomous. They reflect, instead, a growing regional specialization in the United States and the entire world as mutinational interests utilize space and place to improve economic performance.

The Cycles of Growth and Decline. As we have seen, the best way to describe Sunbelt development is in terms of boom and bust cycles that are relatively rapid in fluctuations. Sunbelt residents who have been attracted to the region by visions of affluence may have to tolerate a life of feast or famine. At present the national recession has hit many Sunbelt areas especially hard. The powerful states of Texas and California, once thought immune to downturns, have been in the doldrums since the late 1980s. Unemployment was above the national average for a time. California has experienced two straight years of fiscal crises which required cuts in spending, wage freezes, and a reassessment of the state's credit rating. Social services such as education are now besieged due to lack of funds, and the quality of life has deteriorated accordingly.

The characteristic woes of the region are exemplified by Silicon Valley, also known as Santa Clara County, in California. This region was once touted as the exemplary high tech boom area that even countries should emulate in their development plans. Currently, the region is called the "Valley of Gloom" (Smith, 1992), because of the severity of its recession. Much of its heralded job creation has shifted to other places around the globe, and its businesses are besieged because of declining sales while some have fallen victim to both foreign and domestic competitors. As one newspaper report states,

> Not only has Santa Clara County lost 20,000 manufacturing jobs in the last 18 months, industry analysts estimate that tens of thousands of newly created electronic industry jobs have gone elsewhere in the same period. .... High tech manufacturing in this area is no longer competitive with other areas of the country or the world. Even if the economy rebounds, we're not going back to the double-digit job growth we enjoyed the last two decades (Smith, 1992: A-1).

It may be possible that this area will experience a revival much like the one in Houston (see above), and the cycle of boom and bust will start up again. But as the newspaper report indicates, there is a profound sense of pessimism that paints the future in more modest growth terms. Silicon Valley is typical of other high tech growth poles. Its population is both well educated and diverse—37 percent of those over 18 years have at least a two-year college degree, and 12 percent of its population is foreign born. These residents have been used to several decades of affluence and growth. At present they are learning to suffer with the rest of the nation during the current recession.

The Environmental Costs of Rapid Growth. Because it has been the site of rapid and largely minimally planned growth, the Sunbelt region has also encountered monumental environmental problems. In fact, as of 1991, we may be poised at a point of immense growth difficulties for many areas of the Sunbelt. The environment has long suffered the initial impact of development. Unique and pristine formations, such as Tampa and San Francisco bays, have been almost destroyed biologically in the wake of change. Clear cutting of virgin forests, pollution of lakes and streams, fouling of beaches with oil or sewage, and emission of choking smog are but some of the environmental problems already well established in the South and West. After years of uncertainty regarding published accounts of the effects of smog, for example, it was recently reported that constant exposure produces *permanent* lung damage in both children and adults (*Press Enterprise,* May 17, 1992: AA-1). The population of Los Angeles lives in just such an environment, yet the presence of damaging smog has done little to date to stem the otherwise constant stream of new arrivals to the region (see Chapter 14 for a more detailed discussion of the environment and the sociospatial perspective).

In more recent years other effects of population growth have appeared. Crime is a serious problem, for example. New York City is often stereotyped as an unsafe city. Its murder rate was 26 per 100,000 persons in 1989. Houston's rate, however, was 27 for that year, Dallas' was 35, and New Orleans' was 47. Even Los Angeles had a high rate of 25, less than New York but the same as Chicago and much more than Boston (17). Sunbelt cities may just be the most unsafe and violent in the nation, containing nine of our ten most dangerous metro areas (MacDonald, 1984)—see Chapter 10.

In addition to crime, overcrowding in schools and declining educational quality are a typical Sunbelt lament. These conditions are expected to get worse as the western and southern states encounter intractable budget crises. In 1991 California suffered its largest budget deficit in its history, and educational spending was the first casualty.

In rapidly growing areas traffic congestion is so bad that it is fast approaching gridlock. It's not uncommon for commuters in parts of California to travel four hours both ways by car, especially when no other alternatives to commuting are available. Finally, housing prices have soared in the best locations, making first home purchasing progressively out of reach. Despite these and other constraints, life in the Sunbelt continues to attract new people, especially highly trained professionals who have the ability to find well paying jobs (Kephart, 1991). It is expected that the fifteen states of the Sunbelt will continue to grow in the future. Estimates are that this region wi'' contain half the nation's population by the year 2000.

In sum, since the 1960s the relationships between people, and spatial living and working arrangements have profoundly changed. Gone is the highly compact industrial city with a working-class culture and labor influenced democratic politics. In its place, everyday life now transpires in multinucleated metropolitan regions across the country. Development is dominated by the population shifts to the suburbs and the Sunbelt, while the vision of unending growth and affluence has been tempered by the experience of living through rapid cycles of boom and bust. These changes have been explained by the sociospatial perspective, which emphasizes the pull factors of economic and technological change (as do other approaches) but also the importance of government intervention, real estate, and the restructuring of sociospatial arrangements in business and residential activities.

CHAPTER

6

THE RISE OF URBAN SOCIOLOGY

A special inquiry devoted to urban phenomena was the premier achievement of early U.S. sociology. During the 1920s the University of Chicago started the first sociology department in the country, headed by Albion Small. Almost immediately a prominent role was given to a former journalist, Robert E Park. Small and Park had something in common. They had both gone as students to Germany—in particular to take courses with Max Weber. At that time, the early 1900s, only France and Germany had professional sociologists, and Max Weber was acknowledged as the premier social thinker of his day, although a second sociologist, Emile Durkheim, had accumulated a growing reputation in France.

While in Germany, both Small and Park were informed about a brilliant lecturer, Georg Simmel, and they eagerly became his students. Due to discrimination against Jews in Germany, Simmel was not able to obtain a regular academic appointment. Instead, he lectured part-time at the University in Berlin, usually in the evening. Like Weber, Simmel was also interested in the city, and the two of them produced the only papers addressing directly the issue of urbanism among continental Europeans. One other person must also be mentioned, since he is usually forgotten in discussions of urban sociology, namely, Friedrich Engels, who was working in England. Engels wrote a classic study, *The Condition of the Working Class in England* (1973), which devoted a chapter to what he called "The Great Towns." According to Engels, the evils of industrialization and capitalism were intensified by the space of the city. This is a perspective to which we shall return in the next chapter.

The most influential European in U.S. urban sociology at the beginning was Georg Simmel. He viewed the city in cultural terms and was concerned with the way urban life transformed individual consciousness. That is, for Simmel, everyday existence within the city altered the way people thought and acted as compared to traditional society. Both Park and Small took this "interactive" perspective back home with them.

Georg Simmel.

In the United States the work of the early Chicago School that followed was less concerned with historical and comparative studies in the manner of Weber, and more focused on social behavior and interaction within the urban milieu in the manner of Simmel.

Any good discussion of American urban sociology must begin with explaining an important distinction. There are really *two* distinct organizing topics in the field: *urbanization* and *urbanism. Urbanization* refers to the city formation or building process. It studies the way social activities locate themselves in space and according to interdependent processes of societal development and change. Its analysis is often historical and comparative. Urbanization charts and tries to understand the rise and fall of great cities. Many of the discussions in the previous chapters were about urbanization.

Urbanism in contrast takes the city formation process as given and seeks instead to understand the ways of life that transpire within this container. Urbanism deals with culture, with meanings, symbols, patterns of daily life, adjustment processes to the environment of the city, but also with conflicts, with forms of political organization at the street, neighborhood, and city levels.

While Max Weber and Friedrich Engels both stressed the relation between the historical nature of the city and its ways of life, Simmel was more concerned with the latter. Early U.S. urban sociology followed Simmel most closely and focused on patterns of activity within cities rather than addressing the topic of U.S. urbanization or city formation. Yet for Simmel the study of life within the city was not meant as an "urban sociology." Simmel was concerned with what is called *modernity,* or the transition from a traditional society characterized by social relations based on intimacy or kinship (known as "primary" relations) and by a feudal economy based on barter to an industrial society situated within cities and dominated by impersonal, specialized social relations based on compartmentalized roles (known as "secondary" relations) and by a money economy based on rational calculation of profit and loss. For Simmel the subtle aspects of modernity were displayed most clearly within the large city or metropolis and through consciously directed behaviors. Simmel gives us a social psychology of modernity which Robert Park took to be the sociology of urbanism, or "urban sociology."

Simmel on the City

What was it like to confront modernity and why was Simmel so impressed with the city as the vehicle for change? Consider, if you will, a German farmer from Bavaria. His life was tuned to the daily rhythms of agriculture. Nature and his own physical labor provided the boundaries within which the farming endeavor was framed. The regime of labor on the land was early to bed, because darkness meant little work could be done, and early to rise, because it was necessary to use every second of daylight for work—even dawn and twilight. This farmer was immersed in a social world of primary, kinship relations. His principal contacts were members of his family, both immediate and extended. Perhaps several generations and families lived together in the same location and worked the land. Beyond this primary network, the farmer would interact with individuals who aided his enterprise. Most typically he visited a local service center, perhaps a small town. There he was surely involved in a network of people that knew him well. It was entirely possible in this kind of traditional society that no money changed hands while farm produce and needed commodities were exchanged. Barter, credit, and informal agreements among known persons characterized the social relations of this world.

As Simmel might suggest, suppose that this individual, call him "Hans," lost the farm and his family in some personal tragedy. With a small amount of money he now traveled to Berlin to begin a new life. He went to this modern city precisely because it offered him an alternative to the rural, traditional existence of farming. Karl Marx, writing in the nineteenth century, would have focused on Hans' conversion to an industrial worker. He would have taken us into the factory with Hans and described his encounter with abstract capital (the machine); with the relations of production (the assembly line, the factory building, and the daily schedule of work); and with class relations (interaction with the workers and the boss). Simmel virtually ignored this entire domain of the factory, which could be termed the *immediate* environment of capitalism, and focused instead on the larger context of daily life, the *extended* environment, namely, the city.

Hans stands on the corner of a large boulevard filled with daytime auto traffic in Berlin. He has to dodge the steady stream of pedestrians just to stand still and watch, since everything else is in constant motion. At first shock Hans would be paralyzed by the "excess of nervous stimulation," according to Simmel. Haven't we all had a similar experience upon visiting a large city? Loud noises from traffic, people in the crowds calling after each other, strangers touching him as they passed without an acknowledgment, and more—noise, noise, and noise. Hans would find himself in a totally new environment that *demanded* an adjustment and response.

According to Simmel, small town life required Hans to develop strong, intimate ties to those with whom he interacted. Here in the city, the excess of stimulation requires a defensive response. These are the characteristics of urbanism noted by Simmel. Hans would (1) develop what Simmel called the "blasé" attitude—a blurring of the senses, a filtering out of all that was loud and impinging but also irrelevant to Hans' own personal needs. Emotional reserve and indifference replaces acute attention to the details of the environment.

Hans would require the satisfaction of his needs. Yes, he would encounter capitalism and, no doubt, sell his labor for a wage, as Marx had observed. Simmel agreed with Marx about the necessity of that transaction. It would (2) *reduce the quality* of Hans' capabilities simply *to the quantity* of his labor time—the time he spent at work, for a wage. It would make his work equivalent to a sum of money, no more, no less. That sum of money exchanged for Hans' labor time would be all that the employing capitalist would provide. Hans would quickly see that absolutely no concern for his health-related, spiritual, communal, sexual, or any other type of human need would be involved in his relationship with his employer. In short, the world of capitalism was (3) an impersonal world of pure monetary exchange.

Simmel, unlike Marx, showed how the impersonal money economy extended itself outside the factory to characterize all other transactions in the city. Hans would use his paycheck to buy the needs of life, but here, too, in these transactions impersonal or secondary social relations prevailed. Unless he went to a small store and frequented it every day, he would simply be viewed as (4) an *anonymous* customer being provided with mass produced items for purchase. As a city dweller, he might find himself more frequently going to a department store where (5) a mass *spectacle* of consumption would be on display.

In all these transactions Hans would have to be very careful. His weekly paycheck could only go so far. He would have to count how much each item cost and then budget himself accordingly. This (6) *rational calculation* would be at the heart of his daily life. Everything would be measured by him, just as costs were carefully measured at the factory. Rational calculation of money would require knowledge and technique. If Hans mastered it successfully along with gaining mastery over the consumer world of the city, he could look down at his country bumpkin cousins. City life, for Simmel, was a life of the intellect, and everywhere the relation between the money economy and the rational calculation needed to survive in the world of capitalism prevailed. Those in the city who could not master the technique of money management—of profit and loss—would be surely lost.

We are not finished with the example of Hans. In the traditional society of the country the rhythm of life was provided by nature. The city environment requires adjustments to (7) a *second nature*—the orchestration of daily activities as governed by clock time and as played out within a constructed space. All life in the city follows the schedule of capitalist industrialization or modernity. If Hans didn't own a watch before coming to the city, he now needed one. Time and money constitute the two types of calculation necessary for survival in the second nature of the urban milieu— the built environment of concrete, steel, and glass that is the city. Finally, Simmel also commented on the qualitative value of an experience like Hans'. He did not see the transformation as something that was necessarily bad. Hans would be cast in a calculating and impersonal world, but he would also be (8) *freed* from the restrictions of traditional society and its timebound dictates. Hans would be free to discriminate about the type of friends he chose, about the job he took (within strong constraints, mind you), about where he lived. Modernity meant the possibility of immense individual freedom to Simmel, in addition to constraint.

For Simmel, the freedom of the city meant, above all else, that Hans would be free to pursue and even create his own individuality. Provided he had the money, of course—an occurrence that Marx would doubt—Hans could cultivate himself. He could dress according to some distinct fashion, develop hobbies which he could share with others, perhaps take up the violin and join a neighborhood string quartet; he could enjoy a certain brand of cigar or shoes, or attend night classes at the university—even Simmel's own lectures. Could Hans and Simmel have eventually met? The city allowed the possibility of attaining such cultural freedom, and the signs of individual cultivation—the clothes, cigars, friends, lovers, discussion groups, opera, art, novels—were all together the signs of modernity which we may also call urbanism.

The Chicago School: Park, Burgess, and McKenzie

In Chapter 4 we saw how the early industrialized cities of the United States were the scene of get-rich-quick schemes, poverty, the churning of immigrant groups in and out of neighborhoods, innovation, and large-scale factory production. The members of the sociology department at the University of Chicago became uniquely interested in their city and were inspired to study the great human drama transpiring outside their windows. During the 1920s there were already several efforts to monitor the characteristics and needs of the urban population. The settlement house movement and people like Jane Addams (see Chapter 4) were concerned about urban problems. They conducted some of the earliest surveys in the United States and planned schemes of intervention to aid the large numbers of working poor.

Robert Park and his associates at the University of Chicago were less concerned than was Simmel with the city dweller's encounter with modernity, and more involved in detailed study of the specific Chicago milieu. They were responsible for a number of important conceptual advances in the field of urban sociology.

From the very first, the Chicago School urbanists adopted a conceptual position that we call *human ecology*—the study of the human group-adjustment process to the environment. While European thinkers like Weber, Marx, and Simmel viewed the city as an environment where larger social forces of capitalism played themselves out in a human drama, Chicago School urbanists avoided the study of capitalism *per se,* and preferred instead a biologically based way of conceptualizing urban life. For them urban analysis was a branch of human ecology. Their ideas brought them closest to the work of the philosopher Herbert Spencer, who also viewed society as dominated by biological rather than economic laws of development. Economic competition, in this view, was a special case of the struggle for survival. All individuals in the city were caught up in this struggle and adjusted to it in various ways.

According to Robert Park, the social organization of the city resulted from the struggle for survival which then produced a distinct and highly complex division of labor, because people tried to do what they were best at in order to compete. Urban life for Park was organized on two separate levels: the "biotic" and the "cultural." The *biotic* level refers to the forms of organization produced by species competition over scarce environmental resources. The *cultural* level refers to the symbolic and psycholog-ical adjustment processes and to the organization of urban life according to shared sentiments, much like the qualities Simmel also studied.

In Park's work, the biotic level stressed the importance of biological factors for understanding social organization and the urban effects of economic competition. In contrast, the cultural component of urban life operated in neighborhoods which were held together by cooperative ties involving shared cultural values between people with similar backgrounds. Hence, local community life was organized around what Park called a "moral order" of cooperative, symbolic ties, while the larger city composed of separate communities was organized through competition and functional differentia-tion. In Park's later work, however, the complex notion of *urbanism* as combining competition and cooperation, or the biotic and the cultural levels, was dropped in favor of an emphasis on the biotic level alone as the basic premise of urban ecology. This then led to some of the earliest critiques of the ecological perspective, faulting it for ignoring the role of culture in the city, or what Simmel would call the important influence of modernity, and for neglecting the basis of community (Alihan, 1938) which was social and not biological.

Other members of the early Chicago School translated the social Darwinism of Park into a spatially attuned analysis. For Roderick McKenzie, the fundamental quality of the struggle for existence was position or *location* for either the individual, the group, or some city institution such as a business firm. Economic competition or the struggle for existence affected spatial position. Groups or individuals that were success-ful took over the better positions in the city, such as the higher ground, the choicest business locations, or the preferred neighborhoods. Those less successful were relegated to less desirable positions. In this way the population under pressure of economic competition sorted itself out within the city space.

McKenzie explained land-use patterns as the product of competition and an eco-nomic division of labor, which deployed objects and activities in space according to the roles they played in society. Thus, if a firm needed a particular location in order to perform its function, it competed with others for that location. The patterns resulting from that process were studied by ecologists.

Finally, Ernest W. Burgess developed a theory of city growth and differentiation based on the social Darwinist or biologically derived principles that were common in the work of Park and McKenzie. According to Burgess, the city constantly grew because of population pressures. This, in turn, triggered a dual process of central agglomeration and commercial decentralization; that is, spatial competition attracted new activities, on the one hand, to the center of the city, but also repelled other activities, on the other hand, to the fringe area. As activities themselves located on the fringe, the fringe itself was pushed further out from the city, and so on.

Thus the city continually grew outward as activities which lost out in central city competition were relocated to peripheral areas. This sorting led, in turn, to further spatial and functional differentiation as activities were deployed according to competitive advantages. In Burgess' theory, the city would eventually take on the form of a highly concentrated central business district which would dominate the region and be the site for the highest competitive land prices, while the surrounding area would comprise four distinct concentric rings (1925: 51; and Figure 6.1).

The importance of Burgess' model cannot be overemphasized. First, he explained the pattern of homes, neighborhoods, and industrial and commercial locations in terms of the ecological theory of competition over "position" or location. In short, competition produced a certain space and a certain social organization in space. Both of these dimensions were pictured in the concentric zone model. Those who could afford it lived near the center; those who could not, arranged themselves in concentric zones around the city center. Such a model required among other things that the center had the most jobs and social activities and, hence, that it was the most desirable location.

Ernest Burgess of the Chicago School.

The Growth of the City

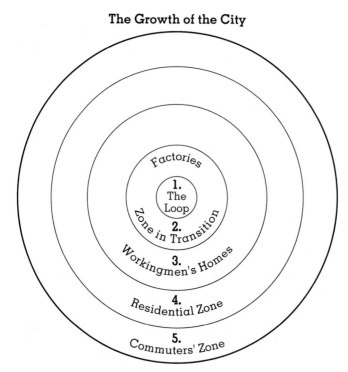

Figure 6.1   Burgess' concentric zone model.

This view will be challenged below in the models of Hoyt (Figure 6.2) and Harris and Ullman (Figure 6.3).

Second, Burgess' model explained the shifting of population and activities within the space of the city according to two distinct but related processes: *centralization* and *decentralization.* His theory explicitly related social processes to spatial patterns—a most important link for all theorizing about the city that was to follow and a view that is quite compatible with the aims of the new urban sociology.

Finally, Burgess revealed that the characteristics of the social organization of the urban population were *spatially* deployed. A gradient running from the center to the periphery characterized the attributes of the urban population. Individual traits such as mental illness, gang membership, criminal behavior, and racial background were found to be clustered along the center/periphery gradient of the city. Cutting across the urban form from the Central Business District (known as the CBD) to the outskirts, Chicago School researchers using census data found that the incidence of social pathology decreased while homeownership and the number of nuclear families increased. The inner zones, therefore, were discovered to be the sites of crime, illness, gang warfare, broken homes, and many other indicators of social disorganization or problems.

In practice, however, research on the internal structure of cities contradicted Burgess' view of concentric zones. Two other models of the city were proposed which argued that cities had multicenters rather than a single focus. The first critique of

Burgess' model was proposed by Homer Hoyt (1933) and was called "sector theory." Hoyt suggested that cities were carved up, not by concentric zones, but by oddly shaped sectors within which different economic activities tended to congregate together, that is, agglomerate (see Figure 6.2). Hoyt suggested that all activities, but especially manufacturing and retailing, had the tendency to spin off away from the center and agglomerate in sectors that expanded outward. Thus the city grew in irregular blobs rather than in Burgess' neat circles.

The idea of multiple nuclei as the shape of the city developed further Hoyt's break with Burgess and is close to the current multicentered approach used in this book (see Chapter 1). It was introduced in a classic paper by Harris and Ullman (1945). They suggested that *within* any city, separate functions and their particular needs require concentration within specific and specialized districts (see Figure 6.3). Thus, within cities, similar activities often locate in the same area, forming agglomerations or minicenters. Cities often grow asymmetrically around these multiple nuclei.

A common assumption of all of these models is that the city remains the central place that dominates in importance all other areas. In recent years this way of thinking about urbanized areas has declined, and a focus on the individual city has given way

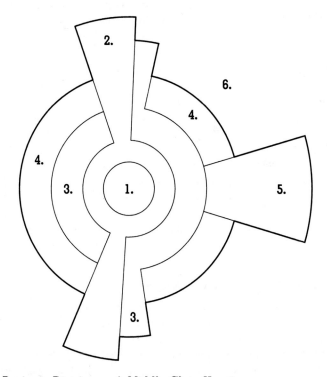

1. Central Business District   4. Middle-Class Housing
2. Industrial Manufacturing   5. Luxury, Upper-Middle- and Upper-Class Housing
3. Working-Class Housing   6. Commuter Zones

Figure 6.2   Hoyt's sector model.

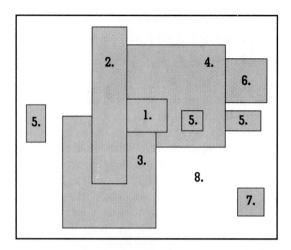

1. Central Business District   5. Luxury, Upper- Middle- and Upper-Class Houses
2. Manufacturing District   6. An Outlying Central Business District
3. Working-Class Houses   7. A Suburban Industrial Park
4. Middle-Class Housing   8. Commuter Zone

Figure 6.3 Harris and Ullman's multiple nuclei model.

to the regional metropolitan perspective which stresses the relative independence of multiple centers, as we have discussed in previous chapters.

While ecologists were concerned with location and with thinking of social activities as located in space, their biologically based explanation for perceived activities and spatial patterns has been rejected in recent years in favor of the new urban sociology (see Gottdiener and Feagin, 1988).

Despite its limitations, under the leadership of the Chicago School pioneers, a large body of research was produced whose hallmark was the connection between social processes of city living and a specific location in urban space. That location, furthermore, was perceived as a consequence of competition over scarce resources, of which one was space itself. Hence place and space saturate the conceptions of the early Chicago School.

The Chicago School: Louis Wirth

A short time after Park, Burgess, and McKenzie worked in tandem to discover the forces creating patterns of daily life within the city, another Chicago School sociologist appeared who defined a different theory of urban space, Louis Wirth. Other ecologists viewed spatial patterns as caused by powerful social factors such as the struggle for survival. The phenomena they observed were the outcome of social forces operating within the city. Thus urban space was viewed by Park and his associates as a *container,* some built environment that encloses the action. Wirth's idea was different. He wanted to know what it was about the city itself that produced unique behaviors which might be called an "urban way of life." In this emphasis Wirth returned to Simmel. However, while Simmel (and Weber, and Marx) attributed much of the city way of life to the

Louis Wirth of the Chicago School.

influence of larger systemic forces, especially capitalism and its money economy, Wirth aimed for a generalized theory that ignored forces having origins outside the city. He studied the characteristics of people in the city and how life there might produce a distinct "urban" culture. Hence "urbanism," or an urban way of life, became the *dependent* variable that was to be explained.

Wirth settled on the isolation of three factors. Urbanism was produced in *relatively large* (population size), *densely* populated settlements containing heterogeneous people (different backgrounds). That is, urbanism was a product of large population size, density, and heterogeneity. Wirth's approach was an important advance because he provided a set of factors that could be analyzed statistically according to their effects. Hence, it was a theory with true predictive power. Given a sample of cities, the higher each one scored on the three factors of size, density, and heterogeneity, the more we could expect it to house a true urban culture. For example, consider the following three cities: Motorville, Cosmotown and Booneycity. They have the factor scores illustrated in Table 6.1. Note that for the purposes of this example, density is defined as population per square mile and heterogeneity as a percentage that reflects the number of classes and the number of ethnic/racial groups.

Motorville is an industrial town with a moderate density. It possesses two main

TABLE 6.1
Wirth's Theory Illustrated

	Population size	Population density	Heterogeneity
Motorville	100,000	10,000 per sq. mi.	.40
Cosmotown	100,000	30,000 per sq. mi.	.80
Booneycity	5,000	1,000 per sq. mi.	.20

classes—workers in the factories and capitalists who own and control industry. The ethnic groups consist almost entirely of Eastern European and Irish workers. The capitalist class is WASP. According to Wirth's point of view, Motorville would exhibit a *moderately* developed urban culture.

Cosmotown is a mixed industrial, service, and retailing center. It has a high density and a very diverse population that works in the varied economy, including three or more classes (a middle and perhaps under class, in addition to workers and capitalists) and many different ethnic groups from Asia, Latin America, Africa, and Europe. Wirth's theory would predict that Cosmotown possesses a *highly* developed urban culture.

Finally, Booneycity scores low on all three factors. Most probably this is a service center in a rural area. Wirth would predict that it has only *weak* urban attributes.

As might be expected, actual cases may not be so clear. Nevertheless researchers could make some predictions through comparative analysis by looking at census data and constructing factor scores such as the ones above. The higher the scores, the more urbanism could be predicted.

Wirth's theory was very impressive for his time (1930s) because of its predictive potential. Problems arose when he tried to define what precisely an urban culture would be like. Recall the example of Hans. Simmel gave us a detailed picture that contained both negative and positive aspects. Essentially, Simmel viewed the city as simply *different.* In his formulation Wirth stressed the dark side of Simmel's vision. Urbanism as a culture would be characterized by aspects of social disorganization. Most central to Wirth's view was the shift from primary to secondary social relations. Wirth tended to see urban anonymity as debilitating. More specifically, the effects of the three factors on social life can be expressed as a series of propositions according to the role of each factor, as indicated in Box 6.1.

In the years following Wirth's work his theory has been exhaustively tested, mainly because it was so clearly stated (Fischer, 1975). Unfortunately, the core assertion that size, density, and heterogeneity cause behaviors considered urban has not been borne out. If we look at the propositions above, many of the assertions seem true of the big city and hence they help provide a more detailed picture of what urbanism as a culture is like. However, while the theory contains some truth, we cannot say along with Wirth that the factors he chose produce such results. The large city merely *concentrates* the effects of societal forces producing city culture. Crime rates provide one illustration. Cosmotown might have a high crime rate, but Motorville might have a higher one (see Table 6.1 above). Using a per capita measure, places like Booneycity might also possess comparatively high rates. Surely, we know that rural areas are just as afflicted by crime as is the central city, although the types of crimes and their intensity may vary.

In other examples, studies of social pathology such as mental illness find that rural areas score higher, in some cases, than do many cities. Other indicators of social disorganization such as high divorce rates are ubiquitous in the society. Density causes stress, but urbanites have also been very resourceful in finding ways to alleviate the potential stress caused by crowding. In short, we should not discard the assertion that different aspects of social organization or disorganization are dispersed in patterns of a spatial nature in our society. However, we can question whether those patterns are related to the difference that cities themselves make (see Fischer, 1976).

BOX 6.1 WIRTH'S PROPOSITIONS

Size Propositions

1. The larger the population, the greater the chances for diversity and individualization.
2. Competition and formal mechanisms of social control would replace primary relations of kinship as a means of organizing society.
3. The larger the population, the greater the specialization and functional diversity of social roles.
4. Anonymity and fragmentation of social interaction increase with size.

Density Propositions

1. Greater density intensifies the effects of large population size.
2. Greater density creates the blasé attitude and the need to tune out excessive stimulation.
3. Greater density produces greater tolerance for living closely with strangers but also greater stress.
4. Escape from density produces development of the fringe and greater land value in suburbia.
5. Density increases competition, compounding the effects of size.

Heterogeneity Propositions

1. The greater the heterogeneity, the more tolerance between groups.
2. Heterogeneity allows ethnic and class barriers to be broken down.
3. Individual roles and contacts become compartmentalized according to different circles of contacts. Anonymity and depersonalization in public life increase.

Finally, it should be noted that Louis Wirth held strongly to the view that the true effects of urbanism would occur as a matter of evolution, as cities operated on immigrant groups to break down traditional ways of interacting over time. He did not see the larger city acting as an environment to bring about immediately the change he predicted. These things would take time, perhaps a generation. In Chapter 8 we shall return to the topic of urbanism and continue discussing the refinement of Wirth's ideas up to the present.

In the main, Wirth can be remembered as showing us a *style* of doing urban research that differed from Chicago School field work. While others took to the streets to record the everyday life found in cities, Wirth inspired a subsequent generation to plow through census data and derive statistical regularities of urban living. Much urban research is like that to this day. In a subsequent chapter we shall return to the theory of urban culture and find aspects of Wirth's theory itself that are still useful as well.

The Chicago School: Other Considerations

The work of the early Chicago School should never be forgotten. For about a decade, beginning with 1925, a veritable flood of work poured out of the sociology department.

Counting some of the books alone (i.e., ignoring masters and Ph.D. theses produced at that time), the following list samples their accomplishments. All these books were published by the University of Chicago press: F. Thrasher (1927), *The Gang;* Louis Wirth (1928), *The Ghetto;* Ruth S. Cavan (1928), *Suicide;* Clifford S. Shaw (1930), *The Jackroller;* Harvey W. Zorbaugh (1929), *The Gold Coast and the Slum;* E. Franklin Frazier (1932), *The Negro Family in Chicago;* Paul G. Cressey (1932), *The Taxi-dance Hall;* Walter C. Reckless (1933), *Vice in Chicago;* Norman Hayner (1936), *Hotel Life;* and then later, St. Clair Drake and Horace R. Cayton (1945), *Black Metropolis.* Regarding this list, it can also be said that while gender issues were not well articulated at that time, women were involved in the Chicago School. The issue of race, however, was clearly drawn, as was the issue of black family life, and three of the above authors were, in fact, African American, although the entire question of racism seemed undeveloped.

This marvelous output was produced with a similar stamp. It took an important social phenomenon, such as suicide, and located the distribution of its incidence in the space of the city. Chicago researchers then analyzed it in terms of the relation between the individual and the larger social forces of integration/disintegration. Most often this meant that phenomena were explained as products of social disorganization, particularly the breaking up of primary social relations through city living, as Wirth's theory suggested. As a result the Chicago School was eventually criticized for reinforcing a negative view of city life.

Despite their limitations, we can also appreciate the positive aspects of these early efforts. Chicago School researchers explicitly connected social phenomena with spatial patterns; that is, they thought in *sociospatial* terms. Second, they took an *interactionist* perspective. Individuals were studied in interaction with others, and the *emergent* forms of sociation coming out of that interaction were observed closely. Finally, they tried to show the *patterns of adjustment* to sociospatial location and developed a rudimentary way of speaking about the role of individual attributes in explaining urban phenomena. It *was* true that they focused almost exclusively on social disorganization and pathology; the break-up of family integration, for example, was given much more attention than questions of race or class.

The principal reason, however, for this ideological slant was that Chicago School sociologists were deeply concerned with improving life in the city. In their time they rejected radical prescriptions for change and believed, instead, that *reformist* efforts prevail. Well-done reports produced by professional sociologists were viewed as one element in this reformist struggle. Perhaps the best example of an academic/reformer was Louis Wirth, himself. Wirth not only contributed to the output of the Chicago School on theory and ethnography but left a sizable body of material addressing the issue of urban planning. He devoted considerable time to trying to improve city planning and saw government intervention as a means of elevating the urban quality of life. This reformist, practical side of Chicago Schoolers like Wirth is often ignored in discussions of their work.

Another way to appreciate their achievements is by returning to their original case studies. A particularly vivid ethnography is Frederick M. Thrasher's 1927 study, *The Gang.* Thrasher spent eight years tracking down the youth gangs of Chicago and in the end was able to identify 1,313 of them. Today, media coverage tends to associate gangs with black or Hispanic teenagers in the inner city and lament their violent ways, as exemplified by such films as *Boyz N The Hood* or *Colors*. Thrasher brings us back to the city of some seventy years ago when gangs were as much a problem, but they were almost all white (see Box 6.2).

Contemporary Urban Ecology

The ecological perspective remains active in urban sociology. Its core biological meta-phor has been retained, as well as its central view that social organization should be understood as a process of adaption to the environment. As Berry and Kasarda (1977: 12) assert in a recent formulation,

> The central problem of contemporary ecological inquiry is understanding how a popula-tion organizes itself in adapting to a constantly changing yet restructuring environment. Adaption is considered to be a collective phenomenon, resulting from the population de-veloping a functionally integrated organization through the accumulative and frequently repetitive actions of large numbers of individuals.

As we can see, ecologists avoid any mention of social groupings such as classes or ethnic, racial, and gender differences. They see life as a process of adaptation rather than competition over scarce resources that often brings conflict. They have a limited conception of the economy, which they conceive principally as the social organization of functions and the division of labor—a conception which neglects the dynamics of capitalism and the global system. Although they emphasize ecological location, they ignore aspects of the real estate industry and its role in developing space. Finally, ecologists seem to ignore the political institutions that administer and regulate society, and affect everyday life through the institutional channeling of resources. Their empha-sis is on the push factors or the demand-side view, which neglects the powerful supply-side causes of growth and change in the metropolis. We shall return to these neglected aspects in the next chapter when we take up the new urban sociology.

After World War II the ecological approach enjoyed something of a renaissance, because ecologists paid careful attention to the census of population and how demo-graphic locational patterns had changed. By 1950, it was found that the U.S. population had matured and spread out across metropolitan regions. In addition to population dispersal, the war years had also changed the locational patterns of U.S. industry. Many plants dispersed to the countryside during the 1940s. As a result of the war effort against Japan, heavy industry was also decentralized and relocated west. Los Angeles, California, in particular, became both a focal point for the burgeoning aerospace industry and an important port for trade with the Pacific Rim markets. All of this restructuring and change called for new research that would chart the emergent patterns.

Working with descriptive tools, urban ecologists produced many studies on the differentiation of social activities across the United States. A great deal of refinement went into statistical analyses of census data that enabled new descriptive models of U.S. metropolitan growth to be devised. Much of this effort followed the style of the

BOX 6.2 CASE STUDY: GANGLAND CHICAGO, 1927

The population of gangs in the 1920s was composed principally of recent immigrants to this country. Of the total gang census taken by Thrasher amounting to 25,000 members in a city of 2 million, roughly 17 percent were known as Polish gangs, 11 percent were known as Italian, 8.5 percent were Irish, 7 percent were black, another 3 percent were mixed white and black, 2 percent were Jewish, and so on, with the largest percentage of *all* gangs composed of "mixed nationalities" known exclusively for their territory, not for their ethnicity (1927: 130). According to Thrasher, roughly 87 percent of all gang members were of foreign extraction! The gang phenomenon was explained in part by the lack of adjustment opportunities for immigrants, in part by the carryover of Old World antagonisms, and also by the need to defend territory against "outsiders."

Thrasher's study demonstrates sociospatial thinking. As Robert Park (Thrasher, 1927: vii) comments in his introduction,

> The title of this book does not describe it. It is a study of the gang, to be sure, but it is at the same time a study of "gangland," that is to say, a study of the gang and its habitat, and in this case the habitat is a city slum.

Note Parks' grounding of the study in a biological metaphor by his use of the word *habitat*. Today we would use the sociospatial perspective and say *territory* or *space*. Gangland is the city space where gangs lived. Their influence was felt all over. What Thrasher did was locate gangs in their space. In fact, he found "three great domains" of gangdom—the "northside jungles," the "southside badlands," and the "westside wilderness." Using Ernest W. Burgess' map of Chicago (see Figure 6.4), Thrasher provided details for each of these areas and the gangs they contained. Within gangland "the street educates with fatal precision" (1927: 101). The northside covered an area directly north of the downtown, or the "loop" on the Burgess map, and behind the wealthy neighborhoods that lined the shore of Lake Michigan. It was home to the "Gloriannas," the site of "Death Corner" and "Bughouse Square," and a gang so threatening that Thrasher disguised its real name.

The westside was the most extensive slum area producing gangs, and it encompassed the west past downtown, spreading out both north and southward. The westside was home to the "Blackspots," the "Sparkplugs," the "Beaners," and the "hard-boiled 'Buckets-of-Blood'" (1927: 9). On the

Chicago School—an emphasis on spatial location, on functional differentiation, and on the use of census data to pinpoint population differences as they are deployed in space.

Eventually some new theoretical ideas were formulated, principally by Amos Hawley (1950), and these became the focus of contemporary urban ecology. Hawley was most interested in explaining two aspects of change in the postwar period: first, the massive growth of suburbanization; and second, the restructuring of central city

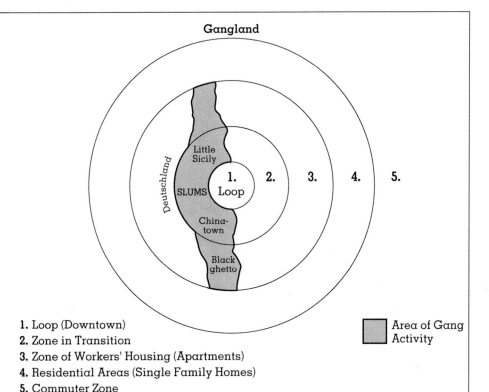

Gangland

Deutschland

Little Sicily

SLUMS

1. Loop

2.

3.

4.

5.

China-town

Black ghetto

1. Loop (Downtown)
2. Zone in Transition
3. Zone of Workers' Housing (Apartments)
4. Residential Areas (Single Family Homes)
5. Commuter Zone

Area of Gang Activity

Figure 6.4 Thrasher's map.

southside of Chicago are located the stockyards and miles of railroad yards. Most of the blacks settled there, but the area remained dominated by Poles and Italians. The latter gangs were known as the "Torpedoes," or the "So So's." Black gangs of the time were the "Wailing Shebas," or the "Wolves."

As a territorially divided area the city of Chicago and its environs pulsed with the give and take confrontations between the various gangs. Only the relative scarcity of killing weapons like handguns kept the constant confrontations from erupting into the type of carnage characteristic of many cities today. For students of contemporary urban sociology there can be no better example of spatially sensitive research than Thrasher's original study. I doubt, too, that in today's urban environment anyone could carry out the kind of exhaustive census on street gangs that Thrasher did. Certainly his study is now outdated. But like the pyramids, it remains an inspiration across time.

areas away from manufacturing and toward administration. In explaining these changes, Hawley dropped the early ecologists' concern for space itself. He viewed social organization as fundamentally dependent on mechanisms of interaction, most importantly, the technology of communications and transport. As the technology of these means changed, so too did the patterns of social organization. Any theory that takes as its principal source or cause one factor, such as technology, can be considered a form of reductionism. Choosing technology specifically produces a *technological re-ductionism.*

Since that time ecologists have moved away from a focus on technology as the principal cause of urban changes. An illustration of how the theory was refined and also how contemporary ecologists use census data to carry out research is provided by the example of the case of the timing of suburbanization.

An Example: The Timing of Suburbanization

The issue of suburbanization is critical to an understanding of the maturation of U.S. settlement space, as we have already noted in previous chapters. After World War II several demographic studies noted the impact suburbanization was having on the nation's cities. In 1956 Amos Hawley published a paper claiming that while decentral-ization of the urban population had been around for some time, it was only with the mass introduction of the automobile that suburbanization took on significant proportions whereby the "outer rings" of the city grew faster than did the center. Hawley's argument, in short, tried to account for fundamental settlement space changes through technologi-cal determinism.

Researchers since then have tried to examine this thesis. Census data showed the pattern Hawley studied for subsequent years after 1950. The theory itself, however, depended on fixing the precise time of rapid suburbanization whose alleged cause was a technological innovation. Ecologists reexamining the data all arrived at the same conclusion. Results were distorted because they did not account for the ability of cities to annex suburban land. Thus, while suburbanization may have been occurring for years, it was disguised in census figures by the city annexation process. Leo Schnore (1957) and subsequently Brian Berry and John Kasarda (1977) set the argument in new terms by correcting census data for annexation. They subtracted all population living in suburbia but counted as part of the central city after annexation. As you might imagine, this necessary correction was most laborious and time consuming. Yet it shows the rigor with which ecologists approached the use of demographic data on cities in the testing of urban theory. In fact, this combination of theory and census data analysis is very much in keeping with the tradition launched by Louis Wirth and is also emphasized in the sociospatial perspective (see Chapter 7).

In the most recent version of the timing thesis by Berry and Kasarda (1977), once annexation is controlled for, it becomes clear that suburbanization has *dominated* urban growth since at least the beginning of this century, that is, since 1900! As Berry and Kasarda note:

> Thus, while the street car, electric trains, and automobile may be credited with lowering initial density levels in cities that developed during those vehicles' respective technologi-cal eras, they were not responsible for "emptying out" or reversing concentration within existing central-city boundaries (1977: 193).

Hence, the contemporary ecologists reject technological determinism. Berry and Kasarda assembled comparative data on all metropolitan regions (known as SMSAs in census terminology) and across time since 1900 (1977: 186). The key feature of their study was to correct for annexation, but it is worthwhile to sample their analysis

TABLE 6.2
City and Suburban Growth Rates by Decade

				Decade			
All areas of U.S.	1960–70	1950–60	1940–50	1930–40	1920–30	1910–20	1900–10
All MSAs	16.3	25.0	21.3	8.3	27.1	24.8	31.1
Cities	0.0	0.8	10.0	4.3	19.7	22.4	29.6
Suburbs	32.5	59.6	41.1	16.0	43.7	30.2	34.5

Source: Adapted from Berry and Kasarda, 1977.

as a way of illustrating how we go about using census data today to test theoretical explanations for urban change. Using data on all SMSAs, they compared the rate of population growth in central cities within SMSAs with the suburban rings located within those same regions for the seventy-year period (and controlling for annexation). Their results can be found in Table 6.2.

On the basis of these data, Berry and Kasarda show that suburbs were growing faster than the central cities in *all* decades since 1900, that is, *before* mass use of the automobile. In every decade suburban rings grew faster than the SMSA as a whole—in many decades twice as fast. Thus central cities, especially most recently, have not grown much in population since the 1930s. Between 1950 and 1970 (continuing even to today) they have virtually ceased to grow. In contrast, suburbs assumed phenomenal growth levels, for example, between 1950 and 1960 increases were as much as 59.6 percent nationwide.

Berry and Kasarda help us learn a lot more about growth trends from their data. For example, they have taken the national data above and divided it by region or "disaggregated it" geographically. From this they discovered that suburbs in the West and South grew most spectacularly since the 1900s. In addition to such geographical variation teased out of the data, Berry and Kasarda find that growth differentials exist by age of city. The younger cities possess a clearer record of suburbanization than do the older ones which practiced annexation.

In the end, and allowing for the effects of annexation, Berry and Kasarda show conclusively that true suburbanization *outside* central city limits started on a mass scale after 1930. But whether we control for annexation or not, there is *no* evidence that such growth patterns are correlated with innovations in transportation technology. This finding challenges not only the theory of contemporary ecology but also a well-known theory of regional development by geographers that is technologically deterministic (Borchert, 1967). Thus, despite the important descriptive work of contemporary ecologists (which should be emulated by urban sociologists). we need to switch to a more comprehensive theory of metropolitan growth and change. More factors have to be considered than those focused on by ecologists. The previous chapters of this text have introduced the sociospatial perspective by way of illustration. Chapter 5 in particular discussed central city, suburban, and Sunbelt changes by focusing on a complex set of factors that explain change. In the next chapter we shall discuss aspects of the new urban sociology in more detail.

CHAPTER

7

CONTEMPORARY URBAN SOCIOLOGY:
The Sociospatial Approach

At the beginning of this text I discussed several conceptual changes that are the hallmark of the new urban sociology. These include a shift to a global perspective on capitalism and the metropolis; the inclusion of factors such as class exploitation, racism, gender, and space in the analysis of metropolitan development; an attempt when possible to integrate economic, political, and cultural factors of analysis; special attention to the pull factors of real estate investment and government intervention; and the shift to a multicentered regional approach to cities and suburbs. In the preceding chapters we have used these concepts, which I call the *sociospatial* approach.

In addition to a change in perspective, the new urban sociology also involves important theoretical changes in the way human environments are analyzed. The previous chapter discussed classical and current urban sociology of a traditional kind. The present chapter will consider the new theoretical ideas that have recently invigorated the urban field.

Since the 1970s a great deal of creative work has been accomplished by numerous writers who have challenged orthodox ideas of city development. One of the most interesting observations about this effort is that much of it has been carried out by people in other fields and even in other countries. Only recently has U.S. urban sociology been affected by new theories. Second, regardless of the international scope and intellectual diversity, most of the new ideas have their origin in the application to city environments of the ideas of Max Weber, Karl Marx, and Friedrich Engels regarding the analysis of capitalism. The following chapter concerns this "political economy" approach. While this perspective represents a considerable advance over those discussed in the previous chapter, mainly because the latter simply ignore the important role of economic and political interests, it is not without its own limitations. Sociologists have tried to tailor the approach of political economy to the needs of their discipline. In concluding sections of this chapter I shall discuss such attempts, especially the growth machine perspective and the sociospatial approach of this text.

Political Economy and the City

Marx, Weber, and Engels

The classical sociologists Karl Marx and Max Weber turned to historical analysis in order to explore their ideas regarding the general laws of social development. Both of them understood that societies were organized around integrated systems of economics, politics, and culture. Marx emphasized the dominance of economic considerations in analysis, while Weber sought to show how cultural and political factors also affected individual behavior and social history along with economic activity. The two approaches served to complement each other.

Marx wrote very little about the city in his classic *Capital* (1967), originally published in 1867, while Weber included some passages about the nature of the city in a much larger text, *Economy and Society* (1968), originally published in separate pieces beginning with the 1880s. For Marx the early history of capitalism was a struggle between social relations that were located within urban areas and those situated in the countryside within feudal manors. For Weber, the city developed because of its political powers—in particular, the independence of city residents and their local government from feudal relations of authority. In both cases, Marx and Weber showed how modes of social organization, such as feudalism or capitalism, work through a form of space—the city—and social relations situated within that spatial form. It is this perspective that informs the approach of political economy to settlement space.

For example, Weber argued that during the feudal period in the European Middle Ages, traders and craftspeople set up towns and bargained for protection from the king against the activities of local feudal lords. It was in these towns that capitalism began to thrive through trade in goods and eventually overtake the feudal economy. Thus, as capitalism became a dominating force in Europe it also created the modern city. In short, the political economy perspective studies social processes within urban space and links them to processes occurring at the general level of society.

While Marx and Weber had comparatively little to say about the industrial city of capitalism, Friedrich Engels devoted some time to the topic. I have already mentioned his study of the working-class situation in nineteenth-century England and his field observations of the "great towns," Manchester in particular. For Engels, the large industrial city was the best place to study the general aspects of capitalism as a social system, just as the factory itself was the best place to study the specific details of the relationship between capital and labor. Engels picked the city of Manchester because it was built up as capitalism developed in England, as opposed to other cities, such as London, which had a longer history.

Engels observed several aspects of capitalism at work within the urban space.

Portrait of Friedrich Engels.

First, he noted that capitalism had a "double tendency" of concentration: it concentrated capital investment or money, and also workers. This centralizing process made industrial production easier because of the large scale and close proximity of money and people. Second, Engels noticed that as Manchester developed, investment moved away from the old center and extended further out to the periphery. Unlike Burgess, but very much like Harris and Ullman and the sociospatial approach, Engels pictured growth as a multiplication of centers. For him this followed no particular plan, and he observed that capitalism unregulated by government planning produced a spatial chaos of multiplying minicenters.

   Third, among other important observations, Engels focused on the social problems created by the breakdown of traditional society and the operation of capitalism. In Manchester he noticed examples of extreme poverty and deprivation: homelessness, orphan beggars, prostitution, alcoholism, and violence. For him this misery was the result of exploitation at the place of work which went largely unseen in the factory itself, along with the failure of capitalism to provide adequate housing for everyone. He thus connected conditions in the workplace with those in the living-space, or what Marxists call the *extended conditions* of capital accumulation, which involve the reproduction of social relations that insure the continued use of the working class across the generations. For example, if problems such as poverty and homelessness become too severe, they can threaten the ability of working-class families to produce new generations of workers. This would then threaten the future of the capitalist system. Hence, neighborhood or living-space relations and the quality of daily life are just as important to the survival of capitalism as are relations at the place of work.

   In addition to the problems of poverty, Engels also observed that the city of

Manchester was a segregated space. The rich and the poor lived in segregated neighborhoods. Engels concluded that capitalism produces this spatial isolation of the classes. The sum total of all these social problems is described by the term *uneven development,* which conveys both the disparity between the rich and the poor and their segregation in space by capitalism. We shall use this concept frequently in subsequent chapters.

Uneven Development

Cities grow and develop because of capital investment. The ebb and flow of money determines community well-being. Not only are jobs created, but economic activity also generates tax revenue. The latter is used partly by local government to fund public projects that improve the quality of community life. But spending, both public and private, is not uniformly distributed across metropolitan space. Some places receive much more investment than others. Even within cities there are great differences between those sections that are beehives of economic activity and those that seem scarcely touched by commerce and industry.

Within any given business there are also great disparities between those who are well paid and workers who get the minimum salary. Wages are carried home to neighborhoods, and a significant portion is spent in the local area. Hence, the well-being of a place depends not only on the amount of investment it can attract but also on the wealth of its residents.

In the metropolitan region the variation in the affluence of particular places is called *uneven development.* It is a characteristic of our type of society with its economic system of capitalism, but as we shall see in chapters 12 and 13, it is also characteristic of other societies, some of which have communist rather than capitalist economies. People with money seek to invest in places and enterprises that will bring them the highest rate of return. Profit drives the capitalist system. But this profit making is usually expected to occur in a short time period and with the largest return possible. Consequently, investors look carefully at opportunities and always try to switch to places where money will achieve its greatest return. This process also causes uneven development. As capital becomes increasingly mobile, it can shift money around more easily with corresponding effects on the quality of life. At present, capital is more mobile than ever before in history and has the ability to move operations from one country or region to another in search of the lowest costs or highest profit margins. This process, of course, can have immense consequences for individual places.

The changes since the late 1960s in Silicon Valley, the high tech showcase of California, are illustrative of this pattern. In the 1960s, when the printed circuit industry was first expanding, all operations including manufacturing, research and development, and marketing were located within Silicon Valley. By the late 1960s, one of the leading manufacturers, Fairchild, transferred its manufacturing operations to plants in Mexico, leaving jobless thousands of U.S. workers. Soon after, other electronic assembly plants followed the Fairchild lead and by the 1970s most of the manufacturing operations of Silicon Valley had been transferred to other countries with cheaper labor. By that time, too, owners of corporations discovered that operating in Mexico was not as cheap as production in the Orient. Hence, many plants were shut down and work transferred to

Hong Kong, South Korea, and Singapore, then later, Malaysia, Indonesia, and more recently Sri Lanka. In Chapter 5 we saw that, today, Silicon Valley residents lament the rapidity with which the boom and bust cycle played itself out in that region. But other areas of the world are caught in a similar process because of the increased mobility of capital.

Silicon Valley residents are well educated, and they have hope that eventually a new round of investment will occur in their space by companies seeking their skills. At that future time, their area of the country may once again prosper. When a place is poor, however, such as an urban ghetto, and its people have limited educations, it is highly unlikely that capital will come there and invest, especially when cheaper wages are available in other countries. This remains so even for "small" capital ventures, such as grocery stores. Ghetto areas, such as the Watts section of Los Angeles, have comparatively few places where residents can provide for their needs. Most often, they must travel out of their community to shop because local convenience stores charge excessive prices.

As a result of the inherent desire not to invest in places that are already depressed and that offer little incentive for profit, uneven development usually becomes more acute over time. This pattern increases the polarization between those places that are poor and those that are thriving. But places are made of people, so that the spatial disparities result in different life chances for metropolitan residents. As Engels observed in Manchester, inequities create a problem of social justice as the less affluent members of the working class find it difficult to raise families that will acquire a reasonable, productive status in society.

Because of uneven development the society would degenerate into a two-tiered structure, with a select group of people and places that are well off while surrounded by a sea of poverty, except that government in the United States has stepped in with a safety net of programs that tries to prop up the bottom stratum. Unemployment insurance, welfare, and job training are but a few of the ways government agencies use tax revenues to fight the inherent tendency of capitalist activities to produce uneven development. Over the years, however, despite periods of prosperity, the problems of the poor have been little affected by government programs (Jencks, 1992). New techniques of public policy, therefore, are sorely needed.

In short, metropolitan areas today are besieged by the cyclical nature of capitalist development because the country is on a downswing that has yet to be reversed. Job security and planning for the future are jeopardized for people in communities across the nation. Extremes of poverty and wealth characterize metropolitan life. This clash between the rich and the poor in the city was also observed over 100 years ago by writers in the industrial towns of England. What is new and different today is the global extent of such uneven development and the way the cyclical nature of growth affects people and places across the world.

The Revival of Urban Political Economy: Henri Lefebvre

In the late 1960s and early 1970s the Marxian tradition was revived in social science. Urban analysis was affected minimally at first in this country, but greatly affected in France by the philosopher Henri Lefebvre.

Henri Lefebvre, the great French philosopher of
daily life who died in 1991 of the age of 89.

Lefebvre, who died recently in Paris at the age of 89, is without question the
seminal source of new thinking on the city from a critical and Marxian perspective
(Lefebvre, 1991). His accomplishments can be broken down into four areas:

1. He went back to the work of Marx and Engels on the city and extracted from
their writing an urban political economy. That is, Lefebvre showed how it was
possible to use economic categories such as capital investment, profit, rent,
wages, class exploitation, and uneven development in the analysis of cities. In effect he argued that the city development process was as much a product of the
capitalist system as anything else—the production of shoes, for example. The
same operation of the economy applies in both cases.

2. Lefebvre showed how Karl Marx's work on the city was limited. He introduced
the idea of the circuits of capital and, particularly, the notion that real estate is a
separate circuit of capital. For example, we often think of economic activity as
involving the use of money by an investor of capital, the hiring of workers,
their production of products in a factory, and the selling of the goods in a market for a profit which can then be used for more investment. Automobile production would be a good example of this circuit. Lefebvre called all such industrial
activity the "primary circuit of capital."

Much of the wealth created in a capitalist society is of this type. But for Lefebvre there was a "second circuit of capital," real estate investment. For example, the investor in land chooses a piece of property and buys it; the land is either simply held on to or it is developed into some other use; it is then sold in a special market for land, the real estate market, or developed as housing for a profit. The circuit is completed when the investor takes that profit and reinvests it in more land-based projects. Lefebvre argued that the second circuit of capital is almost always attractive as investment because there usually is money to be made in real estate, although at present there is a recession in all economic sectors. As we have seen in the development of the United States, investment in land was an important means for the acquisition of wealth. But in addition, it was investment in real estate that pushed the growth of cities in specific ways.

3. Lefebvre also introduced the idea that real estate is a special case of the dynamics of settlement space. For Lefebvre, all social activities are not only about interaction among individuals, but about space as well. Social activities take place in space. They also produce a space by creating objects. The city building process, for example, creates a certain space. When we visit a city, we experience particular attributes of the space that was created in that area. Other city spaces may be different, although places produced by similar social systems tend to resemble each other, such as the close resemblance of suburbias in California and Virginia, or between the United States and Australia, for example.

Lefebvre, therefore, introduced us to the idea of space as a component of social organization, as we have already discussed in Chapter 1. When people discuss social interaction they are implicitly talking about behavior in space as well. Space is involved in a dual sense (see Chapter 1): as an influence on behavior, and, in turn, as the end result of construction behavior because people alter space to suit their own needs.

4. Finally, Lefebvre also discussed the role of government in space. The state uses space for social control. Government places fire stations and police departments in separate locations across the metropolis in order to respond to distress relatively quickly. The state controls a large amount of land and utilizes it in its administration of government. It dispenses resources and collects taxes according to spatial units such as cities, counties, individual states, and regions. Government also makes decisions and relays them to individuals across the network of administrative units, that is, from the national level back down to the separate regions, individual states, counties, cities, and ultimately, neighborhoods.

Lefebvre argued that the way capital investors or businesspeople and the state think about space is according to its abstract qualities of dimension—size, width, area, location—and profit. This he called "abstract space." In addition, however, individual people use the space of their environment as a place to live. Lefebvre called this interactively used space of everyday life "social space." For him the uses proposed by government and business for abstract space, such as in the planning of a large city or suburban development of new houses, may conflict with the existing social space, the way space is currently used by residents. Lefebvre said that the conflict between abstract and social space is a basic one in society and ranks with the separate conflict among classes, but is often different. With this view he also departed from Marxian analysis because the latter stresses class conflict as the basic force in the history of capitalism.

In sum, Lefebvre is responsible for a large number of the ideas that inform the sociospatial perspective used in this text. He also heavily influenced a number of critical and Marxian urbanists to develop ideas of their own. In the following sections we shall discuss some of the most contemporary urban approaches and indicate how the ideas of Lefebvre, in some cases, or the classical thinkers Marx, Engels, and Weber, in other cases, have influenced new theories of urban development.

Class Conflict Theories: Gordon, Storper and Walker, and Castells

A class conflict approach to urban development was introduced by the economist David Gordon (1977, 1984). He suggested that the locations chosen by capitalists for factories were affected not only by economic needs but also by the desire to remove their workers from areas of union organizing. According to Gordon, owners of businesses prefer to locate in places where workers are not as militant as they are in cities with a long labor tradition.

To prove his point he studied a period in U.S. history when workers were especially militant—the latter part of the 1800s to the 1900s. He calculated the number of workers engaged in strikes during those years and matched it with the number of times owners of factories decided to relocate to the suburbs or to more isolated cities. The matchup was significant for the years between 1880 and 1910 (see Table 7.1). Hence, the need to control labor conflict by relocating to the outlying areas of large cities was a very early reason why urban development assumed a regional, multicentered form, because it led to the suburbanization of factories (see Chapter 4).

Two geographers, Michael Storper and David Walker (1983, 1984) have expanded Gordon's approach. They consider labor-force considerations as the principal locational variable. By so doing they argue against the received wisdom of traditional location theory which asserts that businesses choose to locate in a specific place because of

TABLE 7.1
Worker Participation in Strikes, 1881 to 1905, Index of Strikers*

Period	Index of strikers, 5-year averages
1881–1885	56.8
1886–1890	118.6
1891–1895	125.8
1896–1900	124.0
1901–1905	187.4

*The index includes all workers involved in strikes for each year, 1927–29 = 100, averaged over 5-year periods (Gordon, 1984: 38).
Source: Adapted from D. Gordon. 1984. "Capitalist Development and the History of Cities." P. 38 in W. Tabb and L. Sawers, eds., *Marxism and the Metropolis*. New York: Oxford University Press.

marketing and production costs (including transportation), a view that is similar to that of urban ecologists (see last chapter). Walker and Storper's "labor theory of location" argues that the commodity, labor, is unique. Its quality depends not only on the physical attributes of the worker but on his/her training and on his/her interest in being a part of a union, that is, in organizing against capital for rights and benefits.

For example, studies of the shift in manufacturing to Asia note that it is caused predominantly by labor-force considerations (Peet, 1987). These include not only the presence of cheap labor, but also the particular qualities of the workers. In the case of the electronics and garment industries in Asia, the work force is overwhelmingly female, young, and unmarried. These laborers are advertised by development officials as providing a docile, easily controlled work force (Fuentes and Ehrenreich, 1987). According to one Malaysian government brochure: "The manual dexterity of the Oriental female is famous the world over. Her hands are small, and she works fast with extreme care" (Fuentes and Ehrenreich, 1987: 205). Reports on the condition of these women describe a world where they are kept bound by the conditions of work from living productive family and social lives.

According to the class conflict approach, then, any given nation has regions that vary with regard to the quality of labor. In part, the quality of schools and training facilities are responsible for this. However, the presence of a union tradition in the local area is also considered. Finally, particular cultural conditions, such as extreme patriarchy that subjugates women workers, are also important for creating a docile labor force.

Storper and Walker use these ideas to explain the shift of industry to the Sunbelt in the United States, which occurred because the southern and western regions of the country have weak or nonexistent unions. They also suggest that their approach is applicable to the entire globe and that location decisions of multinational companies follow what has been called the "international division of labor" (Frobel, Heinrichs, and Krege, 1980). That is, multinational corporations decide where to locate their activities by choosing places around the globe that specifically have cheap and compliant labor. In short, for these theorists the qualities of labor are the determining factors in industrial location.

In broadest terms, the contentions of class conflict theorists have merit, especially for the case of shifts in the location of manufacturing in recent years. Since the 1970s the advanced industrial societies have lost over 8 million manufacturing jobs. At the same time, Latin American and Asian countries have experienced a 6-million-job growth (Peet, 1987). Table 7.2 illustrates the average hourly earings for manufacturing. The figure for the United States is $8.83, for Mexico $1.59, for South Korea $1.35, and for India, 40 cents. These wage differences provide considerable incentive for global capital to invest in less advanced countries. Regions of low class struggle and of a docile labor force are also attractive.

Class conflict theorists make a mistake common in traditional Marxian analysis. They try to explain *everything* by economic factors alone. In the previous chapter we have seen that some traditional ecologists, such as Amos Hawley, commit the fallacy of technological reductionism; that is, they explain everything in terms of changes in

TABLE 7.2
Average Hourly Earnings (1983, in U.S. dollars)

United States	$8.83
France	4.41
Germany	5.94
Italy	4.95
Hong Kong	1.26
South Korea	1.35
Singapore	1.43
Japan	6.91
India	0.40
Mexico	1.59

Source: Adapted from Peet, 1987, p. 17.

technology. Similarly, traditional Marxists such as Storper and Walker are economic reductionists. Thus, while class conflict may indeed explain many of the moves owners made to outlying areas during periods of intense union strikes, it cannot explain relocations during other periods, and there are certainly additional reasons for such moves, such as the pull factors that we have already discussed in the case of suburbanization: cheap land, low taxes, and other government incentives that subsidize capital.

There is no doubt that labor force considerations are a major reason for the transfer

Striking United Auto Workers from Caterpillar Inc. shout at workers entering the plant in Mossville, Illinois, on April 7, 1992. The labor dispute lasted for five months, and the company threatened to move elsewhere.

of manufacturing activity to less developed countries such as Mexico or Malaysia. This approach, however, cannot explain why many multinationals continue to build plants and offices in places like the United States, Germany, and Japan, which have comparatively high wages (see Table 7.2). Factors including relative government stability and the desire to remain close to markets are also important considerations. For example, recently Japanese companies such as Honda and Mazda have opened up plants in the United States. Most of the popular models from these two companies are made in Ohio and Michigan, respectively, where they are close to the important U.S. markets. These factors also play a role in the well-being of places within a global economy. (We shall discuss some of this behavior in chapters 12 and 13.) Thus, while the cost and quality of labor counts for much in location decisions, other factors are also relevant.

An interesting variation on the conflict perspective was devised by the European sociologist Manuel Castells (1977, 1983). He was familiar with some of the work of Lefebvre since they both lived in Paris, but Castells broke with him and followed the ideas of more orthodox Marxists. Castells suggested, however, that traditional Marxian analysis was limited when dealing with social movements in cities. In particular, advanced countries had highly developed welfare states. That is, the national government supported a variety of social programs for all workers, such as unemployment insurance or subsidized housing, that sustained people's quality of life. Most often welfare programs were administered by local, that is, city governments. Struggles for resources by residents of the city, therefore, often took the form of conflicts aimed at local government, rather than the capitalist class.

For Castells, the unique aspects of urban sociology as a special field of inquiry were defined by the issues arising from city government's administration of worker subsidies, such as housing, mass transportation, education, health, and welfare. This created the conditions for a special kind of conflict that did not fall into the traditional Marxian category of disputes between labor and capital. Yet state-supported resources were necessary for the reproduction of the working class. That is, state intervention provided for the "extended conditions" of capitalism, as we discussed in the case of Engels, above. Thus, urban struggles were a new form of conflict (Castells, 1983) produced by the modern form of capitalist social organization—namely, welfare capitalism. Such social movements are highly significant for the study of urban sociology.

Castells is well known among urbanists, and his ideas have been influential. His approach, however, has become increasingly limited over the years. When he wrote in the 1970s and early 1980s many advanced industrialized countries possessed welfare states of the kind he envisioned. Since that time, however, financial problems have caused societies to cut back and in fact dismantle their welfare states (see Chapter 11). Consequently, local city governments do not engage in as many subsidizing activities of the quality of life as they once did. In turn, local conflicts are much less concerned with disputes between citizens and government, and more concerned with economic or general social needs, such as the fight against racism or the desire for jobs. Instead of the specific "urban question" asked by Castells (1977), there is a more general and farther reaching "social question" asked by critical urbanists today which relates to regional issues and the well-being of the *entire* society. Hence Castells' work, like that of other conflict theorists, is limited and confined to pushing a single aspect of city life rather than a more comprehensive view.

Class Accumulation Theories: Harvey and Scott

When sociologists discuss economics, they usually think in general terms and focus on individuals such as wealthy businesspeople who own companies. Class conflict theories go beyond individuals to discuss group behavior—particularly, the clash between the capitalist class of owners or investors and the class of workers who sell their labor for a wage. In this section we consider other urbanists who use economically based ideas to explain city development but do so with a great deal more detail than traditional sociologists.

David Harvey is a well-known geographer from England. He started out as a mainstream member of his field, concerned with mathematical modeling techniques. During the late 1960s, however, he was greatly influenced by events in the United States, such as the ghetto riots, and by the writings of Henri Lefebvre. In the 1970s he wrote a book and a series of articles that applied Marxian economic analysis to the condition of the cities. He was especially influenced by the earlier writings of Lefebvre on the urban analysis of Karl Marx and Friedrich Engels. See Box 7.1 for an example of his work.

Harvey, like Lefebvre, systematically applied the categories of Marxian economic analysis to the study of urban development. He asserted four things. First, the city is defined in the manner of Engels as a spatial node that concentrates and circulates capital. Second, Harvey applied a conflict perspective to discuss the way the capitalist and the working classes confronted each other in the city (1973, 1976). According to Harvey, and unlike the general way sociologists usually speak about classes, this basic conflict takes many forms as both the capitalist and working classes split up amongst themselves into various groups or factions as a consequence of protracted struggles for advantage. The capitalist class, for example, can be divided between financial investors (finance capital), owners of department stores and other marketing assets (commercial capital), and owners of factories (manufacturing or industrial capital). Workers can also be split, for example, between factory laborers, white collar salespeople, and professional financial analysts, all of whom still work for a wage.

Each of these factions may want different things from urban development, so that conflict and coalition building are always a part of urban life. However, the basic struggle is still between capital and labor, as Gordon, and Storper and Walker, also suggest (see above). As Harvey suggests, "Labor, in seeking to protect and enhance its standard of living, engages in a series of running battles in the living place over a variety of issues that relate to the creation, management and use of the built environment" (1976: 268).

Third, Harvey discusses how the volatile urban mix of economic interests brings about government intervention as a means of quieting things down so that planning can take place and capitalists can get back to their principal task of profit making (1975, 1976). As Harvey suggests, "capital, in general, cannot afford the outcome of

BOX 7.1 DAVID HARVEY'S CASE STUDY OF BALTIMORE

Harvey starts the analysis of the Baltimore housing market with a homage to Lefebvre. He suggests that the concept of the second circuit of capital is very profound, but it is necessary to make it more specific before it can be useful. He asks how returns to the ownership of land or property can be specified within a city where "the distinction between capitalist and landlord has blurred concomitantly with the blurring of the distinctions between land and capital and rent and profit (1985: 65). Harvey defines a specific category called "class-monopoly rent" as the return on property owned in cities. He suggests that the ability to earn this money is contingent on a combination of factors involving both a variety of financial institutions and government subsidies. Hence, the process of earning money from the second circuit of capital is quite complex and varies from location to location. This profit taking pattern in real estate also has implications for the people who live in the city.

To demonstrate this point, Harvey divides Baltimore City into eight real estate submarkets. Each of these submarkets had its own dynamic of investing and selling. Harvey used data for 1970 and obtained the following results:

1. The *inner city* was dominated by cash and private loan transactions with scarcely a vestige of institutional or governmental involvement in the used housing market.

2. The white *ethnic areas* were dominated by homeownership financed mainly by small, community-based savings and loan institutions that operated without a strong profit orientation and which really did offer community service.

3. The black residential area of *West Baltimore* was essentially a creation of the 1960s. Low- to moderate-income blacks did not possess local savings and loan associations, were regarded with suspicion by other financial institutions, and in the early 1960s were discriminated against by the FHA. The only way in which this group could become homeowners was by way of something called a "land-installment contract" (where a white middleman bought the home first and rented it to blacks for a profit until a loan could be secured).

(continued)

struggles around the built environment to be determined simply by the relative powers of labor, the appropriators of rent and the construction fraction" (1976: 272). Therefore, the capitalist class requires government to intervene and aid the profit making process within cities.

Sometimes, however, investment simply will not flow into districts of the city because they are so run-down or unattractive economically. In such cases, Harvey argues, government must step in to make areas profitable again. Usually this form of state intervention involves the tearing down or destruction of existing buildings in order to make way for new construction, such as in the example of government supported urban renewal programs (see Chapter 15). According to Harvey, "under

4. The areas of *high turnover* were serviced mainly by a combination of mortgage banker finance and FHA insurance. . . . In the high turnover submarkets created by these programs there were plenty of opportunities for the speculator to realize a class-monopoly rent.

5. The *middle-income* submarkets of Northeast and Southwest Baltimore were typically the creation of the FHA programs of the 1930s. By the 1960s homeownership was being financed conventionally by federal savings and loan institutions and by some of the smaller ethnic savings and loan institutions. . . .

6. The more affluent groups made use of savings and commercial banks to a much greater degree and rarely resorted to FHA guarantees. Such groups usually had the political and economic power to fend off speculative incursions, and it was unlikely that they would move except as the result of their own changing preferences or from declining services (1985: 72–78).

The figures illustrating the different ways these six housing markets operated are given by Table 7.3 which is adapted from Harvey:

TABLE 7.3
Housing Submarkets in Baltimore City, 1970

Market	Total houses sold	Percentage of cash	Percentage of private financing	Percentage of bank financing*	Percentage of government insurance
Inner city	1,199	65.7	15.0	19.3	4.0
Ethnic	760	39.9	6.1	54.0	3.3
West Balt.	497	30.6	12.1	57.3	30.0
High turn.	2,072	19.1	6.1	74.8	47.7
Middle inc.	1,077	20.8	4.4	74.8	28.9
Upper inc.	361	19.4	6.9	74.7	15.5

*Includes a residual term.
Source: Adapted from Harvey, 1985.

Harvey's approach is important because it supplies details to the economic process of profit making which urban sociologists usually pay attention to only in terms of vague generalities, that is, rarely discussing factions of capital or labor and the special role of real estate. Perhaps this case study tells us much more than we ever cared to know about the functioning of

capitalism there is, then, a perpetual struggle in which capital builds a physical landscape appropriate to its own condition at a particular moment in time, only to have to destroy it, usually in the course of a crisis, at a subsequent point in time" (1981: 14). For Harvey this process of boom and bust, or new construction and urban decay, is basic to urban change in a capitalist system.

Finally, Harvey took a detailed look at the capitalist class and how it made money within the space of the city. He borrowed the concept of circuits of capital from Lefebvre and elaborated on the latter's ideas. In particular, Harvey argued that capitalists involved in the first industrial circuit are principally interested in location within the urban environment and in reducing their costs of manufacturing. Capitalists in the housing markets in Baltimore, but there are several important observations that can be made from the above material. First, urban development is not some monolithic process of growth (as the growth machine perspective suggests). The second circuit of capital is composed of a variety of arrangements, each with its own set of social factors, conflicts, and possibilities in determining the level and quality of investment in real estate.

Second, the second circuit of capital consists of a combination of private financial institutions, community banks, and assorted government programs that support housing in different ways. Real estate is not a pure case of private enterprise but involves the government in direct ways. Speculators, developers, homeowners, and renters react differently in these separate environments, and while some people are simply interested in owning a home, others are out to make money any way they can. Furthermore, real estate can attract investment under a variety of circumstances. As indicated above, even in black ghetto areas the turnover activity is significant. Hence, second circuit activity is relentless, even during recession or under adverse investment conditions.

Third, the housing market in the United States discriminates against blacks and the poor. Inner city blacks have it the worst. They must finance most of their transactions by cash payment. Banks will not lend to them. Poor white ethnics also have trouble obtaining bank support, but they have managed to establish community savings and loans that help them out. Only the middle and upper classes have free access to loans, with fully 75 percent of households obtaining bank financing. Harvey notes that in a certain section of Baltimore, the western part, black and/or poor people were in fact helped by government programs to obtain loans; hence some correctives to the general pattern of discrimination have occurred.

Finally, the discrimination against poor and/or black people is also revealed in the data on government sponsored insurance. Inner city and ethnic areas cannot obtain such support. However, more affluent sections have no trouble in getting FHA or VA insurance. Once again West Baltimore, with its active government programs of renewal, fared much better than other poor areas. In short, the real estate market not only works through a complex assortment of combined public and private resources, but also acts to reinforce the inequities and uneven development of the society. Hence, much can be learned from this kind of study, an inquiry that traditional urban sociology has often neglected.

second circuit hold a different set of priorities relating to the flow of investment and the realization of interest on money loaned or rent on property owned. These differences are reflected in the different ways capital investment circulates within the two circuits. Harvey illustrated these differences in his case study of development in the city of Baltimore during urban renewal (see Box 7.1).

Thus, while investment in factories is often located in places with cheap housing, capitalists in the second circuit often refuse to invest in poorer areas and seek out only the higher rent districts of the city. As a consequence, areas of the city can become run-down and abandoned not because of the actions of industrial capital, the faction that we usually think of as determining city fortunes, but because of actions taken by investors in real estate, as the sociospatial perspective suggests. In the Baltimore study, both suburbanization of the population and central city decay were linked to the priorities of the second circuit of capital as assisted by government programs. Hence, Harvey's work bears out the importance of Lefebvre's ideas on the real estate industry, and also Engels' central insight into the production of uneven development under capitalism.

Another influential geographer is Allen J. Scott, also from England, who has gone even further than Harvey in one sense by detailing the production process and its impact on space. For Scott, all things are explained by the needs of industrial manufacture (1980, 1988). In this case, Scott is also a reductionist, but unlike Harvey, he is not a Marxist. Rather, Scott is a follower of the nineteenth-century economist David Ricardo, who argued that all profit making, and hence, the dynamics of capitalism, can be explained by the process of production, rather than capital circulation as Harvey would have it.

Scott has little to say about the factions of classes, the political context of development, the role of real estate, and the pull factors of government intervention because they are not particularly relevant to the production process per se. Instead, Scott gives us a detailed picture of the spatial impacts of changes in production processes (1988), which, he argues, explain changes in the form of cities.

Allen Scott's approach cannot explain the production of the built environment, despite his claims to the contrary. The missing ingredients to his analysis of changes are the roles of the real estate industry and the action of state government, as the sociospatial perspective suggests (see last section). Nevertheless, his approach is extremely helpful in understanding the new relations between the location of business and the global economy.

In Chapter 4 we saw that social life is organized around a combination of working, shopping, and community service relations. Although changes in each of these *sociospatial* dimensions can affect the organization of everyday life, the structure of the local economy is most important. In Chapter 4 we saw that during the metropolitan phase of growth U.S. corporations lost their purely local character due to the concentration of ownership under monopoly capitalism. Their operations shifted to a national network of manufacturing, marketing, and administrative functions that were *horizontally integrated* by the same company but spatially dispersed across the country.

After 1970, Scott (1988) suggests additional changes occurred in the sociospatial relations of business. These can be characterized best by the phenomenon of *vertical disintegration*. In this process large corporations sell off or abandon many of their activities that supported production, such as the manufacture of parts and materials or the supply of inputs to the production process. Instead, they contract out to suppliers for such inputs and acknowledge the lowest bids. Competition among suppliers results in much lower costs to the firm than producing parts and materials themselves. Because the burden of supply is carried by subcontractors rather than by the manufacturing company itself, the inventory stocks of the company and thus its costs are also lowered.

This arrangement of vertical disintegration in production is coupled with the horizontal integration of manufacturing, marketing, and administration across the globe in the command and control centers of transnational corporations. The new organization of business is a major reason for the success of both new firms and new competitors of western countries, such as Japan, especially in the areas of electronics and automobile production. It is also one reason why large cities have shifted to business service employment (Sassen, 1991).

Vertical disintegration has a number of drawbacks that must be overcome. For one thing, subcontracting the supply of parts and materials reduces the need for large inventories by manufacturers, thereby reducing costs, but those inputs must be available when needed. The Japanese technique of "just-in-time" supply is used to make sure that inputs are at the factory when needed. Often this means that a single supplier will sign on as responsible to the larger company, with the prospect of going bankrupt if performance is not adequate and the contract is not renewed. But it also means that around any large factory may be found a complex of small subcontractors in a complex industrial space offering a variety of employment opportunities. Second, when manufacturers give up producing their own inputs, problems can arise in the coordination of production. This limitation is overcome with the introduction of computerized manufacturing systems or CAM (computer assisted manufacturing) which is able to keep track of all needs. Electronic information processing has revolutionized the manufacturing process in this manner. It has also created new job skills and made new, more sophisticated demands on both workers and their educational systems. All these changes have effects on the local community and the process of the extended reproduction of the work force.

For Scott, the end result of vertical disintegration is the ability of large companies to carry out businesses on a global scale. They can locate manufacturing, administration, and marketing in a host of places across the world. Suppliers of "just-in-time" parts can also be almost anywhere. This makes capital extremely mobile. It puts a great pressure on individual places and individual communities of workers to be productive and attractive for capital investment. When capital is dissatisfied with existing arrangements, it is comparatively easy, according to Scott, to relocate.

In sum, both the class conflict and capital accumulation approaches of the new urban sociology provide impressive improvements over more traditional perspectives. The world today is a volatile one where the predictable accommodations of work, shopping, and residential living characteristic of the industrial city have been shattered. Economic factors such as the ebb and flow of real estate investment and the changing structure of manufacturing in a global system affect the sociospatial features of daily life. So too do the activities of workers involved in the struggle lying at the heart of the capital/labor relationship, and the residents of communities who are concerned about maintaining their quality of life. Each of these aspects helps determine the pattern of sociospatial organization.

Until the development of the new urban sociology the effects of special, powerful interests (such as transnational corporations) on the pattern of growth were ignored by the traditional approach that emphasized biological factors of species competition over territory. But the work of geographers and Marxian analysts places greater importance on economic than on social factors in sociospatial arrangements. As we have discussed, there are several limitations to both the class conflict and capital accumulation approaches. In recent years, therefore, sociologists have added to the new perspective on the city by showing how social factors are also important in the production of settlement space.

Recent Sociological Approaches

There are two sociological perspectives belonging to the new urban approach that are most important—the growth machine and the sociospatial perspective.

The Growth Machine

This approach is most associated with the work of Harvey Molotch and his recent collaboration with John Logan (Logan and Molotch, 1988). Molotch was dissatisfied with the traditional ecological approach to urban development and highly influenced by new work carried out among French urbanists inspired by Lefebvre and Castells (Pickvance, 1977). Molotch was especially taken with the studies by the Frenchman Lamarche (1977) on the role of property development in the city.

According to Molotch's approach, which remains consistent to the present, the focus of urban change involves the activities of a select group of real estate developers who represent a separate class which Marx once called the "rentiers." It is this class that both prepares land for new development and also pushes the public agenda to pursue growth.

For Molotch, the intentions of the rentier class mesh well with the needs of local government. This is so because government is in constant need of new tax revenue sources. As increasingly more people enter an urban area, their demand for services strains fiscal budgets. Without new sources of revenue, city governments cannot maintain the quality of life, and the region is threatened with a decrease in prosperity. Property development is a major source of taxes. New people also bring in new demands for city goods and services, which aids the business community and, in turn, increases revenues to local government. In short, according to Molotch, cities are "growth machines" because they have to be. Pushed from behind by demands for community quality and pulled from the front by the aggressive activities of the rentiers, city governments respond by making growth and development their principal concerns.

Molotch's approach might be considered the exact opposite of the one advocated by Allen Scott. For Scott, spatial development is explained by the internal workings of the production process. For Molotch, industrial production has little to do with urban change. Both perspectives, therefore, are limited by their own brand of reductionism, that is, by focusing only on one aspect of the more complex development process. Logan and Molotch (1988), in more recent work, retain their emphasis on the growth machine as explaining the dynamics of urban development, but they now push the idea that the global context of capitalism accounts for many of the changes occurring in cities. In addition, they have qualified their one-dimensional emphasis on development to account for what they call "tensions" in the growth machine.

Briefly, they acknowledge that the pursuit of growth does not always proceed smoothly. At times, members of the community who are not part of the rentier class may perceive further growth as threatening their own quality of community life. For example, people in a quiet, well-tailored suburban neighborhood might resent the construction of a nearby mall and multiple-family rental apartments. Or residents of a central city area may dislike the tearing down of affordable housing to build new, luxury condos. In these and other cases the pursuit of growth is tempered, and perhaps blocked, by splits in the community supported by groups that oppose growth. Hence, local politics often becomes a battle ground for pro- and anti-growth factions.

The Sociospatial Perspective: Real Estate and Government Intervention

How can we make sense of the various ideas that have been offered by new urban theories? This text adopts the sociospatial perspective (SSP), which attempts to take what is best from the new ideas while avoiding the endemic reductionism characteristic of both traditional ecology and recent Marxian political economy. It does not seek explanation by emphasizing a principal cause such as transportation technology (Hawley), capital circulation (Harvey), or production processes (Scott). Rather, it takes an integrated view of growth as the linked outcome of economic, political, and cultural factors. At one time, it might have been suggested that such an integrated view derives from the tradition of Weber. However, since the 1950s even Marxists have looked for ways to advance an integrated perspective (see Althusser, 1971), and this is especially important for the understanding of space (see Lefebvre, 1990).

The SSP is inspired by the work of Lefebvre as applied to the needs of urban sociology by Feagin (1983, 1988) and Gottdiener (1977, 1985) and their collaboration (1988). The SSP can be distinguished from other approaches by the following characteristics. First, it considers real estate development as the leading edge of changes in the metropolitan region. While other approaches tend to focus only on economic changes

A woman speaks out at a homeowners' association protest against new construction in Lake Forest, California.

The failure of traditional urban sociology to explain urban unrest, such as in Watts (Los Angeles) in 1965, provided an incentive to develop a new approach.

in industry, commerce, and services, the SSP adds to these important dimensions an interest in the way real estate molds metropolitan growth. Second, the SSP considers government intervention and the interests of politicians in growth as a principal factor in metropolitan change. Traditional urban ecology and the newer approaches of urban political economy either ignore completely the role of government in channeling growth or treat the state as simply derivative of economic interests. The SSP considers the state as relatively autonomous, that is, with officials having interests of their own, and more specifically, considers politics as highly linked to the concerns of property development (Gottdiener, 1987).

Third, the SSP considers the role of cultural orientations as critically important for an understanding of metropolitan life. Because of the importance of this subject, culture will be considered in more detail in chapters 8 and 9. Finally, the SSP takes a global view of metropolitan development. The most local areas today are tied to the activities of multinational corporations and banks. Changes in the way they invest affect each of us. By emphasizing global economic changes, however, the SSP also seeks to understand how local and national factors interrelate with international links.

All spatial levels of organization are important in understanding metropolitan development. In the following section let us review some of these features while keeping in mind the differences between the SSP and other sociological perspectives discussed in the previous two chapters. In particular, I shall show how the SSP is a much more sophisticated and useful approach than either the growth machine or traditional ecology.

Real Estate Investment As the Leading Edqe of Growth. From the earliest chapters on urbanization in the United States we have seen that interest in real estate profits played a central part in urban development. George Washington was not only the first president of the country, but also participated in the innovative scheme to develop the swampland that became the site of the nation's capital. During the 1800s great profits were made by businesses as the country industrialized, but they were also made through investment in land. Cyrus McCormick earned millions from the manufacture of his famous reaper, but millions more from his activities in real estate. Railroad tycoons competed with each other by building the infrastructure that opened up the great land mass of the United States to development, but they also established towns and developed real estate as they went along. Finally, over the last few decades we have seen that the shifts to suburbia and the Sunbelt were fueled, in part, by the phenomenal expansion of the single-family home industry and the development of lands outside the large central cities of the Northeast and Midwest.

The SSP argues that other perspectives have neglected the important role played by investment in real estate in the process of regional development. Traditional urban sociology or ecology, for example, overemphasizes the push factor of technology as an agent of change. Marxian political economy pays special attention to the activities of capitalists and the way changes in industrial investment patterns affect local spaces. The SSP acknowledges push factors such as changes in economic production and transportation innovations but also highlights the role of pull factors such as government intervention and the action of real estate—the second circuit of capital—as crucial to explanations of metropolitan growth. Both demand-side and supply-side dynamics are studied in their details.

The SSP stresses the human dimension along with structural arrangements. It wants to know who the actors are and how they behave, not just the facts or figures about aggregate levels of growth and change. Activities involve people acting as part of social classes and class factions, or as gender, racial, and ethnic interests. How people come together to struggle over the patterns of development is an important question for the SSP (see chapters 11 and 15); but this is not viewed as a machine.

Feagin (1983), for example, discusses specifically the variety of ways real estate developers and speculators create development projects and channel money to real estate investment. Agents of growth include *financial conduits* such as commercial banks and trust or pension funds, savings and loan associations, insurance companies, mortgage companies, and real estate investment trusts; *real estate brokers* and chamber of commerce members; and *public utilities* and other relatively immobile public service agencies that cannot move and must work to maintain the attractiveness of specific places. Real estate, therefore, is composed of both individual actors and a structure of financial conduits that channel investment into land.

Gottdiener (1977) also demonstrates the way both structure and agency are important for an understanding of real estate activities. A case study of suburban Long Island, New York, identifies the following types of social roles assumed by investors in the built environment:

1. Land speculators who purchase land or buildings simply to be sold at a later date for a profit.
2. Land developers who purchase land with or without housing and then develop it by constructing housing or other built structures such as factories or malls. To this type can be added developers who restructure the uses of land and buildings, such as those who convert rental into condominium units, single-family into multifamily dwellings, and residential housing into office space.
3. Homeowners and individuals who invest in property as part of an overall scheme for the protection of income and not just to acquire shelter.
4. Local politicians who are dependent on campaign funds from the real estate industry, and lawyers or other professionals who make money from government mandated requirements which need legal services.
5. Finally, there are also individual companies or corporations that do not specialize in real estate but that develop choice locations for their respective businesses, such as office towers or industrial plants, and a host of financial institutions, such as savings and loans, that channel investment into land.

The above list of institutional and private interests involved in the development of the metropolitan region reveals that growth is not simply determined by economic "push" factors of production, as both the class conflict and capital accumulation perspectives maintain, nor by a special class of people called rentiers, as the growth machine approach emphasizes. Development is caused by the pull factor of people's activities involved in the second circuit of capital, real estate. This sector is not simply a select group of investors, as the growth machine believes, but is composed both of *actors* interested in acquiring wealth from real estate and a *structure* that channels money into the built environment. The latter consists of a host of financial intermediaries such as banks, mortgage companies, and real estate investment trusts, which allow a large variety of people to put their money in land. In short, the activities of the second circuit of capital consist of the intersection between structure and agency.

The sociospatial perspective asserts that Molotch and Logan are wrong to hypothesize a separate rentier class that comprises growth interests, since the second circuit of capital enables anyone to invest money in real estate for profit, even homeowners (Gottdiener, 1985). It is just not true that we can separate the people in society into a select few who seek to make money in real estate (exploiting its exchange value), and a majority that only seeks to enjoy the built environment as a staging ground for everyday life (the exploitation of space's use value). Instead, space can be enjoyed for its uses and for its investment potential by both business and local residents. In fact, that's what makes the relationship of society to space so complicated. The latter is *simultaneously* a medium of use and a source of wealth under capitalist commodity arrangements.

Because developing the built environment involves so many different interests, growth or change is always a contentious affair. This criticism has critical theoretical and empirical implications for the study of urban sociology, especially the role of the state, as we shall see next.

Government Intervention and Political Agency. The SSP suggests that metropolitan growth is the outcome of negotiations and contending interests, rather than the product of some well-oiled machine without conflict. Developers, for example, must negotiate with government planners and politicians, citizen groups voice their concerns in public forums, special interests such as utility companies or religious organizations also interject their stakes and culturally defined symbolic visions in metropolitan growth. The end result of these negotiations is a built environment that is *socially constructed,* involving many interests, and also controlled by the quest for profit.

The absence of a separate class of growth mongers means that the conceptualization of local politics by the growth machine perspective is limited. Feagin (1988) shows how powerful economic interests use the state to subsidize growth; hence development often reflects the direct interests of industrial and financial capital rather than some select, separate class of rentiers. Gottdiener (1977, 1985) indicates how local politicians are intimately involved with development interests. The purpose of this alliance is not growth and increased public revenues per se, as it is viewed by the growth machine, but *profit.* In this sense, growth interests represent both factions of capital involved in the accumulation process and also community interests concerned about growth and the quality of life. It is this melding of profit taking and environmental concerns that is most characteristic of settlement space development, and it involves a second source of complexity in the society/space relationship.

The interests aligned around issues of change in the built environment should be seen as *growth networks* rather than as the monolithic entities suggested by the concept of a "machine" (Gottdiener, 1985). The idea of networks captures the way alliances can form around a host of issues associated with development, often splitting classes into factions. The concept of network captures the diversity of people who may join, often only temporarily, to pursue particular growth paths. What counts is not necessarily the push for growth, but both the way different community factions perceive the form growth will take and how they evaluate their own environmental needs. There is a rich complexity of people and interests involved in metropolitan growth and change which is captured neither by ecological or political economy perspectives, because they ignore particular agents, nor by the growth machine approach, which reduces conflict to a simple dichotomy of pro- and anti-growth factions.

For example, each community group may have its own interests which are manifested in local politics. They often join in coalitions to push for some version of growth while opposing other coalitions that have their own vision of the future. Growth is not the result of single-minded efforts by some machine. Rather, development is a contentious process involving many groups in society that push for a variety of forms: rapid growth, managed growth, slow growth, no growth, and so on. Local social movements arise not just because of economic needs, but because of racial, religious, ethnic, and community interests concerned with the quality of life.

Development or change is a constant occurrence of the American landscape. Local politics consists of the clashes between all these separate interests as they play themselves out in the second circuit of capital and within the forum of local government. We shall discuss this process as it relates directly to metropolitan politics more fully in Chapter 11.

The Global Economy

Finally, the SSP agrees with all other perspectives that acknowledge the important role of the global economy, the new mobile or "flexible" arrangements in production, and their effects in the restructuring of settlement space. It argues, however, that the push factors of capital mobility and considerations regarding the international division of labor, discussed above, are not the only ones determining growth. Perspectives that are usually identified with the "new" urban sociology often simply stress the effect of the global system as the key determinant of metropolitan change (see Smith and Feagin, 1987; Palen, 1991). The pull factors of state policies and the second circuit of capital are also important, particularly as manifested at the local, regional, and national levels.

Hence the SSP has a more integrated view of push and pull factors associated with growth. The influence of the global system does have a profound effect on the fortunes of place, but unlike other approaches (see Logan and Molotch, 1987; Sassen, 1991; Smith and Feagin, 1987), the SSP does not believe that it has a sole determining effect.

This feature was illustrated in Chapter 5 with the discussions of suburban and Sunbelt development. At that time it was pointed out that, while the U.S. economy had become integrated into the world system, development patterns of deconcentration to suburbs and Sunbelt regions had been going on for many years, even prior to the 1960s when the restructuring of the global system began to be felt. The shifts to the suburbs and the Sunbelt are the two *most* important sociospatial changes in U.S. history, but neither can be said to have been produced by the power of the global economy. They have their roots in growth trends that have been going on for years and which involve important aspects of both government intervention and the phenomenal draw of real estate investment.

For example, in Chapter 5 we studied the nature of suburban development after recognizing that the majority of Americans live in suburbs, not central cities. Suburbanization in the United States has been going on since the turn of the century. Development accelerated after World War II when the government initiated special loans to veterans and consolidated the income tax subsidy to homeowners, providing families with a cash incentive to invest in real estate. Suburbanization was also promoted by a variety of federal housing acts passed since the 1930s which revitalized the real estate industry, and by the Interstate Highway Act in the 1950s which promoted the construction of freeways. All of these factors fell into place long before the advent of global economic effects.

We have also seen how the Sunbelt prospered as a consequence of government programs and real estate activity. Government military spending during World War II and later during the Cold War propped up the Sunbelt economy by transferring billions of dollars in tax money from the Frostbelt to this region. Real estate investment found riches in a host of Sunbelt schemes for the development of housing and industry. Other factors, such as the prosperity of agribusiness, also helped growth. In short, the most important spatial changes experienced by the United States are the consequence of many factors operating at all spatial levels, as the SSP suggests, rather than at the global level alone.

Of course, since the 1970s changes in the global economy have had a profound effect on the built environment. The decline of manufacturing in the United States and the transfer of many production activities abroad have wiped out the traditional relation between central city working-class communities and their capitalist employers. The economy of our largest cities has restructured away from manufacturing and toward specialization in advanced services and information processing, particularly those business services required by the finance capital faction which coordinates investment activity for the global economy (Sassen, 1991). All these changes affect the nature of the local labor force and alter living and working arrangements. We shall discuss some of these effects on the people of the metropolis in chapters 8 and 9. Other effects of the restructuring initiated within the context of a global economy will be considered in chapters 10 and 11 when we consider metropolitan problems and policies, respectively. Finally, in chapters 12 and 13 we shall discuss the effects of global restructuring on third world cities and settlement spaces in European countries and Japan.

The sociospatial changes produced by the global economy have also been important because of the new spaces that have appeared in recent years. Prior to the 1970s both Santa Clara County and the peripheral areas around the city of Boston were not significant employment centers. During the last two decades they proved themselves to be world class economic spaces, becoming Silicon Valley and the Route 128 high tech corridor. These new spaces produced by high technology industries earned disproportionately large sums of money on the world market for their employment size. At one time these results prompted analysts to suggest that other countries follow suit and promote their own export-oriented high tech corridors as the key to future prosperity (see Chapter 13). Today Silicon Valley and Route 128, along with other such spaces, are experiencing a severe recession. The global economy is now shaky as recession hits worldwide. According to the SSP, alterations and development of new spaces of production and consumption will be produced, not by investment directed at the global level alone, but also by the logic of real estate development and by other pull factors, such as the quality of government intervention, in addition to factors that operate locally, regionally, nationally, and globally, that is, at all sociospatial levels.

Summary

In sum, the sociospatial perspective involves ideas that distinguish it from previous sociological approaches. First, it incorporates a number of different factors, instead of emphasizing one or two, that can account for development and change. It particularly seeks to provide a balanced account of both *push and pull* factors in metropolitan and regional growth. Second, it considers the role of real estate in development as the combined activities of both agency and structure. Investment in land is a sector of capital accumulation with its own factions and cycles of boom and bust. The categories of political economy, such as profit, rent, interest, and value, are just as applicable to metropolitan development as to any other part of the economy.

Third, the SSP strives for a detailed view of politics which emphasizes the activities of individuals and groups in the development process. The SSP focuses on the activities of certain *growth networks* which form coalitions interested in choices that must be made over the direction and effects of change.

The SSP considers cultural factors such as race, gender, and the symbolic context of space just as important as economic and political concerns (see next chapters). It also deals specifically with the special qualities of spatial forms and their role in the organization of society. At present, metropolitan life is played out within the context of an ever expanding multicentered region. We have discussed the historical significance of this form of settlement space in previous chapters and will discuss its signficance for daily life in chapters to come.

Finally the SSP, along with other approaches, adopts a global view of development, but does not claim that the world economy alone is responsible for the restructuring of settlement space. Global changes are particularly relevant for an understanding of how cities, suburbs, and regions have been affected by the economy in recent years. New spaces of industry, commerce, and services have helped redefine settlement patterns as multicentered regional development. Historically, however, the pull factors of government intervention and of investment in real estate have also played an essential part in the restructuring of space.

In remaining chapters we shall examine the role of culture in metropolitan life, address the issues of politics and problems, and then turn our attention to other countries in order to compare the U.S. experience with growth and restructuring elsewhere.

CHAPTER

8

PEOPLE, LIFESTYLES, AND THE METROPOLIS

In previous chapters we have been studying the growth and development of metropolitan regions. The next two chapters concern the people of the metropolis, and they explore the relationship between everyday life and local territory. The sociospatial approach to metropolitan life asserts that diversity in lifestyles and subcultures exists regionwide. This is especially the case since 1980 as suburbs have matured. In this chapter we shall consider the interplay between the social factors of income, gender, age, and race, and the spatial patterns of population concentration or dispersal across the metropolitan region.

A basic tenet of the sociospatial approach is that social factors determining the patterns of population dispersal are also linked to particular spaces. Class or gender relations, for example, are acted out through spatial as well as social means. Lifestyle differences are externalized in a specific environment: the ghetto, the street corner, the mall, the golf course. Furthermore, these places are always *meaningful*. Interaction is shaped through the signs and symbols of sociospatial context (see Chapter 9). In this chapter we shall consider the effect of class standing on lifestyles, gender differences and everyday life, racial and minority distinctions, and new patterns of ethnic bonding and immigration. The effects of class, gender, and race are so powerful in our society that they will also be considered in Chapter 10 when we discuss social problems. We shall see how differences in sociospatial factors affect the way people live, their interaction with others, and their use of space.

Class Differences and Spatial Location

Class Stratification in the United States

The sociologist Max Weber believed that an individual's class standing was important because it helped determine the life chances that could be expected in the future, that is, the possible opportunities or constraints for future achievement open to any individual. He also suggested that economic factors of class status, such as the type of occupation or monetary resources that an individual possessed, were not the only determining factors of overall social status. Standing in the society's hierarchy also depended on particular cultural attributes, such as prestige or symbolic differences, and on the possession of political power. Thus, life chances differ according to economic, political, and cultural factors, but material wealth, as Karl Marx maintained, clearly is the most important of all social variables.

The United States is a stratified society. This means that there is a social hierarchy or ranking determining access to resources. Stratification is often pictured as a pyramid of social standing. Those at the very top control most of the society's resources; they also enjoy the most symbolic prestige and political influence. Those at the bottom are the most numerous and have the least power. In the United States, despite an active ideology that preaches equality, the top 1 percent of the population control over 70 percent of the wealth and the top 5 percent control over 90 percent. Status considerations like driving an expensive car, living in a large home, having fabulous vacations, and wearing expensive clothing are all derived from the media images of affluence and what life is supposed to be like at the top of the stratification pyramid.

Most research on the American class structure divides the society into at least five different groups. Judgments for these divisions are based on what social scientists call *SES*, or socioeconomic status, which is a particular combination of wealth, occupation, education, gender, and race, among other factors (see Robertson, 1987). The five groups are the lower class, the working class, the lower middle, the upper middle, and the ruling class. Only the ruling class controls enough wealth to be considered independent from economic needs; hence many Marxists suggest that we still retain a system of two classes—the working class and the class of independent capitalists. Thus, the middle class in particular remains caught in the social relations of class stratification despite its relatively high SES standing (Ehrenreich, 1989).

These SES standings also involve the ability to sustain a residence in a particular place. Thus socioeconomic status is also about living in a certain space. In our society, due to stratification differences, the choice of residential location is not always voluntary. Restrictions of wealth, race, and gender are particularly potent sifters of population across the metropolitan regions. SES differences and the system of social stratification, therefore, manifest themselves both as differences in individual lifestyles and as differences in neighborhood living or local space. Let us consider some of the distinct ways stratification is reflected in this interaction between social relations and territorial practice, as the sociospatial perspective suggests.

The Wealthy

The upper classes always had the advantage of several homes because they could afford it. Former President George Bush, for example, has for many years maintained residences in Houston, Texas; Washington, D.C.; and Kennebunkport, Maine. Many wealthy people alternate between townhouse, suburban estate, and rural recreational home. In the city the wealthy are associated with the more fashionable districts such

A large suburban home in Westchester County, New York.

as Nob Hill in San Francisco, Beverly Hills in Los Angeles, the Gold Coast near Lake Michigan in Chicago, Beacon Hill in Boston, and Park Avenue in New York City. Their activities, in short, take place within a certain space.

One important way the wealthy manifest their power is by isolating themselves as much as possible from the rest of the population. Their segregation is voluntary. In the city this is accomplished by living in ultraexpensive housing with security guards and controlled entrances. While taxis are available, the wealthy will often utilize private limousine services that go door-to-door. Shopping and recreation are all located in heavily policed areas. In the city, such isolation remains somewhat of a constant chore that taxes the resources of surveillance and control. In the suburbs or at country homes, however, the benefits of isolation are more readily enjoyed. Box 8.1 details one of the very few sociological studies done on the wealthy by E. Digby Baltzell (see also Fussel, 1983). This study indicates that while the wealthy require their own segregated space, the areas they choose for their voluntary isolation vary over the years.

The upper class is not confined to city residence alone. One of the earliest studies of the affluent in suburbia was Thorsten Veblen's *Theory of the Leisure Class* (1899). Although wealth was behind their behavior, the most important characteristics of the lifestyle were symbolic or cultural. Veblen coined the concept *conspicuous consumption* to refer to this particular aspect of the affluent style of suburban life. By this concept is meant an outward display of consumption that demonstrates wealth and power through the wasting of resources and the symbols of upper-class membership. The suburban homes of the wealthy, for example, were endowed with excess. Houses were huge, over 5,000 square feet or more, with many more rooms than were necessary to service the immediate family. Estates had large front and rear lawns that were landscaped and attended to by a staff of gardeners. Conspicuous consumption was symbolized by

BOX 8.1 THE PHILADELPHIA GENTLEMEN

Perhaps the best study by a sociologist of the upper-class lifestyle is E. Digby Baltzell's (1958) *Philadelphia Gentlemen*. The author distinguishes between the elite and the upper class. The former are "those individuals who are the most successful and stand at the top of the *functional* class hierarchy. These individuals are leaders in their chosen occupations or professions" (1958: 6). Baltzell's book is not about the elite but about the upper class, which he defines in contrast as the

> group of *families* whose members are descendants of successful individuals one, two, three or more generations ago. . . . [Individuals in this social grouping are] brought up together, are friends, and are intermarried one with another; and finally, they maintain a distinctive style of life and a kind of primary group solidarity which sets them apart from the rest of the population (1958: 7).

According to Baltzell the upper class in Philadelphia restricted itself to a particular location in the city and tried to remain out of sight. Over the years, however, its choice of location varied. That is, it did not usually stay in the same neighborhood generation after generation, but tended to be subject to the same forces of deconcentration and regional drift as were other individuals in the metropolis. Most American cities have a pattern similar to Philadelphia of once fashionable districts that have declined as the wealthy shuffle around the metropolitan region in search of secure enclaves for their lifestyle. As Baltzell remarks,

> In Philadelphia, the rise and fall of upper-class neighborhoods can be divided, with some overlapping of course, into three periods: (1) during the colonial period and through the first part of the nineteenth century, fashionable

the landscaping of yards precisely because land was allowed to lie uncultivated as a resource—the lawn was just for show.

The wealthy practically invented the stereotypical suburban lifestyle (see Chapter 4). As a sign of conspicuous consumption it is focused on leisure activities; that is, symbols of leisure mean that people do not have to work. An important affluent social institution is the country club, which is costly to belong to and which also restricts its membership. In many parts of the country, clubs such as the Everglades Country Club in Florida prevent African Americans and Jews from belonging even if they can afford membership fees. The fees usually run into the tens of thousands of dollars, thereby automatically keeping the working class out. The leisure activity of choice for the affluent is golf, and in recent years, this game has come to symbolize suburban wealth and leisure itself, because golf is most often played at country clubs. A second important recreational pursuit is tennis, which also requires outdoor maintenance when it is played at the country club, although tennis is also played in the city. In a wealthy area such as Palm Desert, California, located about 100 miles east of Los Angeles, a considerable amount of the town land is devoted to golf courses which require immense amounts

Philadelphians lived in what is now the downtown business district around Independence and Washington Squares; (2) after the Civil War, and until World War I, the upper-class center of gravity, as it were, became the Rittenhouse Square district; (3) after World War I, the center of society moved west once again out to the suburbs along the Main Line and in Chestnut Hill. At the same time, of course, many of the wealthier families had country places even as early as the eighteenth century (1958: 179).

The most characteristic area of upper-class life was the Main Line, which stretched westward from the central city of Philadelphia on the commuter railroad to the suburbs of Overbrook, Merion, Wynnewood, Ardmore, Haverford, Bryn Mawr, Rosemont, and other towns out to Paoli, Pennsylvania. As Baltzell observes,

Exploited in the literature and by the popular press, the famous Main Line is the most popular elite suburb in Philadelphia. Each Sunday, Philadelphians read all about upper-class social life in the Philadelphia *Inquirer's* popular society column, "The Mainliner" (1958: 201).

Baltzell notes that the upper-class lifestyle consisted of a withdrawal from civic affairs and the concentration on business by the males, while females were expected to stay close to home minding the household and entertaining when necessary for the husbands' needs. In addition, however, women were expected to be involved in philanthropic enterprises outside the home, such as organizing charity balls or fund raising activities for the arts. Children were sent to exclusive private schools, and social life meant interacting only with other members of the upper-class *Social Register*. Family time for these people was divided between town and country residences. In this way the upper class maintained its spatial and social isolation from other segments of the society.

of water and daily care. Because Palm Desert is located in the desert, the presence of so many golf courses is indeed a luxury.

At present, wealthy suburbanites maintain their isolation through mechanisms similar to those utilized in the city, such as the high price of homes, surveillance and control by private security forces, gate-guarded and enclosed communities, and the sheer separation that comes from spatial dispersal itself. Whether we are dealing with the city or the suburbs, the wealthy tend to use topography to their advantage. Their homes are located at the greatest heights. In the suburbs this often means that estates are built on the high ground, on hillsides or escarpments. In the city this "god's eye view" is acquired with a penthouse, and in most cases, those apartments higher up in luxury buildings often cost the most.

In short, the wealthy possess a distinct lifestyle founded on class privilege and symbols of high social status. Their daily life manifests itself in space through unique molding of the environment to create isolation and exclusion. The wealthy also overcome the limitations of space by owning several residences, each with its own locational advantages. Whether living in the city or the country, their lifestyle, like any other, is sociospatial; that is, it is organized around expressive symbols, some of which are quite subtle (Fussel, 1983), and particular spaces.

Yuppies, Dinks, and the Suburban Middle Class

A large proportion of central city residents are not members of the upper class but do have money by virtue of occupation and family choice. Since the 1970s, as manufacturing has declined in the city, there has been a phenomenal increase in service related jobs (see chapters 5, 13; also, Sassen, 1991). Many of these are professional positions created by the information-processing economy of the city, such as the financial and legal institutions associated with corporate headquarters. In previous chapters we have discussed how certain kinds of economic activity create or help reinforce a sociospatial tissue of lifestyles, particular labor skills, community relations, and expressive symbols. Recently, the shift to information-processing professional services has also affected city areas by reinforcing certain upper-middle-class patterns of behavior.

The term *yuppies*, or young, urban professionals, has recently acquired a derogatory connotation, but it is a very useful way of describing relatively young (late 20s to early 40s) middle-class professionals who live in the city. The same can be said for the term *dinks*—double income, no kids—which describes yuppie couples without children. Only recently have such components of the middle class achieved the kind of numbers that have attracted attention. According to Sassen (1991), yuppies were responsible

Eighteenth Street in the Adams-Morgan area where many ethnic restaurants are located. One of the oldest Washington, D.C., neighborhoods, the area is now undergoing gentrification.

for upgrading housing in many parts of the city, otherwise known as "gentrification" (see Anderson, 1990); their culinary demands spurred the opening of many new and often exotic restaurants; and their more specialized everyday needs, such as last minute food shopping, health and fitness requirements, and reading and cinema tastes, have opened up new sectors of employment for a host of immigrant groups and working-class urban residents looking for entry level service positions. Box 8.2 details some of the characteristics of the urban professional lifestyle.

In the early 1980s the leaders of many cities believed that the two-pronged explosion of jobs and spending related to the expansion of the business service sector would take the place of manufacturing as the key growth industry of urban areas. Indeed, places such as Pittsburgh (Jezierski, 1988) managed to change from centers of industry to focal points for global banking and investment. Restructuring of the financial and corporate business sectors with a consequent decline in the growth of jobs, however, occurred in the mid 1980s, cutting short this expansion. Especially significant were the changes occurring after the October, 1987, "crash" of the New York stock market, which led to greater computerization of financial transactions, the reining in of risky ventures such as junk bonds, and the failure of several investment firms (Minsky, 1989). All of these changes meant employment declines, with as many as 100,000 people losing their jobs after 1987 in New York City alone. Other areas of the country have been hit in a similar fashion. Hence, despite what was once believed, the place of yuppies in the revitalization of central cities may be overrated.

Most of the middle class do *not* live in the city. Years of white flight to a suburban location for the majority of people who can afford to buy their own home have emptied the central city of much of its middle class. The majority of middle-class Americans have spread out and prospered across the vast expanses of developed housing tracts throughout the metropolitan region.

Middle-class suburban living is in many respects a mimicking of the upper-class lifestyle within a more modest budget. Symbols of status abound in this kind of environment as well. The normative suburban home is a scaled down replica of the estate. It consists of a front yard which is strictly ornamental and a back yard reserved for leisure. In the warmer parts of the country the desirable back yard may contain a built-in swimming pool which usually is no more than thirty feet long. While the upper-class estate involves a team of gardening and maintenance men, the middle-class homeowner is a "do-it-yourselfer." Indeed, a stereotyped activity of the suburban male invariably involves fighting crab grass on the lawn, repairing roofs, and main-taining homeowner appliances. Women in suburbia also have a unique lifestyle, as we shall discuss more fully later when we consider the relationship between gender and space.

For suburbanites, leisure activities are confined to the weekend when there is some free time. In many developments and municipalities, tax monies have been devoted to acquiring the kind of public facilities that the affluent enjoy in private. There may be public golf courses, swimming pools, tennis courts, and parks. In areas close to the ocean or a lake, suburban municipalities often build and service public marinas for boating and other water sports. Suburban life is family life. Box 8.3 details everyday life in suburbia.

A family enjoying their suburban back yard, one of the many attractions of homeownership and suburban location.

The Working Class, The Working Poor, and the Underclass

Traditional urban culture is associated with the large numbers of workers employed in manufacturing. In the nineteenth century, the city was invariably dominated by factories. Modest working-class housing was constructed in grid-pattern rows nearby. Weekly schedules were centered in this space which included the few amenities available to the working class—the pub, the association football park (soccer) or the local baseball diamond, and the streets themselves which functioned for children as the playground (Hareven, 1982).

In the period immediately after World War II, U.S. cities contained a prodigious density of such working-class districts. Since the 1960s, however, such a pattern has been in decline. One reason is that many factory workers attained middle-class status with the ability to purchase single-family homes in the suburbs, often with liberal government-sponsored veterans benefits. A second, more drastic cause has been the decline in manufacturing itself. When the factories closed, working-class life became all the more precarious. Housing and neighborhoods declined. Box 8.4 depicts working-class lifestyles in both the city and the suburb.

Although working-class families have suburbanized in large numbers since the 1960s, there are still many that remain residents of large cities. They are often referred to as the working poor because their standard of living is declining as cities themselves have become expensive places to reside. The quality of life of the working class is dependent on the public services provided by local government. They require mass transportation, for example, which is becoming increasingly expensive. They often

BOX 8.2 THE URBAN UPSCALE LIFESTYLE

Market researchers have studied yuppies in detail because they spend so much of their income on consumer products. They identify characteristic yuppie areas as located in the more affluent sections of the central city (Weiss, 1988). Yuppies live in high-rise buildings in areas of high population concentration. According to one report:

> Almost two thirds live in residences worth more than $200,000, decorating their living rooms according to *Metropolitan Home*, buying their clothes at Brooks Brothers, frequenting the same hand-starch Chinese laundries. In Urban Gold Coast, residents have the lowest incidence of auto ownership in the nation; these cliff-dwellers get around by taxi and rental car (Weiss, 1988: 278).

Market researchers also note the peculiar, service dependent nature of yuppie consumer behavior. For the sake of last minute convenience, they will spend more to eat out or purchase items at close-in grocery stores that charge more than large supermarkets. Convenience is prized by people who make high salaries but have to devote extra hours to their work. According to Weiss:

> Residents usually eat out for lunch and dinner, and their forays to grocery stores mostly yield breakfast items: yogurt, butter, orange juice and English muffins—all bought at slightly above-average rates. Compared to the general population, residents buy barely one-fifth the amount of such pedestrian treats as TV dinners, canned stews and powdered fruit drinks. Where these consumers do excel is at the liquor store: they buy imported champagnes, brandy, beer and table wine at twice the national norm, possibly to take the edge off stress-filled urban living (1988: 281).

The novelist Jay McInerney (1984) has captured the mind-set of individuals who live alone, have high paying jobs, and haunt the central city gentrified districts which contain an implosion of various cultural influences from around the world. As his novel's character, a yuppie writer living in New York City, observes:

> You're dressed and out of the house before ten. The train pulls in just as you make the platform. . . . The car is full of Hasidim from Brooklyn—gnomes in black with briefcases full of diamonds. You take a seat beside one of them. He is reading from his Talmud, running his finger across the page. . . . At Fourteenth Street three Rastafarians get on, and soon the car reeks of sweat and reefer. Sometimes you feel like the only man in the city without group affiliation. . . . The *Post* confirms your sense of impending disaster. There's the Fiery Nightmare on page three—an apartment blaze in Queens; and on page four a Killer Tornado that ravaged Nebraska. In the heartland of the country, carnage is usually the result of acts of God. In the city it's man-made—arson, rape, murder (1984: 56, 7).

need family assistance, such as childcare or welfare. Welfare parents with dependent children cannot work even if they want to without adequate childcare. The level of medical care for this less affluent group is precarious and dependent on city supported hospitals because they work at jobs that do not provide adequate, if any, health insurance. In fact the Health and Hospitals Administration of New York City, which runs the city's medical facilities, has a yearly budget of about 1½ billion dollars, as much as the entire budget of several small countries.

Because so much of their standard of living depends on city services, the working poor are often at odds with public administrators. City politics involves clashes between this public and the municipal administration over the quality of services. Since the latter 1970s, declining fiscal health of cities has made this political conflict worse because of budget crises and cutbacks (as we shall see in Chapter 11). The working poor and their advocates in the city fight a running battle with the mayor over the declines in education, fire and police protection, sanitation, highway maintenance, health care, and recreational amenities.

The "underclass," which is produced by a combination of class and race related factors, consists of the most isolated elements of the poor who have little prospects of employment, are residents of husbandless households, and whose lives are besieged by crime and drugs. This segment of the population was first called to our attention by Ken Auletta's (1983) journalistic account, and later analyzed by the Chicago sociologist William J. Wilson (1987). In recent years the term *underclass* has been dropped because it has assumed the characteristics of a buzzword that blames the victims of racial and economic deprivation, rather than, as originally intended, highlighting the causes of extreme poverty and isolation. In order to avoid the negative connotations of this term, this text refers, instead, to the *ghettoized poor* (see Chapter 10 for a more detailed discussion).

According to Wilson, the plight of the ghettoized urban poor arises from the reproducibility of their condition. They have become so isolated and concentrated in specific areas of the city that their needs fundamentally outstrip the available municipal resources aimed at alleviating the condition of poverty. As a result, they are doomed to raise children without many prospects for a better life unless they turn to criminal activity. Box 8.5 details aspects of the poverty-stricken ghetto resident's lifestyle. Thus, the so-called "underclass" phenomenon is really caused by a combination of sociospatial factors—such as poverty and racial exclusion—and the spatial concentration of large numbers of poor people within specific areas of cities and suburbs, rather than by individual failings (see Chapter 10).

The life of the ghettoized poor is subjected to an almost unending list of pathological consequences of city living, including public health crises such as AIDS, child abuse, tuberculosis, dropouts from education, juvenile crime, drug addiction and the bearing of addicted babies, juvenile motherhood, murder, rape, and robbery (see Chapter 10). The crime and pathology associated with poverty-stricken ghettos make city living difficult for everyone and are largely responsible for the high murder rates in urban areas.

Women, Gender Roles, and Space

The issue of gender roles and territory is a vast topic on which urban sociologists have largely been silent. As recently as the 1970s one well known geographer wrote a book

BOX 8.3 THE MIDDLE-CLASS SUBURBAN LIFESTYLE

A picture of middle-class suburban life was drawn by the geographer Peter Muller:

> The needs and preferences of the nuclear family unit shape modes of social interaction in middle-income residential areas. The management of children is a central group-level concern, and most local social contact occurs through such family-oriented formal organizations as the school PTA, Little League, and the Scouts. However, despite the closer spacing of homes and these integrating activities, middle-class suburbanites . . . are not communally cohesive to any great degree. Emphasis on family privacy and freedom to aggressively pursue its own upwardly mobile aspirations does not encourage the development of extensive local social ties. Neighboring (mostly child-related) is limited and selective, and even socializing with relatives is infrequent. Most social interaction revolves around a nonlocal network of self-selected friends widely distributed in suburban space (1981: 72).

This relative isolation of individuals in suburbia and the exclusive autodependency of the spatial arrangements is particularly hard on teenagers. Ralph Larkin makes these observations about suburban teenagers in a place he calls Utopia:

> The most serious complaint among Utopia High School students is boredom. They are restless. Many complain of having nothing to do. They are forced to compete with each other for grades, sexual attractiveness, hipness, and all the other minutiae that are involved in the status race. Since everyone else is struggling for the same, somehow scarcer rewards, friendship has a hollow quality to it. It is a gloss on a relationship in which vulnerabilities are hidden so they won't be capitalized on by others (1979: 60).

In Jerry Jacob's pioneering study of the suburban shopping mall (1984) he discussed how teenagers fight the boredom of their lives by converging on a certain space, the fully enclosed shopping mall. Jacobs took one particular teenager, Julie, as typical and detailed her activities within this environment as follows:

> First and foremost she and her friends spend "a lot of time" at the (video game) arcade. They often stop in at the "Gift Horse," a shop featuring "jewelry and design shoelaces and calendars and mugs." They might on these walks stop to visit "The Old Erie Coffee House." Ironically, this is not a place to drink coffee although coffee, tea, and their accoutrements are sold there. However, on these jaunts, Julie and her friends usually have a different agenda in mind, and go there to look at "cute stuffed animals, the little animal farm, animals, mugs and stuff, cards and pins." From there they might move on to "Sweet Temptation" and get some "gum or something." By then, it would be approaching lunch-time and they would go to the "T.J.'s" (a hamburger place not unlike McDonald's) where they would get a large french fries and a coke and sit and talk about a variety of topics . . . (1984: 98).

BOX 8.4 THE WORKING CLASS AT HOME IN CITIES AND SUBURBS

Peter Muller characterizes the working-class suburb as closely resembling inner city blue collar neighborhoods. As he states:

> Although working-class suburbs vary according to the state of their local economies, age of housing stock, ethnic composition, and threat of racial change, their lifestyles are quite similar. Unlike the carefully structured modes of socializing in middle-class macro- and microcommunities, working-class ethnic-centered neighborhoods are characterized by a broad social interaction of informal groups congregating at such local meeting places as the church, tavern, street corner, or door stoop. Local group acceptance and integration is the dominant social value, and communal life stresses the availability of a satisfying peer-group society, similar neighbors, maintaining easy access among people well known to each other, and collective defense of neighborhood respectability. . . . The physical and social character of these working-class communities, which Lieberson (1962) found to be virtually identical to blue-collar central city neighborhoods, offsets them sharply from surrounding higher-income suburbs (1981: 74–75).

William F. Whyte (1955) carried out a classic study of a working-class inner city neighborhood in Philadelphia. Over thirty years later the sociologist Elijah Anderson (1978) published another important study of street corner life in a black ghetto of Chicago. Both studies illustrate how the corner space and the small shops that are located there serve as the cornerstones of everyday life in working-class areas. According to Whyte, the street gang is a phenomenon of the corner. While middle-class suburban kids might converge on the mall as their special space for socializing, inner city youth

entitled *This Scene of Man* (Vance, 1977), and not to be outdone, in 1989, an equally famous urban sociologist published a study of Chicago entitled *The Man Made City* (Suttles, 1989). Feminist scholars would indeed agree that the city is man-made because women had little to do with its planning and even less to do with its construction. Yet the lives of women are a critical component of urban and suburban activities. Increasingly, with the prodding of feminist observers, we are gaining greater insight into the role of women, and their needs, in everyday metropolitan life (Hayden, 1981).

Women and the Urban Political Economy

During the nineteenth century in the early stages of industrial manufacturing, it was common for entire families to labor together. Home life was second to the needs of the factory, and even children were pressed into the service of wage labor (Hareven, 1982). Over the years conditions in these Satanic Mills, as Karl Marx (1967) called them, were changed. Child labor laws were passed at the turn of the century in the United States prohibiting school age youth from full-time employment. Many women continued to work, but the growing number of middle-class families during the 1920s choose the nearest street corner and claim it for their group. The close connection between this place and the social group does not seem to decline over the course of time, as Whyte observes:

> The corner-gang structure arises out of the habitual association of the members over a long period of time. The nuclei of most gangs can be traced back to early boyhood, when living close together provided the first opportunities for social contacts. School years modified the original pattern somewhat, but I know of no corner gangs which arose through classroom or school-playground association. The gangs grew up on the corner and remained there with remarkable persistence from early boyhood until the members reached their late twenties or early thirties. ... On any evening on almost any corner one finds corner boys who have come in from other parts of the city or from suburbs to be with their old friends. The residence of the corner boy may also change within the district, but nearly always he retains his allegiance to his original corner (1955: 255).

In contrast, Anderson's account of street life shows how the diverse residents of the ghetto interact at corner establishments to reaffirm their social standing within their own, racially segregated communities. As a consequence the particular space at the corner serves an important function by providing a public venue for the sociability and social order of ghetto areas.

> Urban taverns and bars, like barbershops, carryouts and other such establishments, with their adjacent street corners and alleys, serve as important gathering places for people of the "urban villages" and ghetto areas of the city. ... The urban poor and working class people are likely to experience their local taverns as much more than commercial businesses. They provide settings for sociability and places where neighborhood residents can gain a sense of self-worth (1978: 1).

enabled people to copy the upper-class lifestyle with married women remaining at home. This effect of class, which occurred because of successful economic growth beginning with this century, resulted in the redefinition of the middle-class woman's gender role to that of housewife (Spain, 1992).

Over the years further changes in class standing and in the economy altered the relationship of women to both the family and the larger society. Status differences were caused by the effects of male social dominance, which dictated women's life chances, and by the effects of the economy. For example, among the middle class during the 1920s it was expected that women remain housewives. During World War II, however, many women returned to full-time occupations including manufacturing, as in the image of "Rosie the Riveter." After the war and especially during the suburbanization of the 1950s, middle-class women were once again expected to remain home as housewives. Finally, since the 1970s the middle-class lifestyle has grown increasingly expensive; hence it is common for both parents to pursue full-time employment, and now the majority of adult women work outside the home.

Recent statistics from the U.S. Department of Labor illustrate the phenomenal changes in the labor force participation of women since the 1950s. In 1950 roughly

A central city area of poverty-stricken street people, Portland, Oregon.

30 percent of women worked outside the home, but by 1986 the figure was 55 percent. In 1950 it was relatively rare for married women with children to be employed. Only 28 percent of women in this group with children between the ages of 6 and 17 worked, but by 1986 the figure had jumped to 68 percent. Today roughly 66 percent of all women with children work outside the home, and two-job families (both husband and wife working) comprise 58 percent of all married people with children (see Hochschild and Machung, 1989).

In contrast to the cycles of middle-class gender role differences, working-class women have always had to secure employment outside the home, even if it is only limited to part-time work. Minority women, for example, have always worked, and many are the main sources of income for families, due to discrimination against males. Certain industries, such as garment manufacturing, depend almost exclusively on the exploitation of female labor in factories. In Chapter 7 we discussed the role patriarchal norms of domination play in the global economy. Women in Asia and Latin America, in particular, are exploited as the source of labor for the electronics and garment industries in places like Mexico, Singapore, and South Korea (see Chapter 12). As one scholar suggests (McDowell, 1991), male domination of female roles is an integral part of the global economy and a major reason for the success of recent restructuring which has shipped manufacturing jobs to developing countries. In short, female gender roles are dictated in part by patriarchal social conventions and in part by the needs of the economy.

BOX 8.5 THE GHETTOIZED POOR

The sociologists Terry Williams and William Kornblum carried out a study of poor inner city areas in four cities: Cleveland, Ohio; Louisville, Kentucky; Meridian, Mississippi; and New York City, New York. A common stereotype is that all members of the underclass are poor. While many are, others have made fortunes off of the drug-centered economy within ghetto areas. Williams and Kornblum contrast two individuals living in the same place. Much of daily life revolves around a particular space, the local "candy store" and the street corner on which it is situated. As they observed:

> The neighborhood once was flooded with junkies, but it is changing slowly. The candy store is one of the last institutions in the area to serve this particular consumer group. In fact, the store operates on several levels. It's a hangout for kids, number runners, drug dealers, and winos. The kids can buy reefer; adults can buy wine under the counter; boosters (sellers of stolen goods) sell their wares to customers and managers alike. . . . Seventh was the avenue of the big-time hustlers. There they sported their fine cars and pretty women. . . The names of infamous street hustlers who made it into big time are given legendary status.
>
> C.C. has a long way to go if he wants to make it to the big time. Right now all he can do is talk big. Wearing a floppy hat that he claims is a Christian Dior, a fur-type vest, sneakers, and khaki trousers, he takes a perverse pleasure in shouting obscenities at his peers. As one of them, Zero, dressed in a grey hooded jacked [sic] zipped up to the neck, passes to go into the store, C.C. looks at him. "Yo, what you wearing all of that shit for? This ain't the north pole—you look like a motherfucking polar bear. . . ." Zero gets to the door, steps in for a second, then comes out, grabs C.C. around the neck, and proceeds to twist his head around. As he twists he mumbles something like "I-done-told-you-to-stop-fucking-with-me-ain't-I?" (1985: 48–49).

Williams and Kornblum identify C.C. as "among the losers of the street world," but there are also what they call "winners," such as Darryl:

> Darryl's expensive tastes are evident in his wardrobe—a mink coat, several pairs of three-hundred-dollar boots, a closet filled with silk shirts, and a diamond ring—in addition to his four cars: a 450 SEL Mercedes Benz, a 633 CS1 BMW, a Cadillac Seville, and a Volkswagen Rabbit. He also owns two three-story brownstones and is, in the words of the teenagers, "coming off strong." Darryl has been a dealer in heroin and cocaine for ten years. When he was nine years old he already controlled a crew of kids who sold joints at school. Today, at nineteen, he is a veteran (1985: 49).

Domestic labor is unpaid and has low status. In fact, housework is usually not a family topic of importance. Yet the well-being of the family depends on the cooking, cleaning, nurturing, and monitoring of the household. In most societies it has been women's lot to bear the responsibility for these tasks. Even when women work outside the home, men expect them to do the "double labor" of housework. According to a classic study of this burden (Hochschild and Machung, 1989), married women who work outside the home still do an average of three hours a day of housework compared with seventeen minutes for their male spouses. As one group of observers note:

> As women it is assumed that we will be ultimately responsible for the upkeep and general maintenance of our homes whether we have another job or not. . . . Even when others contribute to this work, the primary responsibility remains with the women. We are conscious of its demands at all times; responsibilities cannot be shut off by retreating into a "room of one's own" (Matrix Collective, 1984).

Domestic or unpaid labor supports child rearing and family life. While these activities are necessary in all societies, the tasks themselves are the primary responsibility of women, who labor for the most part alone. Urban sociologists refer to these activities as the *reproduction of the labor force*, because household work along with education and health care join to nurture children until they themselves enter the labor force. The socialization of women to accept the role of domestic laborer in our society, therefore, is an essential and necessary component of the economy and the proper functioning of metropolitan life.

As discussed above, the participation of middle-class women in the formal economy has been cyclical. Since the 1970s, women have entered the paid labor force in record numbers. As a result of economic restructuring, that is, with the decline in manufacturing and the rise of service industries (see Chapter 5), new opportunities have been created for women. They have responded by moving into the professional service sector. One consequence of this shift has been a change in the way both men and women view household tasks, with a greater willingness of men among the middle class to share in domestic labor, especially a growing percentage of men who "mother" (Lamb, 1986; Grief, 1985). Another consequence has been the multiplication of service related jobs created by working mothers. Many of the pressing household tasks have been farmed out to specialized service workers for a fee. Childcare, household cleaning, shopping assistance, and lawn care are but some of the services that have taken the place of unpaid domestic labor. In addition, fast foods, restaurants, and take-out shops have expanded their operations greatly over the last twenty years. All of these new economic activities have changed the texture of space in both cities and suburbs. Specialty shops and services spring up everywhere to cater to those families with double incomes. Supermarket and giant merchandising stores such as Wal-mart and K-Mart make shopping more efficient. Along with malls they also redefine metropolitan space through the construction of minicenters across the region.

In sum, the role of women in the society has an effect on space (Spain, 1992). In fact, the sociospatial relations of the modern, global economy have as much to do with gender roles and patriarchy as they do with economic and political factors. When women stayed at home and engaged in full-time but unpaid labor, they were responsible for keeping up the appearance of the neighborhood. Once middle-class women in the United States were encouraged to change their social role, although still expected to do a "double shift," energies and resources were transferred to service industries that catered to domestic needs. Neighborhoods changed to accommodate fast food and take-out places, restaurants, laundries and dry cleaners; and supermarkets and malls made shopping progressively more convenient.

Houses in the suburbs required at least two-car garages because both spouses commuted. In both the city and suburb, day care and extended childcare programs changed the place where children went to play—from city streets supervised by mothers, to indoor group play areas supervised by paid day care specialists. Elsewhere, in the global economy, young girls compose the bulk of the manufacturing labor force in electronics and garment industries because patriarchal relations make them docile and low paid workers. The control of women's bodies is as essential to the sustenance of third world countries as it is to the first world patriarchal societies. Everywhere, then, the nature of gender roles has a direct effect on sociospatial relations.

Women and the Environment

The concluding remarks of the last section can be expanded to explore the specific relations between settlement space and female gender. These relations extend from the home to the community to the larger metropolitan region. The home, for example, is the one space in the environment where people can be themselves. It is the private and intimate space. Due to the family division of labor, women have been assigned the main task of decorating the home. Through this activity they have been able to express their own individuality (Matrix Collective, 1984). Housing has several meanings, as we shall see (Chapter 9), including signifying status. But for women, their control over the environmental space of the home has meant an opportunity for self-expression. It has also meant, for the middle class, a restricted domain within which women are allowed to influence their environment.

Black and Hispanic children playing on the street in the Bronx, New York.

If the home space can be viewed in the above way, it is partially because women have been socialized into the role of responsibility for shelter maintenance. Spatial relations, therefore, play a great role in the perpetuation of female socialized roles in our society. However, if the female gender role assigns a certain power to women through control of the home environment the opposite is the case for the larger physical environment of the city and metropolis. Once out in public space women have to beware. They are subject to harassment and, quite often, danger. Women living in large cities must acquire "street smarts" early if they are to successfully negotiate public space. As one commentary noted:

> Whether you wear a slit skirt or are covered from head to foot in a black chador, the message is not that you are attractive enough to make a man lose his self-control, but that the public realm belongs to him and you are there by his permission as long as you follow his rules and as long as you remember your place (Benard and Schlaffer, 1993: 390).

In contrast to men, women are situated in a constrained space and do not enjoy the same freedom of movement. For example, women are cautioned not to go out alone at night, and with good reason. If they walk or jog around the neighborhood, they usually do so only in secure places. The women's movement has been particularly attentive to the needs of females for safe places, such as in the "Take Back the Night" rallies occurring in the 1970s. The constricted and confined safe places for women in our society are another form of oppression. In general, by patterning what activities are allowed, what are isolated, what are considered safe or dangerous, and what are connected to other activities, such as the combination of childcare and shopping found in the mall or the gender segregation of children in elementary schools (Thorne, 1993), space plays a role in gender socialization.

The secondary status of women is also reinforced through spatial design. Community planning invariably assigns the major portion of open space to traditionally male dominated activities, such as sports. Places for mothering are rarely considered at all and are restricted to playgrounds, if they are constructed. Creating safe environments for children and mothers requires some planning. In Columbia, Maryland, one of the totally planned New Towns in the United States, pedestrian and automobile traffic are separated by the segregation of space. This feature of Columbia makes it easier for mothers to protect children at play. It is not so easy to suggest ways the home and community environments can be improved by taking the needs of women more into account, although some progress through feminist activism has been made in sensitizing planners and architects to the specific needs of women (see Matrix Collective, 1984). In sum, current gender role changes and new demands of family life may affect our environment in the years to come (see Chapter 14 for an extended discussion on environmental and planning concerns).

Ethnicity and Immigration

Ethnicity is a phenomenon either of living in a foreign country, or of living in an ethnically diverse society. In relatively homogeneous societies, lifestyle differences may exist but they are usually not expressed as ethnicity—class, gender, religious, subcultural, and age differences may be more important. When indigenous people, such as mainland Chinese, immigrate to another country that contains people from many different origins, like the United States, then subcultural differences take on the dimensions of ethnic differences. These are almost wholly "semiotic" or symbolic in nature (see Chapter 9). In particular, ascribed characteristics and inherited beliefs may make individuals with foreign heritages uniquely different. What counts for the dynamics of ethnicity is the extent to which those symbolic differences clash with the dominant society or the culture of other ethnic groups in a diverse society.

In the United States ethnic lifestyles are closely connected to the waves of immigration from abroad. As Espiritu and Light (1991) suggest, however, our understanding of immigration should include a global perspective that also acknowledges reasons for why people left their land of origin in the first place. For the most part, and principally with the exception of African Americans, immigration has been voluntary.

There have been three distinct waves of immigration to the United States.

First Wave

Many thousands of years ago Asians immigrated to the western hemisphere over a land bridge to Alaska. Beginning with Columbus' fateful voyage in 1492, Western European settlers from the British Isles, Spain, Holland, and France confronted the Native Americans. These European settlers arrived as a consequence of official state policy. Some were convicts taking an alternative sentence to their homeland prison. Others signed on with the promise of free land and other resources such as gold. As is well known, still others, such as William Penn and his Quaker community, came in search of religious freedom.

During the 1840s, the Irish potato famine forced many people from that country to immigrate. The Irish were the first large group of non-Wasp (i.e., White Anglo-Saxon Protestant) immigrants, and they were discriminated against (Higham, 1977). By the time they arrived, the earlier groups had entrenched themselves as the ruling class. Many of them, such as Rockefeller, from Scotland, Vanderbilt, whose family had come from Holland, and Leland Stanford, of English origins, had made fortunes in the burgeoning industrial economy of the United States. The Irish were considered less valuable than the African slaves of the South and they were used for dangerous tasks, such as the building of the railroads, or as the first proletarian factory workers in the northern cities where slaves did not exist.

Second Wave

Around 1870 industrialization was in full bloom and the cities of the United States were expanding. At about that time a second, substantial wave of new immigrants arrived here from the countries of Central and Eastern Europe. As we noted in Chapter 3, the cities of the time were overcrowded. Housing for most immigrants lacked the basic necessities of sanitation and sewage. Public health crises and crime waves were quite common (Monkkonen, 1989). The quality of urban life went into decline.

Most second wave immigrants made their homes in the city. Many had come from rural backgrounds and had to make adjustments to the urban way of life (Handlin,

1951). In addition, they found most jobs in the factories of the largest cities and they had to accommodate themselves to the industrial daily schedule.

It wasn't long before antagonisms developed between immigrant groups organized as workers, and city officials and factory owners. Both the Irish who had arrived somewhat earlier and the second wave of Central and Eastern Europeans were viewed by established residents as threatening to the American way of life. Some second wave immigrants had already been exposed to radical labor movements in Europe, and these, such as the Industrial Workers of the World or the IWW, started up in the United States. Because of the large majority of Catholics among the foreigners, particularly the Irish, Italians, and Poles, a popular antiurban sentiment was expressed at the time about large cities being centers of "Rum, Romanism, and Rebellion."

It may be difficult for us to imagine today, but the older, first wave immigrants, especially those among the elite of the country, propagated racist ideas about the Irish, Italians, Poles, and Jews in the late 1880s. Among the books published was Josiah Strong's (1891) racist diatribe which blamed the white foreigners for diluting the "American Race" and for spawning the crises of the city. In another case, during the 1920s many outspoken anti-Semites operated in the open, including Henry Ford, who financed a successful reprinting of the virulently anti-Semitic forgery, *The Protocols of the Elders of Zion*—a racist book that is still circulated today.

To a great extent such racist and anti-Semitic slanders were propagated in tandem with others accusing the new immigrants of harboring communist and anarchist or anticapitalist ideas. Thus anti-immigrant racism was a strong weapon used to call immigration itself into question. Reaction around the turn of the century was so strong to the second wave of arrivals that it eventually led to a restriction of immigration from Eastern and Southern Europe. This was accomplished in a succession of federal acts which established quotas that favored first wave, Western, and Northern European countries. These quotas actually lasted until the immigration reform bill of 1965, that is, until quite late in our history (Espiritu and Light, 1991).

Fighting between employers and workers was not the only conflict of the time; conflict also took on a spatial manifestation. Areas in the city were marked off by ethnicity, race, and religion. Often these disparate groups would fight each other over territory and public resources. Thrasher's study of Chicago gangs, discussed in Chapter 6, provides an excellent example of these "defended neighborhoods" that are a socio-spatial phenomenon of ethnicity.

Theories of Immigrant Adjustment

The earliest view of the U.S. city as composed of ethnic enclaves emerged at the turn of the century as a consequence of this territorial conflict, and subsequent studies by the Chicago School, in particular, documented its dynamics. Among other things this included a biological analogy for inner city conflict that came to be called "human ecology." Some of the principal authors of this tradition, such as Roderick McKenzie and, much later, Amos Hawley (as discussed in Chapter 6), described the adjustment of people in the city in terms of species competition, with one new group usurping the environment of another through a cycle of invasion-succession (McKenzie, 1933).

BOX 8.6 SPATIAL SEGREGATION AND ETHNICITY

African Americans. Unlike other ethnic groups, African Americans were forcibly removed from their home countries and brought to the United States as slaves during the 1700s. In 1990 their descendants constituted 12.4 percent of the total population. Until the twentieth century the overwhelming majority of blacks, more than 90 percent, lived in the South and most where located in rural areas. Since the turn of the century, however, there has been a steady movement of African Americans to the North in general and to cities in particular (Lemann, 1991b).

In the 1800s many slaves fled the South for freedom. Using such routes as the "underground railroad" they arrived in the cities of the North and some even made it as far as Canada. By the end of the Civil War there were already several communities of African Americans established in northern cities. As a result of discrimination against blacks, however, these areas soon became segregated. A similar pattern of ghettoization occurred in the making of black communities in Chicago (Speer, 1968), Philadelphia (W.E.B. DuBois, 1899), and New York (Drake and Cayton, 1945).

During the turn of the century the mechanization of agriculture coupled with the immense increase in industrialization with its job opportunities both pushed and pulled blacks off southern farms and into northern factories. This process accelerated as a consequence of World War I, fell off during the Great Depression, and resumed with full intensity during World War II. As a result, by the 1950s African Americans were almost as urbanized as were whites, with over 60 percent of their total population living in cities. After 1950 a large percentage of whites began an exodus from the cities to the suburbs, which at the time were almost overwhelmingly closed to black migration. As a result, the percentage of African Americans living in central cities rose. By the 1980s cities such as Los Angeles, Chicago, Atlanta, and Detroit had black mayors, and in the 1990s the list grew to include New York and others.

(Continued)

While the changes occurring in the cities of the time appeared similar to behavior in the animal and plant kingdoms, this "ecological" metaphor was criticized early on as being too mechanical a view for the complicated process of neighborhood change (Alihan, 1938). Today we know that the turmoil of population turnover in the city had more to do with the operation of the real estate market and the competition for housing among large numbers of immigrants than it did with some innate biological contest over territory between separate ethnic groups. However, this now outdated "ecological" metaphor was notable for its appreciation of the role of space in the action of social groups. That is, in the conflict between different residential and commercial interests, control of space was one very important feature, especially for cultural reasons.

The most powerful theory of immigrant conflict and accommodation in the United States was the "melting pot" view. It was believed that change would occur gradually and

As we have seen, racial discrimination is still a potent force which prevents African Americans from integrating into society. For blacks, segregation into distinct ghetto areas of most cities still persists despite their large urban numbers. During the last fifteen years a growing number of blacks have achieved middle-class status (Landry, 1987). However, much of the African-American population remains segregated. In Chapter 10 we shall discuss the immense problems this segregation poses for the quality of urban life. These involuntary places, or ghettos, are filled with the sights and sounds of African-American culture. African connotations, the signs of poverty and discrimination, and the symbols of political struggle mark ghettos from other city districts.

Mexican Americans. Much of the Southwest, including parts of California, Arizona, New Mexico, and Texas, once belonged to the country of Mexico. Over time these lands were taken over by the United States. As a result, a significant Mexican population was included within our borders, and the places in the Southwest bear Mexican names. Mexican Americans suffered discrimination at the hands of the "Anglos" or non-Hispanic Americans. Due to the language barrier they also found it difficult to achieve mobility. Settlement in most of the Southwest was confined to specific ghettos or "barrios," which literally means "neighborhood" (Moore, 1976).

In 1990 Hispanics accounted for over 8 percent of the total population and Mexicans constituted roughly 60 percent of all Hispanics (Bean and Tierida, 1987). Between 1980 and 1990 the Hispanic population as a whole increased by over 50 percent. This figure underestimates the total number of Hispanics because many are illegal aliens. Mexicans continue to cross over to the United States in record numbers, and the community will retain its rapid growth rate in the future. Most settle in the border states of California and Texas, although they are also slowly filtering out into the heartland, and there is a growing Mexican-American community in Chicago (Hutchison, 1988).

In the Southwest, some barrio areas are known for gang related activities and a high rate of murder, principally caused by gang violence (Moore, 1978; Vigil, 1988); others are simply areas where Mexican-American families can find housing. Recently, however, Mexican Americans have achieved

in some cases over successive generations as the children of arrivals would eventually assimilate into the American way of life. Most immigrants might find the United States a strange country and experience certain difficulties upon arrival, such as having to learn English. As a consequence, they would invariably seek out enclaves of their own kind within the city, thus perpetuating the ethnic character of the neighborhood. Over time, however, the melting pot theory suggested, their children would become familiar with U.S. culture and language. They would leave the enclaves and mix or "melt" with the children of others. Melting pot theorists asserted that the forces operating to bring such changes about were both the free market economy and the institution of democratic politics, both of which allowed for active participation and public life.

In sum, accommodation to the United States would occur, according to this view, over several generations with assimilation the end result (Glazer and Moynihan, 1963;

a certain level of mobility and have entered the ranks of the professional middle class. For example, Denver had the first elected Mexican-American mayor, Peña, Tomas Rivera served as a chancellor of the University of California; and several Mexican Americans are now members of Congress and the president's cabinet. As language barriers are overcome, and with their increasing numbers, this group is expected to play a greater role in U.S. society.

Native Americans.   The history of Native Americans is not an urban story. Prior to World War II almost 90 percent lived outside metropolitan areas of the country. According to Snipp (1989), however, those identifying themselves as Native Americans have moved to the cities in record numbers, although at least 50 percent still reside in rural areas. Cities such as Chicago, Albuquerque, and Minneapolis have interesting Native-American communities. Even New York City contains the remnants of a Mohawk enclave brought from upstate to work the heights of skyscraper construction.

From the sociospatial perspective, this group is interesting because, as a conquered nation, Native Americans were offered a spatial solution to their dilemma of being overrun. In 1830 under President Andrew Jackson, the Indian Removal Act was passed, which approved the forced transfer of east coast tribes to the area west of the Mississippi River. Reservations were set up throughout the West, and the Native Americans were forced to live in these administered spaces. During the 1870s the United States ceased to recognize these people as belonging to independent nations, and they came under the administration of the Bureau of Indian Affairs.

Most Native Americans who are found in U.S. cities live in segregated sections, although there are many middle-class people who are Native-American descendants but are not identified as such. Until quite recently (1970) Native Americans were the poorest group living in the United States. (Snipp, 1989). By moving to cities they have improved their economic chances somewhat, but they are still victims of discrimination.

In sum, sociospatial relations play a significant role in the control of certain populations within the United States who are discriminated against. As a modern society we still possess within our borders ghettos, segregated barrios, and state controlled reservations.

Gordon, 1964; Sowell, 1981; Lieberson and Walters, 1988). Implicit in this view was also the notion that the United States was a land of unbridled opportunity and mobility. The much believed "American Dream" fostered the idea that any immigrant who worked hard and lived a responsible life could become a successful U.S. citizen. Beyond this variant of the American Dream was the belief that success in the United States depended principally on individual self-worth or human capital. That is, having certain skills and the desire to work hard (human capital) became all that was needed for success because the opportunities themselves were there for the taking.

Lieberson (1980) and Morawska (1990), among others, have recently challenged this melting pot theory. They suggest that while individual attributes are important to future success, there are also institutional impediments that may prevent immigrants from realizing their full potential, such as economic and political constraints. In particular, mobility and success are often a function of business cycles. When times are rough, newly arrived residents have an almost impossible task improving themselves. But when the economy itself is expanding, as it was for much of the period between 1840 and 1920, immigrants may indeed find golden opportunities.

The melting pot theory is also criticized for failing utterly to explain the condition of African Americans. Originally this group was physically and violently forced to come to this country because of the slave trade. Centuries after they arrived as slaves, they remain highly segregated. Institutional racism in the case of blacks prevented them from melting into the population. Other groups that have been spatially segregated despite a long history in the United States are Mexican Americans and Native Americans. The special histories of these groups, that defy in varying degrees the melting pot theory, are summarized in Box 8.6, which also illustrates how spatial restrictions work to perpetuate racism.

Third Wave

Most of our ideas about ethnicity and the immigrant experience are being challenged by the newest, third wave of immigrants that has arrived since the 1970s. Immigration laws were liberalized in 1965 following almost fifty years of strict quotas. The response was worldwide and somewhat unprecedented. Between 1968 and 1990 almost 10 million people immigrated to the United States. Furthermore, the pace has been growing, with roughly 60 percent entering the United States in the 1980s alone (Dinnerstein,

A Hispanic neighborhood in New York City. Travel agencies are important because of frequent visits back to countries of origin.

Noodle samples are cooked for shoppers at a Japanese supermarket located in suburban Costa Mesa, in Orange County, California.

Nichols, and Reimers, 1990). This rate has not been observed here since the last great influx of people around World War I and should prove to be just as important to the United States as were the previous peak years.

Another surprise of the third wave involves the composition of the newest immigrant groups. During the first and second waves, 75 percent of the arrivals were from somewhere in Europe. Today the same percentage, that is, three-fourths, are coming from Latin America and Asia. In California, for example, during the 1970s, 33 percent of the immigrants came from Asia and 43 percent from Mexico (Espiritu and Light, 1991). In the future the United States will be more culturally diverse, more Asian and more Hispanic than in the past.

A third distinct characteristic of the new immigration is that it is economically diverse as well as culturally contrasting. Many of the recent arrivals exhibit the classic

BOX 8.7 ETHNIC SUBURBS

Recent immigration from Asia has changed the mix of people in the suburban areas of the metropolitan region. Table 8.1 lists changes in New York, New Jersey, and Connecticut (the greater New York metro region).

TABLE 8.1
Changes in Immigrant Population, 1980 to 1990

	New York	New Jersey	Connecticut
Total	2.5%	5.0%	5.8%
Asian Indian	133.0%	169.2%	135.3%
Chinese	91.9%	152.8%	136.2%
Filipino	83.4%	118.0%	64. 8%
Japanese	43.9%	74.2%	104.5%
Korean	180.0%	200.0%	142.3%
Vietnamese	134.1%	154.2%	123.9%

Source: *New York Times*, December 7, 1991, p. L-28.

Table 8.1 uses the example of the New York region to illustrate the immense changes taking place in metropolitan areas as a consequence of immigration since the 1980s. In New York City, although the total population increased by only 2.5 percent, the Asian Indian, Korean, and Vietnamese populations increased by over 100 percent, with the Chinese and Filipino increases not far behind. Traditionally, for the first two waves of immigration it was expected that large cities like New York would attract new arrivals, so the figures above may not be so unexpected. What is new and different, however, is illustrated under the columns for New Jersey and Connecticut. In both states almost every group experienced increases of over 100 percent.

characteristics of the past—limited education, rural backgrounds, and limited resources. A goodly portion, however, are the exact opposite. These well-endowed immigrants are educated—many have college degrees—they are former city dwellers, and they often come with enough personal financial resources to start their own businesses. Thus, many third wave arrivals have achieved success in the United States in a relatively short time. According to Portes and Rumbaut (1990), in the decade between 1980 and 1990, professionals and technicians accounted for only 18 percent of the U.S. labor force but represented 25 percent of the immigrant population.

Espiritu and Light (1991) attribute this "bimodal" distribution, that is, having *two peaks*—one high income, one low income—of immigration to changes in the global system of capitalism. Many countries underwent crash modernization programs in the 1960s and 1970s that were not entirely successful. On the one hand, large numbers of the middle and working classes received technical and professional training. But upon graduation their economies had not expanded fast enough to offer them work. On the other hand, agricultural reform programs and development of interior places forced many impoverished and uneducated rural residents into the cities. They too took the chance on immigrating rather than waiting around in their home countries for work.

Much of this immigration was directly to regional suburbs or medium-sized towns, an influx that details the process of foreign entry-level suburbanization.

Traditional views of the suburbs are that they remain relatively homogeneous in race and income. Most urban sociologists do not talk about suburbia as a place of increasing population diversity, yet in recent years this is exactly what has occurred in the New York metropolitan region and perhaps elsewhere. According to one newspaper account:

> More than anything else, one has only to walk down the street—looking and listening—to realize the growing diversity of the region. In North Tarrytown a video store rents tapes translated into Spanish while a Chilean bakery offers traditional pastries like milhojas and meringues. In the same tiny business district are a Cuban-owned laundromat, a Dominican-owned stationery store, an Argentine-owned television repair shop, a Puerto Rican-owned grocery store. . . . Some longtime residents see such "foreign" influences as an intrusion in their communities; others welcome them. In Larchmont, New York. for instance, many residents feel that the French community of some 400 families in the area lends a certain cachet to their village, one of the most expensive suburbs in Westchester. Not so in the comfortable neighborhoods surrounding the more workingclass village of Mount Kisco in northern Westchester. In the last decade, the Hispanic population there has risen to 1,100 from 400, with many Guatemalans and Salvadorans crowding into apartments. Some residents have organized to expel illegal aliens (*New York Times*, Dec. 7, 1991: L-28).

The report goes on to say that whether or not the immigrants are welcome, the influx is likely to continue in the future because when settlement is successful in particular areas, relatives tell other relatives, and through networking their numbers grow.

Some of the recent immigrants have not only been successful, they have realized opportunities in new ways. For example, a suburb outside Los Angeles, Monterey Park, became a focal point for new Chinese immigration. Between 1960 and 1988 the population went from 85 percent white to 50 percent Chinese, with other Asians also in residence. Consequently, the city is known as the first "suburban Chinatown" (Arax, 1987), and it provides an excellent example of why we can no longer consider large cities as the prime site for ethnic subcultures. Recent arrivals have invested over $1 billion of their own money in the suburb, and it is estimated that the Chinese own at least 66 percent of all business and property there (Espiritu and Light, 1991: 43). Other areas of the country report a similar phenomenon of immigrant suburbanization, where in many cases, new arrivals bypass the large city entirely (see Box 8.7).

The third wave is rewriting the immigrant experience in a fourth and final way. The behavior of new arrivals challenges the melting pot theory. Many immigrants remain isolated in ethnic enclaves by choice. Affluent Asians, in particular, have not cut their ties with the homeland. Instead, they visit it often as part of business as well as to connect with intimates. According to one report, foreign governments have increasingly recognized the presence of native born individuals in countries overseas as important for both investment and the transfer of technology (Weiner, 1985). The growing Little Koreas, Chinatowns, and Hispanic sectors of cities are retaining their character and resisting integration. They are the new ethnic enclaves that will continue to provide diversity across the metropolitan region.

In the years to come the new sources of ethnicity will produce influences on U.S. culture that we have yet to anticipate, just as the formidable influx some eighty years ago once did. For example, as we shall discuss in Chapter 11, new immigrants have changed the complexion of metropolitan politics. Only time will tell what other forms this influence will take, but immigration from Asia and Latin America to the United States continues its active pace in the 1990s.

Summary

Years ago it was proper to speak of an urban mosaic in order to capture the diversity of people and lifestyles in the city. Today it is appropriate to define the entire metropolitan region, both cities and suburbs, in these terms. As we have seen, regional space is stratified by class, race, and gender. It is also differentiated according to ethnicity and age of population. Each lifestyle manifests its own daily rhythm in space. The built environment displays the expressive symbols of this interaction between social factors and local territory. But in addition, settlement space directs behavior in certain ways. Female gender roles, for example, are conditioned as much by spatial restrictions as by patriarchal domination. Sociospatial relations also condition class and race distinctions which range from exclusion to the extreme case of ghettoization.

Economic and political factors influence sociospatial patterns, but so do cultural features. Class, racial, gender, and ethnic differences are expressed as symbols that *mean* difference. The images of a large home, an expensive car, certain styles of clothing, and patterns of everyday consumption are potent signs of status. Racial segregation operates strongly through the regulation of appearance. Gender and ethnic differences are largely symbolic. This semiotic dimension of the sociospatial perspective will be discussed more fully in the next chapter.

The diversity of metropolitan life has been studied in great detail. In fact, such explorations of the everyday texture of urban and suburban lives constitute a central focus for the work of urban sociologists. There is a variety of methodological perspectives that are employed in the study of everyday life, including participant observation, interviews, network analysis, and semiotics. Let us consider these next.

CHAPTER

9

NEIGHBORHOODS, THE PUBLIC ENVIRONMENT, AND THEORIES OF URBAN LIFE

Film directors usually establish a Manhattan location by filming a long shot of some busy street in Midtown or the financial district. In it we see a crowd of people pressed together—a sea of bobbing heads hurrying on their way to and from business. To establish the location of Los Angeles, in contrast, film makers will often take to the air and provide a helicopter shot of clogged freeways, or, at other times, shoot from a car moving slowly on palm tree-lined streets.

Different images reflect spatial differences. Locale, or the sense of place, matters. Preparing ourselves for a trip to New York would involve special things, such as acquiring a rudimentary understanding of the bus and subway systems. For a trip to Los Angeles, preparations would be somewhat different and would certainly involve, for example, arranging for auto transport and learning something about the freeways. A visit to most suburbs would also be different, yet closer to the Los Angeles experience than to New York City. In the suburbs we need to be driven about to get to shopping or entertainment that is not close at hand after a short walk as it is in the city, but attainable only after a drive to shopping centers or malls.

Suppose we took a trip to a large city—Chicago, for example. What would we do there? Figure 9.1 lists some of the activities Chicago has to offer:

A trip to Chicago or any other large United States city would also require preparation for unpleasant things. Chicago is one of the most racially segregated cities. It has a high murder rate—25 per 100,000 people—about the same as Los Angeles and New

---

What to do in Chicago

Population (1989): city: 2,992,000; metro area: 6,177,000

Museums   Chicago has many world famous museums, including the Museum of Science and Industry, a center for the study of science and engineering; and the Chicago Art Museum, which is known for its modern European and American collections.

Music   We could go to a concert by the Chicago Symphony Orchestra. There is great jazz in the city—the Chicago School of jazz, otherwise known as Dixieland, was invented here in the 1920s. There is also great popular music: Junior Walker and Bo Diddley are native sons, and what about the rock group "Chicago"?

Zoo   Lincoln Park Zoo in Chicago is world famous. In the 1950s a TV show about animals originated from there, *Zoo Parade*.

Night Life   Lots of restaurants and bars (did you see the movie *About Last Night?*). There is a Greektown, a Chinatown, a Mexican section, and French, Polish, Jewish, and Middle Eastern restaurants.

Scenery   The Sears Tower is the tallest inhabited building in the world, standing 1,454 feet or 110 stories high. Chicago is on Lake Michigan, which is the third largest of the Great Lakes.

Sports   How can you beat seeing the Chicago Bulls (basketball), Bears (football), Cubs or White Sox (baseball), and Blackhawks (hockey)?

Figure 9.1   What to do in Chicago.

York, but not as high as either Detroit or Houston (see Chapter 10). Many of the downtown streets and parks are not safe after dark, compared to small towns or suburbs. It would be necessary to take precautions against muggers, particularly if you were a tourist and didn't know your way around.

In short, cities have a lot to offer, most of which is fun. In fact, every place possesses some distinguishing feature that can be enjoyed, whether it is the picturesque quality and friendly people of a small town, the quiet and spaciousness of the suburbs, or the hustle and bustle of the large city. A resident of the metropolitan region has a choice on any given day whether to experience the cultural amenities of urban or suburban life. These opportunities are mainly a function of the activities or features that are found in particular places, such as cities or suburbs, rather than arising from the particular environment of a city or suburb itself. But many urban sociologists insist that the nature of space does produce differences in behavior on its own so that the city, any city, would influence behavior in specific ways.

The arguments, both pro and con, regarding whether city or suburban living has the ability to change behavior constitute the focus for the study of metropolitan culture. These discussions make up a considerable part of the contents of urban sociology; that is, investigations of urban and suburban ways of life compose a large part of research work by sociologists. In Chapter 6 we studied the early contributions of sociologists to the study of urbanism, particularly those associated with the Chicago School, which focused exclusively on the city. In this chapter let us consider more contemporary studies that have explored the relationship between spatial location and social interaction for all communities in the metropolitan region, including suburbs and cities.

Does Space Affect Behavior? The Search for Community

Early urban sociologists in the 1920s and 1930s were preoccupied with whether the city produced differences in behavior, specifically when contrasted with the rural way of life. One reason for this interest was that at the time, hundreds of thousands of people left the farms and small towns of America and moved to the large industrial cities looking for work. At that time sociologists worked with an image of small town life that idealized it somewhat, and were suspicious of the city. They believed that small towns offered people a sense of community as manifested in the domination of primary or intimate ties in social relationships. In contrast, cities were viewed by early researchers as destroyers of intimacy and as forcing secondary or anonymous relations on individuals, with a consequent loss of community feeling. In contrast to the "friendly" rural town, city people were supposed to be unfriendly, rushed, uncaring, suspicious, and hard to get to know.

As we also saw in Chapter 6, Louis Wirth, of the Chicago School, went a bit further with this contrast that helped feed an antiurban bias. Wirth believed that living in large cities in particular resulted in forms of social disorganization such as increased crime, divorce, and mental illness because of the decline of close community ties (see Chapter 10). For Wirth it was the city itself, operating through demographic factors such as size and density of population, that produced characteristic urban behavior. According to Wirth, when we go to a store in a city we do not have nor do we seek a close relationship with the salesperson. We simply want service and wish to get what we want to buy as quickly as possible. Rural area residents, in contrast, may have the

"A Vision of Urban Anonymity," by Richard Tooker. Contrast this with the photo on page 190.

opportunity to establish primary relations with local businesses. The same contrast applies to relations with neighbors in the two different locations. As a consequence of the domination of secondary relations in the city, Wirth believed, negative effects would result, such as crime and other interactive problems. This assertion is known as the *social disorganization* thesis of urban life.

Field Research on Community

In the United States after 1950, urban life was not as disruptive as it was during Wirth's time, because of the decline of immigration compared to the turn of the century. A number of sociologists decided to challenge Wirth's theory. Studying local neighborhoods within the larger cities, sociologists were able to discover communities with strong primary relations among the residents (Whyte, 1955; Gans, 1962). What followed in the 1960s and 1970s was a series of case studies on various communities which contradicted the social disorganization thesis of the early Chicago School. Researchers discovered vital, healthy *primary* relations located within urban boundaries and the fostering of local community life. Ulf Hannerz's (1969) remarkable study of an inner city ghetto area in Washington, D.C., exemplifies the case study approach to community. This fine-grained analysis depicts ghetto residents as multidimensional human beings, trapped in the ghetto by racism and poverty. Hannerz could not find a single, characteristic ghetto resident. Rather he discovered a typology of behavioral patterns reflecting differences in individual character and family organization as each person dealt with racial and economic adversity in his or her own way. These results were replicated in other, more recent research (see Anderson, 1990).

From the outside, densely populated inner city neighborhoods seem chaotic. One of the sterling accomplishments of field research has been to document the order wrested from urban chaos by city residents. A classic field study discussed in Box 9.1 was carried out by Herbert J. Gans (1962). Gans challenged the view that the area was a "slum" and discovered that life in this working-class community of Boston was highly organized around peer groups. Adult males spent leisure time with other males, adult females with their female friends, and so on. Once the form of social organization of the community was understood, it became a familiar place. As explained in Box 9.1, the insights for Gans' conclusions were obtained using the methodology of field or participant observation research.

Field research carried out in the 1950s and 1960s in the suburbs also supported the view that all residents had access to primary relations and an intimate community life, even though suburban lifestyles differed somewhat from what was depicted as urban. One of the earliest studies of suburban communities was William H. Whyte's *Organization Man* (1956). For more recent examples see Baumgartner (1988), Jackson (1985), and Fishman (1987). Whyte depicted the classic suburb of the time as a place where nuclear families were housed in single-family, detached homes; where women did not work but spent their time with housekeeping chores and chats over coffee with neighbors; and where men commuted into the city to corporate, professional jobs.

While city based analyses tended to choose the working classes or "ethnics" with extended familial ties to kin and neighbors who lived in close proximity (see Box 9.1),

BOX 9.1 FIELD WORK METHODOLOGY

The methodological approach known as *field work* always situates observations within a particular space and time. A distinguishing feature of field work is that investigators get to know residents intimately because they often live among them for an extended period of time. They also get to know the space well and often supplement observations of behavior by describing the space in which it occurs. Field work is based on the systematic writing of notes that describe in as much detail as possible the day-to-day experience of participant observation. All descriptions, examples, impressions, and conclusions of research must be based on these extensive notes which the researcher guards carefully as the record of investigation.

Herbert J. Gans' (1962) study of a poor Italian neighborhood is a classic. Before Gans' study, the common conception of such areas was that they were slums and that the people living in them needed the aid of middle-class professionals in order to overcome their problems. Such conclusions were reached from afar. Gans, in contrast, actually lived in a so-called slum area, which is what field work is all about. His perception of the "slum" changed quickly from the initial impressions of an outsider to those of one who is intimately familiar with the environment. During his field experience Gans was able to learn that our "outsider's" view of such areas is misguided:

> My first visit to the West End left me with the impression that I was in Europe. Its high buildings set on narrow, irregularly curving streets, its Italian and Jewish restaurants and food stores, and the variety of people who crowded the streets when the weather was good—all gave the area a foreign and exotic flavor. . . . Looking at the area as a tourist, I noted the highly visible and divergent characteristics that set it off from others with which I was familiar.
>
> After a few weeks of living in the West End, my observations—and my perception of the area—changed drastically. The search for an apartment quickly indicated that the individual units were usually in much better condition than the outside or the hallways of the buildings. Subsequently, in wandering through the West End, and in using it as a resident, I developed a kind of selective perception, in which my eye focused only on those parts of the area that were actually being used by people. Vacant buildings and boarded-up stores were no longer so visible, and the totally deserted alleys or streets were outside the set of paths normally traversed, either by myself or by the West Enders.
>
> Since much of the area's life took place on the street, faces became familiar very quickly. I met my neighbors on the stairs and in front of my building. . . . In short, the exotic quality of the stores and the residents also wore off as I became used to seeing them (Gans, 1962: 12).

suburban studies concentrated on the middle-class nuclear family and its communal relations among friends. This division of labor gave the false impression that the classes had stratified in space to an extreme between cities and suburbs. More recently life in both cities and suburbs has been documented in increasing complexity with multiple classes living in the same city and far greater diversity of lifestyles, as we have already seen in Chapter 8.

In sum, after several decades of comparative field work it is clear that cities and suburbs are home to a variety of lifestyles, as the sociospatial perspective suggests, which are more a function of the complex interplay between class, ethnicity, race, and gender than a result of living in a particular environment. Does this conclusion mean that location has no effect whatsoever on personal behavior? Field research tended to debunk the social disorganization thesis of urban life, but another method, network analysis, discovered conditions under which location did play a specific role in people's lives. Let us consider this research tradition next.

Network Analysis: Does Location Matter?

In the 1970s Claude Fischer (1975) claimed that while most of the differences between individuals in the metropolis were caused by background factors such as class and race, there were attributes of behavior that differed among people according to their location. In particular, because of the size of urban populations, residents of the large city were provided with the opportunity to act in ways that rural residents would ordinarily find more difficult. According to this *subcultural perspective* on urban life, people in the city have a greater opportunity to establish relations with a greater variety of people than do those in places with smaller populations. It is these relationships or *networks* that sustain differences in lifestyles observed between city and rural dwellers. Hence, according to Fischer, the subcultural diversity of cities created by large population size does produce differences between urban and rural behaviors.

Following the subcultural perspective, Fischer (1982) documented the effect of location on the quality and structure of personal networks. Individuals in the city, it was found, differed from rural counterparts because they had fewer kin or more unrelated intimates in their personal networks. However, Fischer also discovered that the effect of place alone, when controlling for all other factors, *was quite small.* The single most important predictor of non-kin networks was education: the more years of education, the more nonrelatives in an individual's personal network. A second important factor was income, which also contributed to independence from relatives. Thus, while location does play a role in influencing behavior, it is not as powerful as are the *compositional* factors related to education, income, and other social considerations that we have already discussed in Chapter 8. Box 9.2 illustrates the network methodology used by Fischer and others to show the differences that location makes in lifestyle patterns.

Network analysis has uncovered a second important aspect of urban community relations. As the metropolitan environment of cities and suburbs has matured, people now organize their lives across a greater spatial distance than in the past. Among other things this means that one's intimate relations may involve people at some distance. While community still exists, according to the network analyst Barry Wellman (1988), it may not be composed of one's neighbors. Rather, today we have relations with people without propinquity (i.e., nearness). Network researchers who have studied this more mature phenomenon of U.S. settlement spaces have, therefore, redefined our understanding of community, because in the past, people assumed that you were most friendly with those who live near you as neighbors. According to Wellman (1979;

BOX 9.2 NETWORK ANALYSIS

Network analysis studies individuals rather than the kind of group contexts that are characteristic of field work. Using personal interviews it seeks to discover the links between people—who they interact with on a daily or weekly basis, whether one person's close friend also feels the same way about him/her, how many people a single individual knows, and so on. This method is compared to a chain letter by the anthropologist Ulf Hannerz:

> We are probably all familiar with chain letters. You receive a letter from somebody instructing you to send something—money, a picture postcard, or whatever—to the person at the top of a given list, then remove that name while adding your own at the bottom of the list, and finally pass the new list with instructions along to some number of persons whom you choose yourself. If everything worked according to plan, the chains would rapidly branch out, so that for your trouble you would in due time get a sizable number of responses from others, perhaps people personally unknown to you. But frequently . . . you get nothing at all, because somewhere along the line there are people with no wish to participate (Hannerz, 1980: 163).

Network analysis can give us composite pictures of community relations which may contrast with differences in other regions or even other countries. In short, through network analysis of individuals we can learn many things about the nature of the community in which they live. For example, according to Herbert and Johnston:

> In order to resolve the most fundamental confusion in the notions of the social network and to relate it to more traditional notions of the community, it is necessary to distinguish between *structure* (which is what "close" and "loose" usually are taken to describe) and what we will here call *plexity*. Plexity may be simply understood as the degree of complexity of the connection. . . . If we combine these two, we arrive at a simple typology of the range of social milieux, of local situations in which individuals and families find themselves [see Figure 9.2 below].
>
> A is a traditional community as normally understood: social relationships are multiplex in that, for example, neighbors are workmates, are kinsmen, are leisure-time companions, and the social network has a dense structure in that everyone knows everyone else.
>
> B is a situation of the idealized urban anonymous anomie: social relationships are uniplex (the taxi driver and his fare), fleeting, impersonal and anonymous, and the social network structure is single-stranded in that only one person knows the others (Herbert and Johnston, 1976: 198).

		Structure		
		Dense	Loose Knit	Single
	multiplex	A		
Plexity	simplex			
	uniplex			B

Figure 9.2 Structure and plexity in social networks.

1988), the concept of community must be rethought to emphasize the nonneighborhood basis of personal ties. People's communities consist of networks that are not spatially distinct but which are dispersed across the metropolis and the country.

In sum, current research using network analysis on community relations suggests that while spatial location matters, its effects are *not* large. Social or *compositional* factors such as class, education, gender, and race are most important when explaining urban behavior, as we have seen in Chapter 8. But network researchers only look at the role of space in a very specific way. Hence, they miss some important influences of the environment. The approach advocated in this book, the *sociospatial perspective,* improves on the limitations of network findings by conceiving of the influence of space in a broader, more general way while acknowledging the central role played by social factors. In what follows we shall consider the role of space in social interaction and highlight how the environment interacts with compositional factors, as the sociospatial perspective suggests. I shall discuss the new theory of urbanism and illustrate it with a look at several issues in which spatial or contextual factors count heavily in our understanding of urban and suburban behavior.

Does Space Affect Behavior? A New Theory of Urbanism

The Sociospatial Approach to Metropolitan Culture

The preceding sections have reviewed perspectives on urbanism. Previous research has drawn conclusions from the historical conditions of the time. Wirth observed the city of the 1920s and 1930s when the United States was still experiencing a large rural-to-urban migration. Fischer (1976) made his claims about city/rural differences when that distinction still mattered (prior to 1970) and when suburbs were only recently maturing, a condition that has changed today.

In Chapter 5 we have seen that suburbs have steadily matured and possess patterns of life very much like those of the large city. Fischer's subcultural theory still argues for something unique about cities and neglects large suburbs. The suburban region of Orange County, for example, possesses as varied a subcultural life as is true of any large city, although twenty years ago it may have been less developed than the city (Kling, Olin, and Poster, 1991). Furthermore, entire suburbs, such as Monterey Park, California (see Chapter 8), have become ethnic enclaves, thereby adding to the subcultural diversity of suburban life.

While it is true that city residents enjoy more choices than do people living in lower density areas with regard to their respective circle of friends, this effect is explained best by income differences, because an individual must be able to afford to sustain a network of friends outside the immediate area. Hence, the effects of urbanism that are attributed to subcultural differences are also closely intertwined with the compositional effects of social factors, such as level of income, education, and race.

Today all areas of the metropolitan region have matured and achieved population diversity. Instead of discussing lifestyle differences as a function of urbanism, it makes increasingly more sense to adopt a metropolitan perspective and relate social differences to locational differences in the region. I suggest that lifestyles within the metropolitan region are explained best by a combination of compositional or social factors and the action of the environment. On the one hand, the population size and density of cities do play a role in producing distinctive lifestyles. However, this effect works through the action of space as well as through demographic factors. The quality of the environment conditions the opportunities available for distinctive lifestyles.

For example, Manhattan in New York City is known for its active street culture. Over 1 million inhabitants are squeezed onto an island that is less than 20 square miles in area. One aspect of Manhattan street behavior involves a strong emphasis on fashion and appearance as a way of judging other people (we shall discuss the phenomenon of fashion later). Consequently, New York subcultures possess a highly developed sense of clothing differences. By contrast, Los Angeles dress is notoriously casual. It is not uncommon to see people appearing at fancy restaurants in the least formal attire. Los Angelenos stress the importance of cars in everyday life, and several subcultures have developed around the use of the automobile as an expressive symbol, such as the Chicano lowrider cults. The city of Los Angeles encompasses almost 1,000 square miles, and public transportation is limited. Consequently, it is understandable to find cars playing so important a role in daily life. Manhattan is a pedestrian town while Los Angeles is notorious for its reliance on the automobile, and this helps explain some of the cultural differences between the two places, although there are also other reasons, such as historical and demographic differences.

Second, in addition to the influence of spatial environment on behavior, people's actions are organized according to how they view particular places. The built environment, like other objects in society, possesses a social *meaning*. That is, place or location has a symbolic value that counts in determining behavior. For example, Hummon (1986) did a comparative study of big city, suburban, and small-town residents, using a questionnaire and interview method (see Box 9.3). He discovered that individuals in each location possessed different imagery by which they reinforced their own positive feelings about where they lived and negative feelings about alternative locations. For the most part, residents of big cities, suburbs, and small towns each participated in the construction of positive images of place, rather than all subscribing to some antiurban bias or some universal desire to escape the city for either the suburbs or a small town. Box 9.3 illustrates this third method for studying settlement spaces, namely, interviews or questionnaire analysis.

Third, while all individuals possess a distinctive lifestyle which is based in part on their collectively held symbolic values, they are also constrained by material factors, such as income, in determining where to live or locate economic activity. People in cities and suburbs selectively locate in different areas of the metropolitan region according to both their symbolic and material needs. Some of this selection is voluntary, but in the cases of family income and race, where you choose to live can be where you can afford or where you are allowed to live. As we have seen, residential location can also be an involuntary choice that is dictated by racial or ethnic factors, hence the creation of ghettos and reservations.

In the last chapter we demonstrated the importance of symbolic factors to the patterns of metropolitan life. Let us conclude this chapter by analyzing in more detail how symbolic processes and the sense of place are related to people's behavior in cities and suburbs. I shall examine three aspects of the semiotics of space, including mental maps, the spatial context and behavior in public, and the sense of community.

Mental Maps and the Semiotics of Place

Mental Maps. Cities and suburbs are not only spaces where people organize their lives; they are also physical environments that are *meaningful.* People impute distinct meanings and associate specific emotions with places. Often a single space, such as the New York City skyline, can invoke an incredible variety of such meaningful associations from individuals. The signifier *home,* for example, is attached to the place of residence but it can also signify the block where you live, your neighborhood, or a section of the metropolitan region where your particular living space is located. All the feelings of comfort, security, and familiarity that might be associated with your house or apartment are often also elicited by returning from a trip outside the neighborhood and by glimpsing the familiar objects of the local environment. Sociologists and other urbanists who study the role of meaning and cognition in space use the method of mental mapping which is augmented by the approach of semiotics. A discussion of mental mapping is outlined in Box 9.4.

People negotiate through a metropolitan space of familiar neighborhoods, known work places, leisure and consumption places, and unfamiliar gray areas of little specific meaning. Known places are pictured in great detail by the mind's eye. In between them are gray areas that are not distinctly detailed. These gray areas are negotiated by direct travel routes so that residents pass through them spending the least amount of time possible. Consequently, these zones remain undistinguished. All people, in short, carry with them a "mental map" of their weekly routines that varies in its detailed knowledge of space. We use these maps to negotiate through space and to assign meanings to different places. Often, these maps are a function of power and class differences or social stratification.

The study of mental maps helps augment our understanding of how individuals relate to metropolitan environments containing large numbers of people and differentiated activities. Kevin Lynch (1960), a planner, discovered that variation exists among individuals regarding how they depict a space, but in addition, that places themselves vary with regard to their ability to invoke detailed mental images. Thus, a city with an impressive skyline or distinguishing statues and buildings produces an image that is remembered by visitors and residents alike. In contrast, many places seem so ordinary that their physical appearance is hard to recall even after repeated visits.

Lynch's discovery of the importance of *imageability* implied that some spaces were *better* designed than others because they were more legible; that is, they were easier to understand as built environments. Imageability, therefore, facilitated movement or use. For example, Lynch contrasted the mental maps of residents in two cities— Jersey City, New Jersey; and Boston, Massachusetts. He found that residents of the former, when compared with the latter, had a much less detailed mental image of their space. It was harder for them to visualize the features of places they often passed or went to during the week's routines. Lynch's discovery has important consequences for city planners, architects, and landscapers, as we shall see in Chapter 14.

BOX 9.3 QUESTIONNAIRE AND INTERVIEW METHOD

David Hummon (1986) wanted to test the images of place in different communities. He chose a large city, San Francisco, and three other places in the same area of Northern California, including a middle-class suburb, a working-class suburb, and a small town. It was necessary to study a variety of communities in order to obtain a comparative analysis. Hummon chose an equal number of households at random in each of the four cities from lists using census tract data and field observations to ensure diversity of classes. Because most of the communities were white, he excluded black neighborhoods within the central city in order to control for race. As he states:

> This ensured that urban residents did not differ significantly in minority background from suburban and small-town residents. Households were sent a letter describing the research; up to four call-backs were made to locate residents and this led to slightly over half of the selected households.
>
> The interview focused on issues of community belief and sentiment and utilized open- and closed-ended questions. The former were emphasized to ensure considerable spontaneity, complexity, and richness in responses. Interviews typically lasted one hour and fifteen minutes and, with the permission of the respondents, were taped and transcribed for analysis (1986: 6).

Hummon classified his responses according to whether the interviewees were "pro-urban," "ambivalent or indifferent about where they lived," or "anti-urban." His results are given in Table 9.1, adopted from this study.

TABLE 9.1
Sentimental Posture toward City by Place of Residence

| | Place of residence | | |
Posture	Large city	Suburbs	Small town
Pro-urban	62	15	0
Ambivalent	31	42	25
Anti-urban	8	42	76
Total	101%	99%	101%

In Table 9.1 interviewees were asked several questions regarding preference for locations—the city, the town, and the suburb. The results suggest that where you live *does* influence in a positive way how you feel about your location. The majority of small-town residents reflected anti-urban feelings; residents of a large city (San Francisco) were very pro-urban; while suburbanites were as ambivalent about the city as they were anti-urban. If Hummon were concerned with pursuing a cultural analysis of these results he could have gone further in understanding them. In particular, people probably value where they live because that place has important, personal meanings. Thus, attachment to place involves both social and spatial factors, as semiotics shows (see Box 9.4).

BOX 9.4 THE METHOD OF MENTAL MAPS

The technique of mental mapping is used to discover how residents of any given place conceive of their environment. They are asked to draw their own local neighborhoods and fill the picture in as detailed a way as possible. Studies are done by obtaining mental maps from a sample of residents. In all cases the conception of place will vary from person to person. Researchers study the causes of such variation. For example, the way children draw mental maps of their environment differs from adult maps. Researchers have also uncovered racial differences in the way people conceive of their local space. In one study of the Mission Hill area of Boston, which contains a housing project inhabited primarily by poor African Americans surrounded by a white community, it was discovered that the black residents' view of their environment was greatly restricted and confined, while comparable white residents possessed a much more expansive image of their surroundings (LaGory and Pipkin, 1981: 119). It was concluded by the researchers that minority status also confines people in space because of anxiety about venturing beyond racially mixed areas. This kind of territorial anxiety is also felt by women in the big city, as we discussed in Chapter 8, and felt by people in general because of the increase in random street crime (see Chapter 10).

One of the more common results from mental map research is the discovery that differences in both the conception and meaning of local place are correlated to differences in class status (Golledge and Ruston, 1976). In general, differences in the conception of space reflect social stratification or the felt differences regarding power and class in society. The anthropologist Claude Lévi-Strauss, for example, examined the conception of space among the Winnebago Native-American tribe of the Great Lakes region. Figure 9.3 illustrates his powerful findings which indicate that even traditional societies display status differences regarding the conception of place.

The Semiotics of Place. Mental maps assign meaning to space. But the meaning of objects also comes from the various ways we use them as symbols. Material forms, such as particular buildings and constructed spaces like plazas and freeways, all possess meanings that are ascribed to them by social use. They are known to us by their functions, as the study of spatial semiotics suggests (Barthes, 1986). Hence, the phenomenon of the mental map is but a special case of the more general semiotics of settlement space. Malls, theme parks, architectural forms, and neighborhood places all work to orient our behavior and provide us with a sense of place by conveying certain meanings through objects that act as signs of their function as places of business, recreation, amusement, shopping, and the like. Instead of strangeness and disorientation, the signs of space create order and familiarity, which is so helpful both in reducing the stress of daily living within giant, metropolitan regions and in enabling residents to *use* the built environment effectively.

For example, the suburban shopping mall is a successful adaptation of architectural form to the needs of commercial interests. Malls are the counterpart in low density suburbia of the higher density city center shopping district. The mall works because

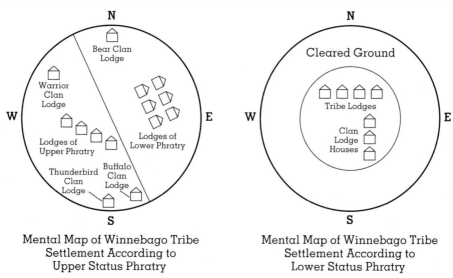

Mental Map of Winnebago Tribe
Settlement According to
Upper Status Phratry

Mental Map of Winnebago Tribe
Settlement According to
Lower Status Phratry

Figure 9.3 Contrasting mental maps according to status in the Winnebago tribe. Adopted from C. Lévi-Strauss, 1963.

Lévi-Strauss (1963: 129) found that the Winnebago tribe was split between two statuses. The higher status people were called the *wangeregi,* or "those who are above," and the lower status people were called the *manegi,* or "those who are on earth." The higher status people drew mental maps of their village which divided it in half according to this status difference. Most of the clan lodges were contained in the upper status half, thereby segregating the *manegi* from powerful institutions. In contrast, the lower status residents made no such distinction. They saw their village (the same village) as unsegregated and composed of two concentric circles. The lodges were contained in the center along with the residential units.

of its skillful use of symbols and signs coupled with environmental forms. Malls are designed with large parking lots and blank external facades that do not distract customers but make them respond to the overarching meaning—"for shopping related activities, enter here." This technique, known as *introversion,* is meant to discourage prospective customers from dawdling in the mall parking lot. On the inside are located additional semiotic devices that control shoppers. Malls usually are organized with some overarching theme. They feature atriums, "food courts," even amusement rides for children. Often they are designed with images that invoke city living—avenues with artificial street lamps and small, neatly spaced trees and benches; and because all shoppers are on foot, they provide inhabitants with a taste of the typical urban street crowd.

Corporate product signs or "logos" are also important in the mall. They label stores or products. Each store has its own symbolic and functional associations that are the consequence of advertising and of what customers know about its price range. Product signs or brand name logos also take advantage of the fact that people have already been conditioned by advertising to associate certain products with store signs. That is, by watching TV or reading magazines, we have all been subjected to advertising

A two-story suburban shopping mall.

that links a product with its sign, and these internalized associations are then used to advantage in the mall by directing our attention to specific stores or products. They hold such power only because we have already become familiar with them in our daily lives, so that we respond to their stimulus and are oriented in our journey through the mall.

Using these various logos, and with the aid of the advertising and theme signs that pepper the mall, customers are able to "read" the space of the mall and make their way through it with ease so that shopping is as stressless as it can be. An example of the way malls manage their environments using appropriate objects as signs is provided by Box 9.5.

Behavior in Public Space

For many years urban sociologists have been aware that the large city with its dense crowds offers special challenges to residents. They have studied the way people negotiate this particular environment, and have found that the techniques of accommodation that are used comprise much of what we might identify as uniquely *urban* behavior. Yet this interaction, which takes place in *public* space where strangers as pedestrians encounter others in places such as malls, department stores, and bars, also occurs in suburbia. For this reason, the study of behavior in public space can take place throughout the metropolitan region and can involve the interaction of people as pedestrians or as drivers/passengers in cars.

Behavior in public depends on the proper expression, interpretation, and negotiation of signs between people interacting with each other and with the built environment. This semiotic aspect of city and suburban living is quite essential to daily life, as the

BOX 9.5 SWADDLING SHOPPERS: A MALL'S COCOON EFFECT

When Richard arrives for work at the mall, he first removes the silver loop with the tiny skull that usually hangs from his earlobe and that definitely does not say "hi." Then he slips into the crisp white shirt of a mall security officer with the blue sergeant's stripes and the gold badge.

The transformation to a reassuring look from a menacing one is something like putting on a costume. But [Richard] and the other security guards at the Danbury Fair Mall here often seem to be playing parts, as interested in the perception as they are in the reality of safety at the mall. "We're the incarnation of a warm safe feeling," [the] Sergeant said, with his skull earring out, the other day. . . . It is as important for shoppers to feel safe as it is for them to be safe (Glaberson, 1992: A10).

sociospatial perspective suggests. According to Anderson, for example, interaction in the public space of a large city requires "street smarts":

One gains street wisdom through a long and sometimes arduous process that begins with a certain "uptightness" about the urban environment, with decisions based on stereotypes and simple rules of public etiquette. Given time and experience, the nervousness and fear give way to a recognition that street life involves situations that require selective and individualized responses—in this complicated environment, applying broad stereotypes simply will not do (1990: 6).

Social psychologists who have studied this interaction in public insist that *all* behavior is interpreted according to the particular spatial context. That is, we interpret someone's actions based on the space where it occurred (Karp, Stone, and Yoels, 1977); hence behavior is a combination of social and spatial factors. If we saw two men fighting each other in a park, we would be concerned and might call the police. The very same action placed inside a boxing arena would be considered entertainment. Thus, we decide how to interpret the behavior of others, which is essential to determining our own behavior, in part by interpreting space as a context for action. In short, spatial context has a very powerful role in the patterning of behavior in public.

Spatial context also determines how individuals behave toward each other. In a classic study, the sociologist Erving Goffman (1963: 36) observed that when ordinary situations become extraordinary, interaction rules between complete strangers in the city change, and they might begin to act intimately. Thus, if a subway train gets stalled, the normally silent passengers might suddenly talk to those strangers sitting next to them about the incident. In a study on bystanders (Darley and Latane, 1970), it was discovered that urbanites are not by nature blasé about other people's troubles on the street. But when an incident occurs, the more bystanders there are to witness it, the less the likelihood that any single one will intervene. Because of the density of city crowds, social responsibility is spread so thin that bystanders may not get involved even when they witness a serious breach of behavior. This phenomenon sometimes makes us wonder about the perceived weakness of social links between people living in large cities. It also suggests that the social disorganization perceived by Chicago

A crowded street in the Wall Street section of Manhattan, New York.

School researchers may have been a temporary or short-term product of spatial context rather than an innate or permanent change in people's behavior produced by the move to the city.

Darley and Latane (1970) applied this insight to explain the behavior of bystanders in the now infamous Queens, New York, case of Kitty Genovese, who was stabbed to death despite her repeated screams for help which were heard by thirty-eight of her neighbors. According to this study, no one intervened because of the sociospatial context, that is, the large number of bystanders who all felt that others bore a greater responsibility for responding to crime.

The most distinctive aspect of city life involves interaction with large numbers of strangers. Whom to trust and whom not to, how to act in a crowd, how to react to people you do not know, and how to interact with strangers in shops, restaurants, museums, and on the street constitutes a major aspect of the metropolitan resident's set of behaviors, whether living in the city or the suburbs. As in other cases, signs and meaningful clues make a difference in the way people feel about and act in public space. Some researchers, for example, have studied interaction with strangers as a problem that can bring unattractive consequences from poor judgment in "reading" the sociospatial context. For example, J. Henslin (1972) studied cab drivers in a big city and discovered that their lives might depend on the way they size up a prospective fare. They do not always stop for everyone. Experiencing this, many African Americans find it difficult to get cabs at night regardless of how wealthy they may be. Also, because many taxi drivers will not travel to ghetto areas or accept fares that do not possess the proper appearance, the unlicensed or "gypsy" cabs have appeared as an alternative industry that has become the ghetto residents' taxi of last resort. Gypsy cabs are part of the informal economy of the city (see Chapter 5), and they involve some risks because they usually have no insurance and do not have to comply with industry regulations.

Appearance and fashion have always figured prominently in the types of judgments people make when dealing with strangers, especially in public space. Goffman (1963) regards the way we look as providing the most concise and meaningful cues to guide the interaction of others in the city (but we can add: the suburbs, too!). In dealing with strangers, fashion provides us with a way to "read" such things as class standing, lifestyle interests, and even whether or not an individual poses a threat to us. As discussed earlier, in large cities with dense pedestrian environments people are more attuned to fashion than in other places such as Los Angeles where automobiles dominate, although there may be several reasons why this is true.

The spatial context is just as important in the organization of suburban life as it is in the city. Instead of subways or buses, for example, suburbanites contend with cars and car pools. When organized privately, the latter involve people who are acquaintances that share driving to work, shopping, school, and recreational activities. Unlike individuals riding in city mass transportation—buses or subways, for example—people in carpools feel compelled to be friendly. It is the sociospatial context and not the proximity of one commuter to another that makes the difference. Yet for carpoolers, being friendly at 6:00 A.M. with little sleep and a full day of work ahead may be a difficult chore. Consequently, car pools have never been as popular as they could be. Recently, a novelist described the hell suburban mothers go through while chauffeuring children around town to and from schools, doctors, shopping, and friends. "With three children in three different schools, she [the heroine of the novel] lives most of her life now in her Honda hatchback. There is no one to talk to but her slobbering dog, which resides in the back seat, and she longs for a drive-in window at the local psychiatric hospital" (Lawson, 1991: C-1).

Neighboring and Community

Perhaps the most characteristic behavior of suburbia is said to be neighboring. Yet this is a phenomenon of the city as well. Only when we speak in generalities can we say that dwellers in large cities know fewer of their neighbors than do residents of smaller places. Most neighboring tends to be done by people raising families. Hence, the stereotypical image of suburbia as a place of neighboring may be based on fact, because families with small children prefer to live there. However, when we look more closely at the city, we can find instances of intense neighboring, such as in the ethnic communities studied by Gans (1962) and others (see Box 9.1). Consequently, spatial location is important for neighboring networks in a variety of metropolitan settings. This topic is another illustration of the important relationship between spatial settings and social processes that is essential to the sociospatial perspective.

Neighboring studies are important because they are related to the issue of community and territory. There is a certain conception of everyday life which places individuals within a nurturing neighborhood of friends and relatives. This conjunction of a certain space with an intimate circle of primary relations became the classic image of the community.

In a previous section, we saw that network researchers such as Wellman (1988) have called this image into question. Community is less dependent on territory and more a function of a network of friends and relatives dispersed in space. According to Fischer (1982), there is some variation in the extent to which local or dispersed networks exist for residents of cities. The territorial reach of friendship networks depends on the presence of *competing commitments*. That is, if an individual is relatively isolated and has few outside involvements, then that person would most likely be dependent on neighbors—it's all that's available. However, the more outside involvements an individual possesses, the less likely that the person will be tied to immediate neighbors. In short, according to the network perspective, neighboring and close ties to community space are a kind of residual effect produced when other, more attractive alternatives are not available.

Fischer's analysis pinpoints how choice of location affects individual network ties, but it is also remarkable for the way it de-emphasizes the effects of class, age, and gender as they are deployed in space—a relationship that is important to the sociospatial perspective. For example, elderly people living in the city are not physically capable of traveling long distances for companionship or help. They are dependent on their local community but they may also prefer things that way. Not everyone assertively seeks to find the most compatible network of people across the metropolitan region. In other cases, people may have an extensive network but may also retain a need for a local community. For example, single career women living in a large city may possess a robust network of friends living throughout the metropolis, but they find it uncomfortable to travel or dine alone. They, too, along with others, may find the need for a close-at-hand network of neighbors.

In reevaluating neighboring studies according to the sociospatial perspective, it is clear that middle-class males are the best candidates for possessing a community without locality, that is, nonspatially specific networks. In contrast, the poor, the elderly, some women, and most certainly, segregated minorities have closer ties to their immediate neighbors, and they are, therefore, the ones to whom community and the local territory of friendship relations matter most.

Other neighborhood researchers have remarked on the role of some of these factors neglected by the network perspective. Susanne Keller (1968), for example, indicates that community relations can be a function of class. She found that middle-class people have more casual acquaintances, while working-class individuals are more dependent on their neighbors. Another observer, Ida Susser (1982), carried out an important field study that clearly indicates the differential roles of class, race, and gender in fostering neighborhood ties. As the sociospatial perspective suggests, these factors operate symbolically and within a specific territory to make behavior meaningful.

Susser lived in and researched an industrial area of Brooklyn, New York. She makes the important point that many studies of neighboring networks aim for some universal results, while the role of community in people's lives very often depends on historical and social circumstances that are specific to places and local economies. The Greenpoint section of Brooklyn, for example, was a traditional working-class community containing several factories. Residents were very attached to their local space, which provided them with ethnic and religious resources such as Italian restaurants and churches with Polish-Catholic congregations. As with other communities of this type, the locals engaged in robust neighboring and mutual aid. Everyday life was organized within this particular space with the aid of expressive symbols of ethnic, racial, gender, and community status.

In addition to these historical circumstances, Susser also describes how the nature of neighboring was affected by the larger social context, in this case, the economic decline of New York City. In the 1960s and 1970s New York, like other industrialized and large cities, was afflicted by the steady decline in manufacturing that we studied in Chapter 5. New York City also experienced a terrible fiscal crisis in the 1970s when it almost ran out of money and credit (see Chapter 10). Adjusting to this dilemma required drastic declines in the city budget, with corresponding cutbacks in city services. As a result of the financial crisis, "municipal workers were laid off . . . city services were drastically cut, tuition was imposed at the City University of New York, and transportation fares were hiked 43 percent" (Susser, 1982: 11).

According to Susser, the changed social conditions increased the degree to which neighbors were dependent on each other. This was especially the case for women and minorities. As men were laid off from jobs, family life suffered. While it is true, as the network researchers might observe, that close ties to place were exhibited by those with limited "competing commitments," in this field study of Brooklyn we can see just how selective with regard to class, race, and gender the effect of "competing opportunities" (see Fischer, 1982) can be. Mothers with small children, poor people unable to afford transportation costs, and minorities trapped in ghetto areas were the least likely to take advantage of acquaintances outside the area, if, indeed, they had any. Instead, Susser observed how these besieged residents relied more heavily on neighbors for support.

This form of community involvement was intensified as individuals fought to protect their quality of life in the face of severe city service cuts due to the fiscal crisis of the city. Active mutual aid among neighbors gave rise to community political action. As Susser observes:

> Relying on community ties between neighbors and relatives, the working-class people I observed were constantly involved in local holding actions as they tried to influence political decisions that would affect their living standards. The formation of block associations, sit-ins to protest inadequate day care, and the occupation of buildings in reaction to the reduction of city services were frequent forms of political expression (1982: 6).

In short, the very general observations about neighboring which downplay attachment to local territory may disguise the specific needs of the poor, of women, and of minorities for strong communities. They may also obscure the actions taken by such groups to *create* strong communities, an interest that is very much a part of both city and suburban politics, as we shall discuss in Chapter 11.

In sum, the semiotic perspective aids our understanding of metropolitan culture by explicitly demonstrating the links between behavior and sociospatial context. All interaction is meaningful. People use expressive symbols to organize their daily life.

The range of signs includes spatial organization or context as well as the use of the common objects of our culture. As an ensemble, the collection of signs helps us to understand behavior in public space and aids in our own orientation to the built environment. It is upon this meaningful foundation that all interaction between people within the metropolitan milieu is based. The specific cultural mechanisms of sociospatial behavior that we have explored above include mental maps, the use of the built environment as expressive symbols, the mechanisms of interaction in public, and particular attachments to community or neighborhood territory.

This relationship between social interaction that is meaningful, community life, and the spatial context of the built environment has been studied best by researchers examining variation in the types of neighborhood relations among people living in cities and suburbs. In comparative studies of neighborhoods we learn about the significant ways the meanings attached to place interact with social or compositional factors of class, race, and gender. Hence they further illustrate the sociospatial perspective. Let us turn to these studies in the concluding section of this chapter.

Types of Neighborhoods and Community Interaction

Albert Hunter (1979: 269) defines the neighborhood as a "uniquely linked unit of social/spatial organization between the forces and institutions of the larger society and the localized routines of individuals in their daily lives." As we have already seen, you do not have to be neighborly to belong to a neighborhood. For Hunter, typologies of neighborhoods can describe local community life, but they neglect to indicate connections to the larger society. Good case studies of neighborhoods, in contrast, provide a glimpse of the links to sociospatial organization in the larger society, an approach very much in keeping with the perspective of this text. As Hunter remarks, "If one does not view the neighborhood within its [social] context, in short, one ends up with description, not explanation" (1979: 269).

Studies of neighborhoods or communities note great variation in the degree to which local residents are attached both to the area and to each other. In order to analyze this variation, researchers have constructed typologies of different communities based on local attachments. They suggest that in addition to rural, suburban, or urban location, there are considerable differences between *all* localities regarding the quality of neighborhood interaction.

Donald and Rachelle Warren (1977) have done the most work on sociospatial aspects of neighborhood typologies. They studied the way communities varied according to three distinct dimensions:

1. *Identity*—or how strong was the sense of connectedness to place; how much did people feel they shared with their neighbors?
2. *Interaction*—or how strong were the interactive ties to neighbors; did they visit often?
3. *Linkages*—or whether or not there were ties between the local area and the general area outside. What were the nature of these ties?

In short, by addressing each of these research questions, they attempted to specify the sociospatial connections to the larger social context.

On the basis of these dimensions the Warrens identified six types of communities: integral, parochial, diffuse, transitory, anomic, and stepping-stone. Their typology is useful because many case studies of community in urban sociology literature fit into one or another of these categories. Using the Warrens' typology as a guide but modifying it slightly to conform to community research carried out more recently yields the following six types. These categories are possibly applicable to suburbs as well as cities.

Ethnic Urban Village. This is very much like the Warrens' parochial community, in which a strong subcultural orientation dominates everyday life. This is a stable community with strong identity and considerable neighboring or interaction. However, the urban village tends to have weak ties to areas surrounding it and to the city as a whole. It does not always possess political influence.

Scores: identity—high, interaction—high, linkage—low. Examples: the classic study is Herbert J. Gans (1962), *The Urban Villagers.*

Interactive Middle-Class Neighborhood. Scores high on every dimension. Active neighboring coupled with a high degree of involvement in community associations. This community also has strong ties with city agencies and the PTA, and possesses active influence in the affairs of the city as a whole.

Children play while mothers watch and socialize in this inner city neighborhood.

Scores: identity—high, interaction—high, linkage—high. Examples: Most of the field study examples of this type come from early studies of suburban communities—Seeley, Sim, and Looseley's (1956) *Crestwood Heights;* and more recently, Baumgartner (1988), Fishman (1987).

Diffuse. The kind of neighborhood studied by network researchers. Here we have examples of community without neighboring. It is not very integrated but there is considerable interaction between residents and others, principally outside the area. Some of these places may possess a strong identity, but this is principally a function of real estate values and status.

Scores: identity—can be high, interaction—high, linkage—low. Examples: Barry Wellman (1988): Yorktown, Toronto.

Anomic. Characteristic of poor areas. This type of neighborhood has low voter turnout and weak community organizations. There is little connection between residents, who live in fear of crimes such as muggings, rapes, drug-related violence, and burglary.

Scores: identity—low, interaction—low, linkage—low. Examples: William J. Wilson (1987), *The Truly Disadvantaged;* Anderson (1990), *Streetwise.*

Transitory. Residents in this neighborhood are highly mobile. They live there for only enough time to acquire suitable resources to move elsewhere. While there may be some neighboring, community identity and linkages are weak.

Scores: identity—weak, interaction—can be high, linkages—weak. Example: Morris Janowitz coined the term the "community of limited liability" to characterize such areas. Many suburban communities would qualify (see Gottdiener, 1977).

In addition to the above types, there is a particular community phenomenon, known as the *defended neighborhood,* a sixth type that is of considerable interest to researchers. These are places that have become communities of high neighboring as a consequence of political action. At times this is temporary, but some communities manage to maintain the strong links to outside city agencies even after mobilization has declined. The example of the Greenpoint neighborhood in Brooklyn, New York, discussed earlier illustrates this phenomenon. According to Gerald Suttles (1973) the defended neighborhood closes itself off as a consequence of some external threat (such as an attempted move by a different racial or ethnic group into an area) or a city agency plan to modify the environment in some way (such as the construction of an incinerator or garbage dump). Defended neighborhoods usually attempt to forge strong links with city government in an effort to use political influence (Susser, 1982; Castells, 1983).

In sum, one way of examining community life involves the quality of local ties to others. There is great variation regarding the nature of these network ties. While it is true that people with alternatives seem to possess networks of intimates that are not constrained by spatial considerations, many individuals in both the city and the suburb need local communities with strong friendship and kinship ties. This sense of place and the variation in neighboring between metropolitan residents is expressed as variation in the different types of communities exemplified by the typology of six categories discussed above.

Summary

In the previous chapter we surveyed the diversity of metropolitan life. We saw that lifestyles are a consequence of the interaction between compositional social factors such as class and race, and particular territorial relations that assign particular individuals to particular places within the metropolitan region. In this chapter we have considered how living and working arrangements foster types of community. Many of the discussions about ways of life have suggested that spatial location can influence behavior. Thus, while Chapter 8 considered how people are organized into places, this chapter deals with the question of how places influence behavior. Such balanced considerations are in keeping with the sociospatial perspective, which claims that space operates in this dual way as both a product and producer of behaviors in society.

According to the arguments of urban sociologists, spatial location per se has little effect on lifestyles, which are better explained by compositional factors. Even one's sense of community has much more to do with one's network of intimate friends and kin than with where one lives. Yet the degree to which a community without place characterizes people's lives varies according to compositional factors such as class and gender, age and race, ethnicity and religion. Hence the localized, territorially specific community remains important to the way people organize their daily lives. This holds equally for single, middle-class professional women alone in the city, for poor black men who are disadvantaged because of racial oppression, and for the aged central city dwellers, all of whom need the sustaining resources of local neighborhoods and vital community relations.

Space affects behavior in other ways. According to the sociospatial approach, we orient ourselves in particular places by assigning meaning to space. All objects are meaningful to us. The meanings of space and the objects of the built environment, studied by semiotics, help us organize our everyday lives. This sociospatial process utilizes particular mechanisms in ordering public interaction. We recognize the cues of behavior and acquire street-wisdom by repeated use of public space. Our interpretations of behavior require repeated learning experiences and an understanding of spatial context. In fact, the latter frames for us the way we should interpret the actions we see around us within the metropolitan environment. Spatial context, in short, is a principal component of meaning.

Finally, we have discussed how the metropolitan region is diversified not only with regard to the individuals who live there (Chapter 8), but also with regard to the types of neighborhood ties and commitments to community that can be found in particular settings. Urban and suburban sociologists have produced a long list of studies that document the diversity of neighborhood types and community relations.

An understanding of such differences helps us overcome stereotypical thinking about the people of cities and suburbs.

The richness of metropolitan life has been detailed in the last two chapters. Urban and suburban life also have their problems and challenges. The next chapter considers metropolitan problems and argues that they are produced by a combination of social and spatial factors.

CHAPTER

10

METROPOLITAN PROBLEMS:
Poverty, Racism, Crime, Housing, and Fiscal Crisis

On October 12, 1962, Ruby moved into a large housing project in Chicago with her four children, all of whom had been born out of wedlock. Her new husband had a job in a nearby factory, and their rent was subsidized. Three years later, her husband abandoned her and Ruby had to go on welfare to support her family, which had grown to seven children.

Over the next decade one son was murdered, another was sent to prison, and two daughters went on welfare to support children of their own. The two daughters live in the same project, raising the third generation on welfare. Only one son managed to escape the inner-city projects and move to a middle-class neighborhood by keeping a steady job. For years Ruby was trapped in the projects, which experienced rising crime, deteriorating maintenance, large-scale drug use and gang-related activities. In 1979, Ruby left her children and returned to the South to live near her relatives (Lemann, 1991).

Ruby's family provides a good example of the types of problems that Americans associate with large cities. Ever since the founding of this nation, the city has been viewed with suspicion as the corrupter of morals and family life. In a recent Gallup Poll (1982), over one-third of all residents of cities with a population of over half a million stated that they would prefer to move out. There is, in short, an *antiurban* bias in American culture which persists in viewing the large city as the source of social disorganization.

In previous chapters I have been developing the themes of the sociospatial approach and, in particular, I have tried to show that problems which appear to afflict individuals like Ruby and her family are caused in part by factors that we cannot readily see. In Ruby's case, she is a victim not only of poor family relations, personal limitations, and bad luck, but also of racism and poverty which severely hinder the life chances of black and poor people in the United States. Consequently, explanation for the social disorganization of Ruby's life lies in the particular combination of adverse social conditions, personal circumstances, and the specific effects of spatial segregation and uneven development. The present chapter will apply this sociospatial approach to metropolitan problems. But first a brief word about the antiurban bias and its relation to sociology.

The Antiurban Bias

Earliest images of the city feature overcrowding: immense traffic jams of primitive Model T automobiles mixed in with horse-drawn carts, teeming immigrant quarters of tenements, and crowds of children swarming across city streets. For almost a century, city life in this country was plagued by frequent public health crises such as cholera outbreaks, high infant mortality rates, alcoholism and family violence, street gang activity, and crime. At around the turn of the century, a wave of murders set an all-time record that was not broken until quite recently. For much of our history, then, city life has virtually been synonymous with social problems. Yet we know that these same problems—crime, disease, family breakup or divorce—are really experienced everywhere, not just in large cities. Hence, the antiurban bias is something of a paradox.

In Chapter 6 we discussed early urban sociology and the members of the Chicago School in the 1930s who believed that the move to the city brought with it social disorganization. While subsequent research showed that this perception was inaccurate, people in the United States still rank small and middle sized cities as providing the highest quality of life (Gallup, 1982). The negative perception of the large city provides the basis for varying mental images of place (see Chapter 9). Yet we have also seen that there are a good many positive aspects of urban living and that the early belief in the loss of community among migrants to the city was unfounded. In this chapter I shall assess the relative sociospatial impacts of social problems as they affect city, suburban, and metropolitan populations. One purpose of this discussion is to explore whether or not large cities in particular and metropolitan regions in general possess unique features that might propagate specifically "urban" problems.

Theories of Urban Problems

Early observers of city life saw immigrants from rural areas with stable family traditions turning to alcoholism, robbery, child abuse, and prostitution. Something about living in a large city, it was suggested, created social disorganization—broken families and broken lives—and this in turn led to all sorts of urban problems.

Several theories explaining the link between urban living and social disorganization have been proposed over the years. Wirthian theory, the compositional approach, subcultural theory, and the sociospatial perspective are the main approaches that we will consider.

Wirthian Theory

According to Louis Wirth, city life is based on social relationships completely different from those in rural areas. As discussed in Chapter 6, Wirth believed that *primary group* or intimate relations were more characteristic of rural areas. In the city, by contrast, most relationships are *secondary* and are based on temporary, superficial, and impersonal connections.

The dominance of secondary relations produces anonymity and distance between urban dwellers, who rarely get to know those with whom they interact, such as shopkeepers, fellow commuters, coworkers, and even neighbors. As a result, city life seems impersonal and uncaring. Wirth believed that secondary relations eventually lead to family breakup, alcoholism, crime, and the other negative aspects of urban life (Wirth, 1938).

The Compositional Approach

In Herbert J. Gans' (1968) compositional thesis, the urban environment does not have a major effect on people's lives. Instead, the differences between city and suburban behavior are attributed to differences in class, age, and lifestyle orientation. According to the compositional view, urban problems are the consequence of factors related to the demographic characteristics of the population such as class standing, marital status, age, poverty, race, and educational level. There are not innate qualities of urban living that cause specific problems such as divorce.

The Subcultural View

Claude Fischer (1975) claimed that the compositional view neglected the special role cities play in social interaction, because life in the city intensified local cultures, as we have discussed in Chapter 8. There is no intrinsic reason why urban life produced problems, as Wirth had suggested. However, according to Fischer, cities could have a negative effect on behavior. City life can, for example, more readily support criminal subcultures.

Although drugs, for instance, are available in all areas of society, they can be more easily obtained in cities. All forms of deviance flourish within urban environments because there are more individuals who support such behaviors. Hence, urban life does not automatically lead to social disorganization, but within cities there are more opportunities to be exposed to deviance and negative influences on one's behavior.

The Sociospatial Perspective

While the chances of being exposed to social problems such as violent crime are greater for the residents of large cities, suburbs have a surprisingly high rate of problems themselves (Fishman, 1987). Cities no longer have an exclusive hold on the rising divorce rate or family violence, for example. Suburbs are now almost as likely as cities to be afflicted by family disorganization and by deviant subcultures, gangs, and drugs (Barbanel, 1992). In short, while there is still some evidence for the subcultural perspective, as the suburbs have continued to mature, their differences from the central city have become less significant. Problems are ubiquitous in the metropolitan region. Hence, the subcultural approach no longer clearly points to *unique* differences between city life and life in other developed places, such as the suburbs (see Chapter 9).

This book emphasizes the sociospatial approach, according to which the spatial environment plays a role in human interaction, provided that it is understood that compositional or social factors are equally important. In effect, both Wirth and Gans were correct. On the one hand, according to the sociospatial approach, lifestyles result from social factors such as race, class, and gender. Social problems in particular are caused by poverty, racial exclusion, gender differences, and the uneven development of capitalist economies which results in differential access to resources and life chances. On the other hand, spatial forms still matter. Environments intensify or dissipate these compositional effects of uneven development. In short, ways of life result from an interaction between social factors and spatial organization.

Cities are not unique in having acute social problems, but the spatial nature of large cities and densely populated suburbs makes the uneven development resulting from the inequities of race, class, gender, and age particularly severe. According to the sociospatial approach, the following factors are the most significant.

First, the principal effect of the city as a built environment is that it *concentrates* people and resources (Lefebvre, 1991; Engels, 1973). Thus, social problems such as drugs and poverty have a greater impact in large central cities and densely populated suburbs than in less dense areas. In confined urban space under the jurisdiction of a single municipal government, it is the sheer numbers that tend to be involved, such as the frequency of murders and rapes or the number of "crack babies," which make social problems a matter of grave concern.

Second, over the years urban populations have been disproportionately affected by social forces stemming from changes in countries around the globe. For example, large metropolitan regions such as Los Angeles or New York are the destinations of choice for most recent immigrants who have left their own countries in search of a better life. With the flow of immigrants comes specific problems, such as the need for bilingual education, that affect these areas more than other places.

Changes in the global cycles of economic investment also affect metropolitan regions because of the scale of activities in the largest places. For example, after Wall Street stocks took a plunge in October, 1987, over 100,000 trained professionals were laid off from brokerage and financial service firms in Manhattan alone. Job loss on this scale presents a particularly acute problem for cities.

Finally, social problems are caused by uneven development, and this pattern of differential resource allocation may be accentuated in dense, built environments. For example, large cities are major centers of the global economy. Extreme wealth is created within their boundaries and the signs of that money are highly visible in the city, such as expensive restaurants, upscale department stores, luxury housing, taxis, and limousines. Close by, in the concentrated space of the city, are also people who suffer the most terrible consequences of abject poverty, such as homelessness, malnutrition, and chronic unemployment. It is this contrast that is so visible within large cities and makes the issue of uneven development particularly pressing to inhabitants.

In summary, problems that can be considered uniquely *urban* derive from the concentrated nature of metropolitan space and the scale of changes in compositional factors. Let us now consider some problems that are usually associated with urban life, including racism and poverty; crime and drugs; fiscal problems such as declines in educational quality; infrastructure problems; housing inequities; and homelessness.

Racism and Poverty

Racism

The United States has a serious racial problem that is compounded by class. The most extreme effects have been felt by African Americans. When given the choice, white people would prefer not to live near blacks (Hacker, 1992). Through the institutions of white society, African Americans have been systematically discriminated against so that their social mobility has been severely constrained.

The most powerful indicator of institutional racism in the United States is a spatial one, population segregation. In Chapters 12 and 13, when discussing cities around the globe, we shall also encounter the phenomenon of population segregation. But nowhere is the racial nature of this sociospatial effect as clear as in the United States.

The classic study of segregation is by the Tauebers (1965). They compiled statistics on American cities with regard to the relative locations of whites and blacks. In order to measure segregation, they constructed a very useful concept, an "index of segregation." If a city had a 30 percent African-American population as a whole, then they expected, in the absence of segregation, that the black population would be evenly distributed across space. The index of segregation refers to the percentage of African Americans who would have to move in order for all neighborhoods to reflect the 30 percent black composition of the entire city. If a neighborhood were 90 percent black, then 67 percent of the black population would have to move, or an index of .67.

On the basis of Taueber and Taueber's study, all U.S. cities were discovered to be highly segregated, that is, with indexes above .5 for African Americans. They replicated their study in the 1970s and found little change in the degree of black population clustering. Some of the most segregated cities during the 1970s were Detroit, Michigan; Chicago, Illinois; Buffalo, New York; Cleveland, Ohio; and Birmingham, Alabama (see Table 10.1 and the discussion below for 1990 figures).

The Tauebers' study cannot be used to prove that all segregation is the result of discrimination, that is, that it is *involuntary* segregation. The spatial clustering of population groups can also be *voluntary*. For the case of African Americans, however, there is ample evidence that the graphic and persisting nature of sociospatial concentration is the result of racism compounded by class factors (Wilson, 1987; Bullard and Feagin, 1991). Bullard and Feagin (1991), for example, discuss various techniques used by housing-related institutions in the United States to prevent blacks from locating where they prefer, thereby fostering involuntary segregation. This is an example of *institutional racism.*

For example, rental and real estate agents use a variety of methods to prevent blacks from locating in white-owned areas. One mechanism is called *steering.* When an African-American couple comes to a rental or real estate agent, the latter will steer the couple to areas of the city that are populated by blacks. Agents will also simply refuse to divulge the existence of housing opportunities in white areas. A recent study indicates that despite gains in family income earnings by a growing number of middle-class blacks, racial segregation remains a fact of life for the majority of African Americans. The report observes:

> The analysis of 219 metropolitan areas shows that despite gains by some, black segrega-
> tion remains the most extreme and enduring of any group in the nation—a wall of pov-
> erty and isolation that remains despite the country's attempts to legislate racial under-
> standing. The depth of white resistance to desegregation has remained so great that even
> the salve of money has failed to heal the differences. Middle-class and affluent blacks
> are only slightly more likely to live next door to whites than poor blacks (*USA Today,*
> Nov 11, 1991, p.2).

The sociospatial effects of racism on African Americans are also illustrated by comparing their position with other minorities. In particular, a recent study looked at metropolitan areas where minorities were at least 20 percent of the population, that is, where they were present in sufficient numbers to perhaps overcome prejudice. Hispanic Americans were highly segregated in only two of the 33 metropolitan areas and the data was not conclusive for Asian Americans due to their relatively low total population. In contrast, "blacks are highly segregated in 31—two-thirds—of the 47 metro areas where they make up at least 20 percent of residents, including Detroit, Chicago, Miami, Birmingham, Ala." (*USA Today,* Nov. 11, 1991, p. 2).

Since the date of the Tauebers' study researchers of spatial segregation have developed more accurate measures of population clustering. The most sophisticated studies combine these measures to arrive at overall estimates of segregation (Harrison and Weinberg, 1992). A study of 254 metropolitan regions (MSAs and PMSAs) by Harrison and Weinberg (1992) using 19 different indexes of residential segregation for four separate racial and ethnic groups documented the extent of racial segregation between 1980 and 1990. The Harrison and Weinberg study also possesses the virtue of a regional perspective, as it uses the metropolitan area rather than the central city as the unit of analysis. The results are illustrated in Tables 10.1 and 10.2.

Table 10.1 lists the twenty most segregated metropolitan areas in 1990 for blacks, Hispanics, Asians/Pacific islanders and for Native Americans. The five most segregated regions for African Americans were located in the East and Midwest of the nation: Milwaukee, Wisconsin; Detroit, Michigan; Buffalo, New York; Cleveland, Ohio; and Newark, New Jersey. Hispanics were also most segregated in those same areas of the country. Their five most segregated metro regions in 1990 were: Newark, New Jersey; Springfield, Massachusetts; New York, New York; Chicago, Illinois; and Lancaster, Pennsylvania. The experience of Asians/Pacific islanders and Native Americans is somewhat different. The areas where the former groups were the most segregated

TABLE 10.1
The Twenty Most Segregated Metro Areas (PMSA) by Ethnic/Racial Group, 1990

For Blacks	For Hispanics	For Asians/Pacific Islanders	For Native Americans
1. Milwaukee, WI	Newark, NJ	Stockton, CA	Phoenix, AZ
2. Detroit, MI	Springfield, MA	San Francisco, CA	Rapid City, ND
3. Buffalo, NY	New York, NY	Fresno, CA	Sioux City, IA–NE
4. Cleveland, OH	Chicago, IL	La Crosse, WI	Anchorage, AL
5. Newark, NJ	Lancaster, PA	Madison, WI	Bellingham, WA
6. St. Louis, MO	Providence-Pawtucket, RI	Sacramento, CA	Great Falls, MT
7. Indianapolis, IN	Reading, PA	Champagne-Urbana, IL	Lawrence, KS
8. Flint, MI	Hartford-New Britain, CT	Lafayette-W. Lafayette, IN	Yuma, AZ
9. Toledo, OH	Los Angeles-Long Beach, CA	Seattle, WA	Billings, MT
10. Gary-Hammond, IN	Milwaukee, WI	New York, NY	Santa Fe, NM
11. Kansas City, MO–KS	Philadelphia, PA	State College, PA	Albuquerque, NM
12. Muskegon, MI	San Antonio, TX	San Diego, CA	Yakima, WA
13. Chicago, IL	Bergen-Passaic, NJ	Fort Smith, AR–OK	Sioux Falls, SD
14. Fort Wayne, IN	Denver, CO	Minneapolis-St. Paul, MN	Green Bay, WI
15. Cincinnati, OH	Lorain-Elyria, PA	Vallejo-Fairfield-Napa, CA	Tuscon, AZ
16. Philadelphia, PA	Buffalo, NY	Los Angeles-Long Beach, CA	Reno, NV
17. Baltimore, MD	Houston, TX	Biloxi-Gulfport, MS	Houma-Thibadoux, LA
18. Harrisburg-Lebanon-Carlisle, PA	Rochester, NY	Bryan-College Station, TX	Duluth, MN–WI
19. Grand Rapids, MI	Allentown-Bethlehem, PA	Ann Arbor, MI	Bismarck, ND
20. Saginaw-Midland, MI	Anaheim-Santa Ana, CA	Merced, CA	Fort Smith, AR–OK

Source: R. Harrison and D. Weinberg, 1992: Appendix, Table 3.

TABLE 10.2
**Average Overall Changes in Segregation by Ethnic/Racial Group for the
10 Largest Metro Areas, 1980–1990**

Metro Area (PMSA)	Blacks	Hispanics	Asians/Pacific Islanders
New York, NY	increase	increase	increase
Los Angeles-Long Beach, CA	decrease	increase	increase
Chicago, IL	decrease	increase	increase
Philadelphia, PA	increase	increase	increase
Detroit, MI	decrease	increase	increase
Washington, DC–MD–VA	decrease	increase	increase
Houston, TX	decrease	increase	increase
Nassau-Suffolk, NY	increase	increase	increase
Boston, MA	decrease	increase	decrease
Atlanta, GA	decrease	no change	NA

Source: Adapted from R. Harrison and D. Weinberg, 1992: Table 12.

include the West and Midwest: Stockton, San Francisco, Fresno in California; and La Crosse and Madison in Wisconsin. Native Americans are most segregated in the metropolitan regions of the West and Northwest: Phoenix, Arizona; Rapid City, North Dakota; Sioux City, Iowa-Nebraska; Anchorage, Alaska; and Bellingham, Washington.

The Harrison and Weinberg (1992) study also analyzed changes in segregation between 1980 and 1990 (see Table 10.2). Overall results were that segregation levels have changed very little in the 254 metropolitan regions during the last decade. This outcome replicates the findings of the Tauebers' studies for the 1960s and 1970s. Of all the minority groups, blacks experienced the most improvements, although Harrison and Weinberg caution that changes were very slight and uneven. Table 10.2 indicates changes for the ten largest metropolitan regions. In the New York area, segregation increased slightly for all three groups (blacks, Hispanics, Asians/Pacific islanders). Blacks experienced slight decreases in segregation in the metro regions of Los Angeles–Long Beach, Chicago, Detroit, Washington, DC–MD–VA, Boston and Atlanta. In contrast, Asians/Pacific islanders experienced a decline in segregation only in the Boston metro region.

As Tables 10.1 and 10.2 show, racial segregation is not restricted to the city, but is region wide. Taken as a whole, in particular, the suburbs are even more segregated than are central cities (see section on housing, later). The techniques of institutional racism have been quite effective in insuring that suburbs remain racially distinct. As noted in Chapter 4, the first mass suburban community of Levittown took special precautions to exclude prospective home-buyers who were African Americans. In fact, as several studies have shown, when blacks do acquire suburban residence, they are most likely to find housing in areas immediately adjacent to urban ghetto concentrations. They simply move across the city border into a "suburban ghetto." It is true that, in recent years, a significant number of African Americans have attained middle-class status and have suburbanized (Landry, 1987). But the effects of institutional racist practices remain so strong in the housing market, that their numbers among middle-class whites have not proportionately increased in most areas of the country. In short, spatial isolation is a very effective means of promoting racist divisions in the United States.

One effect on U.S. culture of these arrangements is that increasingly whites learn about blacks and blacks learn about whites only from the mass media, because they have little direct contact with each other. Styles of dress and language among teenagers, in particular, are highly influenced by the media and the mass marketing of youth related fashions in clothing, the cinema, and music. Recently, an urban style of ghetto dress among black teenagers that is associated with rap music and inner city dance styles has been marketed nationwide. Many youths in suburbia copy the style that is marketed to them through television and films. At the same time, suburban fashions associated with active leisure wear, especially influenced by southern California, such as skateboarding or beachwear dress, are also marketed through the media nationwide. Teenage culture represents a battleground of these and other spatially generated life-styles that are diffused across the country by the mass media (Chambers, 1986), and it is here, in popular culture, that urban African-American culture has its greatest impact on whites.

Poverty

The issue of poverty is not confined to cities alone. People throughout the metropolitan region suffer from the effects of this problem. Poverty is caused by the uneven develop-ment of the economy. In the 1950s, despite growing affluence, large numbers of Americans were poor, with some living in appalling conditions (Harrington, 1962). At that time it was recognized that there were poor people in rural areas as well as urban places. During the 1960s and partly as a result of government antipoverty programs such as the War on Poverty, the poverty rate declined to about 12.1 percent. In the 1970s and 1980s, however, the rate rose again and reached levels comparable to Depression-era statistics; roughly 20 percent of the total population was living at or below the poverty line in the 1980s (Wilson, 1987).

Poverty can be considered an urban problem because so many of the poor are concentrated in large cities, as the sociospatial perspective suggests. The number of central city poor people climbed from 8 million in 1969 to 12.7 million in 1982 (a 59 percent increase). Consequently, the city as a spatial form concentrates the poor in record numbers. As William J. Wilson has observed, "to say that poverty has become increasingly urbanized is to note a remarkable change in the concentration of poor people in the United States in only slightly more than a decade" (1987: 172).

Furthermore, the demographic profile of the poor is also cause for alarm. In 1989, 39 percent of young children were living in poverty; among all age groups, 30.7 percent of African Americans and 26.2 percent of Hispanics were below the poverty line. Because the minority population of the United States is overwhelmingly urban, these figures imply a concentration of poor minority-group members in the large central cities and represent a *major* problem for the entire society, not just for those living in central cities. As one report suggested:

As the problems of the urban poor become more toxic to those inside [the city], their immediate impact on most Americans is becoming more distant and elusive. But even though elusive, the effects of urban poverty can be far-reaching. They strain big-city budgets, produce criminal behavior that is altering urban life, poison race relations and threaten to spawn an undereducated work force that could haunt the nation for decades (Applebome, 1991: A 20).

Economic Restructuring and the Problems of the Poor

While poverty is a phenomenon of uneven development, the last two decades of deindustrialization and manufacturing decline have contributed greatly to the numbers of poor people. During the 1980s many cities were transformed by the new realities of global location decisions (see Chapters 7, 8, and 13). Manufacturing jobs declined drastically and central city economies retooled into service centers. These changes created positions for highly trained professional workers, especially in information processing and banking, along with a limited number of low-skilled, poorly paid jobs in the service sectors of food, tourism, and delivery systems, among others. As job opportunities dried up during the recession-plagued years of the 1980s and 1990s, unemployed workers among the less affluent and less educated found it increasingly difficult to make ends meet, and both poverty and crime increased.

The new conditions of poverty, however, are not just confined to the large cities. Deindustrialization and economic restructuring have also affected towns and suburbs that have relied on manufacturing. In Chapter 5 we discussed the case of Youngstown, Ohio, which was devastated by the closing of its pipe mill. There have been other such cases since the 1980s. The decline of manufacturing has resulted in the crushing of communities and a rise of poverty among working-class populations across the country. For example, Homestead, Pennsylvania, near Pittsburgh, was once a thriving town of 20,000 people. It was the site of a large steel mill that was typical of the kinds of businesses that failed due to deindustrialization. According to one account (Serrin, 1992), the community was simply abandoned by U.S. Steel Corporation in the 1980s. It is now an impoverished, bleak community of less than 4,000 people. The pattern that has been repeated in countless places such as Youngstown and Homestead is one of no planning and no transition phase allowed to workers who suffer job loss due to plant closings. Many communities across the United States have been impoverished, and working-class whites have suffered the most because of this callous process of change.

Poverty and Race

Central city poverty is compounded by the consequences of racial discrimination. Blacks have always been spatially isolated in our society due to racism. Hence, the economic deprivation that they now suffer because of industrial restructuring has forced the quality of life in ghetto areas to decline drastically (Farley and Allen, 1987). The black unemployment rate, for example, has reached more than twice that of whites (except in 1975): from 9 percent for blacks and 5 percent for whites in 1954 to 14.4 percent and 6.5 percent, respectively, in 1984 (Wilson, 1987: 65). Today the structurally unemployed (those who have ceased to look for work as well as those recently out of work) among black city residents has skyrocketed to over 20 percent. Many of these inner city residents are not just poor; they are ill-equipped to participate in the economy

The ghetto section of Naples, Florida. Note the police car on patrol and residents out on the street in front of their apartments.

because of restructuring to services and the decline of manufacturing. They do not have the skills to obtain the jobs they need to rise above poverty. The case of Milwaukee is illustrative. The policy of restructuring in that city has had negative effects on black residents, according to one report:

> It has devastated the city's poor black neighborhoods whose residents thrived in the high wage union jobs of the city's manufacturing heyday, but are now adrift on a rising tide of unemployment, crime and despair. The retooling of factories also hurt unskilled whites, of course. But, the effect was less severe for several reasons. . . . In Milwaukee the result is a city of 600,000 people where black men stand idle on street corners just blocks from the breweries and factories that used to employ them. . . . More than half of all black Milwaukeeans are on some form of public assistance (Wilkerson, 1991: Al).

The alarming increase in poverty among inner city ghetto residents prompted several observers in the 1980s to suggest that there exists an urban "underclass" living in ghetto areas that is afflicted by isolation and deprivation (Wilson, 1987). According to William J. Wilson, the *underclass* consists of a relatively permanent population that (1) is concentrated in poor areas of the city, (2) is chronically removed from the full-time labor force, (3) contains a large proportion of teenage and out-of-wedlock births, and (4) has a comparatively long history of welfare dependency (Wilson, 1987: 172). The underclass is a problem because forces or institutions such as education that give people economic and social opportunities have ceased to function for a sizable propor-tion of the urban poor. As a result, there is no mechanism which might improve the condition of the underclass.

Since Wilson's important study, the term *underclass* has been attacked because of its common usage which blames the victims of poverty and racism rather than the structural causes and callous profit-making corporations which are responsible for the condition in the first place (Feagin, 1992). According to Herbert J. Gans, for example, "While this word can be used as a graphic technical term for the growing number of persistently poor and jobless Americans, it is also a value-laden, increasingly pejorative term that seems to be becoming the newest buzzword for the *undeserving* poor" (Gans, 1990: 271). As a consequence, Wilson and other prominent sociologists have recently called for an abandonment of its usage. I suggest the term *ghettoized poor* as closer to the original intent of the concept. Ghettoization is not just an effect of poverty and lack of skills, but an outcome of overt discrimination against minorities.

The spatial effects of concentrating the poor in a few neighborhoods also contribute to urban problems. For example, ghetto areas are the sites of the most violent criminal and drug-related activities, so that the urban poor are also the most likely to be crime victims and suffer the most from crime (Taylor, 1991). In addition, ghetto areas have worse medical care than do other parts of the city. A study of infant mortality rates in New York, for example, found that the rate was almost twice as high in central Harlem and Bedford-Stuyvesant (23.4 and 21 per 1,000, respectively), both well-known black communities, as the city average of 13.3 per 1,000 (the national average was 10 in 1,000 in 1990).

Despite the recent effort to avoid blaming the victim, the recent hopelessness of limited job opportunities and the decline of ghetto social institutions has resulted in changes among racially segregated ghetto residents that seem a turn for the worse. According to the black urban sociologist Elijah Anderson (1990), ghetto culture possessed a male role model, the "old head," who provided stability and positive values to youth. "Traditionally, the *old head* was a man of stable means who believed in hard work, family life, and the church" (1990: 2). He functioned to socialize young men into productive, responsible lives. Anderson continues:

> But today, as meaningful employment has become increasingly scarce for young blacks and as crime and drugs have become a way of life for many, the "old head" is losing his prestige and authority. With the expansion of the drug culture and its opportunities for large sums of quick money, street-smart young boys are concluding that the old head's lessons about life and the work ethic are no longer relevant (1990: 3).

According to Anderson a different role model has emerged over the last two decades:

> He is young, often a product of the street gang, and at best indifferent to the law and traditional values. This "new" old head is in many respects the antithesis of the traditional one . . . he makes ends meet, part time or full time, in the drug trade or some other area of the underground economy (1990: 3).

In sum, the urban problem of the ghetto poor is a product of the sociospatial effects of racism and economic changes due to the restructuring of the global economy and the decline of manufacturing. At present, potential solutions are unclear because even in times of prosperity, underclass areas lack the human resources to capitalize on opportunities; that is, urban poverty does not seem to decline when the economy as a whole improves (Jencks and Peterson, 1991). As Wilson (1987) and others have maintained, special programs are needed to deal with the intractable problems of the poor. In the meantime, the effects of the pathology emanating from poverty-stricken ghetto areas will continue to drain society's resources for years to come.

As a car burns in the intersection, marchers fill the streets in the Mt. Pleasant neighborhood of Washington, D.C., on May 6, 1991, after clashing with the District of Columbia police for the second straight night.

The potential threat of a large, minority population that is racially and economically deprived has been graphically illustrated many times in the outbreak of violence and riots which can terrorize an entire city. Often, ghetto violence of this nature happens after the police, perceived to be a white racist institution, kill or injure an African-American neighborhood resident. Countless times such incidents have occurred across the nation, most recently during the days from April 30 to May 3, 1992. Following a verdict which acquitted four Los Angeles policemen in a case of excessive force against a motorist, Rodney King, rioting broke out on the streets of the south-central ghetto area. As reported in the daily press:

> Violence mushroomed as marauding gangs torched scores of structures and looted dozens of stores despite an all-night curfew and the deployment of the National Guard. Attacks spread to normally tranquil neighborhoods miles away from the city's mean streets, and law enforcement officials dodged bullets (Wilson, 1992: A1).

All told, at least 53 people were killed and 2,328 were injured in America's bloodiest urban riot. Damage estimates exceeded $1 billion and an extensive area was devastated, including portions of Los Angeles adjacent to the south-central area.

Crime and Drugs

Crime

On the evening of July 31, 1990, John Reisenbach, a 33-year-old advertising executive, left his apartment in the fashionable Greenwich Village section of Manhattan. His phone was out of order, and he had to call an associate. Several feet from the entrance to his building there was a pay phone, and Reisenbach stepped in. While talking, he was approached by an African-American man of about the same age who demanded money. When Reisenbach refused, he was shot dead. In the following weeks four children under the age of 15 were also shot in the city. These innocent bystanders included 3-year-old Octavia Brown and 6-year-old Kevin Acevedo, who were caught between warring drug dealers.

These tragic stories give the impression that crime is rampant in cities and that cities are unsafe as human environments. When people speak of crime, they usually mean *violent crime,* which includes murder, assault, rape, and robbery. However, a large amount of *property crime*—burglary, larceny, and auto theft—also occurs every year in cities and suburbs. White collar criminals, for example, such as insider traders on Wall Street and the bankers involved in the savings and loan scandal, are responsible for the theft of billions of dollars. But these crimes are not usually considered an outcome of life in large cities or suburbs. For the most part, the crimes associated with metropolitan areas are of the violent variety or property crimes such as burglary and auto theft. These crimes affect our view of public safety and the safety of our homes.

Table 10.3 indicates the crime rates for the largest cities in the United States in 1990. The cities of New York, Los Angeles, Chicago, Houston, Philadelphia, and Detroit all had over 500 murders. During that same year Houston, Dallas, and San Antonio had over 100,000 property crimes while New York, Los Angeles, and Chicago had over 200,000.

Many people think that cities have become more dangerous than they were in the past, but how accurate is that assessment? Table 10.4 shows the changes in the per-capita crime rates between 1980 and 1990. While New York City had 2,245 murders in 1990 it was not the nation's most dangerous city—its total crime rate per capita was 10 percent. Dallas (15 percent), Seattle (13 percent), Detroit (12 percent), San Antonio (12 percent) and Boston (12 percent) all had higher per-capita crime rates.

According to Table 10.4, indexes of combined violent and property crimes reveal that between 1980 and 1990 crime declined in only five of the twenty-three largest U.S. cities. In fourteen other large cities, total crimes increased. In some cities the gain was remarkable. Violent crimes increased 43 percent in Houston, 94 percent in San Diego, 52 percent in Phoenix, 99 percent in Jacksonville, and 81 percent in El Paso. Only San Francisco and Cleveland experienced a decline in the violent crime rate. Table 10.4 also shows that there seems to be no relationship between changes in city population and changes in crime rates. Philadelphia, for example, experienced a 6.1 percent loss in population between 1980 and 1990 and an increase in total per-capita crimes. In contrast, the population of San Diego grew by 26.8 percent between 1980 and 1990, but its per-capita total crime rate also increased.

In short, the common conception of cities regarding crime is accurate: they are dangerous places to live and have become increasingly crime ridden in the last ten years. Each day, for example, "5 New Yorkers will be killed, 9 will be raped, 256 will be robbed, and 332 homes will be burglarized, and 367 cars will disappear" (Greenberg, 1990). As criminologist James Q. Wilson stated recently, "People have the notion that things were worse in the old days. That's not true. Things are really bad today" (Greenberg, 1990: 22).

TABLE 10.3
Violent Crimes for the 24 Largest Cities, 1990

City	Crime Index Total	Violent Crime Total	Property Crime Total	Murder	Rape	Robbery	Aggravated Assault
New York, NY	710,222	174,542	535,680	2,245	3,126	100,280	68,891
Los Angeles, CA	321,536	84,792	237,727	983	2,014	36,098	44,714
Chicago, IL	NA	NA	228,829	851	NA	37,156	41,114
Houston, TX	184,869	22,637	162,232	568	1,335	12,921	7,813
Philadelphia, PA	114,032	21,387	92,645	503	734	12,806	7,344
San Diego, CA	101,564	12,047	89,517	135	439	4,331	7,142
Detroit, MI	125,325	27,747	97,578	582	1,657	13,010	12,498
Dallas, TX	156,267	24,550	131,747	447	1,344	10,565	12,194
San Antonio, TX	116,774	5,730	111,044	208	430	2,864	2,228
Phoenix, AZ	105,779	10,665	95,114	128	512	3,383	6,642
Baltimore, MD	77,989	17,942	60,047	305	687	9,477	7,473
San Jose, CA	38,090	4,698	33,392	35	416	1,034	3,213
San Francisco, CA	70,183	12,466	57,717	101	422	7,072	4,871
Indianapolis, IN	32,635	6,224	26,411	58	541	1,642	3,983
Memphis, TN	60,255	9,082	51,173	195	831	4,152	3,904
Jacksonville, FL	66,618	11,654	54,964	176	704	3,963	6,811
Washington, DC	65,389	14,919	50,470	472	303	7,365	6,779
Milwaukee, WI	58,406	6,282	52,124	155	495	4,146	1,486
Boston, MA	68,057	13,664	54,393	143	539	6,022	6,960
Columbus, OH	62,703	7,022	55,681	89	647	3,541	2,745
New Orleans, LA	61,799	11,227	50,572	304	361	6,048	4,514
Cleveland, OH	46,085	9,190	36,895	168	846	4,917	3,259
El Paso, TX	57,921	5,111	52,810	34	256	1,381	3,440
Seattle, WA	65,053	7,780	57,273	53	481	2,695	4,551

Note: Figures for rape not available for Chicago, IL, in 1990.
Source: United States Department of Justice, 1990, *Uniform Crime Reports*, Table 6, Washington, DC.

TABLE 10.4
Per-Capita Crimes, Total Crime Changes and Changes in Violent Crimes for the 24 Largest Cities, 1980 and 1990

City	Per Capita Crime, 1990	Per Capita Crime, 1980	Total Change	Percent Increase Violent Crime	Population Change 1980–1990
New York, NY	.10	.10	0	.17	3.5
Los Angeles, CA	.09	.10	−	.40	17.5
Houston, TX	.11	.09	+	.43	2.2
Philadelphia, PA	.07	.06	+	.24	−6.1
San Diego, CA	.10	.08	+	.94	26.8
Detroit, MI	.12	.11	+	.19	−14.6
Dallas, TX	.15	.12	+	.93	11.4
San Antonio, TX	.12	.07	0	.34	19.1
Phoenix, AZ	.11	.11	0	.52	24.5
Baltimore, MD	.11	.10	+	.08	−6.3
San Jose, CA	.05	.08	−	.24	24.3
San Francisco, CA	.10	.10	0	−.02	6.6
Indianapolis, IN	.04	.05	−	.40	4.4
Memphis, TN	.10	.08	+	.32	−5.6
Jacksonville, FL	.10	.08	+	.99	17.4
Washington, DC	.11	.10	+	.17	−4.9
Milwaukee, WI	.09	.06	+	.90	−1.3
Boston, MA	.12	.13	−	.10	2.0
Columbus, OH	.10	.10	0	.37	12.0
New Orleans, LA	.12	.09	+	.37	−10.9
Cleveland, OH	.09	.10	−	−.20	−11.9
El Paso, TX	.11	.06	+	.81	21.3
Seattle, WA	.13	.10	+	.50	4.5

Note: All figures not available for Chicago, IL, in 1990.
Source: Adapted from United States Department of Justice, 1990. *Uniform Crime Reports*, Table 6, Washington, DC.

To understand the nature of urban crime it is necessary to view it as a *spatial* as well as a social phenomenon. The incidence of crimes varies within any given city by neighborhood. Thus, while all cities have become more dangerous, there are still places that are as safe as any other place in the country. Conversely, certain neighborhoods are scenes of unremitting terror.

Typically, criminal incidents follow the lines of class and racial segregation: the most dangerous places are also the places where the poorest urban residents live. For example, "the typical New York City murder victim is a black man in his late teens or twenties, killed by an acquaintance of the same race with a hand gun during a dispute—most likely over drug-dealing" (Greenberg, 1990: 26). In all cities, racially segregated ghettos are the places where violent crimes are committed the most. Furthermore, most incarcerated felons are either black or Hispanic, and virtually all are poor. They come from the ghetto areas of the city, and their crimes usually were committed in those areas. In sum, not only are cities dangerous today, but the urban environment is partitioned into areas of relative safety and terror. Lately, as several extreme examples of violent crimes show, the islands of safety are shrinking in size and availability, even in the suburbs.

Why Crime Is an Urban Problem: Its Costs

What effect does crime have on everyday urban life? Perhaps the greatest effect has occurred with regard to the use of city space. In less crime-ridden eras, public spaces such as parks, plazas, and streets were enjoyed by everyone. Parks in particular were used by diverse people at all hours of the day and evening. Today the use of public space is limited: people are afraid to venture into parks without friends nearby, and children must be supervised and kept away from strangers. The evening use of public spaces and facilities, such as streets and mass transit systems, has also been negatively affected. People leaving their offices late at night now take cabs or cars rather than public transportation. A few years ago, a young woman out for a jog in Central Park was brutally attacked by a group of teenagers. Beaten within an inch of her life and raped, she miraculously survived, but this urban professional who was employed on Wall Street became a symbol of the toll of crime on the enjoyment of urban space.

Crime pushes up the security budgets of companies and households and results in billions of dollars in unnecessary medical expenses. It can also devastate property values. In areas of the city with high crime rates, the value of property remains low and does not rise during times of prosperity (Taylor, 1991). Thus, innocent households suffer doubly in crime-infested sections because they are victims of crime and because the value of their housing declines. Poor areas remain in poverty because high crime-levels chase away prospective investment. Finally, crime makes the city an unattractive place to live, especially for families with small children. Crime chases families away from the city, which compounds the problem of population loss and the inability of the city to increase its tax base.

Crime and Drugs

As was mentioned above, white collar crime results in terrible costs to this society but is not associated with the quality of urban life. Rather, it is violent crime that scares people away from the city. In addition to murder, which usually is committed among people who know each other, mugging is a particularly frightening crime, especially armed robbery. The frequency of this type of crime in the cities contributes greatly to the image of danger.

According to studies of arrestees, many robberies and burglaries are committed in association with trafficking in drugs. In fact, statistics show a disturbing relationship between violent crime and drug use. The National Institute of Justice surveyed arrestees in the twenty largest American cities and found that at least half of them tested positive for the use of illegal drugs. In New York City, for example, as many as 83 percent of males tested positive at the time of arrest. The range for females was slightly lower, but not by much: a low of 44 percent testing positive in St. Louis and a high of 81 percent in Detroit (National Institute of Justice, 1990).

According to this report, the extent of drug use among arrestees varies from city to city, but the use of drugs by people who commit violent crimes is alarming. The most common drug for both male and female arrestees is cocaine or crack. For example, in the family of Ruby highlighted at the beginning of this chapter, one son and one daughter were addicted to cocaine, and that son was a member of a gang involved in the drug trade.

In short, the lack of safety in large cities results from a high crime rate that is compounded by illegal drug use. When city streets are not considered safe, it is difficult for urban areas to attract new residents and businesses. Consequently, the economic

Police patrol the scene of a 1992 shootout as the body of a victim lies covered in the street after five heavily armed men tried to rob a Queens social club.

life of the city deteriorates further. In addition, when the enjoyment of public space becomes impossible due to crime and drugs, one of the primary enjoyments of urban culture is threatened with extinction.

Suburban Crime

Compared to crime in the large city, little research has been carried out on suburban crime (see Stahura, Huff, and Smith, 1980; Gottdiener, 1982). Most reports on suburban crimes identify the same factors that cause city crimes, that is, racism, poverty, and class conflict. As in the case of urban areas, the rate of suburban crimes has increased dramatically since the 1980s (Barbanel, 1992). There are, however, some ways that crimes in the suburbs differ from those in large cities. First, the property crimes of burglary, auto theft, fraud, and larceny dominate suburban crime, although rape is as serious a problem in suburbs as in cities. Thus, while possessing violent crime in increasing proportion, suburban areas have much less of it than do large cities. In contrast, property crimes are most troublesome.

Second, there is a distinct spatial component to suburban crime that differs from the city. In the latter, high crime areas are associated with urban ghettos. While suburbs have ghettos, not all of these are high crime areas. Instead, according to one study of a mature suburban region outside of Los Angeles (Gottdiener, 1982), police in Orange County, California, associate high crime rates with apartment buildings. These stand out because most residential dwellings in suburbia are single-family homes. In large cities, this distinction would not be effective since most residences are in apartment buildings. According to this study, police in suburbs pay particular attention to apartment dwellings and monitor the activities of their residents. Because of the lower density of suburban areas, surveillance of populations is an easier chore than in the large city (see Davis, 1990).

Aside from the above features, however, suburban crime seems very much like that found in large cities, while perhaps not at the same rate per person. Over the past two decades violent crime, drugs, burglary, rape, and bank robberies have become a significant factor in daily life as suburban areas themselves have matured.

The Fiscal Crisis and Public Service Problems

Urban problems are difficult to solve when insufficient money is available to local governments. A *fiscal crisis* starts when the revenues obtained by government fall short of the expenses of running a city. When this occurs, it is necessary to borrow money and incur debt. *Long-term debt* involves borrowing to improve resources and finance public works such as bridges. This form of borrowing is usually considered healthy as long as the projects are well thought out. Long-term debt is considered an investment in the city's future; if it is successful, the city grows and its economy improves, resulting in an increase in revenues.

In contrast, *short-term debt* involves borrowing to pay general operating expenses which revenues and money transferred to the city from higher levels of government cannot cover. Occasionally, cities must borrow simply to cover operating expenses, such as meeting a payroll, but this usually happens only in an emergency. However, as a regular practice it can ruin the health of a city by limiting the amount of money invested for future needs.

Fiscal Crisis

The fiscal crisis of the cities involves two related aspects. During the 1970s, rising costs coupled with declining revenues caused by the decline in manufacturing and the rapid deterioration of urban economies resulted in many cities facing budgetary shortfalls. These cities were forced to resort to short-term borrowing to cover their costs. Compounding the problem was the flight of child-rearing middle-class taxpayers from the cities to the suburbs, leaving behind less affluent people, many of whom required health care, education, and housing services. Because this shortfall went on for several years, cities appealed to higher levels of government for financial relief. During the 1970s, however, the federal government refused to help, and this precipitated the urban fiscal crisis.

Cities responded to this situation by cutting services and systematically laying off personnel. New York City, for example, almost went bankrupt during 1976 and was placed in the hands of a money management panel appointed by the state to bring expenditures back in line with revenues and limit the amount of borrowing. As a result of the changes caused by this fiscal crisis, New York has less to offer its residents. The closing of firehouses, reductions in the numbers of police officers and the hours of policing, the shortening of library hours, and layoffs and firings at city agencies are some of the austerity measures enacted in response to the urban fiscal crisis.

In the 1980s many cities, such as Cleveland, which had *defaulted* in 1978, and New York, which was forced into austerity, regained their fiscal health. The banking community renewed its faith in the obligations incurred by municipal governments. Short-term borrowing was controlled, and many cities prospered. For a time it appeared that the urban fiscal crisis was resolved (Gottdiener, 1987). However, the problem was simply transferred to higher levels of government. At present many states face a fiscal crisis; New York and California are especially hard hit. These and other states have had to cut back on budgets, with perceptible effects in the quality of life. State governments can no longer aid cities, so local jurisdictions must cut back as well. Hence the effects of the state fiscal crisis have been especially troubling for local communities.

In the 1990s the metropolitan fiscal situation has been compounded by the extended economic recession. As a result of this downturn, the states' fiscal problems have worsened. Furthermore, the federal government has not been able to help since it has acquired serious debt problems of its own for the first time in U.S. history. For example, in 1980 the federal deficit was approximately $40 billion, which was unprecedented but manageable. During the 1980s it rose to more than $150 billion a year. The interest payments alone on this massive debt take up 14 percent of the Gross National Product (GNP), and the United States has become the world's leading debtor nation. As a result, the federal government can no longer aid financially strapped cities, suburbs, and states. In 1993, deficit reduction of the federal budget is President Clinton's primary priority. In places like New York and California, governments at *all* levels are now suffering cutbacks of services and programs as a result of the fiscal crisis. Let us consider the current situation as it affects cities.

Social Service Cutbacks: Education, Infrastructure

Cutbacks in the services that municipal governments provide, such as fire fighting and education, greatly affect the quality of life. Even before the fiscal crisis, however, questions were raised about the relative distribution of such services. Many scholars argued that poorer areas did not get the same level or quality of services that wealthier areas received. Thus, the distribution of city services had a spatial component and the allocation pattern was inequitable. In Chapter 14 we shall also see how this sociospatial discrimination is reflected in environmental conditions that proportionately disadvantage the poor. The municipal cutbacks since the fiscal crisis of the 1970s have thus made an unfair situation much worse (Susser, 1982).

Studies of city spending by neighborhood uncovered spatial inequities in the provision of money for education (Sexton, 1961; Oakes, 1985), in municipal health care (Alford, 1975), and in police protection (Nardulli and Stonecash, 1981). In many cities, spending per child was greater in wealthier districts than in poorer ones (Sexton, 1961). This violates considerations of equity because all these districts are serviced by the *same* city government. In short there is a pattern of *fiscal discrimination* which overlies the existing pattern of racial and income segregation in cities.

Some scholars have disputed the suggestion that city governments abet racial and income segregation through their spending practices, stating that private sector mechanisms, such as the cost of rental housing, actually produce these patterns. Lineberry (1977), for example, found that public bureaucracies did not intentionally create inequities in spending but that these inequities were caused by the past errors of bureaucrats. However, other analysts argue that not all services are equal. Some, such as education, are much more critical to the well-being of future generations than others, such as the availability of parks. Differences in spending per school district constitute a serious problem of equity (Gottdiener, 1987). When the quality of public schools is not maintained, urban problems, such as the presence of poverty-related crime and drugs, are projected into the future. Let us consider two critical city services—education and spending on the infrastructure—and the roles they play in maintaining the quality of urban life.

The City Crisis in Education. The crisis of urban education is a reflection of a national crisis in educational quality. Student performance as a whole has declined over the last several decades, and in world comparisons American grade school students do poorly in science and math. But throughout the metropolitan region, the quality of local schools is a function of where you live. For the most part, the better schools are located in the wealthier areas. Even inner city school systems that have historically functioned at a relatively high level, despite the poverty of their pupils, have had to contend with both a prolonged fiscal crisis and a recession, which have combined to cut into the quality of education. Today the pupils attending urban public schools are predominantly poor minority-group members with low educational attainment.

Problems with performance, then, are compounded by the problems of poverty, of fiscal crisis, and of economic decline. According to one study (Pallas, Natriello, and McDill, 1989), the proportion of American children in poverty is expected to increase from 22 percent in 1983 to 27 percent in the year 2020, and the number of children living with mothers who have not completed high school is expected to rise from 13.6 million to 21.3 million in 2020. Traditionally, students from such backgrounds do poorly in school. Finally, educational problems are compounded by race. Schools are increasingly segregated in metropolitan areas. The shift of many urban whites to private education accentuates this racial problem. According to one report, "after steady progress toward integration in the 1970s, the 1980s saw as many schools resegregating as desegregating. And there are strong signs that the 1990s will be the decade in which America regresses into a network of separate schools—one set for whites, another for minorities" (*Press Enterprise,* Jan. 19, 1992: A-1).

At present a growing percentage of urban students are immigrants, many from non-English-speaking countries. For example, by the year 2020 it is expected that the number of Hispanic children in the school system will triple (Pallas, Natriello, and McDill, 1989). Therefore, in addition to problems of poverty and racial segregation, school systems will have to struggle with language difficulties.

There has also been a failure at the federal level to fund education. Since the 1980s, the budget of the Department of Education as a share of the GNP has dropped, and the federal share of expenditures on elementary and secondary education has declined from 8.7 percent to 6.2 percent. Spending on education has increased at the state level, but it is not clear that the states can continue providing this level of support, especially because of the prolonged recession of the 1990s.

In 1988, for example, states already provided 50 percent and local governments 44 percent of the total costs of education. It is unlikely that they can do more, and because education is an investment in human resources for the future, the urban labor force of the next few decades will not have the same skill levels as in the past; this implies that the economy will be disadvantaged. Hence, the decline in educational quality poses a threat to economic recovery.

The Infrastructure Problem. One outcome of the decline in government spending has been a progressive deterioration of the urban infrastructure, especially roads, water systems, bridges, public buildings, and streets. Since the late 1960s total spending on infrastructure as a share of the GNP has declined from 2.3 percent in 1964 to 1.7 percent in 1987, while the population has grown. Hence, many city facilities are living on borrowed time. The problem of infrastructure needs is compounded by the economic and fiscal dilemmas that cities and suburbs face. They have some money to spend, but it is reserved for economic revitalization. Due to the fiscal crisis, cities simply cannot do everything, and while managing in times of recession, they often sacrifice spending on infrastructure maintenance.

Due to neglect, some spectacular infrastructure failures have already occurred causing a loss of life. For example, in 1989 an elevated section of the New England Thruway in Connecticut collapsed, killing three people. The highway was closed for

On April 3, 1989, a section of this highway bridge near Covington, Tennessee, abruptly collapsed sending four people to their deaths.

almost six months for repairs. Breakdowns in sewer, road, and mass transit systems are now commonplace.

The most recent example of the city infrastructure crisis occurred in Chicago. In February, 1992, a cable television company was working in one of the many empty tunnels that exist beneath the streets of downtown Chicago and below the water level of the Chicago River. They found evidence of a small leak and reported it to the city's Department of General Services. On March 13, the tunnel was inspected and a report was filed with the Department of Transportation. On April 2 the city's chief bridge engineer sent a memo to the commissioner of that department who was in charge of infrastructure repairs to attend to the matter of the tunnel leak because it posed an unknown hazard. The engineer estimated that repairs would cost "approximately $10,000," and take two weeks. Yet nothing was done. The Chicago budget was already severely strained from austerity measures. Spending was shunted toward large investment projects that were aimed at revitalizing the city's economy. But this set of priorities had terrible consequences.

On April 14, the tunnel wall gave way and the Chicago River waters flooded the entire downtown. Buildings had to be evacuated and shut down. An estimated 100,000 office workers were temporarily sent home until repairs could be effected. The Chamber of Commerce estimated that losses in business and productivity amounted to $150 million each day and that the final bill for repairing the leak and cleaning up the damage could run close to $1 billion. It took several weeks before conditions in the Loop (the name for Chicago's downtown) returned to normal. The mayor fired the commissioner who had not responded to the need for repairs, but little else could be done (Wilkerson, 1992).

Housing

In the United States, family well-being depends to a great extent on where one's home is located. Differences in wealth and the location of the family home determine the opportunities available to individuals. Where one lives determines the quality of the school one attends, as we have already discussed, but it also determines the safety of the local streets, and how much one's property will increase in value. Over the years the cost of living in well-situated housing, either owned or rented, has increased substantially as a percentage of income. Consequently, attractive neighborhoods are now out of reach for many people.

Since 1965, for example, the cost of housing has risen more rapidly than has income. As a result, a growing number of people either cannot afford single-family home ownership or must devote more of their income to housing. Shannon, Kleiniewski, and Cross (1991) illustrated the rapid increase in housing prices. In 1970 the median monthly rent in the United States was $108; by 1985 it was three times as high ($350). The median sales price of new homes went up four times, from $23,000 in 1970 to more than $92,000 in 1986. Price rises were most rapid on both the east and west coasts, becoming almost prohibitively high in places such as Orange County, California, and Nassau County, New York.

According to one study (Schwartz, Ferlauto, and Hoffman, 1988), one-third of all households now pay an excessive amount for their housing (i.e., more than 30 percent of their gross salary). Almost one-fourth of all renters are spending more than half their income for shelter. Schwartz et al. (1988: 10) suggest that since 1975 the average family has not been able to afford an average-priced home.

Suburban Inequities

Suburban areas of the metropolitan region present a clearer case than do central cities of differentials in the supply of housing. Each suburban municipality offers a bundle of services to prospective residents, and in many cases a local property tax level which helps finance the quality of life. Those wishing to live in suburbia choose the level of services and taxes that they can afford by purchasing a house in a particular community.

Forty years of suburbanization in the United States have produced a pattern of clear differences between communities with regard to family income levels and race. There is extreme social segregation in suburbia (Muller, 1981); that is, classes as well as races are spatially separated. Due to the power of home rule, which provides local suburban governments with autonomy over land use, several administrative mechanisms have been used to control the racial and economic makeup of prospective residents. Perhaps the most powerful tool is *exclusionary zoning,* which mandates large-lot zoning for residential homes. In general, the larger the lot, the more expensive the home. Moderate income families are automatically priced out of areas with such zoning. After a period of development, many communities passed exclusionary zoning ordinances on remaining vacant land precisely to prevent rapid development of affordable dwellings. The result of such practices is income segregation because the less affluent must search for suburban housing in the few communities that make it available.

Exclusionary zoning is a sociospatial problem of the environment that ranks with other environmental issues (see Chapter 14). In recent years, exclusionary zoning practices have been challenged in the courts as unfair because there are serious equity and social justice questions that arise from sociospatial segregation. Perhaps the most famous case involved the city of Petaluma, California. This town is located north of San Francisco in Marin County, and during the 1960s experienced rapid development. Residents passed a zoning ordinance which mandated large lots for remaining land. They sought to slow down growth and enhance the property values of existing homes. In effect, however, the exclusionary zoning ordinance meant that only a few wealthy families could afford the larger lots, thereby preventing moderate income families from moving to the community.

The zoning ordinance was challenged by open housing advocates. They were defeated and the ordinance was upheld by the Supreme Court in a 1976 decision. The Court ruled that local areas indeed had the right to control their own zoning, despite the issues of social justice that had been raised. Since that time it has been increasingly difficult to provide affordable housing in all suburban communities and no less so because zoning has become a tool for the control of growth (see Gottdiener and Neiman, 1981).

Exclusionary zoning means that the quality of local services varies greatly in suburbia. Many states, such as New York, have tried to preserve minimum levels by enacting statewide standards for such things as educational levels. In practice, however, great variation still exists from suburban community to community. A typical family moving into a suburban town will immediately be told precisely where the best schools are located, and in most places there is great variation in educational quality from school to school. If the education of their children is utmost in importance, they will try to purchase a home in the best district. Of course, this area would be among the most expensive in the town. In this way, segregation of family income by housing tract perpetuates inequalities of social services, and remains an unfortunate characteristic of suburbia.

Homelessness

One of the first things visitors to the city notice are individuals walking on the street with all their possessions. Both disconcerting and pathetic, the sight of homeless people makes us question the well-being of this society as a whole. A recent *New York Times* poll found that about 54 percent of Americans see homeless people in the community or on their way to work (Applebome, 1991).

We cannot say for sure how many homeless people there are at present. We do know, however, that the numbers have not been so high since the Great Depression of the 1930s (Blau, 1992). The homeless cannot be found in any single place; they are mobile. Their condition also varies. Some days or nights they may be inside charity shelters, and at other times they may have enough money for a room in a single-room-occupancy (SRO) hotel. In the mid 1980s one estimate was 350,000 homeless "on a given night" (Peroff, 1987), but later estimates have run much higher to 3 million or more (Flanagan, 1990: 320). In addition, the composition of the homeless population is more representative of the entire cross section of U.S. society than during previous periods, such as the Depression.

A homeless man on the street with his possessions.

In Manhattan, for example, the homeless seem to be everywhere, and the city has opened up public buildings such as armories to provide "temporary" shelter to those in need. One report indicated that as many as 24,000 people a day were being housed in this manner (Berak, 1991). According to this report, the Fort Washington Armory in Manhattan, or "the Fort," is typical. It is a scary place where some men have lived for as long as five years. Roving bands of "jawbreakers" control the shelter, drug use is rampant, noise pierces the night and disturbs sleep, stealing is so endemic that inmates must place their sneakers under their bedposts at night, and security guards are scarce, unarmed, and poorly paid. It is a place, in short, very much like prison. However, the only alternative is to remain on the street at night, a fate that many homeless prefer to shelter life.

Recent reports indicate that both homelessness and squatting, phenomena that were once associated with third world cities, have become increasingly common in European as well as American metropolitan areas (Adams, 1986). There are several reasons for homelessness, some economic and others emotional (Flanagan, 1990; Leshner, 1992). First, job loss since the 1970s has taken a terrible toll on families. Economic restructuring, as we have seen earlier in this chapter, has caused job loss and community decline. In many cases a loss of income results in an inability to afford housing; for some families, even rental housing can be hard to obtain with limited financial means. Second, declines in welfare funding have been a principal cause of homelessness: fiscal austerity and cutbacks in the federal budget have limited the ability of local communities to support people in need. Third, since 1970 mental hospitals have discharged large numbers of patients or switched them to outpatient status as a result of cutbacks and changes in treatment philosophies. Many of these patients have not been able to function on the outside and have become homeless.

Finally, homelessness is also caused by the housing problem and the inequities of the second circuit of capital in the United States. Because the real estate market functions both to drive up the cost of shelter and to foster speculation, units may be either too expensive to rent or own, or they may simply be held vacant as a tax loss. The urbanist Carolyn Adams terms this condition one of "maladjustment" rather than a shortage of housing, because in the United States many housing units remain available. As she suggests,

> The term "maladjustment" is more accurate than "shortage" because in many places the number of existing units is theoretically large enough to house the urban population. Yet many households cannot find housing that is both affordable and suitable for their needs. At the same time, large numbers of housing units stand vacant, awaiting demolition or renovation. The presence of empty housing in cities where large numbers of families and individuals need shelter is an invitation to squatting, and that is precisely what has taken place (1986: 528).

Homelessness combines aspects of economic crisis, mental illness, poverty, and the failures of U.S. health and housing policies. Remedies for this problem require integrated plans that address the root causes. It is clear that with the declining economy, poor people have fewer opportunities to improve their lot, and their relative standing in society is deteriorating.

Housing is a major problem in both urban and suburban areas because the stock of affordable units is on the decline. Due to the relationship between the location of a home and the quality of urban life, the lack of affordability will continue to be an important problem for new families and young couples just starting out in life.

Summary

In conclusion, the effect of differences in the flow of resources to metropolitan communities due to racial and economic problems has created a landscape in which poverty and affluence exist almost side by side. While some individuals and families seem to be doing remarkably well, many are barely holding on to what they have been able to accumulate over years of hard work. Large numbers of Americans now find quality education and affordable housing slipping beyond their grasp or that of their children. In addition, a minority of people do not even have the advantages of this besieged majority. They are mired in an intractable syndrome of isolation and despair. Our central cities are becoming unlivable, with crime and social strife prevailing almost everywhere. In Chapter 14 I shall take up other issues involved in social problems, particularly ones that involve the environment and planning. These issues will be related to the process of uneven development that informs the sociospatial approach. A final chapter (Chapter 15) will consider some possible solutions and the prospect of a positive urban future.

CHAPTER

11

LOCAL POLITICS:
City and Suburban Governments

Until the 1950s urban governments in the United States were quite powerful. This is somewhat remarkable because when the political structure of the country was carved out in the eighteenth century, no provision was made for the autonomy of local government. Power under our *federal republic* is shared between the states and the federal government. City governments exist only by permission of the state in which they are located.

In the 1800s cities were granted specific powers which enabled them to prosper. In particular, it was considered beneficial for the entire society if local government could take care of the environmental needs and provide services which supported the quality of daily life. For example, as cities began to grow, they needed *infrastructure,* that is, paved streets, sewer lines, utilities, bridges, and harbors. Cities also needed services such as garbage collection, police protection, and education.

Through a mutual understanding between the different levels of government, the task of providing for the infrastructure fell to the locality. As a result, in the 1800s, states sanctioned the notion of the *municipal corporation* which provided for city government and its services. In return, those same governments were given limited powers of taxation and, most significantly, control over the regulation of land. Hence, the responsibility for the quality of the local environment fell mainly on municipal shoulders.

From its earliest days the powers of city government were viewed as a prize, even though their scope was limited. It was understood over 100 years ago that in addition to capital and land, control of the bureaucracies and of the decision-making power of government was a separate means of acquiring wealth. The power to tax or regulate both land use and public services gave local government officials significant control over other people's money.

Municipalities could, for example, tax the local economy and reap the benefits of growth in the value of land. In addition, city services expanded their domains through various departments or bureaucracies, thereby making the city a major employer. It was this power that made urban administrations central players in the generation of wealth. This ability no longer exists, as we shall discuss later on, because of the increased mobility of capital.

In previous chapters we have seen how capital investment operates to produce a built environment. Due to the uneven nature of development, growth brings with it problems of equity and social justice. The struggles involving these issues are carried out in the municipal arena. The government must also intervene to keep capitalists from destroying each other's opportunities in the mad rush for profits. As a result, local government becomes the forum within which issues of growth and change, of the local quality of life, of the demands of citizens for relief from inequities, and of the well-being of local neighborhoods are all addressed. Both conflict and accommodation mark the tenor of community public affairs.

Over the years the nature of local government has undergone an evolution. Unprincipled exploitation of municipal decision-making powers was opposed by a series of reform cycles, some of which were more equitable and enlightened than others. But always, individual city residents and interest groups sought over the years to make local government in the United States function better. Out of that struggle the ethos of self-rule has been fashioned, however imperfect the results may be. The following sections discuss the evolution of these changes and then deal with several important issues that surround the exercise of municipal authority today—in particular, the decline of democracy and the growing power of corporate and banking interests to define the local agenda.

The Machine

In the early days of municipal government, political groups that controlled city hall and utilized it to acquire wealth were called *machines*. One of the most notorious machines was the New York based Tweed Ring, run by Boss Tweed. His reign made city government synonymous with corruption. A more typical machine, however, was the one founded by Boss Pendergast in Kansas City (Dorsett, 1968). Jim Pendergast came to that town in the 1880s and opened a popular saloon. It was located in West Bottoms, a typical poor section of the city—typical for any city at that time—with large numbers of low-income working people coming from a variety of backgrounds, including foreign countries. He entered politics by creating a local Democrats club and quickly extended his influence to adjoining wards within the city. Soon his organization was able to mobilize the majority of votes, and he took control of local government. Boss Pendergast's regime was apparently not corrupt and derived its income from the regulation of saloons, gambling, and prostitution. Its support came from the successful mobilization of the low-income masses.

After 1910 Jim died and his brother Tom took over. In the years to follow,

Cartoon of Boss Tweed with his hand in the public till. "I stick my fist in as far as it will go, and pull it out as full as it will hold. I stick to my friends. That's me! There you have Tweed self-painted to the life."

Pendergast remained in control of the city, but increasingly followed the lead of corrupt bosses elsewhere by engaging in fraudulent voting practices and the peddling of influence. That is, when business needed some public decision for its own interests, the local political leaders would ask for money in return. Eventually, charges of corruption destroyed this machine as they did so many others.

The principal characteristic of the machine was that it functioned as a mode of administration rather than social change or political ideology. That is, machines did not stand for anything in particular, although most of them ran on the Democratic party line because it was favored by voters. They worked as organizations that acquired and deployed citizen votes. As Lineberry and Sharkansky (1978: 119) note: "Machines are almost never ideological. They are rather broad umbrellas that are large enough to cover every shade of opinion and interest." The members of machines aggressively sought the loyalty of voters, often by promising employment or other favors. In return, those individuals behind the machine used their political influence to acquire wealth for themselves and their associates in the private sector.

Machines were organized efforts of corruption (Scott, 1972). Their power derived from their ability to mobilize large numbers of voters and thereby win elections. Once in power, they had control over the city resources. Hence, machines could also do some good. They helped redistribute wealth to those who really needed it—for example, by employing hundreds of thousands of recent immigrants in search of work. They institutionalized and enlarged city bureaucracies. These became useful during times of crisis, such as when epidemics occurred, and they brought order to everyday city life.

Progressive Reforms

Beginning with the twentieth century, the corruption of machine politics was attacked at a variety of levels. Businesses that had been growing in strength and scope throughout the nineteenth century no longer sought to associate with corrupt regimes. Much of the city infrastructure was also in place across the country by the turn of the century, and there was less for government to do aside from providing services. One remedy used to combat the machine was the movement to change the structure of local government known as progressivism. As the twentieth century arrived, progressivism attracted large numbers of voters, many of whom had recently attained middle-class status because of economic growth. Eventually the machines whose base remained within working-class districts were thrown out of office. Urban governments transferred control to reformers, many of whom were from citizen and business associations known as "good government" coalitions. Some of the reforms that were enacted involved changing the way local leaders were elected and reorganizing city bureaucracies.

Changes in the Political Apparatus. Under the machines, most cities were carved up into local wards with each sector able to vote for a councilperson who would sit in the government chamber. Most bosses, such as Pendergast in Kansas City, Cox in Cincinnati, and Tweed in New York, started by capturing a single ward. Machines could use their influence on the voters at the local levels to mobilize support for candidates. One characteristic reform of the progressives involved a switch from precinct to at-large elections where candidates had to acquire an overall majority of votes across the city in order to win. It was felt that the open glare of publicity and the need to acquire support from all the citizens of the city would act to curb the insider trading and deal making that were characteristic of the ward system.

In short, what this progressive reform did was change the *structure* of the municipal government apparatus of citizen representation. To this very day the extent to which various individuals and parties influence city elections depends to a significant extent on the structure of local government. Specifically, it depends on how citizens are represented, in addition to other factors such as their desire for change. For example, at-large elections require consensus building that cuts across particular interests, while the ward system favors champions of local constituencies with their specific concerns. We shall return to this point when we discuss power structure studies.

Reforming the City Bureaucracy. The reform discussed above refers to changes in the apparatus of *representation*. A second important progressive reform involved bringing apolitical, professional expertise into local government. That is, the progressives also changed the apparatus of *administration*. Because mayors often represented special interests and because city bureaucracies were often staffed by cronies of the machine holding patronage positions, progressives sought to eliminate such abuse. They instituted "civil service" structures in bureaucracies, which then hired people according to their professional qualifications and which insured job security—especially immunity from being fired after a change in political leadership. Work in city agencies became a *career* as a result.

In place of an elected mayor, many cities turned to a councilmanic structure of government with elected officials serving on a council and the head of government appointed as a "city manager." This manager was chosen on the basis of professional background and experience, thereby bringing technical expertise into city government. To this day, the extent to which professional careerists and city managers are involved in local government or the apparatus of administration constitutes a *second* independent source of political effects in the running of the city, in addition to the structure of representation discussed above. That is, the relationship between elected and appointed career officials represents an important source of variation in the relative success of local government.

For example, city managers are usually career civil servants and have considerable control over the day-to-day budget. When their level of expertise is low, they may be responsible for severe fiscal problems through the mismanagement of finances. Unsound fiscal management has contributed to many of the problems that cities now face. Over the past two decades, professional managers have responded to the fiscal problems of cities by improving their ability to aid local government (Matzer, 1986). Several management techniques have been developed, including (1) trend monitoring systems, which enable financial forecasting and trend analysis; (2) fiscal impact analysis, which predicts how future changes will affect people; and (3) creative capital financing, such as floating capital improvement plans for public investment. In short, professional city managers can make a positive difference in the fight against fiscal distress and budget problems.

To summarize, while the machine embodied a vote-for-favor ethic, progressive reforms restructured the representative and administrative apparatuses of government so that influence operated according to general interests expressed in terms of overarching values that were often ideologies. We cannot say unequivocally whether one system was better than the other, although the serious excesses of machine politics were cleaned up by the progressives. The machine, while flawed, did champion the needs of the masses, while the progressives tended to represent the middle-class business community. What we can stress is that explorations into the nature of political power and influence at the local level must consider the independent effects of structures of representation on the one hand, and the role of city bureaucrats, on the other, in addition to factors related to competition over votes.

The above discussion has demonstrated the importance of structure for understanding the role of local government. Much of politics, however, is high drama and involves constant interactions between various individuals and groups over the satisfaction of respective needs. Politics involves the way these actors utilize power to get what they want. In what follows we shall examine a number of theories of politics that address this important issue of the nature of power.

Theories of Local Politics

Whether we consider city or suburban governments, the central feature of the local state—its ability to acquire wealth and channel social resources—has meant that organized interests are always competing with each other for control. This supplies the drama of politics. There are two main approaches to the issue of control, namely, pluralist theory and elite theory.

Pluralist Theory

According to this view (Dahl, 1961; Polsby, 1980), there are many interests within local areas, and citizen preferences are aggregated effectively in political forums to create public policy. While some groups may in the short run seize power, in the long run all interests are represented in some way. Hence, competition for public office makes control of government by any particular interest unlikely.

Those subscribing to this theory have carried out several case studies that seem to confirm it. However, their results were bound by their methodology. In particular, they looked at overt decisions made by government. For the case of New Haven, Connecticut, Dahl (1961) focused on the way the mayor and city council made decisions related to urban renewal. He found a pluralistic array of separate interests that were integrated by the mayor. Critics, however, charged that this approach is much too narrow and doesn't account for the way many important decisions about city life are *never* brought up for public deliberation at all (Bachrach and Baratz, 1962). Thus there is much that takes place behind the scenes that the public never knows about and which influences government policy.

Elite Theory

A second source of criticism of the pluralist perspective comes from an opposing point of view, elite theory. It asserts that there is always a select group of influentials or a "community power structure" (Hunter, 1953) which possesses the controlling interest in town. It is this elite that really runs the city. The power structure can be identified by a network approach that finds the wealthiest and most influential people in town and uncovers whom they associate with.

Community power structure case studies are also very convincing. Despite criticisms, this perspective has emerged as the best way to explain local political power because it captures the way government and the private sector combine to push development toward specific directions, often in spite of community opposition, but mainly in ways that are never brought to light.

The elite structure of power was discovered by Floyd Hunter (1953) in his study of Atlanta, and was confirmed over thirty years later by Clarence Stone (1989) in that same city as a phenomenon of influence. That is, the most powerful people in the city are also the ones with the most influence over decisions. While not actively involved in all government deliberations, this "elite" monitors them and intervenes through personal influence when it appears that some impending decision or public project will interfere with their needs.

One characteristic of elites is that they get together relatively often to establish and reaffirm *common* interests. In Boston, the elite group was known as the "vault" because they met at some sequestered location. During the 1960s the vault consisted of fourteen corporate leaders who worked to influence both local and state government for their common interests. Among other things, they were successful in persuading the legislature to set up a nonelective superagency to promote development—The Boston Redevelopment Authority (B.R.A.). Like all other such agencies, the B.R.A. had minimal community input.

Houston, Texas, to cite another example, has been touted for years as a "free enterprise city." Joe R. Feagin (1988) discovered that despite the label, there was a select group in control which used the local state to improve its private interest. Members were called the "Suite 8F crowd" because they met regularly at a room in a local hotel. The Houston group was very effective in persuading government to enhance its own business interests by pushing for development projects that it preferred. In fact, this group had so much influence that it even got the federal government to fund the dredging of Houston harbor, turning it into a port that made many locals wealthy.

Although most case studies of cities affirm the power elite view, not every city is controlled by a select group of business and political leaders. Detroit, for example, remains a one-industry town—automobiles—but the business leadership chose long ago not to live in the city. Their commitment to Detroit's future remained narrowly focused on the needs of the auto industry itself. As a result, politics was more pluralistic in Detroit. This state of affairs did not prevent General Motors from demanding that an entire section of the city, Poletown, be destroyed to build a new assembly plant during the 1980s. Despite organized citizen opposition, the plans were carried out by an all-too-willing city government. Hence, elite groups can even function effectively from far away to control local politics and do not need to be residents of the city.

Whenever the day-to-day workings of city hall are examined, it is sometimes difficult to discern whether pluralist or elitist powers are in operation. On the one hand, it often appears that there are many groups seeking to be heard and that the mayor must spend a great deal of time with constituents. On the other hand, when big decisions are made the private sector seems to prevail. Recently a *third* perspective on local government has been proposed that fills in the gaps, so to speak, of these other two theories. It is called the state autonomy or state managerialism thesis.

State Managerialism

According to this view, local government itself possesses some autonomy from both community and business interests. The local state also has interests of its own. For example, since government is a principal employer in town, it seeks to enlarge its power over the private sector just to generate jobs and justify expanding budgets. Leaders of local government are also aware that they must satisfy the majority of the population in order to remain in power. Hence, they find highly visible ways of catering to the populace that might on occasion offend individually powerful groups, such as demanding that developers make small but significant concessions to community interests before project plans can be approved.

Several studies (Lipsky, 1976; Hero and Durand, 1985) have confirmed the presence of "relative" government autonomy. In particular, it was found that bureaucrats in city agencies have considerable leeway in responding to the needs of clients. Public satisfaction with government varies greatly depending on personal experiences. Pluralist theory asserts that elected officials function by integrating conflicting demands. While that may be one response, bureaucrats may also choose to lead according to what they perceive is their own expert opinion. As studies of local government have noted, there is great difficulty in holding public officials strictly accountable for their actions. We often discover their abuses of power only when scandalous incidents of corruption are brought to light. But the ability of city bureaucrats to act on their own has positive advantages as well. We have already discussed in a previous section how greater expertise by city managers in handling fiscal problems has made local governments more efficient and prosperous. The relative autonomy thesis suggests that public bureaucrats' ability to pursue their independent interests is always present.

Which View Is Correct?

Years of community power studies have given us a relatively clear picture of the functions of local government. In sum, we might say that the state and its officials act in a variety of ways depending on how they are viewed and on the methodology used to study the government decision-making process. Most cities are controlled by an elite. This notion is *not* the same as the "growth machine" concept of Logan and Molotch (1988). A true growth machine is dominated by real estate interests. In reality, however, city elites are most often composed of corporate and financial interests, as the sociospatial perspective suggests. Furthermore, the actual composition of elites can change over time. It is recounted in historical studies of change that while elites are focused on some economic interest, the sources of wealth change as the decades go by (Feagin, 1988). Spencer Olin (1991), for example, studied the power structure of Orange County, a suburban region outside of Los Angeles, California, over several decades. He discovered that the elite there changed according to the dominant business interests. Initially, the region was composed of ranches and farms, and the corporate agricultural interest dominated. When it was being developed for suburban housing, a land based elite of construction and real estate interests took over. Lately, however, the region has matured into a multifaceted economy, and the elite has changed again to reflect globally linked corporate and financial interests, although land development continues to take place.

At the present time there is considerable evidence that cities are dominated by banks or finance capital because this faction of the business community still invests in downtown. Suburbs and some of the newer cities of the Sunbelt, on the other hand, possess dominating elites with interests in the corporate and construction industries, and some may indeed be controlled by real estate developers alone. Hence, when studying any local area the sources of elite control are important to identify.

In sum, we have enough information about local government to suggest that as a state structure it possesses the ability to generate and channel resources in society. This power is recognized by the business community and by all those individuals who seek public office as a means of acquiring wealth. Despite an ideology of "free enterprise" that preaches minimal government involvement, local governments have often been used to promote parochial business interests. But because the state can channel resources, the public organizes itself and makes community demands on elected officials. They, in turn, must respond in some way in order to remain in office, thereby providing communities with benefits such as adequate parks or summer programs. The outcomes of politics depend not only on walking this tightrope between public and private needs, but on the particular way the apparatuses of representation and of administration are set up. In the end, though, as a great deal of research shows, when really significant issues are involved, such as those that concern economic growth and fiscal stress, the business community wields the most power over local government regardless of structural shape or form.

The Drama of Local Politics

Empowerment: Ethnic and Racial Changes

The succession of economic elites is just one way of looking at changes in local government, although it is perhaps the most important way. Politics is also a dramatic enterprise. It involves struggle, conciliation, coalition building, and conflict. For many years our cities have been ruled by broadly based coalitions representing local neighborhoods as well as economic interests. The backgrounds of local politicians reflected immigrant origins in the early waves that arrived in this country. The late 1700s and early 1800s witnessed the domination of WASPs such as Boss Tweed in New York. Later on, the Irish became adept at political control, as we have seen in the case of Boss Pendergast. For much of the twentieth century, cities have been run by coalitions of Irish, Eastern Europeans, Italians, and Jews. Mayor Ed Koch, for example, a Jew, led New York City from 1977 to 1990.

Most recently, the population of central cities has changed. Minority groups have become majorities. At present over 300 U.S. cities, including our biggest urban areas, have minority mayors. Many are African Americans such as David Dinkins, New York; Tom Bradley, Los Angeles; Coleman Young, Detroit; Wellington Webb, Denver; and Maynard Jackson, Atlanta. The changeover from the ruling coalitions of Irish, Italians, Jews, and Eastern Europeans to minority leadership reflects today's realities but has not necessarily gone smoothly. Change involved a struggle for political control or empowerment, where influence was captured because of voting power. The drama of minority empowerment often involves compelling stories (Marshall, 1990).

Asians, for example, are often considered a "model minority" because most have done well economically. Yet there are many Asian immigrants who are simply scraping along in the United States and who have needs that are being neglected by the existing power structure in local areas. In one such case, the Cambodians of Long Beach, California, decided to organize for empowerment rather than continue to be represented by other ethnic groups. According to a study by Gerry Riposa (1992), Cambodians represent 10 percent of the Long Beach population. Previous ethnic groups relied on churches, ward machines, "and even saloons" as the places where voting blocs could be organized. The Cambodians had no such power bases.

Under continual pressure to become active in politics because of the status quo's neglect of their needs, they began to organize themselves through the only institutional

Mayor David Dinkins, with other city officials, encounters local residents.

channel at their disposal, the Cambodian refugee agencies. According to Riposa (1992: 16), these organizations blended social services for immigrants and cultural support in the transition to U.S. society. As a result of the struggle for empowerment, they were assigned a third task of political advocacy as the voice of the Cambodian community. Today, these refugee organizations are the new organized interests in Long Beach politics.

Another example is suggested by the case of New York City and the recent success at the polls of the city's first black mayor, David Dinkins. As indicated above, until as late as 1990, the old coalition of Irish, Italians, and Jews remained in control of city hall. Dinkins' victory did not happen overnight, but fulfilled an effort of several decades during which African Americans fought for political empowerment. This case is illustrated in Box 11.1.

Social Movements

The section above depicts one aspect of the drama of local politics, namely, the quest for power and control by organized ruling coalitions. There is another aspect, however, that has its basis in the concerns of citizens regarding their everyday life. Individuals and neighborhood associations often organize to influence local government. Despite the old saying, "You can't fight city hall," many people do just that. When there are large enough numbers and defined demands, mobilized constituencies may even aggregate to the level of an *urban social movement,* that is, an organized mass of citizens making demands on local government for *structural* change (Castells, 1983). In the past, such movements have mobilized around the issues of welfare rights, tenants' rights, community control of schools, tax reduction, and control of growth.

In the majority of cases, local protests are *ad hoc* and related to a specific issue. There may be some persisting irritant that afflicts a community, such as inadequate police protection or garbage removal. Residents will mobilize the community to appeal for more resources and the mayor's attention to their needs. Most often this occurs over a short period of time and is resolved when the mayor's office negotiates with local citizens. These incidents constitute the very backbone of democratic freedom, even if the system itself cannot respond freely to every demand. As might be expected, of course, those neighborhoods that are wealthier or better organized usually will receive more immediate attention. There is, therefore, an incentive for communities to keep a standing association that represents an organized voice for their needs. Many localities in both cities and suburbs have such neighborhood associations, and there is even a national network of block associations representing the voice of local communities (Boyte, 1980; Logan and Rabrenovic, 1990).

More organized efforts can become social movements that address fundamental issues such as rent control. For example, there is a class of protests that has been termed "poor people's movements" (Piven and Cloward, 1977) because such actions are organized efforts on the part of the working class to influence local government (see Box 11.2). In such cases, some issue has an impact on a large percentage of the population, cutting across neighborhood boundaries. Leaders will mobilize concerned citizens who demand structural reform. In fact, it is the demand for fundamental change directed at local government rather than at the business community that is most characteristic of an urban social movement. That is, in this phenomenon, while class divisions are present, issues concerning the quality of life transcend class, and other social factors are involved such as race, gender, and the desire for improvements in the "social space" of community rather than the "abstract space" of corporate control.

Suburban Social Movements

Cities are not the only places where social movements occur. Suburbs also have their share. As with the city, organized efforts at influencing city hall in suburbia can range from specific and temporary incidents to full-fledged movements that unite several communities. One common example of the former is the case of neighborhood organization for greater traffic controls on streets; others involve movements to control development and tax revolts of homeowners.

The Struggle for Traffic Controls. A typical subdivision may have a corner that has become particularly treacherous for pedestrians because of the emergent pattern of traffic flow to and from the houses of the development. A problem like this often occurs only *after* most of a subdivision's residents have moved in, and the rush hour stream of cars makes itself felt on local streets.

In such cases, the residents who are most affected will organize and demand from

BOX 11.1 THE STRUGGLE FOR BLACK EMPOWERMENT: THE CASE OF NEW YORK CITY

New York City is a polyglot community of many ethnic and racial groups. No single group dominates. Politics has always been a place of compromise and coalition building; however, government decisions have also been notorious for following banking, real estate, and corporate interests. In the 1980s the population was 52 percent white, 24 percent black, 20 percent Hispanic, and 4 percent Asian. Since the 1960s the black community has sought empowerment because it was a distressed community. Successive regimes never quite met its needs, although some representation was achieved, especially in the heavily dominated ghetto areas. Harlem in Manhattan and Bedford Stuyvesant in Brooklyn had for years been able to elect congresspeople such as Adam Clayton Powell and Shirley Chisolm to the federal government, and even state representatives. But city hall was a prize that the community slowly turned its sights upon.

The late 1960s was a period when African Americans mobilized themselves for the civil rights struggle. They became a force to be reckoned with in New York politics by the turn of the decade. During the 1970s Percy Sutton was the first black to be president of Manhattan borough. He was a loyal Democratic party supporter with a long career in politics. He hoped to run a successful campaign for mayor in the 1977 election. At that time, however, a great backlash arose against the civil rights protests of the 1960s. Law and order was the concern, as was the blocking of welfare rights activism. In the 1976 Democratic primaries, tantamount to winning the overall election for mayor, Sutton faced stiff opposition from the old ethnic camp represented by Mario Cuomo and Ed Koch, and also from the other main bloc of new ethnics in the Hispanic community represented by Herman Badillo, a Puerto Rican.

Badillo and Sutton split the minority vote. Cuomo and Koch fought furiously for the lead, and Koch finally won. Racial overtones were explicitly a part of the 1977 election. The black community organized itself during Mayor Koch's administration as a response to this racism (Green and Wilson, 1992). The years following involved a struggle between Mayor Koch and the minority community in New York:

> The initial effort to confront the Koch administration and to object to the new racism occurred outside the circle of elected officials. The formation of the Black United Front (BUF) in 1978 was the first organized resistance mounted against the Koch administration (Green and Wilson, 1992).

From the very beginning, the BUF was split between those who wanted to work within the system of ethnic politics in New York and those who sought confrontation regarding incidents of racism. Activists and separatists like Jitu Weusi (founder of the nationalist organization The East) and Rev. Al

Sharpton used opportune occasions to confront Koch directly. As Jim Sleeper (1990), an astute observer of New York politics, noted, Sharpton and other militants fragmented the city further by fueling feelings of division between whites and blacks. According to Green and Wilson (1992: 104), two black professors in New York City, "BUF appealed to the more militant elements in the black community but failed to extend the scope of the organization to encompass a broad spectrum of the black community."

The militant cause was helped along by blatant examples of white racism during the years Koch held office. Many of these involved the defending of local territory in response to alleged fears of racial desegregation. Others were more symbolic and involved images of racial antagonism that had developed in city culture. The Howard Beach incident in 1986 occurred when a mob of whites in a section of Queens nearly killed an innocent black man and chased another one, Michael Griffith, to his death on the freeway. Other racial incidents were also as graphic. A 15-year-old was shot by a white police officer. Yusef Hawkins, another teenager, was clubbed to death in 1989 by a white mob in Brooklyn. And Bernard Goetz, a white man, shot four black youths who threatened him on a subway car.

These and other incidents that mesh struggles over meaningful symbols and local territory, as the sociospatial perspective argues, kept the concern over racial injustice alive in New York, but they also served to split the black community over tactics and strategies. Militants garnered the spotlight after these racist events, but they did little to unite the minority community and they did much to antagonize white voters.

Eventually the citywide BUF coalition broke apart. By the late 1980s minority politics was in disarray (Green and Wilson, 1992: 109). In 1988, however, Jesse Jackson ran a brief campaign for the presidency. His effort was afforded serious consideration by the national Democratic party. Jackson ran in what he called the "Rainbow Coalition," which united whites, blacks, Hispanics, and Asians. When visiting New York City, however, the candidate succumbed to the kind of polarized racial politics that plagued the city and that had mired the campaigns of other politicians. He made a derogatory remark against Jews which unfortunately lost him a great deal of local support.

Jackson's effort was not all lost, however. The Rainbow Coalition still exists and has established a legacy that enables moderate black and Hispanic politicians to work together. The organization that was left behind after 1988 and the changing demographics of the city which gave blacks and Hispanics a numerical plurality grew strong.

During the 1990 Democratic primary Dinkins ran against the incumbent, Ed Koch. The campaign was noteworthy for its lack of racism (Green and Wilson, 1992). The two men stuck to the issues. Dinkins won and went on to defeat his Republican opponent in the 1990 election to become mayor. To this day, however, the condition of many African Americans has changed little in New York. Problems of the ghettoized poor still remain, for example, and crime is as horrible an affliction in all neighborhoods as ever. The success of black empowerment, therefore, has ushered in a more realistic era in which people understand that urban problems will not be solved overnight, regardless of greater minority participation in local government.

BOX 11.2 THE CAMPAIGN FOR WELFARE RIGHTS

In the 1940s and 1950s many southern blacks were driven off of farms and moved to the North to find jobs. During the recession of the 1950s employment sources began to dry up and African Americans found themselves trapped in northern cities facing economic hardships. Before the 1960s there were few programs that aided poor people. One such effort was the Aid to Families with Dependent Children (AFDC), which was created by the Social Security Act of 1935, commonly known as "welfare."

In 1950 only 635,000 families were on the welfare rolls. In the 1960s, however, civil rights activities and ghetto riots called attention to the plight of poor black people in the nation's cities. Efforts were launched in association with President Lyndon Johnson's War on Poverty to alleviate some of the economic and social problems identified by the civil rights movement. One outcome of the antipoverty programs was the organization of poor people to obtain relief from AFDC. According to Piven and Cloward:

> As thousands of social workers and community aides who were hired by community action agencies across the country came into contact with the poor, they were compelled to begin to learn the welfare regulations and to learn how to fight to obtain aid for their new clients. . . . Eventually anti-poverty lawyers also became active in these efforts. Thus, when community action workers could not succeed in establishing a family's eligibility for assistance, attorneys instituted test cases and won stunning victories in state courts and then in the federal courts, including the Supreme Court (1977: 271).

War on Poverty programs combined with the expertise of community organizers, social workers, and antipoverty lawyers to promote obtaining welfare as a means of fighting poverty in the 1960s. The success of this effort

city hall aids to control the traffic, such as stop signs or a traffic light. In one suburban case study (Gottdiener, 1977), the affected residents could not acquire the support of their subdivision neighbors living on unaffected streets because the latter preferred the others' street as a traffic corridor. The result was political conflict between two neighborhoods *within* a subdivision, and this touchy affair became a power struggle that for a time polarized the community.

Growth Control Movements. To a great extent, suburban politics is homeowner politics because most of the issues that mobilize citizens concern their interest as owners of single-family homes. One issue that has successfully mobilized suburban residents across subdivisions is that of "growth control." In such cases, we can say that organized efforts to control growth qualify as a suburban social movement. Simply put, when suburban areas grow, the increase in residents brings problems that have an impact on the quality of life for those people who settled there first. Increased traffic, pollution, taxes, crowding in schools, and overburdening of public facilities such as recreational was most dramatic. In 1960, 588,000 families applied for AFDC; in 1963, 788,000 applied; and in 1968 applications had doubled the rate of eight years earlier, totaling 1,088,000. The acceptance rate over these same years also improved greatly. In 1960 only 55 percent who applied got relief. By 1968 the level had increased to 70 percent of those who applied.

During this effort, civil rights organizers came to the realization that welfare programs provided the opening they needed to achieve a guaranteed *minimum* income level for all Americans. As a consequence, they launched the National Welfare Rights Organization (NWRO), whose aim was to mobilize the poor of the country, regardless of race, in order to demand income relief. According to Piven and Cloward (1977: 284), organizing the poor focused on getting them on welfare rolls rather than on demanding that they join the organization. The leaders of NWRO believed that by so doing, they would succeed in realizing their aim—a guaranteed national income standard.

As we have seen, by 1968, the last years of the ghetto riots, over 1 million people were added to welfare rolls, and that figure was maintained for the next few years. In the 1970s, however, the federal government had still not passed an annual income guarantee, and there was an increasing backlash to welfare rights, which by themselves were never popular among the hard-working majority of Americans. Under the administration of Richard Nixon poverty programs were cut back severely. Conservative leaders highlighted welfare cheating as a principal social problem. Governors in New York and California vowed to cut welfare rolls. As increasing numbers of poor people were discouraged from obtaining relief, the mass effort of the NWRO dwindled and finally died. So too did the dream of a national guaranteed income standard for every American.

One bitter legacy of this fight remains, however. During the years since, the issue of welfare rights and the perception that many who are on welfare should not be getting assistance remain volatile factors in the politics of the nation (see Jencks, 1992). At present, many areas have been or are moving rapidly towards welfare reform and a restructuring of the entire system.

areas are but some of the problems that result when a region experiences sustained development. Often, original inhabitants of a suburb will try to prevent future growth from occurring by passing a growth control measure or amendment to the town's zoning code.

For example, in the medium sized city of Riverside, a rapidly growing suburban area in Southern California, a movement arose to limit the development of hillsides and wild arroyos in the town. A growth control initiative was placed on the ballot for the 1980 election. Opposition to the measure was expressed by real estate interests and retailers who wanted to keep up the pace of growth. The initiative to block growth was passed by a majority of voters coming from a variety of backgrounds. In a statistical study of the election, class differences among voters were *not* found to be a significant factor (Gottdiener and Neiman, 1982). Rather, among all social groups in the community a concern for maintaining the quality of life dominated, and this interest remains central to local suburban politics. That is, a principal function of local government is preserving or enhancing the quality of life, and support for this effort comes from all segments

Racial harmony demonstration in 1991 in Brooklyn, New York.

of the community. The nonclass based nature of suburban social movements has commonalities with those of the central city in the United States and other countries that are also concerned with government's role in maintaining the quality of life (see Chapter 7, discussion of Manuel Castells, 1983, and Chapter 14).

Growth control measures often result in "up-zoning," that is, the restructuring of land use to allow only large plots for homes. Such measures prevent the construction of many homes on the same quantity of land, thereby reducing growth pressures. But they also push the value of new homes sky-high. For this reason, many communities that are in the path of development often opt for growth controls. This places them at odds with state legislatures concerned about equal access to housing and developers who seek to build as many houses as they can. What we have then is a potent brew for local political conflict.

Tax Revolts and the Crisis of Suburban Social Services. In several states the demand of homeowners for tax relief not only cut across local suburban jurisdictions, but struck a responsive chord in the majority of residents regardless of class. Such cases are social movements that result in a "tax revolt." California voters, for example, passed the Jarvis-Gann initiative—Proposition 13—in 1979. This measure restricted the property tax that could be charged to existing owners, while allowing increases when property was bought by new owners. In effect, Proposition 13 made new buyers of property the bearers of increased taxes, and in June, 1992, the United States Supreme Court upheld its constitutionality. The initiative was so successful that it sparked tax revolts in other states. Proposition 13 affects all the residents of the State of California because it places limits on the ability of local government to raise and spend tax revenue. At the same time, it has benefited immeasurably all long-time residents because their property taxes are so low.

Local politics in both cities and suburbs is directed at concerns regarding the quality of life and limiting taxes. City government is expected to provide services, maintain law and order, and promote economic development, while not adding to the tax burdens of local residents. This highlights the great contradiction of local politics in the United States. On the one hand, people want government to improve their quality of life; on the other, they are not willing to pay for it in taxes.

Social movements that spring up from time to time which seek reforms and change are motivated by the same concerns that form the basis of local politics, namely, the role of city government in promoting the quality of life and in limiting taxation. One important outcome of research on urban and suburban social movements is that they are not usually class based. That is, their constituencies often cut across class lines. Hence, they constitute a *second* source of politics in society alongside worker-led industrial conflict.

The cross-class basis of local social movements is clearest in the suburban case of homeowner politics. As we have seen, concern over controlling the property tax or the rate of town development is shared by a variety of social groups. Threats to the quality of life cut across class lines. This is clearest in the city when diverse communities unite to block proposed projects that would overdevelop local areas or when traffic, crime, and other urban ills threaten neighborhood tranquility. We cannot deny that in certain cases, such as the campaign for welfare rights, a class basis can be found for protest. But even in this example, the target was local government and not the business community.

It is for these reasons that urban and suburban social movements rank as a unique form of politics which differs from industrial conflict even when they are class based. Whereas the latter involves workers clashing with capitalists over wages and benefits, the former unites people of diverse backgrounds and confronts the state because of concerns regarding taxation or the quality of life. This outcome occurs because it is perceived by Americans that the function of local government is to sustain the quality of life. Examples from this chapter of homeowner struggles for traffic controls and African Americans for empowerment, among others, illustrate how local political movements cut across class lines.

In the end, however, there is also an underlying class nature to all community politics. This is so because ultimately the quality of community life is a consequence of uneven development, as the sociospatial perspective suggests. Thus, while local struggles often cut across class lines and are directed toward municipal government, they would do better to hold wealthy corporations and banks responsible for the effects of uneven development. Business interests, therefore, play a role in how well communities prosper, and there are limits to what government alone can do. In many cases, people do understand this and they work through their local governments to pressure business interests such as real estate developers to channel their investments for the public good. Whenever this occurs and uneven development is assuaged, democratic politics performs the function for which it was intended.

Suburbanites in Westchester County, New York, protest for more library funds.

The Declining Power of Local Politics

There is a drama to local politics, as we have seen, because control of city and suburban government brings with it certain benefits from control over public decisions. The quality of life can be either enhanced or frustrated by the acts of those holding public office. Hence, there is an incentive for citizens to become involved in local politics, even when the apparatus of government discourages direct participation. In addition, as we have seen, involvement in politics is a means of acquiring wealth. Lawyers and politicians along with their friends in real estate, construction, public services such as medicine, and banking and commercial interests may benefit greatly from influence or control of city government. Hence, there is an incentive to fight for the right to manage city hall.

Despite the basis for participatory democracy, the power of local government has been trivialized over the years. The drama of politics has been replaced by infighting over dwindling public resources, some of which unfortunately heightens racial and ethnic divisions. In the past forty years both city and suburban governments have been hemmed in by constraints, making local politics weak. There are three major reasons for this decline of city politics. First, participation in local elections is quite limited. Voter turnout is consistently less than half of all those eligible to participate. Community life was once characterized by high levels of citizen involvement, but if we consider voting, then participation in the community has declined drastically. While some analysts do not consider this phenomenon as cause for alarm, it does signal that a significant number of people have become alienated from the institution of politics and have limited faith in political leaders.

A second limitation of local politics is that if we consider metropolitan regions as a whole, we discover that they are excessively fragmented by multiple municipal jurisdictions and overlapped with special service districts. Some places, such as the Chicago region, possess a chaotic array of over 1,000 separate public service districts. This makes metropolitan coordination of service delivery very difficult and regional planning almost impossible. In addition, central city governments are being overshadowed by their outlying suburban counties which have matured and developed a strong array of services that rival those of the large city. For example, a recent study of Atlanta, Georgia (Fleischmann, 1991), revealed that in 1966 the city outspent its suburban counties by 2 to 1 in services. By 1987, however, the city of Atlanta represented only 10 percent of spending on services among all places located within the Atlanta metropolitan area (MSA). A single suburban county, Fulton, spent almost as much ($409.5 million) as the city of Atlanta itself ($586.7 million).

The third limitation of local politics is the ideology of privatism. According to Squires (1991: 197), "the central tenet of privatism is the belief in the supremacy of the private sector and market forces in nurturing development, with the public sector as a junior partner whose principal obligation is to facilitate private capital accumulation." This ideology, which prevails in most places around the country, asserts that the well-being of the local area is defined as an economic concern, so that the city's main job should be supporting the private sector and its wishes.

Because of the dominance of privatism, social issues such as education, welfare, and crime which require the redistribution of wealth are considered secondary concerns. When times are good, local governments may pay attention to the latter and promote projects of community welfare. However, when budgets are strained, these are quickly sacrificed for the benefit of promoting growth. No connection is made, however, between the need to promote the general quality of life and the desire of businesses to locate in areas that are attractive places to live as well as work. The ideology of privatism, therefore, is a very limited way of conceptualizing the guiding vision of local politics (see Chapter 15 for a more detailed discussion of public policy). It implies not simply the domination of business interests, but limited political leadership and vision in addressing the social issues of growth.

For example, according to Gregory Squires (1992: 28), "no area of public life has suffered more from the current approach to economic development than the public schools." Local government has been spending its limited resources on subsidies to business, such as tax reductions or freezes in the tax rate. Often, this results in a fiscal crisis as overall tax revenues in the local area fall. "As public officials grapple with growing financial problems, they often look to teachers' salaries as a source of savings. Strikes follow, morale on the part of teachers and confidence in the schools on the part of parents suffer, and the quality of public education deteriorates" (Squires, 1992: 28).

Despite these efforts public subsidies to business have had only limited success in revitalizing cities (see Chapter 15). Redevelopment usually is centered on the downtown area and the construction of hotels, luxury housing, and tourist attractions such as convention centers. These areas seem to function effectively by day, but are devoid of life during other times. They are places besieged by crime, the homeless, and deteriorating public facilities. Elsewhere in the city, neighborhoods and infrastructure deteriorate and education declines for lack of funds. In short, downtown business may have been improved by the policy of privatism, but the rest of the city has gone to hell.

The final problem with privatism as it relates to the decline of local political power is that it removes the goals and operation of government from both the political process and public accountability. Government becomes merely a technical matter of choosing which economic policy to pursue. Public/private partnerships involve understandings made in the backrooms of political and corporate corridors. An increasing number of decisions that previously involved the public have now been transferred to administration. Redevelopment has created nonelective superagencies such as the Boston Redevelopment Authority or the Port Authority of New York and New Jersey, which carry out massive projects such as the construction of the World Trade Center in Manhattan with only a minimum of public input. Consequently, the quality of politics has declined and communities no longer enjoy a democratic involvement in urban policies. In short, at present there is a crisis of political process and leadership at the local level, and an alarming deterioration in the community quality of life for most residents of cities and suburbs.

Summary

Since the 1950s, the power of city government has progressively declined. At the same time, the demands on it to insure the quality of life persist unabated. In fact, as suburbanization drained the tax-paying middle class from the city, the population that remained largely represented the neediest elements of society—the poor, minorities, and the aged. As a result, urban governments now find that they are asked to do more and more with less and less.

Suburban governments have not fared much better. Although residents tend to be more affluent than in the city, jurisdictions are relatively small and their economic base is weak. Competition among suburban areas for new investment is always keen and usually results in beggar-thy-neighbor outcomes for everyone. As a consequence, suburban government also possesses a limited scope. Only the wealthiest communities are able to provide the kind of extensive services that rival the central city.

Some people assert that limited government is a good thing and that only liberals seek an extended political sphere which usually does no more than tax excessively and fritter away public money. However, the kind of decline that is referred to in this chapter is not about the limitations of government intervention, but about the diminished quality of local democracy. The former topic will be discussed in Chapter 15 when we consider public policy. At the local level, the declining power of government has meant constraints on the political process and on the democratic participation of all citizens in choosing the future of their own communities.

Local politics is the sphere within which the structural forces discussed in chapters 1 through 7 and the human diversity of metropolitan communities discussed in chapters 8 and 9 meet. As we have seen, government supplies needed services to the private sector and residential neighborhoods. The history of municipal politics in the United States involves a struggle over the form that the representative and administrative apparatuses will take. Each of these is important for an understanding of the daily operation of government. In addition, however, local politics also encapsulates dramatic struggles and themes. Because of the power of political decision-making, both the business and the local residential community strive to make their respective needs known. Municipal government can be the forum within which the desires of ordinary citizens are expressed and the injustices of uneven economic development are remedied. That is a democratic ideal. However, often local politics is controlled by business interests and poor political leadership. Municipal policy merely helps subsidize the needs of the most powerful. This crisis of democracy not only is the consequence of business domination but also represents a failure of citizen participation and political leadership.

City and suburban politics have certain commonalities but also differences. In the city, government has reflected the popular interests of traditional immigrant groups. Recently, leadership and power have shifted into the hands of minorities that have become empowered after a long struggle. Still, corporate, banking, and real estate needs continue to set the city agenda. Greater participation of minorities in city government has not led to the alleviation of social problems.

In the suburbs, concerns over the community quality of life dominate. Once, this issue was defined as one of promoting growth. More recently, growth itself has been perceived as a threat to the quality of life, and suburban politics has shifted to ways of managing growth. Political concerns in the suburbs also hold in common with the large city the need to overcome the injustices of uneven development. In both cases, these concerns are not based on class alone but also cut across class lines to involve a cross section of community interests.

In the 1800s, municipal boundaries enclosed the significant economic resources of manufacturing and banking activities centralized in cities, so that they had the capacity to enrich themselves as the economy prospered. Not so today. At present, capital investing and manufacturing are dispersed across world space. Attachment of capital to place is quite limited, although some businesses such as public utilities, newspapers, and banks have a permanent stake in neighborhood prosperity and growth. Consequently, local government does not have the same ability to raise revenue from the private sector that it once had.

Other factors also add to the limitations of local politics, such as the current recession which impoverishes localities and creates a fiscal crisis, the growing power of quasi-public agencies that push for economic development without community involvement, and the ideology of privatism which restricts the redistributive role of local government and identifies its interest as the need to subsidize business.

The limitations on local government discussed in this chapter require reforms that address the nature of the local political process. Aid for the social problems discussed in Chapter 10, for example, can only come if we understand how government might work better in the future, rather than by endorsing wholesale spending programs such as the urban renewal of the 1960s. Our discussion of problems and politics over the last several chapters, in other words, creates the need to examine the nature of metropolitan policy. I shall do so in the concluding chapter of this text (see Chapter 15). But first, let us examine the patterns of metropolitan growth in other countries of the world in order to obtain a comparative perspective on the issues raised in the preceding chapters.

CHAPTER

12

THIRD WORLD URBANIZATION

U rban development in the United States illustrates the spatial pattern of deconcentrated development characteristic of an advanced capitalist society. While large cities remain important centers of commerce and culture, many of them have reached slow or stable population growth. Despite continual renovation and gentrification in the centers, most development occurs outside the large city in the suburbanized metropolitan region. Land use is mixed and shared between densely populated cities, minicenters of various kinds, and expanding suburban regions of residential housing. As we have seen, our society possesses problems which are accentuated by locational inequities. Both income and racial segregation are common and lead to serious problems in unequal opportunities for employment, housing, education, medical care, and recreation. Despite the problems, most Americans are well housed and well fed. While unemployment is high in recent years, the majority can find work and even pursue careers.

In many parts of the world, cities have a different relationship to society, and people's individual fortunes are plagued by dangers and disparities unheard of in more affluent societies. Box 12.1 depicts life in Lagos, Nigeria, a place of great opportunity but also serious problems. We shall examine the urban condition in Asia, Africa, and Latin America. These regions contain three-fourths of the world's population and most of its land mass. The societies range from democracies to totalitarian dictatorships. What they have in common is an inability to sustain economic development, and with some notable exceptions, a declining quality of life for most of their urban residents.

Changing Perspectives on Third World Urbanization

In approaching the issue of urbanization in developing countries there are a number of misconceptions that must be dispelled. A common conception of such societies is that they are primitively developed compared to the United States. It might be surprising to learn that countries such as Brazil, Mexico, and Korea are highly industrialized, with factory workers numbering in the hundreds of thousands. Some of the largest cities in the world, such as São Paulo and New Delhi, are not only located in developing countries but are also vibrant, dynamic urban centers (see next section). What these societies seem to have in common is a pattern of uneven development that is even more extreme than that found in the older, developed nations. We shall discuss this issue below.

Second, the ecological theory discussed in Chapter 6 argues that developing countries are very much like the developed societies, only they are at an earlier stage and will "modernize" in time (Kasarda and Crenshaw, 1991). The sociospatial perspective disagrees with this view because it considers factors such as the role of the state, of classes, of global capital investment, and of economic changes in the first world—all of which are neglected by the ecological approach—as critical for an understanding of urbanization in developing countries. Thus, it suggests that countries which have a different economic structure will develop in different ways. Close observers of growth patterns in areas such as Latin America (Roberts, 1978) or Asia (Berry, 1989) seem to agree that the explanatory variables stressed by the sociospatial approach are most important, while not necessarily subscribing to the perspective itself. In opposition to the ecological view of similar modernization trajectories, the process of urbanization is *different* from the first world pattern and involves factors such as elite power, differences in state policies, the effect of the global economy, and the effects of class structure (Smith and Timberlake, 1993).

Lagos, Nigeria, including the port district and downtown.

BOX 12.1 LAGOS, NIGERIA

Lagos was unlike anything I had seen before in Africa; it was more like an overcrowded city in India. It is an island with a lagoon between it and the mainland. Perhaps 400,000 people are jammed into this area, almost all of them selling something to someone. . . . Whole sections of the town are devoted to headscarves, and women walk nonchalantly down the street with two- or even three-foot piles of these scarves on their heads. . . . All night the city is alluring: candle flames flickering in small shops or on stalls by the roadside, green or pink electric light bulbs casting eerie shadows in beerparlors. . . . Always the city is intensely vital. All night long, people move up and down, never still (Baker, 1974: 16).

Lagos is the capital of Nigeria, one of the most populous countries in Africa. Due to extensive supplies of crude oil, it is also one of the richest countries on that continent. The British took control of Nigeria from the Portuguese and established a colony at Lagos in 1866. In 1960 Nigeria achieved independence. By 1972 the greater Lagos region contained 1.8 million people. By 1985 the population was 4 million and still growing. At present it is an example, all too frequently repeated in other areas of the third world, of urbanization out of control. As one observer notes:

Lagos today continues to function as the nerve center of the most populous and prosperous country in sub-Saharan Africa. But it presents a disturbing picture of a community overwhelmed by urban problems encountered in both the developed and developing worlds. Like many western cities, it is suffering from serious housing shortages, chronic traffic jams, an increase in the crime rate, inner city decay, pollution, weak financial resources, and a largely unstable urban population. These difficulties are compounded by uncontrolled expansion and growth, painfully poor social services, an inadequate administrative staff, unsanitary environmental conditions, corruption in official circles, and widespread unemployment, particularly among young school leavers who form the bulk of newly arrived immigrants (Baker, 1974: viii).

A third change in perspective concerns the increasing relevance of the global economy. Prior to the 1970s there seemed to be a sharp distinction between first and third world economies. Countries like the United States were still operating under "Fordist" arrangements during this time, which meant that most manufacturing was carried out domestically and that foreign countries were viewed principally as markets for our goods. Less developed countries were sources for agricultural goods such as coffee or winter fruits, but were otherwise disconnected from our own society, except perhaps as places for tourists to visit. Several developmental theories of the time, such as the limited "peripheral urbanization" concept, emphasized the marginal nature of the third world (Harvey, 1973; Castells, 1977; Walton, 1982).

Since the 1970s, however, vast changes have occurred in the United States as Fordist arrangements were dropped and we underwent deindustrialization (see previous chapters). During the 1970s and 1980s, much U.S. manufacturing employment was shipped overseas, and countries like Mexico, Malaysia, Singapore, Brazil, and the Dominican Republic were used as effective sites for labor. By the 1990s it had become commonplace for consumers in the United States to find that the products they purchased, whether these were articles of clothing, sports equipment, or cars, were assembled in foreign places. Thus, a pattern of manufacturing for world markets was established in many areas of the third world, and our lives in the United States were connected by multinational corporations to formerly peripheral societies (Peet, 1987).

Recent studies of third world urbanization now reject previous approaches that emphasized world system marginality or dependency (Datta, 1990). Instead, it is argued that these countries are increasingly linked to the global economy (Smith and Timberlake, 1993). The cycle of investment, manufacturing, consumption, and profit making which leads to more investment integrates U.S. consumers and producers with manufacturing, banking, and consumption activities in other countries, including the third world. This effect is often called the "internationalization of capital" (see Chapter 1). As Smith and Timberlake remark, "Thus, to the extent global linkages are considered, the once sharp distinction between the 'comparative' study of urbanization and urbanization in the U.S. is beginning to break down" (1993: 15). In this and the next chapter we shall highlight these commonalities as well as discuss the differences from the U.S. experience.

While the sociospatial perspective acknowledges the influence of the global system on locality, it does not subscribe to the world system theory which considers that level as paramount (see Chapter 1). Urbanization processes in both developed and developing countries involve combinations of global, national, and local factors that are relatively independent. Thus, for example, the kinds of governments that third world countries have at the national level play a key role in how successful they are in their development schemes. Korea (Barone, 1983) and Singapore (see below) have aggressive national policies in pursuit of growth, and governments that actively aid capital investment. Other countries, such as many Latin American societies, are plagued by government corruption and dictatorships that squander national wealth.

At the most local level there are also independent effects that are related to but not determined by the global level. For example, it was recently observed (Roberts, 1991) that third world cities are moving rapidly from the stage of developing economies to postindustrial relations, that is, skipping many of the features of industrialization that inform the experience of western, developed nations. Large cities in the third world, like their first world counterparts, are experiencing shifts to a service oriented employment base due to their increasing role as command and control centers of capital investment. As a result of new employment opportunities created for professional workers, there is a growing wage differential between well-paid and working-poor residents. How this increasingly diverse class structure manifests itself politically varies from country to country and involves new patterns of local political activity that are independent of and in some cases oppositional to global system needs (see the section on social movements below).

In sum, the sociospatial perspective on third world urbanization considers important the factors of global linkage, differences in the class structure, the effect of national state arrangements, and differences in local politics for an understanding of current trends. Third world urbanization processes also have many features in common that contrast with first world experiences. These can be identified by considering the nature of population growth and change, or demography, as we shall do next.

Demography and Third World Urbanization

When dealing with rapid population changes such as those that affected the United States in the 1800s and affect developing countries today, the science of demography becomes most important. Demographers track the dynamics of population growth. They concentrate on rates of change, such as the frequency of births, deaths, and average babies per mother. Demographers are also interested in rates of migration, especially changes in the rural and urban populations. For any given population, the rate of increase which depends on the number of births minus deaths is known as the *natural increase*. Population changes within any given place can arise from natural increase or from migration.

For most of the history of underdeveloped countries, and we could also say for developed countries during their undeveloped period, the natural increase was relatively stable. More specifically, they had a high birth rate which was offset in many cases by an equally high death rate. Following World War II, the introduction of modern medical techniques and preventive measures to the third world resulted in a population explosion that is called the *demographic transition*. Simply put, new techniques of medical intervention lowered the death rates in these countries, with the result that their societies experienced a *permanent* rise in the rate of natural increase because they maintained a high birth rate. In the developed world the demographic transition was eventually adjusted to by means of a declining birth rate or the social norm of smaller families as industrialization prospered over several centuries. That stage has yet to occur in the third world, although some countries such as Brazil have drastically lowered their rates in recent years. For most of the third world, birth rates still outstrip death rates by a large factor.

The demographic problems of the third world are compounded by the limited success of economic development. With a population explosion, rural areas have been hard pressed to grow enough food for everyone. Despite the best efforts of developmental economists, the standard of living in rural areas has declined drastically since the 1950s in most third world countries. People simply have too many mouths to feed. The dilemma facing families was poignantly depicted in a Mexican film by Luis Buñuel, *Los Olvidados*. A farmer comes to the city with his young son. They move toward a crowd in the center of the city. When the father is satisfied that his son is distracted, he seizes his chance and runs away. Many third world cities are teeming with such abandoned children. As expected, they have a short life span.

The failure of rural agricultural efforts to mass produce enough to sustain the quality of life has led excess population to migrate to the cities. Despite the hardships of life to be found there, the move holds out the promise of improvement, and this encourages others to come. As a result, third world cities suffer from a *double* population explosion—a high rate of natural increase *and* a high rate of in-migration. In the city

Pedestrians and rickshaws in the busy shopping center of Chandni-Chowk in Old Delhi, India.

there is little room for poor people's housing. Migrants find space on the outskirts and put up makeshift shelters that lack the basic necessities of homes, such as running water, sanitation facilities, and even adequate ventilation for heating. These shantytowns have many names all over the world—favellas (Brazil), bustees (India), barriadas (Mexico), poblaciones (Chile), villas miseria (Argentina), bidonvilles (Africa), and Kampongs (Southeast Asia). But they have many features in common, including frequent public health crises, crime, crushing poverty, and no future for the next generation since few countries provide them with schools. We shall discuss shantytowns in more detail below.

A third effect of demographic changes in third world countries involves their common history in colonialism. Western European powers and, in some cases, the United States (for China, the Caribbean, the Philippines) carved up the world and took control of underdeveloped countries beginning in the sixteenth century. Their principal goal was to acquire natural resources such as gold, spices, and, later, cheaply produced manufactured goods. This period of colonialism or imperialism depended on trade with the conquering country. Hence, effective links to the global world system were established early. A result of colonialism was the construction of large cities that were usually located near the coast, such as Hong Kong, Manila, Lagos, Singapore, Bombay, and Bangkok. Over the years these cities grew immensely. At the same time, few other cities were founded because the colonial powers did not deem them necessary.

Over the years third world countries have been able to launch development schemes that have overcome the legacy of colonial control. However, the limited success of these efforts due to a combination of global and national factors has hindered the balanced growth of cities in these countries. As a result, many third world countries today possess a single, gigantic *primate city* that is *overurbanized* or excessively populated and which remains the center for most investment and economic growth, while retaining a relatively *underurbanized* interior with no large cities. Primate cities are characteristic of an unbalanced pattern of urbanization that remains quite different from that found in the developed countries of the world. Let us examine this unique feature in more detail. In addition, we shall consider several other common features of third world urbanization including shantytown development, household coping strategies and the informal economy, and new urban social movements.

Primate City Development Patterns

Primate cities in a given country range as much as thirty times greater in population than the same country's next largest city, such as in the case of Bangkok, Thailand (population 4,697,071 in 1984). They are the *only* destination for rural migrants. Hence, they keep on growing. In developed countries such as the United States, there is an even distribution in the number of cities according to size (see Chapter 4). Some, like New York with over 7 million people, are quite large; but others fill in the ranks lower down with populations of between 1 million and 500,000, such as San Diego, or between 100,000 to 500,000, as in the case of Minneapolis, and so on down the hierarchy. Such a profile constitutes "balanced" urbanization, and it provides both businesses and people with a *variety* of locational choices and urban environments.

Countries with primate cities lack such locational flexibility. As a result, primate cities are locked in a migratory cycle. By functioning like a magnet, they pull the mobile population to them at the expense of other locations. Table 12.1 compares balanced urbanization, such as that found in the first world, with overurbanization, like that found in the third world.

Primate city development questions the legitimacy of ecological theory (Kasarda and Crenshaw, 1991), as discussed above. According to this perspective developed

TABLE 12.1
Comparison Between Balanced Urbanization and Overurbanization

Balanced Country A		Overurbanized Country B	
City	Population	City	Population
Metropolis	3,000,000	Primateville	12,000,000
Metroville	1,000,000	Regioncity	500,000
Metrotown	1,000,000	Ruraltown	10,000
Regionville	500,000	Villageville	10,000
Provincetown	300,000	Hutville	5,000
Industry City	200,000	Tenttown	2,000
Servicetown	100,000	(The remainder: less than 2,000 per	
Homeville	50,000	settlement)	
Suburbtown	50,000		
(The remainder: less than 50,000)			

nations should be the model for poorer countries. They should industrialize and urbanize as rapidly as possible. When they do, ecological theory suggests that the population in industrialized cities will increase their income and acquire a better quality of life. By encouraging urban growth, the entire society benefits.

The sociospatial perspective disagrees with this view. Third world countries can grow economically but only in conjunction with world system priorities and investment flows. Consequently, rapid urbanization may have negative effects because its principal cause is the needs of global capital and not the quality of life for local populations (Smith, 1985). As a result, third world countries can suffer from extreme examples of uneven development despite impressive modernization efforts, and primate cities are often the sociospatial consequence. While the *average* income of primate city residents may be greater than rural counterparts, the inequality of income and of quality of life is so severe in primate cities that the standard of living is less than in rural areas (Bradshaw and Fraser, 1989). Thus, the growth of primate city economies does not help the majority of citizens who are victims of uneven and inequitable development.

Shantytown Development

Despite the dreadful picture drawn of shantytown life, they continue to grow in population. Why is that? The common conception that life in these places is totally peripheral to the vibrancy of urban economies is a gross distortion. In fact, shantytowns are robust economies in themselves—including areas of real estate investment—and are also large residential districts where the working class often lives. Marginality of shantytown inhabitants is largely a myth (Perlman, 1976).

The status of shantytowns varies from city to city and country to country. In many places they are simply illegal settlements that have been built on the outskirts of cities, and they exist under the threat of their annihilation by state authorities. In other places, however, shantytowns have acquired legitimate status through political activism, and they constitute working-class suburbs that have many services, including electrical power, running water, and schools.

Shantytowns also possess a robust social order (Aina, 1990; Cooper, 1987). They are the location for small businesses. In recent years manufacturing has developed in many third world cities, and shantytowns are often the site for small and medium sized factories. In addition, recent penetration of multinational corporations as part of the restructuring of the global economy has brought with it the support of subcontracting in third world countries (Safa, 1987). This phenomenon of vertical disintegration (Chapter 7) creates new manufacturing jobs and helps local entrepreneurs, while integrating shantytowns into the world economy.

Shantytowns are also often the only places where the working class can find affordable housing. Consequently, many of the individuals who build these settlements are real estate entrepreneurs. According to one estimate (Datta, 1990), the majority of shantytown dwellers live in rental housing. Real estate investment brings in much needed income. However, as with the case of the first world, there are also problems with a privatized housing market. According to Schteingart (1990), for example, due

A shantytown at the edge of the city in Caracas, Venezuela.

to the increasing cost of construction materials, shantytown housing around Mexico City has become excessively expensive and new pressures have been placed on the government to address the issue of affordable housing in that country.

In general, shantytowns continue to grow because that is where the growing working-class populations and rural migrants to the city can obtain shelter (Nash, 1992). They must be viewed, therefore, less as slums than as worker's suburbs that require greater attention and services from local government.

The Informal Economy and Coping Strategies

In previous chapters we noted that many urban sociologists follow the ecological approach. They focus on individual behavior and the aggregation of separate interests in the public and private sectors. The sociospatial perspective, in contrast, recognizes that ultimately society is composed of individuals, but finds that a focus on groups, such as classes and networks, is a preferred way of understanding metropolitan dynamics. In the previous chapter, we saw that urban politics has a class component but cannot always be explained by class conflict alone. Homeowner politics and the struggle to control territory and its quality of life are also important political considerations. When studying the third world, the nature of class structure and especially the control by select elites through the government are important factors. However, researchers also assert that third world urban dynamics is not exclusively a class phenomenon. They suggest that the basic unit of analysis for the study of urban populations is another group, the household (Datta, 1990).

As Roberts (1991) argues, the household and its coping strategies are basic to an understanding of urban life everywhere, that is, in the first as well as the third world. Households are collective units that share housing and food, that trade clothing and other consumer durables, and that are composed of individuals who pool monetary resources. According to Mingione (1988), not all the members of a given household are immediate family. Households may contain distant relatives and even friends. Furthermore, collective pooling of resources does not preclude differences between household members, such as conflicts between men and women. What counts most with this emphasis is that it conforms better to the reality of urban life in many countries than does the focus of either mainstream sociology on individual decision making, or Marxists on class alone.

The study of household survival strategies shows that the poor do not accept their adversity in a passive manner. They innovate and find ways of supporting themselves and others. This dynamism makes shantytown life quite complex and leads to both positive and negative outcomes such as, respectively, the reproduction of generations despite poverty, and the existence of criminal activity. Households cope with adversity by making collective decisions rather than allowing the burden of poverty to fall on each individual's shoulders alone. For example, in order to reduce expenses they may engage in *self-provisioning* which "includes domestic processing or production of food, making clothes, undertaking repairs, self-construction of housing" (Roberts, 1991: 142). Other household coping strategies include reducing the number of members (often children, as in the example of the Bunuel film above) and connecting with the *informal economy*.

The issue of the informal economy is an important focus of third world urbanization research, and is increasingly an equally relevant topic for the first world (Safa, 1987). In this sector, whose activities are considered "off the books" or illegal, people sell everything from drugs, to cigarettes and other convenience store items (such as sodas), to produce (such as fruits and vegetables)—and even their own bodies for sex. As the postindustrial elements of global restructuring expand in third world cities, bringing with them highly paid professional services, poor people find informal or casual employment as shoeshiners, messengers, delivery persons, and domestic helpers, in addition to the burgeoning demand for restaurant and other commercial laborers. Many laborers, especially domestic servants and babysitters, are hired off the record.

The informal sector is dominated by the market economy, which is not the same as capitalism (Korff, 1990) because barter or trade as well as monetary exchange prevails and there are no elites that dominate pricing. Work is precarious, especially in the drug or prostitution trade, and does not bring with it the kinds of benefits that people in the first world often associate with jobs, such as health insurance or social security. Finally, researchers of this phenomenon note that in all countries since the 1980s, the numbers of people and activities of the informal sector are growing (Datta, 1990: 15), a fact we have noted in connection with the illegal drug industry's role in poor ghetto areas of the United States.

In sum, the study of household coping strategies and the informal economy paints a multidimensional picture of shantytown life and illustrates how individuals may take advantage of opportunities in cities that are not usually noted when attention is given only to formal economies and our own limited, culture-bound conceptions of every-day life.

Urban Social Movements and Politics

Another important topic that is often neglected in discussing the third world is the significance of political struggles within the city (see Castells, 1983; Walton, 1987; Cooper, 1987). According to one observer, third-world urban movements are character-ized by a

> gradual transition during the last decade from essentially comprising local movements with limited socio-political goals to being more conscious movements making much greater demands on the state and with social and political effects no longer limited to the local arena (Datta, 1990: 44).

An example of this change concerns the broadening movement for affordable housing (Castells, 1983; Ramirez, 1990) and the drive to make squatter and shantytown settlements legal. Organized efforts of poor people have pitted them against the govern-ment with demands for better health, education, and neighborhood services—a phenom-enon which is also characteristic of first world communities, and which transcends class distinctions. Another recent development is the growing number of class based union activities that take place in cities, even though they are not about the built environment as such. Deindustrialization has meant the decline of manufacturing jobs in the first world and with it the drastic decline in the power of unions. But as manufacturing jobs have been shunted to the third world, an associated rise in union activity and class struggles has resulted. Countries such as Brazil and India, for example, have formidable industrial labor forces, and with them have come active trade union movements and class based political action.

Special attention can be given to the role of women in third world politics. Recent research notes that when women migrate to the city in traditional third world countries, they acquire new opportunities for marriage and male-female relations, "even if social conservatism may also be exacerbated by the novelty and difficulties of urban life" (Coquery-Vidrovitch, 1990: 77). African and Latin American studies show that women take advantage both of the informal economy and of shantytown dwellings to earn a living (Schlyter, 1990), although many fall victim to male domination and criminal exploitation such as prostitution. One important measure of the freer status of city women is their respectable role in urban social movements (see the discussion of the mayoral election in Rio de Janeiro, below). Coquery-Vidrovitch (1990: 77) suggests that this important representation may be the result of the active involvement of women in voluntary associations connected with urban shantytown life.

To a great extent, uneven development and the proliferation of shantytowns lead to political instability. The national government is not viewed as an avenue for the solving of ordinary people's problems. This makes struggles at the most local level increasingly important as a vehicle for change. According to one African study (Mabo-gunje, 1990: 361), the government of Nigeria is seen as no more than the instrument of the dominant class, committed to perpetuating an unbalanced distribution of income and wealth and preserving the dominance of capitalist ideology and political power. Reports of the performance in government of different groups, whether military or civilian, reveal a cynical use of state apparatus to enrich individuals at the expense of the commonwealth.

From time to time leaders arise claiming to address the immense disparities of wealth. Commonly, this occurs at the local level and urban social movements help organize residents to fight for political influence. Most recently, for example, a black woman, Beneditas Das Silvas, from the major favella in Rio de Janeiro, Brazil, ran for the office of mayor in December, 1992, on the socialist party (PT) ticket. Although she was defeated, she lost by close voting and hopes to win in the next election. Beneditas, as her supporters call her, symbolizes the forces of change that challenge the inequities of uneven development. Her presence in a local election shows how relevant this issue is for growing urban areas.

A final feature of urban social movements concerns their connections to the global economy. Workers in third world countries comprise a complex social order with many different class statuses (Portes and Walton, 1981). Changes in the activities linked to global investment have differential effects on the third world working class. These differences are reflected in different political positions and complex ideological issues among trade union parties, some of whom are active socialist or communist organizations, although there are conservative and reactionary political elements as well. That is, third world national and urban politics involves a variety of organized political positions despite the greater presence in many countries of worker oriented or left wing movements than in the developed nations.

The global economy can also affect urban social movements directly through its agents of international control. In the 1970s, for example, the International Monetary Fund (IMF), which controls most of the third world debt and national financing, called for austerity measures and reductions in state expenditures among all its client countries in the third world. In turn, national governments responded by eliminating subsidies on many consumer goods, particularly food. This placed a severe burden on households. The results were quite unfortunate. In response to the threat of hunger or increased misery, residents of cities began rioting in protest of food subsidy cutbacks. These "IMF" riots (Walton, 1987; Cleaver, 1989), as they came to be called, were powerful political events that affected the stability of state regimes in diverse places around the globe, including Africa, Latin America, and Asia. As summarized by Datta (1990: 45):

> food riots caused the fall of the Tolbert regime in Liberia in 1979 and threatened the imminent collapse of the regimes in Tunisia and Morocco in 1981, in the Dominican Republic in 1984 and 1985, in Brazil in 1983, in Chile in 1983 and 1985.

As a result of organized opposition to global restructuring agents such as the IMF or to multinational corporations and industrial development, urban social movements have broadened their perspectives to deal with a variety of issues that affect all levels of society, including the local, the national, and the global.

Urban social movements are important in the third world. They take many forms. In Chile, for example, 400,000 people between the years 1968 and 1972 converged on the city of Santiago and established free squatter settlements or "campamentos" (Schneier, 1990: 349). Similar self-governing squatter communities can be found in Mexico, where they are a powerful political force in urban areas (Castells, 1983). In Nigeria, shantytowns have been organized into neighborhoods which have demanded greater political representation. According to one African study, "The mobilization of people at such a level within a city should at least encourage improved information flows and increase the prospect of greater participation by all in the governance (as distinct from the government) of the city" (Mabogunje, 1990: 364). Thus, as we have seen in Chapter 11, urban social movements are common among city dwellers in both the developed and undeveloped countries of the world.

In sum, we have been discussing phenomena that third world countries have in common. These include the presence of primate cities, the complex social order of shantytowns, household coping strategies and the informal economy, and finally, the changing complexion of urban social movements and politics. Much of the research on these topics has been published only since the 1970s, when they were brought into sharper focus for the audience in developed, westernized countries.

Above all, studies show that the "comparative" perspective on global urbanization which conceptualized a break between the first and third worlds should give way to the sociospatial perspective which acknowledges the growing commonalities and links between metropolitan restructuring patterns in both the first and the third worlds. Along with increasing acknowledgment of global links, there is also the recognition of certain differences that exist between countries. Not everything is determined by global processes alone. National and local differences also add to the complexity of third world urbanization. In the final section of this chapter, let us look briefly at these local sources of variation in a region-by-region analysis.

Patterns of Third World Urbanization

Latin America

Latin America contains the world's largest city, Mexico City, with a population of 26 million in 1990, and several of the world's most rapidly growing metropolises: Rio de Janeiro and São Paulo in Brazil, Buenos Aires in Argentina, Caracas in Venezuela, and Bogotá in Colombia. The continent of South America along with Central America and Mexico was urbanized hundreds of years ago as a result of the Aztec, Mayan, and Inca civilizations which founded great cities during the European Middle Ages (see Chapter 2). Later, in the seventeenth and eighteenth centuries, the Spanish and Portuguese conquests aided the urbanization process by founding new towns. The relations of colonialism created primate cities in most countries, and these places were planned enclaves, usually with a standard grid layout that facilitated easy movement. Many of the cities were also located on the coast because of the dominance of trade with the colonial power, although Mexico City, the capital of the ancient Aztec empire, remains an inland magnet for migration.

In recent years countries such as Brazil, Argentina, and Mexico have benefited from

U.S. deindustrialization and the global search for cheap labor. Mexico, for example, is host to the successful "maquilladoras" program which locates primary manufacturing in a band of space along the U.S. border for shipment back to the United States as finished products to be sold in that country. Maquilladoras systems, such as enterprise zones, are becoming increasingly popular with third world countries as first world deindustrialization continues. They allow first world multinationals to retain control of production and marketing while still benefiting from the exploitation of cheap labor in foreign countries with the active support of their governments. The maquilladoras program, for example, relies heavily on the use of female labor which has been made compliant by the culture of paternalism (Fernandez-Kelly, 1991) and enjoys active subsidies from both the Mexican and U.S. governments.

Some Latin American countries such as Argentina and Brazil have industrialized. However, in order to be successful and compete with foreign competition, they must use the most sophisticated techniques to make products that will sell on the global market. Most often this means using capital intensive methods such as automation that do not require much labor. Consequently, even in countries which have achieved some industrialization, factories are run without significant labor forces. New jobs, then, are not created at a pace that could absorb the excess rural population. The result is the perpetuation of shantytown growth despite industrial development.

Brazil is a graphic example of the dilemma presented by world system competition. Brazil has a rather successful indigenous steel industry. It can compete on the world market principally because it is capital intensive and uses the latest techniques of production. But this also means that it employs comparatively few people. Hence, it is not a major source of employment, something Brazil also desperately needs. As Cochrane (1982: 16) illustrates, in the 1870s England was the world's leader in steel production, reaching the million-ton mark. At that time England's steel industry employed 400,000 workers. Brazil today routinely produces four times that amount of steel, but does so using only around 28,000 workers. Modern technology and production techniques make a difference that is surely a mixed blessing to developing countries, and the need to compete in the world system constrains the types of development policies those countries can pursue.

Latin America is the scene of the most explosive growth on this planet. São Paulo in Brazil had a population of less than 3 million in 1950, for example. Today its population is approaching 24 million (Dogan and Kasarda, 1988). Estimates assert that the total Brazilian population, which was 136 million in 1985, will almost double to 246 million by the year 2025 (United Nations, 1985). Of this population it is estimated that over 90 percent will reside in urban areas. In short, Brazil in the next thirty years will become a country of giant cities. To feed these people, Brazil can exploit its arable land mass. However, as the world has recently acknowledged in alarm, these new lands are the rain forest. A potential ecological disaster of global magnitude is in the making.

Mexico's population is simply out of control (McDowell, 1984). It too expects to double its 1985 population by the year 2025 (from 79 million to 154 million). Unlike Brazil, however, the country is semiarid and does not possess appreciable agricultural resources. It has already cultivated virtually all of the available land. Population pressures will force people into the cities and into migration "El Norte," or north, to the United States. As observers note:

> The urban population is expected to increase from 55 million in 1985 to 131 in 2025, the equivalent of 13 cities of ten million each. Is there a limit to Mexico City's growth, this bowl constrained by a circle of pollutant-trapping mountains? Guadalajara and Veracruz might become enormous metropolises. How many new cities of over a million will spring up in the Mexican "desert"? How many Mexicans will head for California, either legally or clandestinely? (Dogan and Kasarda, 1988: 24–25).

In addition to immense population pressures, Latin American countries share a history of political instability. They have been controlled for over a century by the dictates of U.S. foreign policy and by the demands of its corporations. Over the years developmental strategies have been hemmed in by such global constraints. There is a great need to nurture domestic industrial schemes. Yet political problems and periodic military coups seem to hamstring such efforts. Instability is also fostered by the class system, which is one of the most skewed in the world. Thus, the factors of class structure, government control, and global power figure prominently in understanding development in Latin America.

For example, Argentina after World War II possessed the ingredients to become a world power. It had an industrialized labor force, a large proportion of European trained professionals, and abundant natural resources. The country quickly fell victim to totalitarian government under Juan and Eva Peron and a succession of military dictatorships. The corruption and inefficiency of such regimes failed to realize the Argentinian promise.

At present, democracies in countries such as Peru (with recent martial law proclaimed by its president), Brazil, Colombia, and Chile remain unstable. This affects long term chances for economic development, because capital is reluctant to flow into such countries. As observers have noted (Geisse and Sabatini, 1988), the primate cities of Latin America generate economic growth, but when industrialization strategies are sandbagged by corruption and totalitarian politics, and when the quality of life declines for most of the population due to uneven development, the prospects for realizing the economic potential of urban areas remain bleak.

Asia

The global region of Asia represents great diversity and contains at least half of the world's population. The two largest countries, China and India, share a similar pattern of settlement. They are "underurbanized" as nations, with a large segment of the population remaining in rural areas *and,* in the case of India more so than China, "overurbanized" because of the presence of primate cities. In China, close to 80 percent of the population resides in rural areas. The remaining 20 percent are heavily concentrated in the few cities such as Shanghai and Beijing with populations of over 500,000. In India, slightly less than 80 percent of the population lives in rural areas, while the majority of urbanites reside in cities of over 1 million in population.

India and China display differences in their patterns of urbanization because of different national policies; that is, as with the case of Latin America, attention to the factors of state control and local class structure explain a great deal about development. China's communist government, for example, has restricted the size of its largest cities. In the 1980s, China's largest city, Shanghai, had a population of under 7 million, Beijing was 5,550,000, and Tianjin was 5,130,000 in 1982 (Chen, 1988: 233), although their surrounding areas also had large populations. In contrast, India's largest city, Calcutta, contained over 9 million people in the 1980s, while Bombay had 8.2 million, and Delhi had 5.1 million (Nagpaul, 1988: 254). By the year 2000 it is estimated that these three cities will have populations of 19.6, 19.0, and 13.2 million, respectively (Nagpaul, 1988: 256).

Of all the rapidly growing population areas of the globe, only China seems to have controlled the rate of urbanization to match its development potential in the past. China's government pursues a balanced growth process of rural and urban development. Under the "hukou" system, the rural population is prevented by law from moving to cities (Kim, 1988). This outlaws the kind of in-migration to the cities from rural areas that is common in the rest of the developing world.

Such balanced growth has had positive effects. As one study suggests (Bradshaw and Fraser, 1989), in China large cities improve the quality of life. More recently, however, China has launched an extensive drive to integrate into the world economy, particularly by manufacturing consumer items. Recently the government has adopted rapid modernization policies that have canceled China's measured urban growth. It is now estimated that by the year 2000, China's two main cities will have populations that will be slightly larger than India's, that is, 23.7 million for Shanghai and 20.9 million projected for Beijing (Chen, 1988: 247), although it remains to be seen whether or not they will also develop the characteristic pattern of uneven development that plagues other societies.

China and India can also be contrasted with regard to the quality of life in their cities. Extreme forms of poverty are the images that are conjured up by the mention of India's cities: Calcutta, Bombay, Delhi. To an extent these images are accurate. The first two cities have large homeless populations, and all possess a declining quality of life. India's cities are surrounded by shantytowns, called bustees, which grow each day. Their presence has not prevented the city center from experiencing terrible over-crowding. The population density of Calcutta, for example, has been estimated at 45,000 residents per square kilometer, with the overwhelming majority living below the poverty line. Misery, disease, squalor, and malnourishment afflict the hordes of urban street people. The urban implosion of India is the consequence of rural push factors as well as urban pull. The "green revolution" which modernized India's agriculture has been relatively successful, which has led to a decline in the number of people needed to grow food in rural areas. As a result more Indians in recent years are looking toward the cities for livelihood. Estimates are that by the year 2001 the urban population will have increased to 33.1 percent from 23.3 percent in 1981, or a *doubling* of the population living in cities (Nath, 1989: 258).

The uncontrolled influx of people to India's cities is making a bad situation worse. As one observer notes:

The most serious problems are related directly or indirectly to the extreme shortage of housing, and to inadequacy of physical and social infrastructures to meet the needs of the urban low- and middle-income groups. . . . The shortages are the principal cause of the progressive deterioration of the urban environment during the past 20-25 years. Proliferation of slums is the most visible symptom of the environmental deterioration. The other major symptom is the rapid increase in the levels of air and water pollution in or near the cities, far above the internationally accepted levels for maintaining human health and safety (Nath, 1989: 264).

Some of India's cities, however, such as Delhi, have large areas that are middle class and quite prosperous. Bombay was planned by the British as a colonial center and still retains its planned streets and residential districts which allow services to be delivered with some efficiency. It is a major center of industrial and service employment. In short, despite the declining quality of life, India's cities are not all mired in extreme poverty and deprivation (Misra, 1978).

Under the communists, the Chinese cities have fared comparatively better. One of the first acts of the Maoist regime in the 1950s was to eradicate the poverty and prostitution endemic to the streets of Shanghai, the focal point of global colonial interests. City services throughout China are regulated by the state and function to maintain the quality of life. There is little crime and few signs of poverty. The Chinese government has also pushed strict measures of birth control. In fact, most families are not permitted to have more than one child. This state policy of restricting population growth in a country of over 1 billion people has had some success in the cities, but is less successful in the countryside.

There is a visible contrast between India and China, as noted by Whyte and Parish (1984: 2–3) with regard to Chinese cities:

Slums and squatter settlements seemed absent, conspicuous consumption and foreign oriented life styles were not visible, a high degree of economic equality and security seemed to prevail, unemployment seemed absent, close-knit neighborhoods and families seemed to persist, and crime, drug addiction, prostitution, and other forms of deviance seemed minor or nonexistent.

In one area, however, Chinese cities seem to be worse than their counterparts elsewhere—pollution. Under the communists no environmental regulations or controls were imposed on industrial development. The outcome has produced levels of pollution that are so high, they threaten the well-being of the population (see Chapter 14 for an extended discussion of the environment).

Shanghai, for example, may just be the world's most polluted city. Less than 5 percent of the city's sewage is treated, and 4 million cubic meters of raw sewage enter the city's river, the Huangpu, daily (Murphy, 1988: 175). The Huangpu is Shanghai's principal source of drinking water. Industrial plants upstream also discharge untreated chemical wastes directly into the river. The long-term effects of this pollution on the population have yet to be documented. In addition to the problem of drinking water, Shanghai shares with other Chinese cities an increasingly threatening air pollution problem. The major source of heating fuel is soft coal. This is an especially dirty energy source, spewing ash and poisonous gases like sulfur dioxide into the air. One estimate is that 16 hundred tons of fly ash and 15 hundred tons of sulfur dioxide for each square kilometer of the city fall each year—a level unprecedented across the globe. Beijing has similar air pollution problems, especially during the cold winter when the sun itself is obscured by coal smoke. At present, the Chinese government continues to ignore pollution problems and has done little in the way of environmental regulation.

Asia contains other rapidly growing regions (see Table 12.2). By the year 2000, the British Crown Colony of Hong Kong is expected to have 6.5 million people; Japan's urban population will be 111 million; North Korea's, 19.9 million; South Korea's, 36.2 million; Indonesia's, 64.1 million; Malaysia's, 8.8 million; the Philippines', 37.8 million; the city state of Singapore's, 2.3 million; and Thailand's, 15.9 million. In all these countries the primate cities—Tokyo-Yokohama, Pyongyang, Seoul, Taipei, Jakarta, Kuala Lumpur, Manila, and Bangkok—represent the centers of economic growth and development (Yeung, 1988: 162). For example, Tokyo accounts for 60 percent of Japan's elite business leaders and 60 percent of the total capital invested, along with a third of all department store sales. Seoul contains 78 percent of South Korean business headquarters and 90 percent of all large enterprises, while accounting for 27.9 percent of South Korea's GNP. Finally, Bangkok houses one-third of Thailand's manufacturing and almost 80 percent of its banking, and contributes 26.8 percent toward the country's GNP (Yeung, 1988: 162).

In recent years several Asian nations such as Korea, Taiwan, and Singapore

TABLE 12.2
Cities in Asia with Population over 5 Million by Location
(Population in millions)

City and country	Rank	1990	2000 (projection)	Density (sq. miles)
Tokyo-Yokohama, Japan	1	26,952	29,971	24,463
Seoul, South Korea	4	16,268	21,976	45,953
Osaka-Kobe-Kyoto, Japan	6	13,826	14,287	27,833
Bombay, India	7	11,777	15,357	120,299
Calcutta, India	8	11,663	14,088	54,607
Manila, Philippines	14	9,880	12,846	50,978
Jakarta, Indonesia	15	9,588	12,804	122,033
Delhi, India	19	8,475	11,849	59,102
Shanghai, China	23	6,873	7,540	87,659
Taipei, Taiwan	26	6,513	8,516	45,710
Bangkok, Thailand	28	5,791	7,587	55,126
Beijing, China	29	5,736	5,993	37,816
Hong Kong, Hong Kong	30	5,656	5,956	280,350
Madras, India	31	5,743	7,384	48,541
Tianjin, China	32	4,804	5,298	97,291
Nagoya, Japan	36	4,736	5,303	15,236
Pusan, South Korea	37	4,838	6,700	86,284

Source: *Statistical Abstract of the U.S., 1991.* U.S. Department of Commerce, Economics and Statistics Administration, Bureau of the Census, Table 1437, pp. 835–836.

BOX 12.2 SINGAPORE

Singapore is an island nation that is also a metropolitan area. For that reason it is unique in the world. In 1965 the city/island of Singapore with an area of 240 square miles became independent of Malaysia. In 1984 its population was 2,616,000, composed mainly of Chinese, Malay, Tamil, and English people, and since its founding it has been ruled by Prime Minister Lee Kwan Yew, the head of a socialist party. From its beginnings it already possessed the best harbor in Southeast Asia and a flourishing international trade. Over the last twenty years it has become a banking and manufacturing center which attracts considerable foreign capital. As a result, Singapore has achieved the second highest per-capita income (after Japan) in Asia.

Part of the reason for its success lies with the strict government control that is exercised over people's lives. In Singapore the national government operates a compulsory savings scheme, with all workers contributing 16.5 percent of their wages and employers contributing an additional 20.5 percent. The hundreds of millions of dollars collected each year from this scheme by the government are then used for economic development. These compulsory savings cannot be drawn out by workers until their retirement. However, they are allowed to borrow from the fund to pay for government constructed housing. As a result, about half the population lives in such government housing (Palen, 1990).

Singapore is a contradiction. It is a society that works extremely well as a dynamic economy with adequate housing, education, and medical care. The price that has been paid for such development is the complete government regulation of everyday life in the city, where the length of men's hair is fixed by law and even chewing gum is illegal. As one observer notes:

> To the visitor Singapore is clean, green (for years the government planted trees and bushes and grass in preference to making pavements), orderly, efficient and apparently perfectly safe . . . this general impression of safety, tolerance and efficiency is accurate enough. But behind this screen hides another Singapore, a city of violence, with a prison population proportionately half as big again as that of Britain. . . . Keeping Singapore clean and green needs more than propaganda broadcast over radio and television, though this goes on the whole time. For tossing his cigarette butt into a drain, Ng Ah Chai was fined $40. He was lucky; he could have been fined $500 (Josey, 1980: 8).

have exploded the myth of third world dependency and the notion of "peripheral" development by growing rapidly as industrialized countries. They have been helped along by the influx of capital investment from Japan (see Chapter 13) and the search by multinationals for cheap labor. Many of the enterprises are joint domestic and foreign operations. Analysts today refer to the four "Asian tigers"—Hong Kong, Taiwan, South Korea, and Singapore—as especially successful areas of industrial development. In the 1980s the Asian tigers led the world in percentage growth of Gross Domestic Product at 7 percent a year (Berry, 1989: 176), helped along by the continuing demand for consumer goods—especially electronics, textiles, and clothing. This pattern of "export led" development has also been tried successfully in Spain and Italy (see Chapter 13) among other countries.

An important characteristic of the Asian tiger development is the large role played by the national government in promoting growth. This intervention is not restricted to subsidization of capital investment and development, but also includes strong control of unions and often, harsh methods of regulating the working-class population (see Box 12.2 on Singapore; Lee, 1981; Palen, 1990).

The presence of the Asian tigers changes the dynamics of global capital investment. In the future, countries such as South Korea may prove to be as competitive in manufacturing as established first world societies or more so. This Asian *Pacific Rim,* which is linked to Japan (see Chapter 13) as well as the United States, contains economic forces that are emerging as a major sphere of power and development for the next century (Berry, 1989). Box 12.2 illustrates the dynamic aspect of Asian growth with the case of Singapore.

Africa and the Arab Countries

Of all the continents, Africa presents the clearest case of the overurbanization/underurbanization dilemma. For the most part, this represents a legacy of years of colonial rule (Simon, 1989). South of the Sahara, the primate cities were all founded as trading centers and located near the coasts or with easy access by water to the coast. Some countries such as Nigeria have a moderately developed urban hierarchy containing several cities: Lagos, Ibadan, Kano, Oshogbo. Most, however, such as Kenya, are classic cases of primate city development. Kenya's capital, Nairobi, contains over half (57%) of the country's population. Here, as in most of Africa, the intermediate level of the urban hierarchy (i.e., cities with populations greater than 100,000 but less than 1,000,000) is notably absent.

Africa contains fifty-four separate countries, and it is sometimes difficult to generalize about the scale of development or urbanization. The north, which contains Arab countries, is highly urbanized. In 1980, 54 percent of the Libyan population and 53 percent of Tunisia were living in cities. Egypt contains one of the world's most populated cities, Cairo, with over 8 million people in 1984. At the other extreme, only 2 percent of the population in Burundi and 4 percent of the Rwandan population in eastern and central Africa were urbanized.

By the year 2000, it is estimated that almost one half the African countries will contain an urban population of at least 50 percent of the total (Rondinelli, 1988: 295). In addition, urbanization is now proceeding rapidly. In 1950 there were only 9 cities with a population of over one million. Estimates are that "by the end of the 1990s, 29 cities will have a population of between one and two million, another 17 cities will have between two and four million residents, and 11 more will exceed four million (Rondinelli, 1988: 300).

Most African countries have a primate city land-use pattern that is similar to other third world countries. The center consists of wide boulevards loaded with traffic and passing in between high skyscrapers built in the common "international style" of the developed West. Affluent natives and the foreign community make their home there. Beyond the glitter domes of development, the core is surrounded by mile upon mile of shantytowns—the most depressing agglomeration of ersatz housing imaginable— where entire families follow a precarious existence and play the "life lottery," hoping to acquire some meager portion of the wealth circulating through the center.

According to O'Connor (1978: 86), around the central city

> is an extensive peripheral zone of crudely built shacks sometimes disparagingly termed a "septic fringe." In several cities such areas . . . now house over half the urban population and informal sector housebuilding constitutes a major economic activity.

Years of dominance by colonial powers coupled with poor local leadership have left Africa in an undeveloped state. Countries continue to rely on natural resources and tourism for economic growth. With the discovery and exploitation of oil, the country of Nigeria has acquired considerable capital, just as is the case with Libya. However, most countries remain locked in the grip of poverty with limited industrial schemes and weak rural economies. Without extensive agricultural development, migration to the cities is an inevitable result. Extensive squatter settlements, or "bidonvilles," are characteristic of urban development (Aina, 1990; Schlyter, 1990).

The Arab cities are also scenes of uneven development. Cairo is known for its cosmopolitan population but also for its squatter settlements, such as the inhabitants of the immense cemetery, the City of the Dead, or the people known as the "zebaleen" who live off of other people's garbage at the extensive city dump (Abu-Lughod, 1969). Most Arab countries have medium sized cities and have not experienced a massive rural exodus because their hinterlands have always been sparsely settled. The oil kingdoms of the Middle East have utilized their great wealth to create cities with modern architecture, such as Riyadh in Saudi Arabia and Baghdad in Iraq. These cities have remained showcases that are dependent on the oil industry monoculture.

Islamic civilization advanced through the founding of cities, so that most Arab places have a long history of urban life. These were either trading or administrative centers (see Chapter 2). Cities were divided into quarters and provided people with stable neighborhoods. The *casbah* or fortified area is probably the most familiar name for such city quarters. Semiotic signs and symbols enable the pedestrian to negotiate what is often a maze of twisting streets (Boudon, 1986). Because of their age, many of the city thoroughfares were designed for donkey traffic and are quite narrow and confining. Finally, Arab cities contain the original shopping malls or *bazaars*. They can be quite expansive, as in Istanbul, Turkey, occupying many city blocks where just about everything is bought and sold. In sum, quarters; narrow, winding streets; zigzags, courtyards, and alleyways; and bazaars are the distinguishing features of traditional Arab cities. To this urban fabric has been added, in some of the countries, the modern highways and megastructures financed by the oil monoculture.

Summary

Third world countries are mired in the vicious cycle of overurbanization/underurbanization. The failure of agriculture means future populations face starvation or migration.

The limited success of urban economic growth means that third world cities will continue to play a marginal role in the global economy. Without balanced policies of development, these countries will face a bleak future. The issue is not simply growth and industrial development financed by the wealthy first world. Rather, there is a need for linked policies that improve agricultural production on the one hand, and urban economies on the other. Especially in places such as Asia and Africa, it is essential that rural populations are stabilized so that the migration pressures on cities can be relieved. Yet development that is simply led by global capital investment will not head countries in that much needed direction.

For example, two decades ago the World Bank and the International Monetary Fund encouraged developing countries to build enterprise zones of manufacturing that would capture global investment. Many of these efforts were successful, and it is estimated that over 1 million people are now employed in industrial free trade zones across the third world (Peet, 1987: 203). However, this development has occurred with a price. Much of the labor force consists of young women between 16 and 25 years old. In previous chapters we have discussed how world searches for cheap supplies of labor often end by exploiting the patriachical dominance over females in third world countries. These women once constituted the backbone of traditional agriculture. With the young female population working in factories, rural agriculture in many countries is on the verge of collapse (Fuentes and Ehrenreich, 1987: 203). Decline of rural economies pushes more and more people into the cities looking for a livelihood. As we have seen, this cycle of growth has disastrous results.

Analysts tell us that shantytowns are growing rapidly in response to continued population expansion. São Paulo, Brazil, and Calcutta, India, respectively, have over 1 and 2 million residents in their favellas and bustees, while Mexico City's barriadas contain over 4 million. The pattern of shantytown/central core *uneven* development is the exact opposite of the United States. As we have seen, the latter possesses maturing and relatively affluent suburbs surrounding a declining urban core. Third world cities reverse this pattern. But more graphically, the gap between the wealthy and the majority of the population is quite enormous.

For the most part, third world governments have failed their people. Ruling class domination of the economy and government leads to harsh measures of social control, hyperaggressive police, death squads, and repressive political dictatorship, rather than enlightened policies of social reform. The passion of the third world peoples manifests itself as a political clash between the fortunate few backed up by the government, and the afflicted and disadvantaged many who face a declining quality of urban life.

CHAPTER

13

URBANIZATION IN THE INDUSTRIALIZED WORLD:
Western and Eastern Europe and Japan

For many years the study of urbanization in Europe was a relatively predictable affair. This is the oldest part of the globe having fully urbanized societies. In recent years, however, profound changes have been taking place in both Western and Eastern Europe. As we shall see, transformations are similar to the experience of the United States. Shifts in industry to high technology, declines in manufacturing employment, and growth in services are common to both the United States and Europe. Social changes also share commonalities, such as the growing uneven development in cities that results from the division between highly paid professionals and low paid service workers; the increasing presence of immigrants, both legal and illegal, in city populations; and the intractable problems of the poor who are often segregated in sections of the city resulting from the combination of job loss in manufacturing and cutbacks in welfare services.

This chapter will examine the case of Western Europe, which is closest to the U.S. experience. In subsequent sections we shall discuss Eastern Europe, or the former Soviet bloc countries, and describe urban conditions there. A final section deals with the case of Japan, which exhibits certain similarities to but also differences from the pattern of metropolitan changes in the United States.

Western Europe

All of the countries of Western Europe have been urbanized for centuries. In addition, lacking a colonial past, they have a well-developed urban hierarchy with city populations ranging from over 5,000 to 100,000 to over one million. Recently, however, this region has experienced a restructuring of population and economic activities similar to what has been occurring in the United States. In particular, many central cities are declining, and there is a marked increase in the rate of suburbanization. At the same time, many new towns are experiencing rapid growth so that the entire urban configuration is altering (Komninos, 1989).

According to Hall (1988), this pattern of change varies. Some countries, such as the United Kingdom, Germany, and to a lesser extent Italy, have experienced decentralization of the population away from the large urban centers. Others, such as Belgium and Luxembourg and to an extent, France, continue to experience robust central city growth. Between 1970 and 1980, for example, Liverpool, Manchester, Birmingham, Belfast, and other cities in the U.K. all lost population. In Germany, Berlin, Essen, Dortmund, and others also declined (Hall, 1988: 121). Of course, since the unification, things have changed considerably in Germany, and urban decline may be stemmed in the west of Germany while being shifted to the formerly eastern sectors.

As with the U.S. case, most of this change can be attributed to the restructuring of space as a consequence of global economic shifts. Manufacturing has declined drastically in the United Kingdom and less extremely in other European countries. Cities have reduced their labor forces and converted to service economies, but with smaller employment bases than in the past. High technology corridors, the European equivalent of Silicon Valley, and other "new spaces" of production have recently emerged. These have become new sources of employment and growth based on a professional, skilled labor force along with low wage services. Industrial restructuring

These two men recently lost their jobs at the Newcastle docks, which were closed due to deindustrialization in England.

TABLE 13.1
Cities and Their Transnational Corporate Headquarters: United States, Europe, and Japan

City	Metropolitan Population	Number of Headquarters
New York City	17,082,000	59
London (England)	11,100,000	37
Tokyo (Japan)	26,200,000	34
Paris (France)	9,650,000	26
Chicago, IL	7,865,000	18
Essen (Germany)	5,050,000	18
Osaka (Japan)	15,900,000	15
Los Angeles, CA	10,519,000	14
Hamburg (Germany)	2,250,000	10
Dallas, TX	3,232,000	9
Frankfurt (Germany)	1,880,000	7
Rome (Italy)	3,115,000	6
Stockholm (Sweden)	1,402,000	6
Turin (Italy)	1,191,000	5
Hartford, CT	1,020,000	5

Source: Adapted from Smith and Feagin, 1988, pp. 6–7.

has resulted in declining urban cores with considerable unemployment of the working class, while the periphery grows and develops into an affluent, middle-class population base. Welfare state programs have been cut back, leading to increasing problems with poverty and crime.

Much of this change is attributed to the shifting patterns of investment in the global economy or the internationalization of capital. Many large corporations have become transnational and direct activities across a broad range of countries, including the location of manufacturing in low wage, third world nations. One indicator of the global integration of development is illustrated by Table 13.1 which shows the number of transnational corporations headquartered in cities of Europe, the United States, and Japan (compare this with Table 1.3 that lists the largest cities of the world). While U.S. cities figure prominently in this list, Table 13.1 also shows the important role played by companies in England, France, Germany, and Japan.

Let us look at these individual countries in more detail.

Great Britain

Deindustrialization has been drastic in the United Kingdom. All the older industrial centers have experienced sharp employment declines due to factory shutdowns and wholesale job loss. Between 1978 and 1985 alone, manufacturing in Great Britain declined by 24 percent (Sassen, 1991: 131). This followed a decade of comparable job loss. During this same period, employment in business services increased by 44 percent. Hence, Britain like the United States has undergone a shift from manufacturing to service industries.

Statistics for London are most revealing. Since 1960 London lost over 800,000 jobs in manufacturing (Sassen, 1991: 205). After 1980 it reaped a harvest of new jobs in the expanding service sector. By 1985, and for the first time in twenty-five years, net gains in employment finally outstripped net losses. The shift from manufacturing to services in the city of London is graphically represented by the following figures: "In 1971 27% of all London jobs were in manufacturing and 68.6% were in services. By 1986 the shares were 15% and 80% respectively" (Sassen, 1991: 205). Almost all of the new employment in services for London is a result of the continued historical functioning of the district known as "the City" as a global center of financial activities. According to Saskia Sassen (1991), London joins New York City and Tokyo as one of three global centers for finance capital whose companies command and coordinate the increasingly dispersed world economy of manufacturing and marketing.

During the same period of restructuring that has changed the fortunes of British cities, new manufacturing centers have arisen which are tied to high tech development. The M-4 highway corridor between London and Reading represents a center for electronics development that is similar to the I-128 peripheral outside of Boston, Massachusetts. In Cambridge, the government linked up with private venture capital and with the university to build a "science park." It contains thirty new enterprises on fifty-five hectares, and is similar to the "research triangle" located near Duke University and the college town of Chapel Hill in North Carolina.

New employment bases have not been able to compensate for job loss due to deindustrialization. England is currently undergoing a change that requires retraining of the labor force along with a smaller industrial sector. The need for drastic changes has provided support for the Conservative Party, which has enjoyed leadership of the country since the 1980s. The Conservatives have dismantled the British welfare state with increased privatization and reduction in publicly supported benefits (King, 1990). This record is comparable to the downsizing of domestic programs during the recent Reagan and Bush administrations in the United States. While a complete transfer from public financing to market based services has not occurred in either Great Britain or the United States, many welfare state programs have been partially converted to a pay-for-service basis or simply eliminated (Forrest, 1991). In addition, the selling off of formerly nationalized companies has enabled the conservative regimes in the United Kingdom to avoid massive debt financing of the economy in the 1980s, unlike the case of the United States.

Privatization has brought increasing misery to the majority of the British working class. The appearance of uneven development on a national scale has also brought with it social changes to the entire country. According to one observer, shifts in national attitudes involve the replacement of a moral ethos that supported the welfare state and its reliance on redistributive policies to overcome uneven development with a new ethos based on social Darwinism, limited public programs, and a full reliance on the market economy (Mellor, 1989).

The outcome of restructuring over the last decade in the United Kingdom is that the police have had to expand their role as controllers of the population while crime and civil unrest have increased. As Mellor (1989: 591) notes, "U.K. towns were, in international terms, safe places. Now burglary, often minimal in material effect, violates personal space and enforces discipline in the use of house and effects; assaults and/or harassment limit the freedom of movement of the elderly, children, black people, women and, increasingly, white men."

There is also growing evidence that Britain, after years of successful redistributive policies under the welfare state, is producing a homegrown urban "underclass," or more accurately, a population of ghettoized poor much like the one in the United States. A survey of households (Dale and Banford, 1989) has revealed that those families with at least one fully engaged wage earner during the last decade of restructuring have managed to place other family members in employment positions of some kind. Conversely, those families where the major breadwinner has lost a job have had only limited success in placing any member in gainful employment. At present, England is facing the "spectre of an increasing number of households where *no*-one works, while there are also households with multiple wage earners" (Dale and Banford, 1989: 482). In short, when a family can consistently count on the resources of a single wage earner, it has the resources to support the employment of others, even if their positions are not in high-earning capacities. However, those families suffering from job loss and periodic unemployment are falling behind and submerging in a sea of chronic poverty.

As of the 1990s there have been few political repercussions from these changes in the United Kingdom. Urban riots did occur, however, in 1989, when the Thatcher government attempted to levy an excessive poll tax on local voters. Urban violence has occasionally flared up in racially mixed neighborhoods such as Brixton. There have also been protracted and very painful strikes, such as the national strike of coal miners in the 1980s which ended badly for the workers. In the main, however, the social and political effects of restructuring are a question for future studies.

Italy

For decades Italy remained one of the underdeveloped regions of Western Europe. Its problem was reflected in the uneven development of its regions. The north was highly industrialized with an urbanized labor force centering on Milan and Turin. The south, in contrast, remained rural and dependent on agriculture (Martinelli, 1985). Population in the south was unstable as native sons often left home to migrate northward for jobs, or left the country.

Since the 1960s the same force of economic restructuring that has operated in the rest of the industrialized West has changed the sociospatial pattern of development in Italy as well. The middle and southern regions, known as the *mezzogiorno,* have developed a vibrant industrial employment base (Piore and Sabel, 1984). Manufacturing is concentrated in the small-craft tradition of the mezzogiorno region, including apparel, textiles, footwear, wood products such as furniture, metal working, and clay and glass products. The firms in this region have been very successful by adopting custom design and flexible industrial methods. They engage in small batch-production which can be changed and customized for new orders relatively easily. Some observers believe that these firms are a model for the new type of "flexible" manufacturing that will prosper in the global economy (Scott, 1988; Piore and Sabel, 1984), called Post-fordism.

Due to foreign competition, especially in the automobile industry, the northern region has been threatened with decline. For some time during the 1970s, the cities of Turin and Milan were no longer the employment meccas that they had been in the past. Changes were made in the industrial base to regain the competitive edge of such companies as Fiat Automobiles and Pirelli Tires. In Turin (see Table 13.1) existing plants were modernized according to the Japanese style that has also been copied by American automakers. Automation was introduced and aspects of the assembly line were turned over to robotics. Wholesale use of electronic or computer assisted manufacturing (known as CAD) was also incorporated into production. Finally, the "just-in-time" system (discussed in Chapter 7) was adopted by assembly plants to reduce operating costs by eliminating inventory problems. According to this system, assembly plants do away with holding large inventories of items they require in production. Instead, they work with suppliers outside the plant but within the region to provide what they need at the time they require it in the assembly process. Coordination of supplies is accomplished with the use of computers that monitor all aspects of the distribution and production schedules.

The success of Italian industry has stabilized the migration patterns within the country. Transformations as a consequence of restructuring have been celebrated by some observers as a new model of growth that should be copied by other advanced nations undergoing change (Piore and Sabel, 1984). As in the Italian case, the fate of cities depends progressively more on their ability to attract and retain mobile capital investment, while capital, in turn, must restructure and acquire greater flexibility in responding to the increasing demands for small batch, customized production. Caught by the declines in manufacturing employment and the threat of plant closings or layoffs, workers must settle for less job security and a growing need to work closely with business for the sake of their mutual survival.

Much of Italian industry is oriented toward exports, despite the large domestic market. In the 1990s the slowdown in the global economy hit Italy hard, especially in the mezzogiorno region. Once again the specter of layoffs and recession has destabilized politics as the workers' standard of living is threatened. Recently, Italy has been the location for a burgeoning antiforeigner and racist social movement, as is the case elsewhere in Europe (see Germany, below). Fascist skinheads have been notably active, and anti-Semitism is on the rise, despite the very small Jewish population. Not all of this activity is directly related to the current recession, and other, as yet undocumented factors may be playing a role as Italy enters a new period of social transformation.

France

France, like England, has been transformed by industrial decline. Coal mining, steel production, and textiles, located in the north and west, have been particularly hard hit by plant closings and layoffs. In one year alone (1982–1983) over 185,000 industrial jobs were lost (Body-Gendrot, 1987: 244). Cities such as Metz, Dunkirk, Nancy, Lille, and Roubaix have taken on the feel of declining rustbelt cities elsewhere. For a period in the 1980s, the French government sought to intervene and prop up failing industries in order to retain jobs and the community quality of life. These policies were not successful (Zukin, 1985) and supports were abandoned in favor of a competitive gleaning of unproductive businesses.

BOX 13.1 PARIS AND CULTURE

When we think of France, we think of Paris, and when we imagine Paris, we associate that city with the benefits of Western culture. Paris, France, is the very epitome of urban life. Consider the artist Manet:

> All those who knew him agreed that Manet was more than a resident of Paris; he "personified the sentiments and customs of Parisians, raised to their highest power." . . . The boulevards from the Porte Saint-Denis to the Madeleine, and especially the few hundred yards between the rue de Richelieu and the Chaussée d'Antin comprising the boulevard des Italiens, had been the center of Manet's social life since the late 1850s, as indeed they had been for several generations of worldly and talented Parisians for twenty years before that. Here were concentrated the most fashionable theaters, restaurants, and cafés—above all the Café Tortoni on the corner of the rue Taitbout, the very heart of boulevard society and of Manet's as well.
>
> It was also on the boulevard des Italiens, in the enterprising Galerie Martinet, a forerunner of those which later supported impressionism, that Manet had his first one-man exhibition in March 1863. Among the pictures he showed was the one in which, for the first time, he portrayed himself amid this boulevard society and made its elegant, allusive style his own—the *Concert in the Tuileries*. Some of those who have been identified in it were indeed among the leaders of that society: Gautier, the bohemian turned court writer and entertainer; Offenbach, the composer of lighthearted operettas; Aurelian Scholl, the journalist admired for his wit; Baudelaire, the poet and self-styled dandy; and Manet himself, the unofficial painter of this elite circle (Sharpe and Wallock, 1987: 136–138).

Music at the Tuileries Gardens by Edouard Manet.

Industrial decline has resulted in a social crisis for many working-class families. According to one observer, "austerity brought about a deterioration of the social fabric: ... racism, demonstrations of workers against arbitrary decisions benefitting other workers, and petty delinquency. At the workplace, competition rose between the working classes: ... young vs. old, white vs. non-white, men vs. women, all fighting as the size of the pie was shrinking" (Body-Gendrot, 1987: 244). The rise of politically right-wing racists can be attributed in part to this upheaval. Today racism is a major problem in France. Hate crimes target immigrants from North Africa, Jews, and Arabs.

As in the Turin case, some French industry has responded by modernization schemes, especially the French automakers—Renault and Citroën. Post-fordist changes, such as flexible production, just-in-time supplying, and computer assisted manufacturing in the manner of the Japanese industries have also been adopted (see Leborgne and Lipietz, 1988). In addition, the French government has been very aggressive in supporting electronic related industries, software companies, and biotechnology. In conjunction with universities and business venture capital, new technopoles have sprung up in the Grenoble, Montpellier, and Toulouse regions, among others. These resemble the complex around Oxbridge (i.e., around Oxford and Cambridge in Great Britain) and are similar to the larger university/high tech industry regions of Silicon Valley, adjacent to Stanford University, and the North Carolina research triangle near Duke University in the United States.

The push to high technology industries has affected higher education in the country. As elsewhere, more emphasis is now placed on technologically sophisticated degrees in engineering and science. To date, the changeover to a modernized, flexible, and high tech economy has met with some success; for example, the French military industries are world leaders. But the older industrialized cities and their problems of decline, unemployment, and renewed racism remain.

Germany

In western Germany restructuring has had a most pronounced spatial change. Called the "süd-nord-gefälle" or the south/north cleavage, this pattern is very similar to the way economic changes have affected the United States. In the latter case, the rust belt cities once heavily based on manufacturing have all declined, while the Sunbelt has prospered. In Germany, it is the older, northern industrial cities such as Bremen and Hamburg that have been hardest hit by restructuring, while southern towns such as those in the region of Bavaria (Munich and Frankfurt, for example) have become affluent.

According to Hausserman and Siebel (1990), the north/south split has occurred as a consequence of Germany's shift to an export oriented economy, similar to the Italian case. In Germany the southern region contains the automobile industry and also high-technology-based manufacturing—two economic sectors that have done well in the global economy. Steel production and the shipping industry, which are concentrated in the north, have not been able to compete effectively in the world system; consequently, cities based on these sectors have declined. For example, Table 13.2 illustrates differences in the total employment rate of growth. The northern region containing the cities of Bremen, Hamburg, and Bonn experienced a 6.4 percent decline in employment,

Daimler-Benz truck assembly plant in Worth, Germany.

while the southern region containing the cities of Munich, Baden, Frankfurt, and Stuttgart enjoyed an increase in employment of 2.3 percent since 1980 (Haussermann and Siebel, 1990: 377).

Although the cities of the south are expected to grow in the future, it remains unclear how the unification with East Germany will affect urban areas. Most probably, population will shift to centers of increasing employment wherever they are located in the nation. Currently, Germany is experiencing difficulty in absorbing the formerly East German labor force. Unemployment is on the rise and so is racism as hate groups target immigrants and even the few Jews that reside there, despite the history of the Holocaust. The recent activities of fascist skinheads in perpetrating violence and hate crimes against immigrants and Jews threatened to destabilize the government in 1992. As in the case of Italy and France, the renewal of racism in Germany has complex causes, although the recession is a contributing factor. Most Germans believe their

TABLE 13.2
The South-North Split in Germany:
Total Employment Changes, 1988

	Employment change
Northern region	−6.4 percent
Southern region	2.3 percent

Source: Adpated from Hausserman and Siebel, 1990.

economy can absorb the former population of East Germany in the future; nevertheless, the global recession remains unpredictable in its effects.

Spain

Unlike the northern European countries, Spain is not highly industrialized and retains a large proportion of the population engaged in agriculture. Most of the manufacturing has been centered over the years in the Madrid region, which could be called Spain's primate city. Hence the urbanization pattern in this country is not as balanced as in the other European nations we have so far considered. In recent years, however, Spain has also been affected by the worldwide restructuring of the global economy. As a result, sociospatial changes are occurring.

Three changes in the Madrid area have been noted (Tobio, 1989). First, the older industrial districts, such as Villaverde, have declined and are plagued by job loss and poverty. Second, small manufacturers, much like the businesses of Italy's mezzogiorno, have remained successful, especially those involved in metal working, crafts, and printing. In addition, a new, high tech corridor running from Madrid past the airport and toward Barcelona has appeared recently which is expanding in employment. Third, the city of Madrid itself has been changing from a manufacturing economy to a service economy. Increases in service related employment are related to a building boom of office towers along La Castellana boulevard and are caused by the growing importance of finance related business services, as is the case in other large cities.

Spain is an interesting case because of the success of its industries during the 1980s under the direction of a socialist government. The 1992 summer Olympics served to showcase Spain's other large metropolis, Barcelona, as well as stimulate the nation's economy. The global recession, however, has hit this country hard, as it has all other export oriented economies. Consequently, there is a current slowdown in the sociospatial restructuring of metropolitan areas.

In sum, Western European countries have undergone economic restructuring to service based economies with a reduced scale of government aid that is similar to the United States. New techniques of post-fordist manufacturing have been introduced in the successful industries, including automation and Japanese-style flexible methods of production. High technology corridors, like the United States' Silicon Valley, have also appeared, such as the M-4 corridor in England. Finally, there is an increasing integration of large corporations or transnational firms that are conducting business, like their American counterparts, around the globe.

As in the U.S. case, restructuring has also brought with it an increasing array of urban problems. Crime, poverty, and the declining quality of life, almost unheard of as European concerns, are now becoming serious. Hate crimes and anti-immigrant feelings and racism are on the rise. Poverty and unemployment are growing because of related economic changes which have hit the working class especially hard. In Ireland, for example, 33 percent of households are receiving some form of public assistance; in Denmark the figure is 25 percent; and about that amount is also characteristic of Germany and England (Abrahamson, 1988: 21).

Cutbacks in the traditional European welfare state have made the problem of poverty more severe. Since the level of funding for public assistance now varies greatly between the countries of Western Europe, fears have been expressed about the possibility of "social dumping." This phenomenon arises when one geographical area has appreciably better social programs than another during a time of economic hardship. Poor populations migrate to the area with better benefits. As the European community moves to common market integration, it is feared that large movements of relatively poor people will occur and inundate places such as Scandinavia that have attractive welfare programs still in place (Abrahamson, 1988: 7). Such movements would strain the political and social fabrics of host countries and lead to government instability. They also lead to anti-immigrant hate crimes and social unrest that are unfortunate reminders of World War II.

One form of social dumping has already been experienced by European countries and to an extent the United States as well. Since the 1970s large numbers of workers from the third world have entered developed societies in the hope of obtaining work, as we discussed in Chapter 12. Several million Turks, Kurds, and Greeks, for example, live in Germany. Millions of North Africans have migrated to France, and even the Danes, who have always lived in a homogeneous society, are now concerned about the high Muslim birth rate in their country. It is now quite common to have African, Middle Eastern, or Asian cab drivers in cities like Paris, London, Berlin, and also New York and L.A. Domestic servants, undocumented workers, and low skilled, labor intensive factories or sweat shops composed of third world workers are increasingly common in all these cities. Even Japan, which restricts immigration, has a growing number of illegal aliens from Asia (Sassen, 1991) who come there in search of work.

Global economic restructuring, therefore, brings with it an increasingly mobile flow not only of capital investment and goods but also of people. Immigration from third world countries to Europe has affected the social order of these once relatively homogeneous societies in interesting ways. The growing presence of foreigners is reflected in the increasing mix of ethnic restaurants that have sprung up in city centers. This drawing together of the first and third worlds in a common urban experience is increasingly characteristic of contemporary Western cities.

Eastern Europe

Eastern Europe was under communist domination for the last seventy years, but has now joined the capitalist West. Most of the countries exhibit a pattern of primate city development (French and Hamilton, 1979). Only Russia seems to have been able to develop a balanced urban hierarchy. However, its capital, Moscow, remains quite large, with a population estimated in 1990 to be over 8 million. Table 13.3 illustrates the populations for the four largest cities: Budapest, Hungary; Moscow, Russia; Prague, Czech Republic; and Warsaw, Poland.

Discussion about Eastern European cities among urbanists most often centers on whether there is a specific difference in patterns of growth that can be attributed to communism. According to Friedrichs, however, "except for a short period in the early

TABLE 13.3
Population of Major Eastern European Cities, 1960 and 1980 (in thousands)

	Budapest	Moscow	Prague	Warsaw
1960	1,805	6,242	1,133	1,139
1980	2,064	8,302	1,186	1,629

Source: Adapted from Friedrichs, 1988.

1920s, there are no specific socialist types of land use, distribution of new housing, internal organization of residential blocks, or location of companies" (1988: 128). Consequently, communist societies have built environments with features that are similar to those in capitalist countries. Yet Friedrich's statement is an oversimplification. There were fundamental differences between communism and capitalism, especially with regard to the absence in the former of separate factions of capital and separate markets. Consequently, there are some peculiarities of land use and population distribution among such cities that differ from patterns in the West. These involve the nature of the central city due to an absence of the finance capital sector, the pattern of population distribution and the housing shortage, and most importantly, an absence of a capitalist real estate market.

Central City Decline

All Eastern European countries have large central cities. Some, such as Hungary and Poland, approach the condition of primate status due to the dominance of their main centers—Budapest and Warsaw, respectively. Others, such as the Czech Republic and Russia, have a more balanced system of cities. In every case, the central sections of the major cities are quite old, dating back several hundred years to their founding. Under the communist governments original buildings in the city center were not torn down. They remain standing and are, in most cases, in terrible shape. The lack of ambitious office building schemes, characteristic of the communist city, stands in contrast to the capitalist city. In the latter case, as we have seen, finance capital and its associated business services such as accounting and legal consulting have taken over the downtown. In most communist countries, the state directed investment instead of a finance capital sector; thus, their downtowns do not contain an active real estate market of office buildings that services the needs of corporate and finance capital. As a result, the shift to the service oriented economy is occurring more slowly in these countries than elsewhere in Europe.

The Demographic Pattern of Land Use

Scholars of Eastern European cities have pointed out that family income differences are not as segregated as in the rest of Europe or as in the United States (Ladanyi, 1989). In particular, United States cities exhibit a U-shaped curve of segregation. That is, both the wealthy and the poorest classes are highly segregated, with the majority middle class more spread out across the city. Eastern European cities, such as Budapest, exhibit more of an L-shaped curve. That is, the upper classes are highly segregated (the long end of the L) and the poorest people are somewhat segregated (the short end of the L distribution). In between, the rest of the population is evenly spread out in the city despite some differences in family income.

The reason for this contrast seems to be the operation of government subsidies for housing which has prevented the poorest people from being ghettoized to the extent they are in the United States. Thus, a major difference between formerly communist societies and capitalist ones like the United States is the active role of government in providing affordable housing for the poor (although, as we shall see below, the total volume of housing provided was inadequate). Paradoxically, however, observers add that under the communist governments, the more affluent people also enjoyed consider-able state housing subsidies (Ladanyi, 1989). Consequently, it was not the market that created uneven development in formerly communist countries, as it does under capitalism, but state intervention itself. This kind of uneven development and privilege produced by state favors for the elite has been a common complaint about communist practice for decades.

Recently, with the fall of communism, housing subsidies of all kinds are declining, and as the market takes over, segregation is also increasing. More privately produced housing is promoting a positive outcome in one respect. It represents the hope of alleviating the chronic shortage of housing in these societies, as we shall see next. However, a shift to an active, capitalist real estate market is also producing the first significant signs of capitalist-style uneven development, such as a growing number of homeless people and a sharp rise in the cost of rental housing which hits elderly pensioners particularly hard.

Housing Shortage

Unlike those in Western Europe, the cities of the communist societies have suffered a housing shortage for many years. State planned construction has never been able to keep pace with demand, unlike the market experience of the capitalist West. In addition, countries like Russia have restricted the growth of cities. Yet population has increased as migrants from agricultural areas move to the city looking for work. In Table 13.4, the deficit in housing stock is detailed for Warsaw (Poland), Budapest (Hungary), and

TABLE 13.4
Housing Shortages for Warsaw, Budapest, and Moscow, 1960 and 1980

	Year	Households	Dwellers	Deficit
Warsaw	1960	396,100	307,500	88,600
	1980	594,200	514,000	80,700
Budapest	1960	659,000	535,000	154,000
	1980	807,000	727,000	96,000
Moscow	1960	2,214,000	880,000	1,333,900
	1980	3,323,000	2,479,000	844,000

Source: Adapted from Friedrichs, 1988.

Moscow (Russia). As can be seen, while significant strides have been made since 1960, the deficit ranges from over 80,000 for Warsaw, to 96,000 for Budapest and 844,000 for Moscow in the 1980s. This peculiar communist-produced shortage has, over the decades, resulted in an unexpected style of life: households often double up and share one apartment, and married children often live with their parents for years.

According to Friedrichs (1988: 150), migration to the city and natural increase produce this housing shortage, much as they do in the third world. But the failure of state-directed housing programs also compounds in the shortage. Under communism, because land use was strictly controlled by the state, no shantytowns or street people were tolerated. This is currently changing with the switch to a free market in real estate, as we have discussed. In addition, as the urban economy grew under communism, new industry had to locate on the outskirts because of the lack of space within the central city and the absence of any kind of urban renewal that is characteristic of Western capitalism. As a consequence, population has been slowly deconcentrating and following employment opportunities to the outer rim. This is the reverse of the occupational/residence pattern of the old industrial city during the early stages of communist rule which maintained its working-class districts and employment opportunities within the city center (Friedrichs, 1988: 150).

The Emergence of Free Markets

Eastern Europe is now the scene of immense social changes as the changeover is made from communism to a market economy. The most significant change is the growth of a free real estate market and, by implication, a new, second circuit of capital for formerly communist countries. It remains to be seen how this restructuring will affect settlement space areas; however, we can use the U.S. case as a guide for future projections. Some indications already suggest that emergent patterns will be similar to the existing ones in the rest of the industrialized world. That is, within the large cities, segregation will increase, deconcentration of population will accelerate as suburbanization occurs, and the service economy will replace manufacturing as the principal sector. It remains to be seen how slowly or quickly land use in the center of cities like Budapest, Warsaw, Prague, and Moscow will also change. Old buildings remain, and to date there is little new office construction, but this situation most likely cannot last as the capitalist urban land market takes over and the pressures to switch to a service based economy prevail there as they have in the capitalist West. No doubt we can soon expect drastic renovation or renewal programs, led by private investment, for the construction of high rise office towers in the Eastern European cities of the future.

Japan

One of the world's greatest economic powers, the country of Japan has contained large cities for hundreds of years (Bestor, 1985). Tokyo, for example, had over 1 million people as early as the 1700s when it served as the capital (called Edo at the time) of the shogun empire. Since World War II, Japanese cities have developed as large regional agglomerations. The Tokyo/Yokohama metropolitan area, for example, contains over

Tens of thousands of shoppers swarm in Tokyo's busiest shopping street of Ame-yoko on the year's last Sunday, as they prepare foodstuffs for the coming New Year holiday.

25 percent of the entire population of Japan, or over 17 million people, while the city of Tokyo alone contained 11,828,000 in 1985. The Osaka metropolitan area to the south contained 15,900,000 people in 1984. The urbanization of the Japanese population, 77 percent of the total, is roughly comparable to that of Western countries such as the United States and Britain (Population Reference Bureau, 1990).

Japanese cities grew as trading and commercial centers during the sixteenth and seventeenth centuries, despite the country's isolation from the rest of the world. When industrialization was occurring in the nineteenth century, it was embraced by Japanese business along with the aid of the monarchy. By the beginning of the twentieth century Japan was already a major industrial power, but its ranking skyrocketed after its defeat in World War II as the consequence of ambitious, export-industry-led industrialization schemes that were remarkably successful (Lee, 1981; Berry, 1989). Box 13.2 details the city of Tokyo and some of its problems.

Japanese cities are not deconcentrated in the pattern of the United States, nor have they undergone a shift on the same scale to services as has the United States and older industrialized countries. Today, manufacturing remains important to the Japanese economy. In addition, work is highly centralized within city boundaries even though there is a growing suburban population. For example, Tokyo employed almost 6 million people in 1985 (Sassen, 1991: 161), many of whom had manufacturing jobs. Each day several million commuters ride into the central city by public transportation, often traveling as much as two hours each way. Japan is unlike the United States in other respects. Due to a free market in real estate, a general shortage of land in the country, and the centralization of employment within large cities, housing and rental prices are astronomically high. It has become increasingly difficult to own your own home there, and most housing space, in terms of square feet, is extremely small by U.S. standards.

The success of Japan's export oriented industries in the global economy since the 1960s has resulted in important changes in settlement space patterns for the entire Pacific Rim. Japanese industry innovated a number of techniques, such as "just-in-time" methods, that helped their competitiveness. They also embarked on regional schemes of manufacturing in search of cheap labor (much like U.S. companies), which had an impact on other Asian countries, in particular South Korea and Taiwan. But the real impact occurred because of Japan's success in foreign trade earnings. Within a few decades it became a major repository of the world's finance capital. For example, Tokyo alone contains almost half of the top fifty banks of the world, and since 1985 it ranks number one in total banking assets (Sassen, 1991: 176), surpassing London and New York (although the asset figure partially reflects the strength of the yen as against the dollar and the pound).

Regardless of its standing among the top three centers for finance capital, this flow of money into Japan has meant a major source of development funds for surrounding areas in the Pacific. As discussed in Chapter 12, not only Japan, but the new "Asian tigers"—South Korea, Singapore, Hong Kong, and Taiwan—grew at rapid rates during the 1980s. While the U.S. economy inched along at an annual increase of only 2 percent of its Gross Domestic Product, Japan's economy grew by 6 percent and the Asian tigers', by 7 percent (Berry, 1989: 176). Most gains were in those export oriented industries that have proved successful for Japan, namely, textiles, clothing, automobile manufacturing, and consumer electronics.

At present there are several interesting trends that characterize Japanese industrial and urban development. The global recession has affected Japan's economy, but not to the extent that it has Italy's or Spain's. Export industries are still doing well. More significant is the profits squeeze from the increasing costs of Japanese labor. This has very recently resulted in the kind of response enacted by U.S. firms, namely, the shift of some production to other countries with cheaper and more compliant sources of labor. While marketing and control remain located in Japan, recent years have witnessed an increase in the amount of component part production farmed out to Taiwan, South Korea, and Singapore (Douglas, 1988; Berry, 1989: 203).

Along with this similarity there has also been another trend common to the United States and Europe. Japan has always restricted its immigration, which is why its labor force and urban populations have remained more stable than in places like the United States with more open borders. Lately, however, illegal immigration is becoming noticeable as the global flow of investment and people integrates the Pacific Rim countries. Typically, such immigration occurs because the low wage, menial jobs that are necessary in a developed economy are no longer being filled by the domestic

BOX 13.2 TOKYO

Of all the world cities, Tokyo is richest in paradoxes. In terms of population it is the largest city authority, and the second largest metropolitan area in the world; but its public services are structured for a city between one-fifth and one-half the present size. Its factories produce some of the most technologically sophisticated products in the world; yet its wage levels and living standards are noticeably below those of the other world cities . . . and they contrast sharply in turn with relative poverty in Japan's provincial agrarian regions, only a few hundred miles away. Its rate of population growth is by far the highest of any of the very big cities of the world; it has the biggest problems in accommodating the extra millions. It is a metropolis where, in 1964, an elaborate network of expressways is in an advanced stage of construction, but where only 23 percent of the city's ten million people enjoy main drainage. Of all world cities it is the one whose citizens have devised the most varied and original solutions to their problems; but also the one where almost all schemes have a habit of failing for lack of funds (Hall, 1966).

population because of increases in the quality of life and training levels. This is the experience of the United States and increasingly of Japan. As Sassen (1991: 308) notes, since the late 1980s there has been a rapid increase in the number of illegal aliens working in Japan:

> Typically, they have entered the country with tourist visas and overstayed their officially permitted time. The estimate is that by mid-1988 there were 200,000 illegal male workers in Japan in manual work, from construction to restaurant kitchens. Almost all of these were from Asia. The estimate is that the largest single groups were from Taiwan, South Korea, Bangladesh, the Philippines, and Pakistan.

Japanese cities are not characterized by the kind of social segregation found in the West, although the wealthy are isolated from the rest of the masses. However, they exhibit an uneven development of sorts with regard to the lack of services and facilities. It is estimated, for example, that almost half of the Tokyo population lacks flush toilets (Kasarda, 1988), and as mentioned above, extreme housing and space shortages affect the city's inhabitants. There are few parks, medical facilities, and community centers in Tokyo. The city does contain an extensive mass transit network, as do other Japanese cities, but despite such impressive facilities, Tokyo like other Japanese cities suffers from pollution, smog, noise, and overcrowding (Nakamura and White, 1988). The rest of the country is plagued by extensive pollution that has resulted from industrial development which has not been controlled by the government.

Much recent development in Japan involves the construction of new spaces that bypass traditional urban agglomerations. This is especially the case for the new technopoles that have been energetically constructed with massive government help, a feature that differs from the United States which has yet to undertake such federally sponsored development. Most projects are joint ventures by the state, universities, and private capital, such as the giant Tsukuba "science city" centered on "Skuba" university outside of Tokyo. More recently, technopoles have been developed in the peripheral regions of Japan—those areas that have been previously bypassed by development—such as Hokkaido, Tohoku, Kyushu, and the area along the Sea of Japan. One of the most ambitious of these projects is the "silicon island" developed on Kyushu, centered on

Kumamoto City. This region has become a leading producer of microchips and contains a population of over 700,000 people (Fujita, 1988).

In short, Japan exhibits some of the characteristics of Western industrialized countries. Its traditional urban centers continue to grow. At the same time, new spaces have been created to house the "knowledge industries." These are similar to technopoles found elsewhere, but Japan's government is energetic in its support of such new development. Japan's urban system shows symptoms of overurbanization and it is dominated by Tokyo and other large agglomerations, such as Osaka and Nagoya. Due to the high cost of land and the very expensive price for housing, there is little suburbanization and residential construction. As a result, Japanese people must contend with long commutes in crowded facilities to work and cramped living quarters at home.

Summary

The last two chapters have presented a comparative perspective on urbanization. Once, such an approach would have stressed the unique differences between advanced countries like the United States and developing nations such as Ghana in Africa. To be sure, such differences still exist. The formerly communist countries of Eastern Europe, for example, contain cities that have a primate role and centers that are neglected— in stark contrast to other nations of the world. Yet we have also seen in these two chapters that differences can be increasingly explained by a common connection to global processes of economic restructuring. As manufacturing decentralizes in search of cheap and compliant labor, investment circulates from country to country. Command and control centers coordinate the new flows of capital and commodities, with some (such as the finance capital concentrations in New York City, London, and Tokyo) becoming global cities. Thus, marked discontinuities no longer characterize the comparative perspective on urbanization; increasingly, we live in one world, not three.

Western Europe, which has been urbanized for centuries, has recently undergone the same kind of shifts as has the United States. Manufacturing has declined and service employment is on the rise. New industrial spaces centered on high technology industries have appeared and are growing. Suburbanization of people and activities is increasing. New forces of centralization associated with command and control functions for the finance capital sector keep inner city development alive. Finally, the integration of economies due to world trade and the growing differentiation of labor has resulted in the flow of migrants across national borders.

All of these elements have combined to produce changes in the social order of once homogeneous European societies. Uneven development in wage levels creates a growing disparity between the well-off professionals and low wage service workers. Migration and ethnic cultural influences have been responded to with increasing numbers of hate crimes, racism, and, most ironically, anti-Semitism in a post-Holocaust Europe.

Asian urban development is led by the modern economy of Japan. It too suffers from uneven development. Japanese housing and real estate issues are worrisome and the shortage of affordable units will provoke a crisis of business location as fewer and fewer workers find places to live within commuting distances of jobs. But negative effects are outweighed by the success of Japanese economic growth. Industrial expansion continues and brings with it the persisting metropolitan regional growth of Japan's traditional manufacturing centers—Tokyo, Osaka, Nagoya. Financial investment flowing from Japan fuels the economies of the new Asian tigers, and thereby restructures the entire Pacific Rim (including the United States, Canada, and Australia, in addition to less developed countries of Asia and Latin America) for a new round of growth.

Common problems abound in Europe, Japan, and the United States, including the growing lack of affordable housing, challenges from the flow of immigrants who are often illegal aliens, current declines in manufacturing due to the global recession, and the uneven development of city populations due to the restructuring of the economy and the emphasis on high tech skills. With few exceptions, however, no industrialized country has experienced the kind of decay in the social conditions of everyday life that is comparable to the U.S. experience over the last two decades. In this respect it is the United States that presents a unique case to the world, although parallels can be found in third world cities like Calcutta or Nairobi. In the final two chapters of this text we shall examine ways of responding to this unique U.S. dilemma. Chapter 14 considers the issues of environment and planning, while the last, Chapter 15, addresses itself to public policy and the nature of government intervention in light of the social problems that were discussed in Chapter 10 and the political condition of local areas discussed in Chapter 11.

CHAPTER

14

ENVIRONMENTAL ISSUES AND METROPOLITAN PLANNING

On October 1, 1980, the Love Canal section of the small town of Niagara, New York, located near the Canadian border, was declared an environmental disaster by President Carter. He ordered the permanent evacuation of all families from their homes. This action followed after two previous evacuations beginning in 1978 (Gibbs, 1982: 5). Between 1920 and 1953 the area, an uncompleted canal, was a major dump site for toxic chemicals from both the private sector and the federal government, particularly the U.S. Army. Homes had been built on top of landfill after the site was no longer used for dumping. Residents who lived along the canal had been exposed for many years to carcinogens from the toxic wastes which leaked into groundwater and oozed to the surface. In the 1970s some of the 1,000 families that lived near the canal site began to complain about the high incidence of cancer, birth defects, miscarriages, and central nervous system diseases (Gibbs, 1982: 3). Once the full extent of the poisoning became known, evacuations proceeded, but this action came too late to save many people from contracting cancer and other environmentally caused health problems from the area.

On April 26, 1986, a nuclear power plant located in Chernobyl, near the Ukrainian capital city of Kiev, exploded (Marples, 1988). The blast ignited the graphite moderating core of the reactor and resulted in the unleashing of intense radiation across a wide area of the former U.S.S.R. and Western Europe. Fallout from the disaster was measured as far away as the United States, and showed up in the dairy production of countries such as Norway, but the most severe effects were to hundreds of thousands of people living in the small towns of the area. Had the winds been blowing northward at the

Damaged reactor at the Chernobyl nuclear power station is below the chimney at the center of this photo taken on May 9, 1986. The accident caused damage to the building, destroyed the reactor, killed at least 31 people, and raised levels of radiation throughout Europe.

time, the Ukrainian people's historic city of Kiev (population: 2.4 million) would have been destroyed along with countless lives.

Official figures from the U.S.S.R. listed 31 people killed by the accident, but other estimates are as high as 500 (Marples, 1988: 42). It was also estimated that as many as 50,000 people may have been directly exposed to excessive radiation, with as many as 500,000 long-term deaths predicted over the next few decades. The disaster forced a permanent evacuation of a thirty-kilometer zone, but over 100,000 children outside this area were also taken from their families in order to avoid exposure. Thousands of people were treated for radiation sickness. To this day the region contains "hot spots" that are a threat to life.

The above examples are not, unfortunately, isolated cases. The United States, for instance, has had its own potential nuclear catastrophe when the Three Mile Island reactor near Middletown, Pennsylvania, began emitting radioactive steam on March 28, 1979. That emergency was controlled without immediate loss of life or property. Many countries around the world, too many, in fact, have toxic pollution sites and unsafe radioactive facilities within their borders that affect the health of citizens every day. According to the Environmental Protection Agency, the United States alone contains between 30,000 and 50,000 toxic waste dumps (Gibbs, 1982: 1).

In our discussions, so far, we have concentrated on the metropolitan aspects of settlement space. It is necessary, however, to incorporate an enlightened sensibility toward environmental issues into the sociospatial perspective, because the effects of living and working arrangements in modern societies have impacts on the health and well-being of all residents. Questions raised about environmental quality have as much to do with spatial issues as does the nature of economic development.

There is a variety of issues raised by the environmental question and its relation to space. One set inquires about the nature of constructed space or "second nature" as Lefebvre (1991) calls it. These issues involve the activity of *planning* which seeks to obtain the best living and working arrangements in developing cities. The built environment, any built environment, such as a city or a mall, possesses attributes that might enhance or hinder the functioning of its use. Elements of the environmental fabric such as streets, pedestrian pathways, automobile corridors, and housing complexes can be placed in harmony with each other so as to facilitate the movement of people and vehicular traffic throughout the constructed space. Planning and architectural design address these kinds of issues and we shall consider them in the second section of this chapter.

A separate set of questions involves the inherent *quality of the environment.* How nurturing are the outcomes and by-products of social activities? What effects do the activities of some segments of society, such as manufacturing, have on other segments within their vicinity? Who pays the environmental costs for development? What is the environmental impact of growth on the health and well-being of citizens? These and other questions frame the discussion of settlement space as a built environment. Let us consider this topic first and relate it to metropolitan considerations.

Environmental Quality

All societies of the globe seek to improve their quality of life through industrial development. Some countries like the United States already possess a heritage of over 100 years of industrialization. While all human activities produce waste products that may adversely affect others, such as the effluent problem in an ancient city like Beijing, the scale and intensity of the environmental costs of industrialization have been historically unprecedented. Manufacturing results in by-products, for example, that are toxic to animal and plant life; energy generation affects the temperature and quality of water and air with consequent effects on living things; and the extraction of "natural" resources, such as gold, results in environmental damage, such as the releasing of mercury into forest streams.

Societies around the globe have always put developmental desires above environmental concerns. In places like China, Brazil, and sections of Europe, the health related impacts of industrialization weren't even publicly recognized until quite recently, as we saw in the Chapter 12 discussion of Shanghai. For many centuries all societies have held an unwavering belief in the idea of progress. Technology, science, and industrial growth, it is commonly understood, hold the promise of making our lives better and better. At present this assumption, which is at the core of modernist ideology (see below), has been called into question by some environmentally conscious individuals. According to Murray Bookchin (1990: 20), for example, "the certainty that technology and science would improve the human condition is mocked by the proliferation of nuclear weapons, by massive hunger in the Third World, and by poverty in the First World."

Most Americans appreciate the quality of life made available to them by the accomplishments of industrialization, but environmental activists suggest that this comfort for the relative few, globally speaking, has been acquired at a phenomenal cost to the many around the world. Furthermore, the unprecedented scale of human development today has resulted in global effects such as the widening hole in the ozone layer, global warming, acid rain, the eradication of entire plant and animal species, and the increasing threats to fresh drinking water. In response, environmentalists have called for a new ordering of global priorities that would seek out environmentally enhancing methods of industrial production and safe technologies (Naess, 1989; Gore, 1992). This means redefining the relationship between humans and settlement space on this planet.

As the level of awareness increases in society and across the globe, perhaps the issues of growth and development will be reexamined. New, environmentally sound methods of production and safe technologies such as rechargeable electric cars may usher in a transformed relation between people and the earth that preserves the well-being of both. There is already some indication that environmental concerns can translate into new jobs and industries (Kazis and Grossman, 1983) so that persisting development can be compatible with saving the planet.

The above concerns have been part of the environmental movement in the United States for some time. They comprise both the *classical* and *mature* phases of activism (Bullard, 1990). In the former period, which began in the 1800s, Americans sought to protect large areas of the country from development and endangered species from destruction. Naturalists like John Muir (1838–1914), who won protection for places like Yosemite and led the fight to establish the National Parks System, and organizations like the Audubon Society, which has been at the forefront of the fight to save native birds and other wildlife, are examples of the classical phase of environmentalism.

In the twentieth century, the mature phase of activism attacked the unbridled nature of industrialization in the United States. Concerned citizens fought for regulatory agencies, the passage of environmental statutes, and the establishment of industrial standards for control of pollutants. Over the years a host of regulations and legally binding statutes have been passed by both the federal and state levels of government. In 1970 the mature phase efforts culminated in the establishment of a separate federal agency under the executive branch, the Environmental Protection Agency (EPA), which serves as the public's advocate and coordinates research on environmental issues. In the 1970s the EPA was granted powers to regulate mileage standards for automobiles, thereby leading to the production of fuel efficient engines. In sum, while there is still much work that is required, and an imminent need for residents of the United States to rethink their relationship with the settlement space of advanced industrial society, the classical and mature phases of activism have accomplished a great deal. This is especially the case when we consider the sensitivity many Americans have acquired in the last several decades to the need for fuel economy, recycling of waste products, and the search for safe technologies.

There is a third type of activism, *grassroots* or community efforts, which addresses a separate issue that is also relevant. As advocates of grassroots mobilization point out, social concern about environmental quality is quite high in the United States. Still lacking, however, is an appreciation for the social equity and social justice aspects of environmental impacts (Gale, 1983). The latter are distributed inequitably across settlement space so that there is a particular sociospatial dimension to the differential impact of costs. As one observer puts it:

> An abundance of documentation shows blacks, lower-income groups and working-class persons are subjected to a disproportionately large amount of pollution and other environmental stressors in their neighborhoods as well as in their workplaces (Bullard, 1990: 1).

The classical and mature phases of environmentalism have drawn in thousands of people, but the overwhelming majority of them and the concerns they express are middle class. As yet, the environmental costs paid by poor and minority people have been ignored. This sociospatial pattern of environmental costs is most revealing. Love Canal in New York State was situated within a white, working-class community and these people paid the price of toxic pollution. In Alabama, the town of Triana is judged the "unhealthiest town in America" (Reynolds, 1980: 38). The residents of Triana are black, and they have been poisoned by the pesticide DDT and the chemical PCB from a creek whose quality is the responsibility of the federal government. Time and again research shows that society continues to produce toxic pollution and that poor and minority communities are its victims (Bullard, 1990; Berry, 1977; Blum, 1978).

Many of the hazards that differentially affect minorities and the poor are the consequence of industrial location patterns. Factories, chemical plants, mills, and the like are located in areas isolated from middle-class residential communities. Often these are also places where poor people live. Chemical emissions, spillovers of toxic by-products, unpleasant smells, and loud noises are some of the hazards that afflict these relatively powerless communities. In addition, however, poor and minority people are picked on by levels of government responsible for managing pollution. Locally unwanted land uses or LULUs such as landfills, toxic waste dumps, and effluent treatment plants are invariably located in minority and poor areas. Hence, even though regulations have increased for safeguarding environmental quality, they have also led to injustices in the disposal of environmental threats, especially because of the inequitable siting of toxic dumps and landfills. For example:

> Four landfills in minority zip code areas represented 63 percent of the South's total hazardous-waste disposal capacity. Moreover, the landfills located in the mostly black zip code areas of Emelle (Alabama), Alsen (Louisiana), and Pinewood (South Carolina) in 1987 accounted for 58.6 percent of the region's hazardous-waste landfill capacity (Bullard, 1990: 40).

The differential locational impacts of environmental costs and the issues of social equity that they raise have yet to be addressed. Most communities seek to avoid becoming hosts to activities that represent social problems, such as outpatient mental clinics, halfway houses for criminals, and drug treatment centers. They advocate "not in my backyard" or NIMBY politics which makes location a struggle that is lost by the least powerful community. The same is true for LULUs such as hazardous waste dumps or landfills. But allowing the stronger to make the weaker pay for all of society's costs violates principles of social justice.

In recent years grassroots activists have organized poor and minority communities to fight for their rights. They are forcing the larger society to rethink environmental issues. If toxic dumps are unfair to any community, why not design production operations to minimize environmental damage? If landfills are becoming a problem, can't recycling and other even more imaginative schemes be considered for the ever increasing volume of garbage we all produce? How can we reorder our priorities to avoid having people pay unfairly for pollution? These and other questions will frame the agenda for grassroots organizing and environmental activism in the years to come. This agenda will be aided by the way we have tried to relate the effects of our activities to the sociospatial organization of society.

Environmental concerns also raise issues related to the way we have designed settlement space and how best we can improve our arrangements for living and working together. These questions concern the activity of planning, which shall be considered next.

Metropolitan Planning

Pruitt-Igoe was a massive public housing project constructed in the early 1950s in St. Louis, Missouri. It was inspired by the work of the leading architect of the postwar generation, Le Corbusier of France, and executed in design by several famous architects, including Minoru Yamasaki. The project consisted of 33 eleven-story buildings with a total of 2,700 apartment units on a site that stretched out to almost sixty acres (about one-tenth of a square mile). The project represented the zenith of government-sponsored high rise/low income housing construction. Yet residents experienced problems almost immediately after Pruitt-Igoe opened in 1954 (Montgomery, 1985). Elevators broke and were not repaired. Injuries to children occurred when they played in corridors or stairwells that could not be monitored adequately by adults. Crime began to terrorize residents due to the large scale of design which allowed muggers to remain hidden. People complained of isolation from friends and neighbors. In addition, structural hazards of the buildings took their toll in accidents.

Within five short years after opening, occupancy rates were already on the decline despite the subsidized rent. By 1970 vacancy rates in the buildings had reached more than 50 percent. The St. Louis housing authority made the fateful decision that the problems with the project were insurmountable and ordered its complete demolition. By 1976 the entire project was torn down. Architectural critic Charles Jencks sets this date as the time when modernist ideas about the promise of architecture as promoting social progress gave way to the postmodern period with its abandonment of such lofty aspirations (Hoston, 1989). With the failure of Pruitt-Igoe, in short, came the realization that modernist architecture and government intervention in public housing required reexamination.

This chapter and the next are about people's attempts to change their circumstances

The demolition of Pruitt-Igoe on April 21, 1972. Compare this case with the vision of Le Corbusier, on page 304.

through the specific manipulation of space, design, and public policy. In the remainder of this chapter we consider the case of planning, that is, the use of rational schemes of land use, home construction, and environmental design to make metropolitan life better in general and to improve the lot of specific groups of individuals in particular. In Chapter 15 we will consider public policy, or the active intervention of the government at various levels to bring about positive social changes through public means.

Both of these efforts have usually been combined. Thus, Pruitt-Igoe was a combination of architectural design following modernist principles that pursued progress in human/space relations, and simultaneously a type of government intervention which made available to poor people apartments at subsidized rent. For the purposes of discussion, however, let us deal with planning and policy separately, while keeping in mind that they are related.

Planning in the United States

If we were to examine the constitution of city and suburban governments, we would find separate agencies devoted to planning that employ significant work forces. Yet our metropolitan environments seem to be characteristically unplanned. This "planning paradox" (see Gottdiener, 1977) exists because in the United States planners have very little direct power to enact their schemes and are confined for the most part instead to advisory roles. The civic culture of the United States has always resisted direct intervention in the market by government. In the early stages of urbanization, during the nineteenth century, most cities were constructed with little planning. Yet the market, as economists know, does not provide adequate amounts of the infrastructure—roads, streets, utilities, and transportation facilities—needed by society.

In addition, early industrial cities possessed a special chaos of different land uses.

Working-class homes were sited next to factories belching pollution. Narrow streets wandered in and out of districts without plan, so movement was restricted. Construction was not attuned to the aesthetic principles of architectural design. This ugliness and haphazard growth finally stimulated a response. Around the turn of the century, the "City Beautiful" movement sought to inspire localities to adopt aesthetically pleasing architecture and land use planning principles. These ideas were showcased in the 1898 World's Fair of Chicago (see Chapter 3). Proper design was touted as the means of improving the urban quality of life, and the leaders of many cities were inspired by this exposition to give planning a try.

In short, because the U.S. culture has a commitment to free-market solutions, only when the problems of growth were acknowledged did adequate community support for planning appear. Since the turn of the century, most cities and counties have retained a planning staff to help with the problems of development. But rather than discuss the history of planning per se, let us consider some sociological aspects of the profession.

The Sociology of Land Use Planning

The most basic kind of planning involves *zoning* for land use. Based on the principles that like activities should be located near each other and that industrial activities and residential areas should be separated, zoning partitions metropolitan space into distinct areas for each activity. In any community, for example, space is partitioned into zones reserved for residential use, commercial activities, and industrial work, among other functions. Planners use detailed maps to draw up land use guides that constitute the zoning master plan. In most cases such a plan needs to be adopted by local residents or their elected representatives. Changes and modifications are always a possibility with land use schemes, but once zoning has been adopted, it carries the weight of law. Through the political power to control the use of land, planning agencies can shape the pattern of metropolitan development. Their powers, however, are dependent on the local political authority.

Planners also work on a larger scale with elected officials and representatives from the business community to develop new uses of land. They may help design an industrial park for factories and businesses, an office tower or city skyscraper complex, a mall or a large residential development. New developments require infrastructure planning as well as the construction of the buildings themselves. Roads have to be put in along with sewer and utility lines and the like. The impact on the surrounding area also requires careful thought and planning. New developments, just like zoning schemes, must be approved by local political authorities. Sometimes citizens object to new growth, and developments can be blocked or changed according to local resident desires. Most of the time, however, local elected representatives approve growth, since that is the priority of city government. In short, planners can plan but only political representatives have the power to enact their schemes.

Sociologists who have studied the process of planning have noticed two dilemmas facing the profession. The first is called the "physicalist fallacy," and the second, the "elitist/populist dilemma."

Physicalist Fallacy

Planners concern themselves only with the proper use of space under the implicit assumption that adequate living and working arrangements for people can be achieved through the use of construction, design, and landscaping technology. This approach assumes that people's behavior can be controlled or channeled into desirable forms through the manipulation of physical design. As Herbert Gans (1968: 28–33) has argued, this commits the fallacy of assuming that design will determine personal behavior. As social scientists are aware, the latter is determined by a complex relation of various social processes interacting in and with spatial forms, rather than the influence of environment alone. In practice, planners and architects seem to ignore the social basis of behavior and falsely believe that construction design, by itself, can bring about desired change, such as increasing the frequency of neighborly interaction. This fallacy, which privileges abstract over social space, has been responsible for some spectacular failures of planning, including Pruitt-Igoe, and we shall discuss some of them below when we consider the "utopian" impulse in the design of human environments.

Elitist/Populist Dilemma

Professional planners must work within a political milieu because local citizens are endowed with the authority to approve many development schemes. Yet planners are provided with the elitist assumption that they know best what a good plan should be like since they are the technical experts. They, along with the politicians or elected representatives, also assume that there is some easily defined public interest which planning can fulfill. But there are many dimensions to the democratic process of planning that are often ignored, such as public participation in the selection of develop-ment goals—that is, the open discussion of what kind of community people really want and the open search for alternatives to any proposed growth scheme. A true democratic relationship between planners, politicians, and the public would involve such an open search for desirable goals and alternative growth schemes.

The elitist/populist dilemma (Gottdiener, 1977: 119–120) concerns the contradic-tory role of planners who function as technical experts who know what is best for the community, but who must nevertheless acquire community support for their plans. This *politics of planning* does not always achieve the best results. Planners must court citizen support in order for a plan to be approved, but planners and citizens rarely work together in an open process of preparing for the community's future. Because this process is a limited version of what democratic planning would be like, it represents a dilemma. There are only some instances when citizens and planners have achieved an appropriate balance of democratic process, citizen participation, and planners' goals, such as in the active planning for rent control in the city of Santa Monica, California, and in the efforts toward balanced growth achieved by Burlington, Vermont (Clavel, 1986). Box 14.1 illustrates the case of Bellevue, Washington, where citizens worked together with planners and local politicians to preserve the city's quality of life.

The planning process is a complex one, and sociologists studying the three-way relation between politicians, planners, and the public have observed interesting aspects of social decision-making (Gans, 1968). Because development goals are often the

BOX 14.1 THE CASE OF BELLEVUE, WASHINGTON

In much of the United States, recent patterns of development have fostered suburbanization which has torn the city apart. Few cities have been able to resist this process which eventually leads to the deterioration of the downtown. When faced with this dilemma, the citizens of Bellevue, Washington, decided that they wanted to preserve the city and its urban way of life in the face of suburbanization pressures. They enacted a series of land use regulations and initiated projects that channeled development into preserving the urban form. The city was small enough and people were able to cooperate enough with politicians, planners, and each other to make this happen. According to the account of William H. Whyte (1988: 307):

> The central business district that Bellevue is building does not sprawl; it has a tight pattern of development with well-defined edges. Within the core of the CBD, developers can put up buildings with a floor-area ratio as high as 8 by providing bonusable amenities—up to 10 by providing specified public spaces. Beyond the CBD, however, developers must build low, with the maximum floor-area ratio a meager .5. This represents a clear public decision to concentrate and direct development rather than simply let it happen.
>
> Downtown, as a consequence, remains quite compact—an easy walk from one side of it to the other. . . . Bellevue people insist that there is indeed more walking and that within the past two years the increase in walking in the core area has been quite noticeable. Because of the concentration, there are more people there and more amenities to prompt them to walk. . . . They

expression of special interests, and because projects are often renegotiated in response to the public's concerns, the outcome of metropolitan planning appears to lack the coherence that technical ideas profess. An example of the *unintended* consequences of planning due to community politics is represented by a case study of a suburban area on Long Island, New York (Gottdiener, 1977). In this town, planners worked with local politicians and business to build a shopping center adjacent to a large residential development. The residents were in favor of the center, but after it opened, they discovered that it increased traffic on their local streets. This outcome was not considered in the original plans.

Residents rallied to place political pressure on the local government to supply traffic lights in order to slow traffic down. Their concerns were not addressed until the residents had organized themselves so that they could maintain constant pressure on local politicians. The planners and government refused to install the stop lights, however, because the volume was not great enough. In a compromise, stop signs were installed within the development. No one wanted stop signs, and from a planning point of view they are not the best controls of traffic, but that is what the residents received after the negotiation process. A result that no one desired became the outcome of compromise because negotiations and political struggle are also part of the planning process, in addition to technical recommendations.

believe the very structure of downtown is likely to induce more walking. Bisecting downtown is a central pedestrian corridor. At one end there is an attractive shopping mall; at the other, a unique transit center, with lots of seating and overhead cover. Developers along the corridor contribute segments to it, and via incentive zoning, bonuses are given to provide a rich townscape of trees, handsome paving, lighting, and canopies to temper the Northwest's drizzle.

Bellevue has also begun a large central park. Several years ago a fifteen-acre school site became surplus. In many a city a rapacious city hall would have sold it off for a massive development. Bellevue bought it from the school district and held a national competition to select a winning design. The first elements of the park were opened in mid-1987 and have already been discovered by strollers, joggers, and brown baggers. It is even getting use at night.

The car is being tamed. Instead of more parking, the city is mandating less. New buildings used to have to provide a standard five spaces per thousand square feet of office space. This has been cut to three spaces. To pinch matters further, commercial parking lots and garages are forbidden in the CBD. About half of all new employees working in downtown will have to join car pools or take a bus to get there (1988: 308).

The case of Bellevue represents some important ways urban life is being preserved, such as livable streets, the discouragement of deconcentration, and the development of attractive amenities downtown. The success of this make-over, however, depends on the support of the people, because planning is political as well as technical. So far, according to Whyte, Bellevue has been successful.

Utopian Schemes: Howard, Le Corbusier, and Wright

Idealistic thinkers in centuries past often lamented the evils of civilization and thereby created a genre of literature known as *utopian* writing. Plato's *Republic* might be the earliest example, but the consummate vision belongs to Thomas More's *Utopia*. These accounts of some fictional paradise provide us with a means of measuring the prospects of human endeavor; that is, they point to ways in which we can perfect ourselves and our society even while exploring our all too frail shortcomings as a species. Over the centuries utopian literature has provided important inspiration to socially concerned individuals, as has the equally fascinating genre of dystopian writing, especially science fiction's dystopian accounts of life in future cities (such as the film *Blade Runner*).

Utopia, from the Greek word meaning "no place," and *dystopia,* a more recently coined expression that means an imaginary place of dread, are examples of places that exist elsewhere in time and space. While the former usually signals the modernist theme of progress, the latter is representative of our fears about the myth of progress. This yearning for the perfection of settlement space and the realization that it may never be attained due to the limitations of our civilization constitute an important strain in Western literature and cinema. The philosopher Henri Lefebvre (1991) calls all such spaces that exist "elsewhere" and in our minds as imaginary places, *heterotopias.* As mental conceptions, heterotopias have the ability to influence our behavior and to define prospective schemes for architects and planners.

In nineteenth-century Europe, when the evils of industrialization and urbanization became a major social concern, individuals exercised the utopian spirit by conceiving of alternative urban environments. Some of these modernist visions were highly influential on the planning and architectural professions, and, indeed, by the twentieth century, architects no longer confined themselves to the design of individual buildings but composed manifestos and schemes that addressed the living and working arrangements of the entire city space itself. Among the important conceptualizers of new urban environments are Ebenezer Howard, Le Corbusier, and Frank Lloyd Wright. The modernist vision of each was expressed respectively as the Garden City, the Radiant City, and Broadacre City.

Garden City. Ebenezer Howard, who lived during the turn of the last century, was a social reformer in England. Like others of his time, including Friedrich Engels, he was appalled at the social costs of British industrialization. Some thinkers, such as Robert Owen, responded by founding a utopian movement that advocated the construction of communities (such as New Harmony, Indiana) that would counteract the evils of the industrial city but which required a fundamental break with acceptable ways of family or social life. Howard's response was to propose an alternative way of living that could be followed by everyone, even those uninterested in the utopian movement's social change.

To Howard, the city represented the future of economic growth, but it was, to express it directly, a lousy place to live. In contrast, the rural areas remained in organic harmony with their surroundings, but they were afflicted with limited economic opportunity. Howard's vision combined the two. He proposed that all new industrial growth be siphoned off from the older and larger cities and channeled to new places in outlying areas that would combine industrial employment with country living on a moderate, human scale. These "Garden Cities" would represent the very best of city and country living.

The concept of the Garden City proved to be a powerful one in the annals of urban planning. Capitalist industrialization in the nineteenth century knew no bounds, and large cities gobbled up their adjacent countrysides in a relentless process of accretion. Because planners understood that growth was inevitable anyway, they were attracted to Howard's idea of breaking urban expansion off and aspiring to locate new industry and housing in moderate sized communities.

Howard's ideas influenced the "new town" movement in England, which has been responsible for building hundreds of such places, as well as the measured establishment of medium sized cities in Russia, although the latter case does not embody the ideal of the "garden" or suburbanized urban environment. In the United States a group of architects, notably Clarence Stein, popularized Howard's approach. Working with local authorities and developers, they constructed several places across the country including Garden City, New York, outside of Manhattan, and Baldwin Hills, California, which is located in Los Angeles. Ebenezer Howard lived to see the opening of the New York community in 1928.

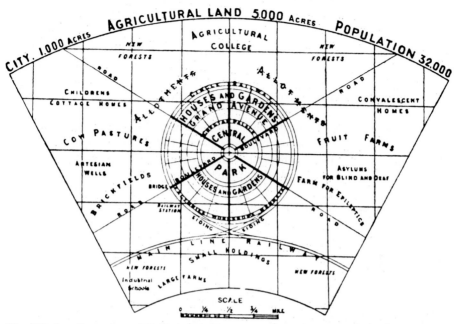

The Garden City plan of E. Howard. Housing was integrated with parks and gardens, while railway lines and manufacturing were zoned out to the periphery.

In practice most of the American garden cities lack their own industry and hence are little more than middle-class suburban housing developments with some interesting features, such as shared public spaces. These ideas, all derivative of Ebenezer Howard's vision, are still put in practice by developers of large suburban residential projects such as planned unit developments or PUDs, which we shall discuss below.

Radiant City. Le Corbusier was the professional name of the Swiss-born French architect Charles-Édouard Jeanneret (1887–1965). Along with several German architects, such as Walter Gropius and Ludwig Mies van der Rohe, Le Corbusier is considered the founder of the *International Style* of design and one of the leaders of the modernist movement in architecture. The type of building associated with this movement is familiar to anyone who has seen the skyline of a large city, because the design concepts took over the world. International Style buildings are clean, straightforward rectangular shapes with flat roofs. They are framed in steel and feature large glass windows which are sealed shut. Not until the postmodern architectural revolt of the 1980s were downtown office buildings liberated from the dictates of this concept.

Le Corbusier was influential because he propagated certain ideas about city living instead of confining his practice to building design. He believed in the triumph of technology over social conditions of industrialization. Buildings themselves were to be "machines for living," that is, the most efficient designs for the sustenance of everyday activities. The urban environment would have to be changed, so he thought, to conform to the dictates of more enlightened architectural design. Because Le Corbusier lamented the terrible social costs of industrialization that he witnessed around him, he proclaimed the modernist rallying cry, "Architecture or Revolution," sincerely believing that capitalist countries had little choice but to follow his ideas or face the revolt of the urban masses.

Le Corbusier's ideas and those of his contemporaries constituted the ideology of *modernism,* which legitimated the notion of progress and the improvement of human conditions year after year through the intervention of technology. Modernist ideology asserted that the lot of individuals could be improved by the acquisition and application of knowledge—scientific, technological, architectural, social, psychological. Part of modernist culture was the celebration of architecture and "modern" ideas about city planning.

Le Corbusier's plan for an entire metropolis, the Radiant City, reordered the space of the large, industrial conurbation. Instead of the relatively low density of housing and chaotic land use that was characteristic of the cities at that time, Le Corbusier proposed that buildings should be high rises. By condensing the living space using building height, open spaces would be liberated, and Le Corbusier envisioned these as parks that would surround residential clusters, thereby making the congested, sprawling industrial city into an open, airy, and efficient place of mobility and light.

A second important feature of the new design followed from Le Corbusier's and the modernist belief in the virtues of technology, in this case, the architect's love affair with the automobile. Le Corbusier believed that the widespread use of public transportation and auto modes of transport would vastly improve the efficiency of urban scale. He proclaimed the "death of the street," that is, the pedestrian thoroughfare

A Radiant City. Le Corbusier's plan for Antwerp (1933), never built. From La ville radieuse (1935). See the photo on page 297 for comparison of how Le Corbusier's ideas went wrong.

characteristic of all cities in the past. His vision instead was of rapid movement facilitated by autos, trains, highways, and feeder roads of people and commodities between the various nodes of urban space—residences, factories, shops, and government buildings.

The lesson of Pruitt-Igoe (discussed above) illustrates the deeply ingrained physicalist fallacy of Le Corbusier. Construction design, which disregards social process, cannot change everyday life alone. Unfortunately, the modernist ideas of the International Style and especially the concepts of Le Corbusier were highly influential. Along with Pruitt-Igoe, another major tragedy of planning in this vein is exemplified by the case of Brasília, the capital city of Brazil, which was constructed as a radiant city.

Designed by the architects Lucio Costa and Oscar Niemeyer in 1960 and located in the interior 600 miles from the Rio de Janeiro coast, Brasília looks like a giant bird from an aerial view. But on the ground its limitations have become legendary (Hoston, 1989). The "death of the street" was a major error which produced an austere, alienating environment in which urban life is shrouded in anonymity. Neighboring and community interaction have all but disappeared because of the inability to overcome the automobile based lifestyle and the imposing superhuman social scale, which has led to feelings of isolation and anonymity among residents.

Crime plagues the vacant parks, ramps, and open spaces. With all buildings looking the same, a horrible ennui afflicts local residents who live and work in interchangeable modules. For the most part, the city exists because it remains the country's capital, hence government administrators and their support staffs find employment there. However, Brasília has failed to attract the diverse kinds of industry and everyday life that would convert it to a major city. In short, Brasília, among other austere creations of modernist city planning, reminds us graphically of the physicalist fallacy and the need for architects to work in conjunction with social science in order to bring about an improvement of urban conditions.

Broadacre City. Frank Lloyd Wright (1869–1959), a native of Wisconsin, lived almost a century and was the premiere U.S. architect. His ideas, unlike Le Corbusier's, remain appreciated today, even if some of his designs have become outdated. Wright was no modernist. In fact, he was much influenced by the crafts movement in the United States and by Oriental architecture, particularly the Japanese use of interior space. Wright believed that structures should be organic extensions of natural environments. Houses, for example, should emerge from the crown of the hill rather than being built at the top, since the latter should be reserved for nature. They should embody a fluid connection with the world outside, and their construction should celebrate natural materials and settings, as exemplified by the Kaufmann home, Falling Water House (built in 1936), outside Pittsburgh, Pennsylvania. This summer home is made of concrete that is stacked like pancakes on three levels (called cantilevering) so that it sits on a rock above a forest stream. The water flows under the lower level and out over a falls. Sitting in the living room it is possible to watch the water flow and hear the stream take its perennial dive over the rocks.

Wright's vision of the new city possesses some similarities with that of Ebenezer Howard, especially the desire to merge the city and the country, except Wright thought

Frank Lloyd Wright's Broadacre City. The plan combined the city and the country without suburbs and introduced ideas such as regional shopping malls and freeways.

in modular terms. Instead of a single, human scale community, Wright envisioned an immense metropolis whose internal structure reduces space to a human scale through modular design. Each family would be assigned a single-family home on an acre of land! The space would enable families to grow their own food and to modify their surroundings according to their own personal tastes. Houses would be arrayed on an expansive grid. Wright also liked the possibilities of the auto, and his Broadacre City assumed that the car would be the basic means of transportation. Each place would be accessible by interconnected roads and highways feeding into and out of grids. Commercial shopping would take place in regularly spaced shopping centers, and industry would be isolated in specifically designed factory areas that were zoned exclusively for business.

Wright's scheme seems almost like the massive suburban environments of today. He was one of the earliest architects to think up the concept of the shopping center, and his factory zoned area is recognizable as the industrial park of the present, a common feature of metropolitan environments. The key element of Wright's vision, however, seems elusive—namely, the one-acre allotment of land which resolved the city/country dilemma at the smallest scale of each individual family. While suburban residences often have ample backyards, these are reserved for leisure activities including, perhaps, a swimming pool. But Wright's vision of every family providing for its sustenance through backyard farming seems far removed from the realities of metropolitan life and extremely naive as an image of what most Americans might aspire to pursue, since they have always traded off work for more leisure time.

Our review of architectural visionaries provides us with some alternative ways of thinking about massive metropolitan environments and points out, by way of contrast, that urbanized landscapes do not necessarily have to assume the form that they now possess. The present-day givens of metropolitan development patterns seem to find no other way of building except unending and congested sprawl. But alternatives are possible; only the physicalist fallacy which wrongly suggests that architecture can alter social processes needs to be abandoned. Developers combining proper design with environmentally aware social science that uses the legacy of utopian ideas have had some successes, such as the new towns of Columbia, Maryland, or Garden City, New York. But planning exhibits the conflict between abstract and social space.

Planning Critics: Jacobs, Krier, and the Goodmans

In addition to the contribution of visionaries, ideas about planning have benefited from the work of critics who have taken both architects and the planning profession to task for neglecting the human values of environmental design; that is, social space (Mayo, 1988). Four of the most influential critics are Jane Jacobs, Leon Krier, and the team of Paul and Percival Goodman.

Jane Jacobs. Jane Jacobs' (1961) main concern is in preserving the city as a viable place to live. She believes that the best cities have a vital and active street life. Her critique of urban planning involves the charge that too many projects have ignored the role of human interaction as providing the life blood of city culture when most city inhabitants live in apartments with restricted space. For Jacobs, active urban life can never be planned because people invent uses for space. They accommodate the pursuit of their needs to the streets, parks, and playgrounds that they find around them. City planning that discourages this social interaction through the limiting of public or social space winds up also destroying the city itself.

For example, adolescents in the city spend a good deal of time out on the streets where they live. An incredible variety of street games has arisen over the years using this space, and many of these have been handed down through the generations, such as "Ring-a-Levio," "Johnny on the Pony," "Hop-Scotch," rope-jumping games, and "stick ball." Planned projects that think only in terms of efficient automobile traffic (such as Le Corbusier's radiant city or Brasília, the capital of Brazil) arrange for wide thoroughfares that are heavily traveled. But such efficiency in the name of transportation destroys the ability of children to use the streets for play. Can you imagine active street games in the immense auto corridors of Los Angeles or on the well traveled two-way streets in your own community, for example? In contrast, Jacobs celebrates the streets and advocates blocking them off on a periodic and temporary basis to allow for neighborhood interaction.

According to Jacobs, human-scale public spaces in the city, such as sidewalks, parks, and playgrounds, provide people with a number of resources: (1) they constitute learning environments for children, (2) they allow for parents' surveillance of the neighborhood and their children's activities, and (3) they facilitate intimate, primary relations between neighbors, thereby providing a strong sense of community (see the case studies of street corner societies in Chapter 8).

Jane Jacobs' ideas have had a strong impact on the way urbanists and planners think about city life. Local governments encourage park use, street festivals, temporary blocking of community roads, and toleration of sidewalk vendors. Not all of Jacobs' ideas, however, have been accepted. Some of her followers advocated the elimination of elevators in apartment buildings to facilitate neighborly interaction, but with disastrous results. Second, the high level of crime in most cities destroys the desire to use the streets for social interaction. As we discussed in Chapter 10, crime destroys cities because it destroys the public use of space. Those planners who emphasize revitalizing streets and city parks must take the high crime rate into account.

Third, Jacobs' ideas about community may also be passé. Many city residents engage in socializing with networks of friends and relatives who do not live nearby, as we have seen in Chapter 9. Even teenagers may prefer to travel to their own friendship networks rather than socialize on the street. On the whole, however, Jane Jacobs' ideas have influenced urbanists because she has captured the heart and soul of city culture. Her importance lies in convincing us that city culture depends on the relationship between personal interaction and public space. The fact that this culture is in danger of dying today is certainly not the fault of her conception.

Leon Krier. As a contemporary architect practicing in Germany, Krier's ideas have been highly influential in recent years in the United States. Like Jacobs, his main concern is in revitalizing urban culture. He views this as principally a problem of scale. The contemporary city has grown too large to shelter a livable environment. According to Krier, it is necessary to return urban building to a human scale. Krier's model of the city is the preindustrial town, and he advocates a return to the type of building characteristic of societies hundreds of years ago. In this sense Krier is a critic of modernist ideology and one of the inspirations for *postmodern* architecture.

According to Krier, settlement space should be divided up into quarters with no more than 15,000 people in each subdivision. Ample use is made of squares, monuments, and public spaces. Buildings and squares should have the proportions of the classical preindustrial towns. All of these changes inspired by "retro" thinking would return urban space to a human scale.

Krier also has his critics (see Dutton, 1989). More so than Jacobs, he commits the physicalist fallacy. He ignores social process and the larger societal forces which make up the modern city and which would make the kind of transition in scale that he envisages difficult for all but the most affluent residents. Krier's proposal, like those of most architects, also commits the elitist/populist fallacy. He never asks what people want; he only dictates design prescriptions through abstract space.

Despite these drawbacks, Leon Krier's work has had an enormous influence on architects who design new communities in the United States that seek to overcome modernist ideology. Among the most significant is the team of Andres Duany and Elizabeth Plater-Zyberk, who are identified with the New Traditionalist Movement (Langdon, 1988). The new traditionalists are especially concerned with the design and social failures of suburbia. They consider suburbs to be sterile environments which prevent an active community life and which, by their very nature, promote the excessive use of the automobile.

Duany and Plater-Zyberk have designed a successful community, Seaside (one among many projects), which is located 100 miles west of Tallahassee, Florida. Seaside is a community of 300 homes and 200 apartments that lies on eighty acres. Its human scale is accentuated by the building of housing that copy the forms of 100 years past. All the homes have front porches and most are located on pedestrian paths rather than roads. There are ample walking paths in the community and places where residents can meet and enjoy interaction in public space.

The new traditionalists' ideas have been influential because there is a growing sense that typical suburban communities have isolated people unnecessarily. At the same time, these ideas, like those of Leon Krier, seem destined to be enjoyed by the most affluent but unavailable to the average family interested in a suburban home. Communities such as Seaside also incorporate many construction features which are dictated by the architects and which play an uncertain role in promoting a new sense of neighborhood, such as the mandated use of tin roofs, or tall and narrow house-windows. This elitism of architectural choice may not appeal to everyone. Yet despite the drawbacks of Krier and the new traditionalists, their work is notable because at long last they have provided alternatives to the ways cities and suburbs have been built, and they remind us of the need for human scale and community feeling.

Paul and Percival Goodman. Most of the planners and critics we have discussed so far focus on construction design and the living arrangements of cities. Recall in the utopian vision of Ebenezer Howard that plans for garden cities included a balanced relationship between residences and industry. Paul and Percival Goodman (1974) asserted that planning could never be effective if it did not integrate working and living arrangements. The focus on residential construction alone ignores the most basic characteristic of social life—namely, that people must work for a living and take care of their families.

The Goodmans also avoided the physicalist fallacy. They argued that good plans try to address political and social relations, not just architectural design needs. Community life should be political in the positive sense; that is, it should be involving. They proposed the construction of communities that would employ participatory democracy both at the place of work and within the local community. Their ambitious scheme involves the creation of a societal decision-making apparatus entirely different from the one we now possess. In the new, democractic-anarchist social order, all decisions related to work and community needs would be based on strict participatory democracy. Needless to say, their ideas have not been applied in the United States, because they would involve a change in the structure of government. However, the Goodmans' work, along with the continuing legacy of Ebenezer Howard, has been influential in the balanced construction of new developments in some formerly socialist countries such as Sweden and Israel—in particular, the Israeli kibbutz (Strong, 1968).

Trends in Planning Today

In recent years development projects in both the city and the suburbs have involved an increase in scale. Projects such as the building of a garden city—Columbia, Maryland—or the construction of Battery Park City at the tip of Manhattan are large in scope and involve many acres. Land has been freed up from agricultural use in the suburbs or as the result of slum clearance and renovation in the cities. These megaprojects usually incorporate mixed use developments of housing and commercial shops. Due to the influence of planning critics, however, many of these designs incorporate human scaling despite their large size.

Among the most successful developers of large but human scale projects is James Rouse, whose corporation built the Baltimore Inner Harbor, Faneuil Hall in Boston, the New York South Street Seaport in Manhattan, and the Santa Monica Mall. The Baltimore, Boston, and New York projects in particular were constructed on deteriorating, unused land that was revitalized. Rouse's success involved a blending of open spaces, reasonably priced eating places of great variety, and upscale shops. Such redevelopment transformed spaces of bleak prospect into vital urban centers with an active public life. The Baltimore Harbor project, for example, consists of a large horseshoe of open space that comprises the shore of the harbor inlet. Concrete steps lead to benches and play areas. One section is devoted to an array of alternative and moderately priced eateries. Two attractions, the Baltimore Aquarium and the Revolutionary War battleship *Concord,* also draw in visitors.

Rouse also successfully developed Columbia, Maryland, a new town which mixes apartment and single-family home construction with accessible and usable open space and shopping areas. The entire project has been planned to conform to human scale and includes pathways totally dedicated to pedestrian use that link the various sections of the town. As one observer notes:

> In Columbia the size of residential areas was determined primarily by the number of households needed to support an elementary school. The Rouse Co., as developer, insisted that within a block of the school there be a swimming pool, a community building, and a convenience store, and that people be able to walk or bike to these facilities without crossing any major streets. Three to five neighborhoods made up a village, which offered more facilities, including a supermarket, a bank branch, and other businesses—also accessible by the community's forty-seven miles of walking and biking paths, as well as by car (Langdon, 1988: 52).

The success of the Rouse Corporation has influenced the way other megaprojects have been designed. In New York City, for example, a ninety-two-acre section of the dilapidated downtown with few residential units was demolished to build Battery Park City. The project consists of high rise apartments, offices, and shopping facilities. Located at the tip of Manhattan, the new development makes ample use of its view of the Hudson River. Residential blocks are integrated with an esplanade that includes spaces to sit and socialize with neighbors. Many other projects across the country, such as Riverplace in Portland along the Willamette River and Riverplace in Minneapolis along the Mississippi River, also use the successful approach of human-scale residential blocks, mixed commercial and housing land use, and pedestrian amenities to provide a more attractive environment for residents.

While the above cases provide examples of developers' attempts to encourage community, other trends are symptoms of the many problems cities and suburbs face. For example, it is also popular to construct "gate-guarded" developments where security and surveillance are given prime importance. These barricaded communities (called "condominium fechado" in Rio de Janeiro) do not seek an integration with city surroundings and an active street life, but instead isolate themselves from the urban fabric. Fences protect the perimeter. Guards supervise the coming and going of both residents and their guests. The uninvited are simply not allowed in. Typically, these residential communities possess empty and austere open spaces between the dwellings. One such project, Studio Colony, is located in the Studio City section of Los Angeles and consists of 450 upper-middle-income apartments. The residences are sealed off in high rise buildings with parking garages located underneath the guarded structures. Studio Colony provides security from the high crime rate of Los Angeles, but as one observer notes:

> What Studio Colony does not do is shape the outdoor areas into coherent, genuinely inviting spaces; it is hard to imagine that anyone would want to walk from one end of Studio Colony to the other even once (Langdon, 1988: 59).

In sum, principally due to the increase in the social problems of metropolitan living, architectural schemes for communities have changed in recent years. The shift is from the utopian influenced plans of the nineteenth century to the current mix of postmodern design which seeks a return to human scale, and the barricaded, guarded environments which seek isolation from the dystopia of the city.

Summary

People in the United States regard planning with suspicion. They prefer to defend individual property rights and the home rule prerogative of local government control over land use. While every jurisdiction, no matter how small, seems to have its own planning department, professional experts are relegated to an advisory position in our society. Planners must maneuver within this politically constrained milieu by exercising their influence on developers, speculators, homeowners, renters, local community activists, and public officials (Weiss, 1987). It is not an easy task. In the main, the professional planners employed by business and government devote their time to working out the ordinary details of mandated land use and construction requirements. They pursue the unglamorous job of drafting site usage plans for developers, reviewing and updating zoning maps for local governments, and assessing traffic studies. They also collect and review demographic information on the present and future growth patterns of individual towns. But this bureaucratic domain of activity remains removed from the active task of fashioning environments in which other people will live.

As we have seen, the limitations placed on professional planners have not stopped individuals from dreaming their dreams of the perfect city. Visionaries and utopian thinkers have tried their best to lead citizens of modern society toward some Eden that actualizes the promise of industrial progress. Some ideas, such as Howard's Garden City, have been influential enough to affect future generations. Colossal failures, such as the superhuman building blocks of Le Corbusier's Radiant City (which can be found actualized in every high-rise public housing project, not to mention the ashes of Pruitt-Igoe), have also been helpful because they have shown what we cannot or should not do. Happily, visionary plans are tried sometimes, and even more happily, most of the time on a small scale so that the human cost of failure is not dear. We learn from mistakes and successes as the knowledge of planning human environments accumulates.

One important lesson that has recently been learned concerns the yearning for human-scale places in the face of unending metropolitan sprawl and the experience of immense, impersonal city space. Developments today feature an informed use of space. Macro environments, such as the Santa Monica enclosed mall, are composed of many mini environments that nurture sociability. The monstrous Battery Park City project opens itself out to the surrounding urban fabric and natural setting, providing for social interaction via micro public spaces and the extended esplanade on the Hudson River. Finally, as we have seen, new towns developed in their entirety (such as Columbia, Maryland) succeed by devoting space to pedestrians and thereby providing alternatives to automobile transportation for the enactment of everyday tasks such as shopping, leisure activities, or the trip to elementary school.

But a return to human scale alone through the best efforts of planners will not save the declining quality of life in either our central cities or massive, sprawling suburbs. As revealed in Chapter 10, the high level of crime has taken an immense toll on the free use of urban space, not to mention its cost in lives. We can rightly wonder what will happen to the Hudson River Esplanade and its pedestrian traffic if it becomes a haven for muggers. How enjoyable would the miles of pedestrian paths of Columbia, Maryland, be if the community were not isolated from the scenes of homelessness and destitution characteristic of inner city residents? The growing problems of land use, congestion, traffic jams, housing blight, environmental pollution, and sprawl spur the public to search for planned solutions to urban growth. These and other problems may yet force local citizens to give up their traditional and narrow concern with protecting their own property rights at the expense of a more coordinated approach to development. Yet the problems of the metropolitan region have societal roots that are not easily addressed by technical recommendations without massive social change.

These contradictions are clearest when we study the impact of environmental pollutants on communities. As we have discussed, the burden of costs for society's progress seems to fall on poor and minority neighborhoods. Often, government at all levels participates in producing this pattern of discrimination. In other areas, such as the Southern California basin around the metropolis of Los Angeles, air pollution affects and endangers the lives of everyone, rich or poor. Environmental problems are common to us all and require economic, political, and social responses in addition to better-quality spatial design.

Professional planners, government officials, and architects would probably remain limited by their own outlook, as sociologists have noted, even if they were provided with more power. They preach the physicalist fallacy, which holds a blind faith in the power of construction technology and design to alter social relationships. Rarely do they profess what the Goodman brothers or Frank Lloyd Wright saw as the organic, holistic needs of individuals. They are more comfortable with limited prescriptions that conform to the dictates of their professions—building design and construction for architects, landscaping or land use schemes for planners, political expediency for politicians. Much more is needed to control the forces of development in the United States, but little public debate seems to be devoted to the issue of planning or the search for alternatives to our deteriorating environment. Without more public involvement in the planning question, little progress will be made. It is up to the leaders of our society, therefore, to involve the citizens in a protracted dialogue regarding the kind of environments they would prefer to have, much like the model of Bellevue, Washington (see Box 14.1).

One last source of reform remains unexamined so far, namely, the activities surrounding the drafting and execution of public policy and state intervention. We shall consider this topic next.

CHAPTER

15

METROPOLITAN SOCIAL POLICY AND THE FUTURE OF URBAN SOCIOLOGY

In the previous chapter we considered one form of intervention—planning. We have examined both its prospects and limitations. Attempts by society to fashion a living environment that is beneficial to citizens do not end by exhausting planning options. A separate approach, one that is often initiated in conjunction with planning, involves government intervention guided by policy. The state has the authority to apply rational decision-making procedures and allocate money from tax revenues and deficit spending to address social needs. Government actions not only can direct behavior by prohibition, that is, by passing laws that prohibit certain acts, but they can also provide incentives and opportunities to channel resources in specific ways. This push versus pull feature of policy is an important one to keep in mind when examining the issue of political intervention. While this chapter will be devoted to the role of government in improving metropolitan life, it is worthwhile noting that intervention, such as the publicly directed dumping of toxic waste in poor communities, can also create problems. Just "how much" intervention is needed and in "what forms" remain critical issues for any discussion of government policy.

The Tragedy of the Commons and Uneven Development

U.S. society possesses a civic culture that is adverse to government intervention in the market. We have identified this perspective as "privatism," namely, the belief that government should restrict its role to helping the business community and seeking market solutions to social problems. But this reliance on the market leads to certain problems. In the previous chapter we saw that the desire to plan the development of metropolitan regions arose because the private market is not capable of providing adequate amounts of infrastructure. There are other problems with the market as a mechanism for allocating resources. Two associated limitations involve, on the one hand, the difficulty of maintaining the quality of life when public resources are involved, and on the other, the problem of uneven development in a capitalist society.

The Tragedy of the Commons

There is an old fable in academic circles that economists use to show why individual choice can lead to socially undesirable effects. The fable has many variations; here's ours: Consider a village of farmers each with a herd of cows and an open field adjacent to the village which is held in common. Each farmer seeks to use the public resource of the field to private advantage. Therefore, they all attempt to graze their cows as often and as long as possible on the common green. Pretty soon, as a result of this practice, the grass is all eaten and the common field is reduced to a muddy, barren plot of land.

If the farmers are interested in improving their situation, they have few alternatives. They could each buy a farm that would be owned privately with sufficient grazing land— an expensive move. Or they could band together and create a community scheduling agreement by which the need of each farmer *and* the need of the field to regenerate itself would be recognized. Because the users of this public resource might have disputes, the individuals involved would also have to arrange for arbitration in the event of disagreements or abuse. In short, this tragedy of the commons points to the need for the social institution of public authority or local government, which safeguards the benefits to the many from the abuses of the few.

Settlement spaces in modern society contain many public resources such as air quality, water quality, and recreational areas. Safeguarding these common environmental resources becomes increasingly difficult as the population and frequency of use rise (see Chapter 14). As a consequence, government must develop active public policies to deal with the many problems arising from large populations living in the same settlement space. Often these policies involve laws that are passed which restrict individual rights but which are considered necessary to preserve public resources.

To take one brief example: In New York City, partly as a consequence of a rising crime rate, apartment dwellers purchased dogs in great numbers. By the 1970s, walking the city streets had turned into a hazardous affair simply because there was so much dog excrement lying around. The city was compelled to pass a "pooper scooper" law which mandated that owners clean up after their dogs in public. This law made it a crime not to comply. To this day, any tourist can observe dog owners from all social backgrounds scooping up after their animals in order to keep the streets clean. The law is an infringement on individual rights, but it is sanctioned by our society because it leads to a greater good—public enjoyment of a common resource, public space. Most environmental policy is of this type, and support for such measures requires a public culture that is committed to protecting environmental resources.

In the United States, many such laws exist which limit the free market for the public good. Some of the most restrictive are the Southern California anti-air-pollution statutes which are regulated by an independent state agency and which affect everything from automobile exhaust systems to by-products of industrial activity to homeowner burning of trash and outdoor barbecue use. The air-quality control board has authority to limit daily activities when pollution is hazardous in the Los Angeles metropolitan region. Over the years, Southern California has lost many businesses because they prefer to move rather than pay the extra cost of compliance. But that has not diminished public support for government policy. Rather, in such an environment, where pollution is a clear and present danger, intervention is the only solution until the causes of air pollution are eliminated by other means. Hence, while we dislike government intervention, we find it useful. Sustaining the quality of life in metropolitan regions is an especially difficult task without the aid of government policy and regulation of free markets.

Uneven Development and Policy: Redistributive Programs

The activities of society do not only threaten public resources that we all hold in common; they also affect individuals in different ways. In capitalist society, resources tend to flow to those who are most powerful. There are many reasons for this and not all of them imply wrongdoing on anyone's part. In addition, under pure market conditions when individuals compete in business with each other, one's prosperity is supposed to spur the others to copy success. Thus, the market serves to discipline business people to adopt the best and most efficient means of pursuing a profit. What holds for business, however, does not necessarily apply to individual people. Issues of inequality plague our society (as we have seen in Chapter 10) and those of other countries (see chapters 12 and 13). They also undermine the social order and lead to conflict.

While we have a public philosophy of privatism in this country, we also have a public commitment, guaranteed by the constitution, to equality of opportunity. This last feature leads to dilemmas for Americans because inequality and powerful special interests produce patterns of uneven development.

It is supposed to be a right, for example, for all children within the same public school district to receive the same quality education. What do we do when we find that schools in richer neighborhoods have more resources than schools in the poorer ones? And shouldn't all children in the United States receive the same quality schooling? Can we all afford to move to the best districts? Should we do so as the only solution, even if we could? Should only the more affluent receive an adequate education, including college, especially when public higher education is supported by everyone's taxes?

Doctors in the United States are capitalists; they charge what the market will bear. Those people who have the most money can get the best medical care. But what happens to people who are too poor to pay? Why is it that some people have adequate insurance while others do not? Shouldn't all Americans have adequate health care? Or should quality of care depend on ability to pay?

In a final example, the housing industry in our society is also a capitalist enterprise. Those individuals who can afford a private home can get one. The more you can afford to spend, the better your home will be. But what about those individuals who cannot afford the price? What happens to the truly poor who cannot even afford rent? Should we sanction poverty, homelessness, premature death, or the ruination of the elderly who must pay for health and housing expenses they cannot afford?

Over the years all capitalist societies have had to face the social costs of uneven development. In the United States, government has enacted legislation at all levels supporting social programs that address social ills. Social welfare programs are designed to pool resources or redistribute them. Using certain criteria of inclusion, government officials decide what is needed and who should be eligible to receive assistance. These programs are supported by taxing the more affluent or by special government borrowing; hence they *redistribute* the wealth from the relatively well-off to the poor, although as we shall discuss below, such schemes are not without their abuses or critics (Jencks, 1992).

The issue of uneven development and public policy in its most basic form, then, involves a question of money, because sustaining the quality of life has private and social costs. Government programs may address the issue of inequitable wealth, but as Christopher Jencks has argued (1992), only income redistribution can directly address the problem of poverty. Hence, many social programs are destined to fail.

Public interventionist schemes are drawn up by government representatives in conjunction with research staffs and various academic aides. Some policies find the government directly intervening in the production of new resources such as the building of dams, highways, housing, and nuclear energy facilities. These directly aid private sector business interests as well as the general welfare. In other cases, incentives are created to channel individual behavior in certain directions, such as the tax subsidy provided to people who purchase single-family homes. The enactment of programs also requires a staff. Government at all levels is a major employer in the United States, accounting for more than 25 percent of the entire work force. Social programs run by government also support immense bureaucracies such as the state welfare department. Hence not only the less affluent but also state workers benefit from public intervention.

There are many ways that government policy redistributes wealth and channels resources toward the public good. The welfare program and Medicaid are meant to protect the quality of life among those individuals who are less affluent or restricted in their incomes because they are single parents or are retired and elderly. State boards of education try to equalize school resources among different public districts, regardless of neighborhood family incomes. Public health crises such as the AIDS epidemic are also addressed by government policy. Finally, housing programs exist in a variety of forms, and there are even public programs to deal with homelessness.

In addition, government policies aid the business community directly and subsidize its activities, as the discussion on privatism suggests (see below). Furthermore, the implementation of public programs aimed at aiding individuals in need is often twisted by private sector involvement toward the pursuit of profit by business. This *coopting* of government intervention is a serious limitation of public policy in the United States, and it alone causes programs to fail, as the recent experience with low-income housing programs run by HUD shows (see Box 15.1, pp. 322–323). There are other limitations, including the failure of individual programs themselves because they cannot attain desired goals—as in the case of welfare aid—or because intervention actually makes problems worse (Jencks, 1992).

State intervention is also the focus for community politics, and as we discussed in chapters 11 and 12, local community organizing for more resources from government is an important source of political disputes in the United States and the third world. In this sense, the politics of policy never ends and government intervention remains the focus for debate, reappraisal, and reform.

Most of the examples we have discussed so far concern the general problems of inequity in our society rather than issues specifically relevant to metropolitan areas. Let us look more closely at some of the programs aimed particularly at the needs of both cities and suburbs, and the various political, economic, and social ramifications of government policy in metropolitan areas. In the previous chapter, we discussed how the desire for planning is associated with the "modernist" belief that increased rationality of land use and architectural design can improve our lives and lead to progress for all. Some countries, such as the welfare capitalist societies of Scandinavia, hold a modernist belief in government policy as also aiding progress through rational state intervention. The United States is characterized by a different public ideology called *privatism* which requires government to aid business interests through the market. While our approach has had some success, it also leaves public programs vulnerable to cooptation by powerful interests. As we shall see below, due to the characteristics of public policy, the pursuit of social justice often fails even when government intervenes with the best of intentions.

Urban and Metropolitan Policy

There is no escaping the fact that public policy in the United States and in other countries as well is shaped by fundamental philosophical positions and ideologically held beliefs regarding government intervention. As we have seen, the dominant belief in the United States is that government should always play a limited role in the economy and that market solutions are usually best. This attitude contrasts with those of industrialized countries in Western Europe, for example, which have more active public policy and more publicly supported benefits such as national health care schemes (although as we discussed in Chapter 13, some of these countries, such as the United Kingdom, have lately limited their public welfare programs).

The United States, therefore, is *ambivalent* regarding government intervention. Different political positions support different types of criticisms directed against state programs. On the one hand, many liberals lament the takeover of public programs by powerful business interests. On the other, many conservatives point to the inefficient and deleterious effects of government intervention. In addition to the philosophy of privatism, a second drawback to intervention is that under the federalist arrangements between the national government and the states the condition of cities is the responsibility of the states, yet many of the problems, such as crime or health care, are national in scope. Over the years the respective roles of the federal versus state level have become an issue of political debate (see concluding section).

The urban renewal program of the '50s, '60s, and '70s provides an illustrative case of the relationship between business and government as well as the limitations of policy. Urban renewal grew out of the 1930s Roosevelt administration's commitment to rescue the housing and banking industry from the Depression, a serious economic crisis indeed. The Housing Act of 1934, for example, established the Federal Housing Authority which guaranteed home loans. The 1937 Housing Act mandated the government to provide funds for the support of low-income house construction and slum clearance. These powers were amplified in the Housing Act of 1949 under Title I assistance and in subsequent acts passed in 1954, 1961, 1968, and 1970. The Department of Housing and Urban Development or HUD grew into a massive bureaucracy that oversaw the many programs associated with renewal.

It is important to note that housing intervention was aimed primarily at aiding the real estate industry, one of the three largest in the U.S. economy, rather than being a showcase of modernist ideas mixing planning with policy, as in the Scandinavian countries, for example. Providing homes for people and caring for their community needs was only a secondary goal of the U.S. program. As a result of this contradiction, metropolitan housing policy has enjoyed mixed results. It proved to be a great boon to business but was less effective in attaining its social goals. Box 15.1 discusses the case study of federal support for public housing in more detail.

During the period from 1950 to 1990 government intervention aimed at aiding cities underwent three separate phases of evolution, each of which reflects the dominant role of business in defining the interventionist agenda. Initially, funds targeted slum removal and affordable housing construction; then, social goals were dropped and the focus turned to the support of economic development for local business; finally, government funds were used to subsidize economic development for global competition. In all three phases local government operated less as a vehicle for social justice than as an aid to businesses experiencing declining profits.

Support for Slum Removal

Beginning with the late 1950s, the amount of federal money allocated for central city slum clearance and renewal increased greatly each year. Combined expenditures, for instance, were $706 million in 1960, $1.8 billion in 1966, and $3.8 billion by 1970, or an increase of over 500 percent in 10 years (Mollenkopf, 1975).

There were many reasons for HUD's spending spree. By the 1950s central cities were being devastated by the immense outflow of people to the suburbs. This shift, as we have already discussed, was made possible by government highway and housing programs. As a result, downtown retailers and their department stores were in danger of being shut down because of the success of suburban shopping malls, while entire residential sections of the city were given over to blight and decline as middle-class people moved out. City politicians appealed to the federal government for help in rescuing downtown areas. A second cause involved the national response to the ghetto riots of the 1960s, which also highlighted the deterioration of inner city areas. Funding for HUD projects more than doubled after 1966, the year of the worst rioting.

During the 1950s, urban renewal was aimed at revitalizing the downtown areas

Older housing in this area of Pittsburgh was torn down by an urban renewal project in the 1960s. Instead of being replaced by low-income housing, the lots remained vacant for years.

of cities and clearing away slums or blighted dwellings. Programs were supposed to replace cleared land with affordable housing and income-earning civic projects. According to some estimates, over 5 million low- to moderate-income housing units in U.S. cities were candidates for destruction and replacement (Flanagan, 1990: 292). By the end of 1961, renewal programs had eliminated over 126,000 substandard housing units, but only 28,000 new dwellings were built (Robertson and Judd, 1989: 307).

At that time observers noted that the policy seemed to be more effective in the removal of black and/or poor residents than at replacing slums with affordable housing. In fact, during the 1960s urban renewal was dubbed "Negro removal." Over 75 percent of all people displaced by renewal projects were black (Robertson and Judd, 1989: 307). In subsequent years programs followed this pattern of removing minorities and the poor from the central city but not replacing much needed low-income housing (see Box 15.1).

Thus, while some low income residents were helped by the ambitious redevelopment schemes which were subsidized by the federal government, much of urban renewal involved the clearing away of slums to allow private real estate interests to use downtown land for profit making, including the building of middle- and upper-middle-income housing projects and the regeneration of central city commerce through the construction of plazas, civic centers, and pedestrian malls.

Paradoxically, at the same time that HUD programs were intervening in renewal, other federal housing policy in the form of tax subsidies to homeowners was destroying city neighborhoods by promoting suburbanization. These subsidies, which amounted

BOX 15.1 THE CASE OF PUBLIC HOUSING

As part of the recovery from the Great Depression, the federal government passed a number of acts that aimed to fight social problems such as unemployment, as well as spur industrial growth. During World War II much American industry benefited from the allied effort; however, the housing industry was still in the doldrums. Congress passed the 1949 Housing Act to stimulate that industry. As drafted, it embodied the contradiction of U.S. public policy because it was a measure aimed principally at subsidizing the housing industry, but it also proposed to alleviate the problem of slums. The act authorized the construction of 135,000 public housing units each year.

The architects of the bill were two famous senators, Robert Taft and Paul Douglas. Both men believed that living in a "decent home" was the right of every American. According to Charles Abrams' commentary:

> Senator Robert Taft, who had been the measure's most forceful advocate, would not allow himself to be distracted by those who had pressed for an enlargement of purpose beyond housing, for the good senator was a Christian at heart to whom "no room at the inn" was a gnawing deficiency in a great and progressive society.
>
> "I do not believe that public housing is socialism," Senator Taft told me in an interview, "if it is confined to the furnishing of decent housing only to that group unable to provide housing by its own means" (1965: 81).

Soon after, however, the commitment to public housing was watered down by Congress. After 1954 the authorization was cut to between 35,000 to 45,000 units per year, hardly enough to accommodate those slum dwellers displaced by renewal.

In subsequent years the commitment to the construction of public housing became a low priority compared to the use of urban renewal legislation to make the housing industry profitable. According to Abrams:

> It was only one of many examples of how legislation passed with the best of intentions is ultimately perverted during the administrative process. In the long run, the profit motive somehow operates as the designated but effective legislator while the public obligation is pushed under the rug (1965: 84).

Another drawback to the housing legislation was that the programs were not monitored carefully regarding their impact both on the industry and on the public housing tenants. In the latter case, we have already seen how life in the few, large public projects led to a high crime rate and disaffection of the tenants—many of whom moved out, as in the case of

Pruitt-Igoe. In Chapter 10 we also learned of Ruby and her family who lived in the massive Cabrini public housing project of Chicago and who lapsed into welfare dependency, drug use, and poverty for several generations. While public housing did *not* cause these problems, it concentrated them and made their solution difficult, especially because of the ghettoization of the poor, as we have seen.

But the abuses of profit entrepreneurs are also cause for alarm when public programs are not adequately monitored. In the case of the 1949 and 1954 housing acts, discussed above, scandal eventually tarnished the intentions of Taft and Douglas. The acts amplified a wartime provision that provided federal funds for military housing, notoriously known as Section 608. This provision was meant to stimulate the rapid construction of rental housing, and it provided for as much as 90 percent of the costs to be covered by the government. The postwar housing acts sought to use Section 608 to stimulate the construction of affordable rental housing after urban renewal had torn slums down.

The program was renewed in 1946 but not monitored for twelve years. Frequent abuse by the private sector occurred, such as the use of dummy leases, purposely enacted defaults to acquire FHA insurance, and the selling of units to wholly-owned subsidiaries in order to hide profits. According to Abrams:

> Three speculators [in one illustration of the rip-off] put up only $6,000 for a $12,500,000 project [in 1954 dollars] in Virginia. They each went on the payroll for $20,000 a year; each got his $6,000 back in a few weeks, and when the building was completed, there was $2,250,000 left over from the mortgage, which they promptly pocketed (1965: 88–89).

The above illustrates an important point about the abuses of government programs. They are not committed solely by those blamed in public discourse as "welfare cheats," for example, but are associated as well with the plundering of millions of dollars from the public by white collar criminals. The abuses of Section 608 seem reminiscent of the present-day savings and loan scandal, which will require billions of public dollars to remedy. These scandals remind us of the power of the business establishment to coopt government programs in order to increase personal wealth through both legal and illegal means.

The public housing program has failed, but not because of the particular evils of either white collar criminals or welfare dependency. It has failed because our society cannot commit exclusively to a social welfare program of such magnitude. Rather, government policy is most often directed at subsidizing industries, such as housing. Instead of doing both of these well, government funds wind up lining the pockets of rip-off artists, often to the detriment of honest people. Without adequate monitoring of programs, the abuses often amount to billions of dollars.

to billions of dollars each year, were responsible for the massive shift to the suburbs, or white flight. By the 1970s it was already clear that the United States had become segregated by race and class, with middle-class whites dominating the suburbs while the inner cities were increasingly populated by minorities and those whites who either could not afford to move to suburbia or preferred to live in the city in newly built or renovated upper-middle-income housing. Thus, government intervention was not only less interested in social justice than in subsidizing business, but it was also not rational and it worked against itself in the fight to save the city.

Support for Economic Development

By the late 1960s the goals of urban policy had changed as a result of political pressures. Commitment to the revitalization of slums was abandoned in favor of using government programs to bolster private business interests in the city. It was now apparent that urban economies, which had been dependent on manufacturing, were in decline. Deindustrialization had taken over the country and cities needed to retool themselves in order to grow. Downtown business interests along with local politicians regrouped and worked together to use federal funds for revitalization projects. The focus of renewal shifted from slum clearance to support for economic development such as the construction of sports stadiums, hotel and tourist complexes, and high rise service centers. For example, in the 1960s the city of Los Angeles used urban renewal funds to bulldoze the blighted section of Bunker Hill near the downtown. But instead of replacing the structures with affordable housing and preserving the community, the city and its partners in the business sector constructed a music center, high rise banking offices, and expensive high rise apartment complexes. Slightly east of this redevelopment, the city eradicated another blighted section and constructed Dodger Stadium instead of low income housing (Davis, 1990).

Such projects, backed by powerful political and business interests, were responsible for the eradication of inner city neighborhoods and small businesses, while the signs of "progress" greeted all residents with visible advertising for the joint government/ business ventures. In many cases, city neighborhoods which did not represent high yield profit making for business were bulldozed despite the objections of local residents. Box 15.2 illustrates this trend with the example of World Trade tower construction in Manhattan, but examples from every city abound (Robertson and Judd, 1989; Stone, 1989; Davis, 1990).

Economic development as an urban policy in the 1960s and 1970s meant that privatism had taken over, not just through cooptation as it had in previous periods, but overtly as part of city revival schemes. As the argument went, business concerns come first in a period of recession because when business prospers, the tax coffers of the city are also enriched. Housing programs and community redevelopment, however, had to take a back seat, as did the fight for social justice and against the problems of uneven development. As in other periods, while some federal programs aided business directly, others also helped the middle class. Indeed, the city government could not stem the tide of middle-class white flight during this period because the pull of subsidized suburbanization was too powerful (see Chapter 5). Government could try to make the city a better place to do business, but it could not make it a better place to live.

Support for Global Competition

By the 1980s cities were running out of options for economic development projects. The shift to a financial and service economy for the downtown had now turned global. Each place was in competition for limited investment that was attuned to worldwide opportunities. During the middle 1970s, however, the federal government ceased to fund cities in the manner it had been. The support of business switched to national programs in an effort to bypass local bureaucracies and downsize the role of government planning. Issues of social justice were ignored. This restructuring of the federal/city government relationship reached its zenith during the eight years of the Reagan administration and resulted in the cutback of urban policy until there was little left of renewal funding.

Several reasons have been advanced for the federal abandonment of HUD city-renewal programs, most of which are political. The Republican administration in the 1980s ran on a platform that de-emphasized the needs of cities. The plurality of active voters lived in the suburbs, and they were attracted by President Reagan's call to get government "off the backs" of people. This meant that under the Reagan and Bush administrations there were severe cuts in public welfare programs but not in military spending. The new regime favored market solutions to social ills according to conservative philosophy. It also reaffirmed the political principle of federalism (mentioned at the beginning of this chapter) which made the condition of cities a responsibility of the states. Hence it determined that local and state governments were better able to deal with local problems, if necessary, and that urban revitalization should be market driven rather than pulled along by federally financed and planned projects. Such sentiments were supported by a majority of voters, who backed President Reagan's conservative agenda and who later elected George Bush.

During the 1980s, the cuts to federal programs were unprecedented. As Robertson and Judd (1989: 314) observe about national aid to cities:

> Overall spending dropped from $6.1 billion in fiscal year 1981 to $5.2 billion in fiscal year 1984. The $5.2 billion spent for the fiscal year 1984–1985 amounted to a decline of almost 20 percent when corrected for inflation. By the 1989 budget year, money for urban programs was cut $4.4 billion—a further reduction of about 40 percent when the effects of inflation are considered.
>
> Nearly all subsidies for the construction of public housing were ended. . . . Urban mass transit grants were reduced 28 percent from 1981–1983 and were cut another 20 percent by 1986. CETA [Comprehensive Employment and Training Act] funds were eliminated after 1983.

During the past decade, cities and states have had to fend for themselves in supporting metropolitan programs. As discussed in Chapter 10, the fiscal crisis which set in during the 1970s severely restricted the ability of local areas to finance policy aimed at social goals, even when good ideas circulated freely. As the fiscal crisis spread to the states in the 1980s and 1990s, they could no longer support social-justice-oriented policies at the local level. With little public money around, both cities and states had to scrap many social projects and have since concentrated on economic development.

Local governments in particular were faced with a crisis when the federal level

BOX 15.2 THE WORLD TRADE TOWERS

The World Trade Center was proposed as a complex of twin towers, each of 110 stories. They were constructed on the lower westside corner of Manhattan Island in 1972, adding 4.5 million square feet of office space to the downtown area. The site on which they were built was not vacant. It consisted of blighted buildings along with several vibrant neighborhoods including the Cortlandt Street complex of independent and highly competitive small businesses dealing in electronics.

One might think that this trade-off of small commercial interests and ethnic neighborhoods for a world class center of international banking was exactly the kind of project urban renewal programs had in mind. According to a report by Ralph Nader and associates (Leinsdorf et al., 1973), however, local residents opposed the project: New York City did not require such a massive increase in office space at the time and there were limited transportation facilities servicing the site area. To this day the towers are plagued by excessive vacancy rates, and they have failed to spark development in the surrounding area.

The project was the brain child of a group of private sector banks including First National City, Chase Manhattan, Morgan Guaranty Trust, Chemical Bank, and Marine Midland Grace (Leinsdorf et al., 1973: 143). However, this group, known as the Downtown Lower Manhattan Association (DLMA), did not build the towers. Instead, they convinced a quasi-public agency, the Port Authority of New York, to construct the complex on land cleared by urban renewal. This quasi-public agency has the government's powers of *eminent domain* (i.e., the right to take over private property for public use despite owner objections) and the ability to extend tax exemptions; it is not directly responsible to the public but has the authority to collect user fees for the area's infrastructure of bridges, tunnels, and roads and use the money for development projects.

In order to finance the project, the Authority borrowed millions of dollars from a consortium of thirteen banks, most of which were members of the DLMA. As the Nader report observes,

> On December, 31, 1968, the Port Authority had 276 million dollars, or 93 percent of its time deposits in the same banks that were receiving tax-exempt in-

slashed urban funds and proclaimed a "market led transition to a postindustrial economy" (Barnekov and Rich, 1989). City politicians now work directly with business to revive ailing urban economies. This represents an extreme example of privatism, because the reduction or elimination of policy aimed at improving social well-being has occurred since the 1980s at *every* government level. It is one thing for the federal government to claim that the local quality of life is a matter for local jurisdictions, but it is quite another matter when no level of government addresses this need due to fiscal crisis cutbacks and the subsidization by taxpayers of economic recovery.

According to Desmond King (1990), local policy now comprises either supply- or demand-side incentives to business. The former consists of packaging incentives such as tax breaks, rent free land, and local bond financing that will attract capital to terest on the 210 million dollar loan. . . . The Authority deposited the proceeds from its bonds in the same banks that were receiving its tax-exempt interest payments. If the banks took tax deductions for the interest they paid on the Port Authority's time deposits, then they were violating the law (Leinsdorf et al., 1973: 148).

Even if the Nader group conclusion was wrong and no laws were violated, this example illustrates how special and powerful interests were able to use the ethos of urban renewal to further their own desires. In particular, the construction of the twin towers is only one example of a pattern that was repeated in many cities, namely, the influence of banking interests or the finance capital faction in channeling public resources toward the preservation of central city land values. According to a newspaper report about downtown Los Angeles, for example, "Federal law prohibits banks from speculating on real estate, but they may own property they use for bank business. Such bank holdings account for perhaps one-fifth of total property values downtown" (*Los Angeles Times*, April 25, 1982, Section A-3).

In sum, not only did urban renewal programs fail to achieve their purpose, namely, the replacement of blighted structures with renovated and affordable housing and revitalized commercial districts (an observation that supports the conservative argument against government intervention), but many of the initiatives were controlled by powerful interests for their own purposes while using public authority and tax subsidies (an observation made by liberal critics of the government program). As a result, many cities have downtowns that are now dominated by bank buildings and their associated services, while neighborhood life and small business districts within the central city have largely disappeared.

While there are many critics of renewal (see Anderson, 1968, for example), there are also some positive accomplishments. According to Abrams (1965), renewal provided an aesthetic to downtown by fostering comprehensive planning in place of a piecemeal renewal process; it brought the participation of local citizens' groups into the development process; when it worked right, it also cleared blight and replaced it with impressive projects that enriched the city, such as Lincoln Center in New York, which replaced a slum with six modern buildings dedicated to the performing arts; finally, renewal stimulated industry and thereby increased the tax revenues of local governments.

the area. The latter consists of city development activities that attempt to create new industries with the aid of the private sector by underwriting development costs, such as in the creation of high tech industrial parks. In both cases the policies of the 1990s are in stark contrast to those of thirty years ago, because the emphasis is on economic recovery without the rhetoric that once obscured the emphasis on privatism by, at least, acknowledging issues of social equity and injustice.

Privatism and Issues of Social Justice

Has the current abandonment of active intervention in cities been successful? Our analysis of metropolitan problems (Chapter 10) shows just the opposite. What are

Mayors Louise Gardner, Jefferson City, Missouri, Raymond Flynn, Boston, Sue Myrick, Charlotte, North Carolina, W. Wilson Goode, Philadelphia, Pennsylvania, Kathy Whitmire, Houston, Texas, Richard M. Daley, Chicago, Illinois, and Maureen O'Connor, San Diego, California (left to right), march in Chicago's "Say No To Drugs" parade.

the limitations of the ideology of privatism and the present constraints on pursuing social justice?

There are several limitations of privatism and its current policy of government subsidy for economic development (Barnekov and Rich, 1989), including the failure to realize benefits from development, especially by low income residents; the proliferation of beggar-thy-neighbor competition between different cities, which does not benefit local areas; the subsidization of capital investment which is not reinvested locally; and the destruction of public resources without benefit from the public subsidization of private sector growth.

Lack of Community Benefits from Public Investment

In one case, Oakland, California, obtained a package of loans and tax subsidies to support the private development of airport improvements and an industrial park (Pressman and Wildavsky, 1973). The rationale for the public subsidy of the project was that it would help provide steady work for the city's hard-core unemployed. According to Pressman and Wildavsky (1973), however, only an estimated sixty-five jobs out of many hundreds that were created went to hard-core unemployed workers.

Other studies also bear out the Oakland case conclusion that publicly supported growth does not bring the kind of benefits purported by boosters of public/private partnerships. Feagin (1988) studied the extreme case of Houston, which claims to be a city based on private enterprise. He shows how business has used government funds in many ways to develop infrastructure, subsidize industry, and grease the wheels of profit making. During the city's growth, furthermore, the costs of development were passed along to residents. By maintaining a low tax rate on business, the city also failed to plan adequately for highways, sewage systems, garbage collection, water quality, and road maintenance. Houston's traffic jams are legendary. And future residents will be saddled with the immense public bill to finance the missing infrastructure and the costs of growth. The experience of Houston has been duplicated in other U.S. cities, which now face immense infrastructure problems of their own while at the same time continuing to spend millions in taxpayer money on "development" projects such as sports stadiums, convention centers, and luxury housing. The alleged "crisis" of the infrastructure and of public support for the quality of life is not, as some political leaders maintain, a crisis of funding alone, but represents some skewed priorities when all available money is spent on civic development projects of dubious value.

Lack of Economic Return on Public Investment

Another, more extreme case of privatism's failure involves the city of Detroit's subsidy of a new General Motors assembly plant (Hill, 1986). A community known as Poletown (because of the predominance of an ethnic Polish population in the area) was chosen for the new plant. The city government, against the wishes of the local community, designated the site for demolition. Over 1,000 homes, 155 businesses, several churches, and a hospital were demolished, and over 3,500 people were displaced (Hill, 1986: 111). Residents observed that even in the former Soviet Union no government official dared to destroy churches, but the Poletown project did so with impunity. The rationale for all this devastation was that the new plant would employ at least 6,000 new workers and retain a manufacturing base within the city at a time when nothing but job loss in industry had prevailed. Despite this rationale, the plant never attained a full schedule of production and today employs only half of the projected workers. Recently, the sluggish economy has forced General Motors to cut back and lay off more workers.

Other case studies reveal that privatism twists the intent of public/private partnerships to the full benefit of business. As Barnekov and Rich (1989: 216) observe:

> Local economic development programs designed to use public funds to leverage private investment frequently result in reverse leverage—that is, private enterprise often leverages public funds to accomplish its own development objectives and, in the process, may hold local governments hostage if they do not come forth with generous subsidies.

Fostering of Cutthroat Competition

Case studies have shown how the competition for investment dollars simply forces local jurisdictions to make excessive sacrifices. This is especially the case as capital has become increasingly mobile in the global economy. Some observers have called this ruthless competition between places for investment the "new arms race." In the chase after global dollars, social equity programs are cut or abandoned. As a result, cities have a diminished capacity to support socially beneficial programs and to sustain the community quality of life (Kanter, 1987: 510–511). At present, the problems of metro areas resulting from uneven development are of deep concern (Chapter 10).

The Decline of Democracy in Local Politics

The new public/private partnerships in pursuit of economic development usually work outside the democratic process of government decision making. Nonelective super agencies such as the Port Authority of New York and New Jersey (see Box 15.2) and similar ad hoc development agencies are not monitored by the voters. This means that the democratic process is itself diminished in the pursuit of growth (see Chapter 11).

In sum, the present direction of metropolitan policy involves the abandonment by the federal government of urban programs with social goals and the boosting of public/private partnerships in support of business growth. Always ambivalent about whether federal policy is meant to support business or deal with social ills, programs have targeted the former since the 1980s in the belief that market solutions will lead to economic recovery. The costs of development are being borne by average residents and the benefits of privatism have not been realized in most cities.

Recently, as a consequence of the Los Angeles riots during April of 1992, the federal government has suggested it is time to reevaluate its urban policy. High hopes prevail with the change in presidential administrations in the beginning of 1993. President Clinton, it is widely believed, signals a return to liberal-type domestic policy that is concerned with social justice. Urban leaders believe that they will now get a fair hearing from Washington, and most recently Clinton has asked the nation's mayors to draw up a list of their concerns as a first step toward policy change. To date, however, few changes have been made, and the issue of the deficit looms large over any attempts by Clinton to alter government spending priorities.

In brief, then, government policy involves an often unproductive struggle between the dominant priority to support business and the lesser goal, often passionately pursued by social movements, of social justice. Spatial competition between places for limited public and private investment also affects the success of policy, because the United States has no overarching national program for metropolitan revitalization. In the 1950s competition was between central cities and their suburbs; in the 1960s it was between regions of the country—especially between areas which were not experiencing a decline in manufacturing (such as the Sunbelt) and those that were (i.e., the Frostbelt). By the 1980s and 1990s, however, all places were involved in a universal global competition for scarce resources. Beggar-thy-neighbor policies pitted place against place to the advantage of capital and at the expense of local taxpayers. Only recently have government policy experts been willing to reexamine this one-sided relation between people and increasingly mobile capital, because the benefits of business decisions to locate have been stripped away in many areas by the costs of incentive packages. This self-evaluation, which is occurring during the new presidential regime of Bill Clinton, is also reconsidering the limited commitment to social programs during the 1980s and 1990s.

As crime, homelessness, housing deterioration, and other urban problems (see

Chapter 10) increase in their intensity, renewed pressure is being placed on the federal government to intervene once more in order to stem the decline in the quality of community life. To be sure, however, if there is such a turnaround during the Clinton administration, it will come only with a renewed debate on the philosophy of intervention. Conservative and liberal positions differ greatly on the nature of public policy. In conclusion, let us examine these differences, because the precise role of government policy remains unclear in the United States.

Urban Policy: The Political Debate

Over the past twenty years a debate has raged regarding whether traditional liberal or conservative solutions to the urban crisis should be applied. Most analysts of urban problems discuss solutions in terms of precisely this clash of ideologies. In this section I shall discuss policy recommendations along ideological lines. In a later section I shall point to a course of action which offers the possibility of rising above this clash of perspectives by addressing the limitations of present public policy arrangements.

Liberal Positions on Urban Problems

Liberals tend to focus on the limitations of the present society and to seek remedies that equalize the ability of all citizens to overcome those limitations. They support government intervention and spending as a means of combating social ills. Most urban problems are caused, in this view, by the inequities of the resource distribution system in our society. Economic rewards and social opportunities are not equally available to all citizens. This can cause poverty and associated problems of uneven development.

For example, there is considerable evidence that economic deprivation is a contributing factor in the rise of crime and drug use rates. Programs could be designed, as they were in the 1960s, for job training, long-term unemployment assistance, and even government subsidized corporate internships that might provide hope and job possibilities for the most disadvantaged city residents. In addition, government subsidized medical care, family assistance, and aid for the homeless, such as the present program of Aid to Dependent Children, could provide a social safety net below which U.S. citizens would not fall. This would improve the life chances of the less affluent and remove from the city streets some of the worst cases of need that threaten the quality of life for everyone.

In short, the liberal agenda uses government intervention as a tool to overcome uneven development. It supports active involvement of policy to identify, address, and help resolve serious urban problems of the less affluent.

Conservative Approaches to Urban Problems

Conservatives, in contrast, believe in limited government intervention and severely restricted government spending. They accuse liberals of squandering society's wealth through excessive public spending. Consequently, they are opposed to the kinds of programs sponsored by liberals precisely because they cost money and must be supported by relatively high taxes. Furthermore, conservatives also address the issue of uneven development. In their view such sociospatial patterns mean that less advantaged people and places must make themselves more competitive so that they will be in the contest for capital investment. It's up to people and places, themselves, to become more attractive.

According to conservatives, many of the problems of the poor reside in their *own* personalities and family traits. Analysts such as Edward Banfield (1974), for example, suggest that poor people are not motivated to find legitimate jobs and that they prefer welfare programs because they have been encouraged to do so by eager liberals seeking to exercise their agenda and support the growth of government bureaucracy (see Jencks, 1992).

Recently, a variant of the conservative position has been taken up by black critics of liberalism such as Shelby Steele (1990). They argue that urban liberals and their programs such as affirmative action have ruined the moral character of blacks while the latter have languished in the ghettos of northern cities. Blacks have been made dependent and are losing the ability to cultivate their own inner resources as a consequence of city bureaucracies and their liberal programs of aid. Consequently, the immense problems of the ghettoized poor (formerly called the "underclass"), for example, are really the outcome of decades of liberal policies that have forced blacks to become wards of the state.

Finally, it must be pointed out that even if people are in favor of government intervention for the pursuit of social justice, our study of the record of government metropolitan policy over the last fifty years shows that expensive public programs have continually been coopted by the business community. Hence, there is considerable evidence against returning to the blind faith of liberals and active public spending to combat social ills, even if we could.

Overcoming the Liberal/Conservative Impasse

What hope exists for the urban future? The lessons of history tell us that either/or choices are unfair. We must look beyond the clash of liberal and conservative ideology and beyond all ideological means of understanding urban problems as a whole. What possible solutions are there that can overcome the liberal/conservative ideological impasse?

An important but neglected dimension to the debate on urban problems involves recognizing the limited ability of local governments to plan adequately for social change. The ideological debate between liberals and conservatives misses an important dimension, namely, the limitations of local government as administrative structures. It also fails to address the particular relationships between the federal, state, and local levels which have always worked against adequate planning and public policy in the United States.

Within metropolitan areas there are so many governments, each with its own limited administration, that power is both highly fragmented and weakly applied. Social programs initiated by cities are ineffective because they must tackle problems that are regional in scope. So cities simply control too small a piece of the regional pie to fight the immense problems of uneven development, such as the need for affordable housing. In fact, it can be argued that the city is not the place to initiate programs aimed at social problems of broad scope or at alleviating the inequities of uneven development. Suburbs and cities share similar problems and the growth patterns of one are linked to those of the other. Hence a *metropolitan* perspective on improving the quality of life becomes imperative for adequate public policy. Beyond that, problems that are national in scope, such as crime or the crisis of health care, must be returned to the responsibility of the national and state levels of government where they belong. In short, by understanding the relationship between spatial and social levels in the study of policy, we can sort out what should and should not be the responsibility of local government. And by adopting a metropolitan, regional perspective we can design better ways of attacking the problems of social justice and uneven development.

A recent report, for example, provides evidence that governmental fragmentation of U.S. cities has promoted uneven sociospatial development. A comparison was made between Detroit and Toronto, Canada, which lies 230 miles away. Detroit has long been in the throes of crisis. Since 1950, it has lost half its population. Its murder rate has increased tenfold during this same period, to 60 per 100,000 people in 1989. It is now overwhelmingly black and poor—virtually an entire city of the "underclass."

In contrast, Toronto has doubled its population since 1950, going from slightly more than 1 million to 2.3 million in 1990. Compared to Detroit, Toronto is relatively crime free with a murder rate of less than 5 per 100,000 people, lower than any U.S. city of 1 million or more population. Yet Toronto has a diversity of people with a mix of racial, ethnic, and class groups living within its borders.

According to the report:

> One thing does much to explain Toronto's success: the enactment in 1953 of a federal form of government for the 13 previously independent municipalities in the area. The original 13 have consolidated into six. They are responsible for local affairs, while the Metro council handles area affairs, including Metro-wide planning (*The Economist,* May, 1990: 17).

The Metro-wide government consolidates resources in the entire region and coordinates the growth of both the central city and its suburbs. As a result, many of the problems brought about by uneven sociospatial development that have plagued Detroit have been avoided by the Toronto region. For example:

> Metro-wide co-ordination of the education system has given Toronto civilized schools. Detroit has some civilized and well financed schools too, but they are in the suburbs; the city schools are mainly deprived, like their pupils (*The Economist,* May, 1990: 18).

Hence, regional government has worked in Toronto. In contrast, Detroit cannot possibly find the resources to address its ills because it is cut off from the affluent suburbs. As tables 1.1 and 1.2 showed earlier, the city of Detroit has been losing population for several decades and is down to about 1 million inhabitants. In contrast, the metro region of Detroit contains over 4 million people and considerable resources. Should this society tolerate the extreme forms of deprivation and affluence that can be readily seen in this region, even if all metro Detroit people suffer from the current recession and the severe problems of the auto industry?

Due to the autonomous home-rule of local communities which discourages regional forms of government, suburbs have effectively insulated themselves from the need to address the problems of uneven sociospatial development. But the contrast is not only one of spatial organization. Canada has a system of national health care that is run by the national government; the United States does not. The two governments differ regarding what they have chosen to bear as national responsibilities, and this also affects the quality of life for metropolitan individuals. In fact, the latter issue of national concern for social justice cannot be separated from the former one of local policy.

In sum, we may not know all the answers to the present case of urban decline, but one very good try at finding a solution that avoids ideological debates focuses on the *structural* limitations of city government and the excessive fragmentation of local jurisdictions. Along with these sociospatial concerns at the local level are also jurisdictional dilemmas between local, state, and national levels that must be faced in order to determine who shares the burden of responsibility for the quality of life in the United States—the individual alone (as conservative policy dictates), the city, the state, or the federal government.

Without metropolitan coordination, and lacking support from higher levels of government, cities simply do not possess the resources they need to address commanding problems of everyday life. At some point in the future, perhaps during the Clinton administration, government will provide the vision necessary to share the responsibility for social concerns at the federal and state levels, where it belongs. Until then, the quality of life in central cities depends on the well-being of the local economy.

Future Prospects

It is customary for urban sociology textbooks to end with a discussion of the future of the city. We must depart from this tradition to deal with two overarching aspects. First, this book has stressed the importance of a regional perspective which includes suburbs as well as large cities. It is the future of the metropolitan region that must be assessed. Second, this book has argued for a new approach to urban sociology, the sociospatial perspective, and we must assess the future of this inquiry.

Future Prospects of the Metropolis

In the nineteenth century, industrial manufacturing was concentrated in the large city. This form of settlement space also concentrated capital and the essential resource of labor. The social world of urban life revolved around home, work, and neighborhood, all located within the space of a short walk or ride on public transport.

After World War II the scale of urban life changed forever. The mass movement to the suburbs and the decline of central city manufacturing transformed the way home, work, and neighborhood were knit together. Automobile commutation or complex mass transportation lines of railroads, subways, and buses became the threads that helped weave a new, regional urban fabric. People's homes were located miles from their jobs, while the place where they lived took on new importance as a commodity with the mass introduction of home ownership. Jobs changed from an almost exclusive

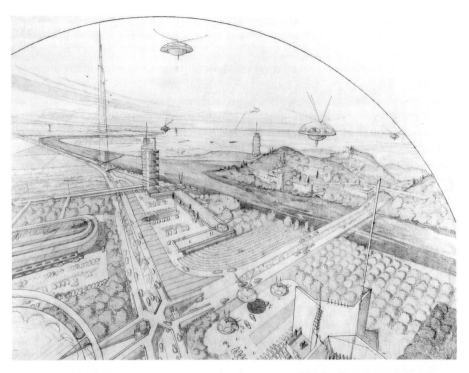

Two contrasting views of the future: Frank Lloyd Wright's vision (top) and the dystopia depicted in *Blade Runner* (bottom).

reliance on manufacturing to the more educationally demanding careers of service industries and their deskilled counterparts in office work and clerking. Finally, it was not so much that the neighborhood changed, as it was that the activity of neighboring changed. People no longer relied on those most adjacent to them to fulfill the needs of intimacy and sociality. They ranged across the metropolitan region participating in friendship networks that were deployed across space.

The new scale of settlement space life was propelled by the process of deconcentration, which we have defined as combining both decentralization of people and resources and recentralization in new spaces of agglomeration. Deconcentration disassembled the old, compact industrial city and replaced this political-economy complex with a regional, multi-centered form of social organization. Factories, department stores, religious institutions, hospitals, universities, banks, and specialty stores no longer needed the proximity of central city location. They decentralized and dispersed throughout the metropolitan region. Deconcentration was helped along by the flight of people, who were overwhelmingly white and middle class, to the suburbs thereby providing both a market and a labor force for relocated business activity. Department stores, malls, and fast food outlets peppered the metropolitan region with branch outlets engineered to capture dispersed consumer markets.

At the same time the process of deconcentration also transformed the large, central city. Its population has become a study in contrasts—between the affluent and the poor, especially, but also between the housed or pampered and the homeless, the high-status professional and the new working class of service employees, and the established and the new immigrant. A shift to service industries within the central city has meant demanding, professional employment opportunities for those with skills, and a burgeoning but relatively low-paid array of jobs in services that cater to the needs of the professional class. As central cities fell under the domination of finance capital and its links to global patterns of investment, the population stabilized or declined. In contrast, metropolitan regions which included these large cities grew steadily, if not rapidly, over the last two decades.

By the 1990s the growth of multi-centered metropolitan regions is occurring unabated. Global economic changes have caused the transformation of cities both in the United States and elsewhere. Large, central cities have become the command and control centers of the world economy. New centralized spaces have sprung up based on new ways of making money centered on increasingly automated or high technology industries. Located principally in the suburbs, the new spaces like Silicon Valley or Route 128 in the United States, Oxbridge complex in England, and the Scuba complex outside of Tokyo became the growth poles of the new advanced economies. The minicenters of employment in the United States helped to define suburban space as a series of residential developments serviced by commercial centers and malls, fast-food outlets, branch banking and drive-in services.

Tying all this together are the seemingly limitless miles of highway, commuter rail lines, and invisible microwave and fiber optic links that stretch across the metropolitan landscape and around the globe. Business is conducted at the office, in the car, and at home using telephone modems, fax machines, cellular phones, desktop PCs, laptops, and revolving pools of clerical helpers and subcontractors. For many people these new arrangements seem the natural outcome of available choices. The concentrated city of the nineteenth century has exploded. But each individual must make his/her own choice about where to live, where to work, where to go to school, where to go shopping, and where to worship within the expanding matrix of separate places that make up the metropolitan region.

The puzzle comes together through personal decisions constrained by available budgets, and invariably involves a good deal of commuting if gainful employment can be obtained. Only the purchase of a home seems to anchor families within a chosen sphere of travel. While an incredible variety of jobs, leisure activities, shopping outlets, and recreational amenities are available to metropolitan residents, they are rarely all found in the same place. Thus, everyday life at present depends on the daily round of commuting and chauffeuring between activities, some of which are located in far-flung places of the metropolis.

The future prospects of this new, multicentered mode of settlement space involve issues of equity, planning, and policy. In recent years, for example, not only have extreme forms of inequality, such as homelessness, surfaced in the United States and elsewhere, but other more subtle forms, such as the inability of first-time buyers to find affordable housing, have also appeared. The quality of community life has been on the decline in central cities for over a decade but is now also plaguing the suburban areas of the metropolis. Educational, transportation, environmental, recreational, crime, and employment issues increasingly define the dilemmas of daily life. The problem of uneven development not only haunts the central city, where the disparities of life chances are on view in the extreme, but also characterizes the suburbs and increasingly defines the nature of all societies, rich and poor alike. At various times the more affluent have been relatively sheltered from social problems such as violent crime, whether they lived in barricaded urban enclaves such as the security-guarded high rises of U.S. cities or the "condominium fechado" of Rio in Brazil, or in the supreme isolation of affluent suburbs. Today this shielding is increasingly less possible.

One possible future prospect is for everyday life to become progressively more inconvenient for all members of the metropolitan region as its problems have effects on more people. Another prospect is that policy may continue to make problems manageable in the future. However, there now are several limitations placed on policy interventions. Perhaps the most formidable is the fiscal crisis of the state, which prevents adequate funding of programs. Another drawback is the inadequacies of government intervention, perceived by both progressives and conservatives. The very idea of intervention must be rethought, with special attention to the sociospatial or structural arrangements of policy. Modernist ideas of unbridled progress arising from government intervention and rational planning seem unable to work (just as public programs are easily coopted by business) even when they have some promise of success.

The massive, complex weave of the multi-centered, regional fabric must be retailored to provide a more human scale of daily life and a more equitable manner of living and working arrangements. People have always been satisfied with the very minimum of planning, especially when they have been willing to sacrifice community goals entirely in return for the ability to purchase an affordable home. In the future we should not settle for so little. Instead, we should return to the fundamental lessons of the sociospatial approach which prefers that decisions about the built environment be made by the majority rather than by the current, select few who pursue profit at the expense of social equity.

In sum, we may decide to jettison the utopian impulse altogether and allow the metropolis to find its own level of prospect and decline; this would amount to a policy of limited intervention. Or we might return to some well thought out ideas about shaping present growth for future prospects and the renewed use of a government role in advancing the quality of life. As with other philosophical and political decisions, the choice will be ours to make if we don't surrender to the wishes of special interests.

The Future of the Urban Inquiry

The present text has introduced a new perspective to the field of urban sociology. Called the sociospatial approach, it has been contrasted with previous perspectives. For many urbanists, analyzing metropolitan phenomena involves a choice between the competing paradigms of human ecology and political economy. I have tried to point out a third way. While human ecology has been useful because it appreciates the role location plays in social interaction, it under-theorizes this role and adopts one-dimensional, technologically deterministic explanations for sociospatial processes. In contrast, the political economy approach deals with a host of important concepts and issues that ecology neglects, such as the role of capital and class in the urban drama. It too is limited, however, because it neglects aspects of culture and politics that cannot be reduced to class phenomena. Sadly, it also ignores the important features of spatial relations by considering location merely as a container for economic processes.

By taking account of space (as the sociospatial perspective does), especially the second circuit of real estate and the concept of location, we pass beyond the limitations of political economy to explain how the built environment changes and develops. Political economy's focus on the restructuring of global capitalism cannot alone explain the changes experienced by metropolitan development. The missing element is supplied by a focus on real estate interests as the leading edge of change which channels growth in specific directions. Once spatial patterns are altered in one region of the metropolis, this alteration affects all other parts. Hence space operates as both a product and producer of changes in the metropolitan environment.

Another limitation of both ecological and political economy perspectives is the weak role they assign to the state as an agent of change. Ecology simply ignores government intervention. Political economy either ignores it or treats the state as simply the direct agent of capitalist interests. In the preceding chapters we have seen that the involvement of the state in sociospatial development is both critical and complex. Government policies help provide the "pull" factors of growth. Second, they are the focus of urban and suburban social movements that aim for a redistribution of both wealth and social costs. Third, government officials are relatively autonomous agents who do not simply follow the needs of capital alone, but have interests of their own which they they pursue to bring about social change. Finally, national policies of taxation and spending can transfer wealth from one region of the country to another; hence programs such as military spending are critical causes of regional growth or decline, in addition to private sector investment patterns. In fact, as we have seen demonstrated in a variety of contexts, private and public sector efforts often work hand in hand.

The sociospatial perspective also tries to understand the role of culture in metropolitan phenomena. It utilizes a semiotic approach to analyze the way ideology symbolically defines sociospatial processes, such as the appeals to progress and modernism in urban renewal or the use of a cosmological code to structure the ancient cities of 4,000 years ago. In addition, the sociospatial approach considers all built environments as meaningful. Behavior is a function of sociospatial context. Public space is defined by its symbolic qualities, as are all objects in society, even if that symbol is nothing more than the object's function. Beyond making these points, the sociospatial approach tries to capture the special articulation between territory and culture that produces lifestyle networks and variation in community daily life within the metropolis. Lifestyles, such as ethnic, gender oriented, or racially defined modes of living, enact themselves within certain spaces. Interaction must have a ground of being in some manifestation of the built environment. The street corner, the mall, the game arcade, the local bar, the school cafeteria, the commuter train, car, or bus are all special venues where social networks interact.

Finally, the sociospatial perspective takes an integrated view of the metropolitan region. We have considered both cities and suburbs. This regional approach suggests that the traditional field of urban sociology possessed too narrow a focus on the central city. Urban texts invariably treat suburbs only in a special chapter devoted to that purpose, while the remainder of the text specializes in the study of the large, central city. As Table 1.2 showed, the plurality of residents live within expanding metropolitan environments. Urban or suburban concerns are largely metropolitan concerns, and any governmental efforts should begin from a regional rather than a local perspective.

The future of the metropolitan inquiry, if the sociospatial perspective has any influence at all, will mean important conceptual changes. In place of urban sociology, we should have a field called the sociology of settlement space which would deal with all forms of human settlement—tribal spaces, cities, suburbs, metropolises, megalopolises, and so on—so that we no longer privilege the city. In place of a contentious and often confusing clash of different paradigms (ecology for aggregate data analysis, political economy for economic issues, and the culturist approach for ethnography) we can look forward to integrated discussions of all levels (micro, macro, and meso) following the synthesis of the sociospatial approach. Finally, by critically evaluating planning efforts because they neglect the importance of space, we have a means by which we can construct and live in more humane and enjoyable environments that face, rather than hide from, the seemingly intractable issues of social justice.

BIBLIOGRAPHY

Abrahamson, P. 1988. *Welfare States in Crisis: The Crumbling of the Scandinavian Model.* Copenhagen: Forlaget Sociologi.

Abrams, C. 1965. *The City Is the Frontier.* New York: Harper Colophon Books.

Abu-Lughod, J. 1969. "Testing the Theory of Social Area Analysis: The Ecology of Cairo, Egypt." *American Sociological Review.* 34 (April): 313–343.

Adams, C. 1986. "Homelessness in the Postindustrial City." *Urban Affairs Quarterly* 21: 527–549.

Aina, T. 1990. "Shanty Town Economy: The Case of Metropolitan Lagos, Nigeria." Pp. 113–148 in S. Datta, ed., *Third World Urbanization: Reappraisals and New Perspectives.* Stockholm: HSFR.

Alford, R. 1975. *Health Care Politics.* Chicago: University of Chicago Press.

Alihan, M. 1938. *Social Ecology.* New York: Columbia University Press.

Allen, O. 1990. *New York, New York.* New York: Atheneum.

Althusser, L. 1971. *Lenin and Philosophy.* New York: Monthly Review Press.

Anderson, E. 1990. *Streetwise: Race, Class and Change in an Urban Community.* Chicago: University of Chicago Press.

———. 1978. *A Place on the Corner.* Chicago: University of Chicago Press.

Anderson, M. 1968. *The Federal Bulldozer.* Cambridge, MA: MIT Press.

Applebome, P. 1991. "Although Urban Blight Worsens, Most People Don't Feel Its Impact." *New York Times* January 28, 1991: A20.

Arax, M. 1987, April 6. "Monterey Park: Nation's First Suburban Chinatown." *Los Angeles Times.*

Armstrong, R. 1972. *The Office Industry.* Cambridge, MA: MIT Press.

———. 1979. "National Trends in Office Construction, Employment and Headquarters Location in the United States Metropolitan Areas." In P. Daniels, ed., *Spatial Patterns of Office Growth and Location.* New York: John Wiley.

Auletta, K. 1983. *The Underclass.* New York: Random House.

Bachrach, P. and M. Baratz. 1962. "Two Faces of Power." *American Political Science Review* 56: 947–952.

Baker, P. 1974. *Urbanization and Political Change.* Los Angeles and Berkeley, CA: University of California Press.

Baltzell, E.D. 1958. *Philadelphia Gentlemen.* Glencoe, IL: Free Press.

Banfield, E. 1974. *The Unheavenly City Revisited.* Boston: Little, Brown.

Baran, P. and P. Sweezy. 1966. *Monopoly Capitalism.* New York: Monthly Review Press.

Barbanel, J. 1992. "Robberies on the Rise on Long Island." *New York Times* February 18, 1992: A15.

Barnekov, T. and D. Rich. 1989. "Privatism and the Limits of Local Economic Development Policy." *Urban Affairs Quarterly* 25: 212–238.

Barone, C. 1983. "Dependency, Marxist Theory, and Salvaging the Idea of Capitalism in South Korea." *Review of Radical Political Economy.* Vol. 16: 1.

Barthes, R. 1973. *L'Empire des Signes.* Geneva: Albert Skira.

———. 1986. "Semiology and the Urban." Pp. 87–98 in M. Gottdiener and A. Lagopoulos *The City and the Sign.* New York: Columbia University Press.

Baumgartner, M. 1988. *The Moral Order of a Suburb.* Oxford: Oxford University Press.

Bean, F. and M. Tienda. 1987. *The Hispanic Population of the US.* New York: Russell Sage.

Benard, D. and E. Schlaffer. 1993. " 'The Man in the Street': Why He Harasses." Pp. 338–391 in L. Richardson and V. Taylor *Feminist Frontiers III.* New York: McGraw-Hill.

Berak, B. 1991. "A Shelter for Rage, Fear, Crack." *New York Times* May 5, 1991: A1, A24.

Berman, M. 1985. *All That Is Solid Melts into Air.* New York: Vintage.

Bernard, R. and B. Rice. 1983. *Sunbelt Cities: Politics and Growth Since World War II.* Austin: University of Texas Press.

Berry, B. 1977 ed. *The Social Burden of Environmental Pollution.* Cambridge, MA: Ballinger.

Berry, B. and J. Kasanda. 1977. *Contemporary Urban Ecology.* New York: Macmillan.

Berry, M. 1989. "Industrialization, De-industrialization and Uneven Development: The Case of the Pacific Rim." Pp. 171–216 in M. Gottdiener and N. Komninos, eds., *Capitalist Development and Crisis Theory.* New York and London: Macmillan.

Berry, W. 1972. *The Unsettling of America.* New York: Avon.

Bestor, T. 1985. *Japanese Urban Life.* Palo Alto: Stanford University Press.

Blake, W. 1977. "London." P. 150 in *Songs of Innocence and of Experience.* New York: Oxford.

Blau, J. 1992. *The Visible Poor: Homelessness in the United States.* New York: Oxford University Press.

Bluestone, B. and B. Harrison. 1982. *The Deindustrialization of America.* New York: Basic Books.

Blum, B. 1978. *Cities: An Environmental Wilderness.* Washington, DC: Environmental Protection Agency.

Body-Gendrot, S. 1987. "Plant Closures in Socialist France," Pp. 237–251 in M. Smith and J. Feagin, eds., *The Capitalist City.* Oxford: Blackwell.

Boer, L. 1990. "(In)formalization: The Forces Beyond." *International Journal of Urban and Regional Research* 14: 404–422.

Bollens, J. and H. Schmandt. 1965. *The Metropolis.* New York: Harper and Row.

Bookchin, M. 1974. *The Limits of the City.* New York: Harper and Row.

———. 1990. *The Philosophy of Social Ecology: Essays on Dialectical Materialism.* New York: Black Rose Books.

Borchert, J. 1967. "American Metropolitan Evolution." *Geographical Review* 57: 301–332.

Boudon, P. 1986. "Rewriting of a City: The Medina of Tunis." Pp. 303–322 in M. Gottdiener and A. Lagopoulos, eds., *The City and the Sign.* New York: Columbia University Press.

Bourne, L. and J. Simmons. 1978. *Systems of Cities.* New York: Oxford University.

Boyle, H. 1980. *The Backyard Revolution.* Philadelphia: Temple University Press.

Bradshaw, Y. and E. Fraser. 1989. "City Size, Economic Development, and Quality of Life in China: New Empirical Evidence." *American Sociological Review* 54: 986–1003.

Braudel, F. 1973. *Capitalism and Material Life: 1400–1800.* New York: Harper.

Bullard, R. 1990. *Dumping in Dixie.* Boulder, CO: Westview Press.

Bullard, R. and J. Feagin. 1991. "Racism and the City." Pp. 55–76 in M. Gottdiener and C.G. Pickvance, eds., *Urban Life in Transition.* Newbury Park, CA: Sage.

Burgess, E. 1925. "The Growth of the City: An Introduction to a Research Project." In R. Park, E. Burgess, and R. McKenzie, eds., *The City.* Chicago: University of Chicago Press.

Buss, T. and F.S. Redburn. 1983. *Shutdown at Youngstown.* Albany: SUNY Press.

Castells, M. 1977. *The Urban Question.* Cambridge, MA: MIT Press.

————. 1983. *The City and the Grass Roots.* Berkeley and Los Angeles: University of California Press.

Cavan, R.S. 1928. *Suicide.* Chicago: University of Chicago Press.

Chambers, I. 1986. *Popular Culture: The Metropolitan Experience.* London: Methuen.

Chase-Dunn, C. 1985. "The System of World Cities, A.D. 800–1975." Pp. 269–292 in M. Timberlake, ed., *Urbanization in the World Economy.* Orlando: Academic Press.

Chen, X. 1988. "Giant Cities and the Urban Hierarchy in China." Pp. 225–251 in M. Dogan and J. Kasarda, eds., *The Metropolis Era.* Newbury Park, CA: Sage.

Childe, V.G. 1950. "The Urban Revolution." *Town Planning Review* 21: 4–17.

————. 1954. *What Happened in History.* New York: Penguin Books.

Clavel, P. 1986. *The Progressive City: Planning and Participation, 1969–1984.* New Brunswick, NJ: Rutgers University Press.

Cleaver, H. 1989. "Close the IMF, Abolish Debt, and End Development: A Class Analysis of the International Debt Crisis." *Capital and Class.* No. 39.

Cochrane, A. 1982. *Patterns of Urban Development.* Unit 29, Block 7. Milton Keynes: Open University Press.

Cooper, F. 1987. *On the African Waterfront: Urban Disorders and the Transformation of Work in Colonial Mombasa.* New Haven, CT: Yale.

Coquery-Vidrovitch, C. 1990. "A History of African Urbanization: Labor, Women and the Informal Sector—A Survey of Recent Studies." Pp. 75–89 in S. Datta, ed., *Third World Urbanization: Reappraisals and New Perspectives.* Stockholm: HSFR.

Coughlin, R. 1979. "Agricultural Land Conversion in the Urban Fringe." In M. Schept, ed., *Farmlands, Food and the Future.* Ankers, IA: Soil Conservation Society of America.

Cressey, P. 1932. *The Taxi-Dance Hall.* Chicago: University of Chicago Press.

Crump, S. 1962. *Ride the Big Red Cars: How Trolleys Helped Build Southern California.* Los Angeles: Crest Publications.

Dahl, R. 1961. *Who Governs?* New Haven, CT: Yale University Press.

Dale, A. and C. Banford. 1989. "Social Polarization in Britain: 1973–82, Evidence from the General Household Survey." *International Journal of Urban and Regional Research* 13: 482–494.

Darley, J. and B. Latane. 1970. *The Unresponsive Bystander: Why Doesn't He Help?* New York: Appleton-Century-Crofts.

Datta, S. 1990. *Third World Urbanization: Reappraisals and New Perspectives.* Stockholm: HSFR.

Davis, M. 1986. *Prisoners of the American Dream.* London: New Left Books.

———. 1990. *City of Quartz: Excavating the Future in Los Angeles.* New York: Venso.

———. 1987. "Chinatown, Part Two? The Internationalization of Downtown Los Angeles." *New Left Review* 164: 65–84.

Dinnerstein, L., R. Nichols, and D. Reimers. 1990. *Natives and Strangers: Blacks, Indians and Immigrants in America.* New York: Oxford University Press.

Dogan, M. and J. Kasarda. 1988. *The Metropolis Era,* Vols. 1 and 2. Newbury Park, CA: Sage.

Dooley, D. and R. Catalano. 1980. "Economic Change as a Cause of Behavioral Disorder." *Psychological Bulletin* 87: 450–468.

Dorsett, L. 1968. *The Pendergast Machine.* New York: Oxford University Press.

Douglas, M. 1988. "Transnational Capital and Urbanization on the Pacific Rim: An Introduction." *International Journal of Urban and Regional Research* 12: 343–355.

Drake, St. Clair and H. Cayton. 1945. *Black Metropolis.* Chicago: University of Chicago Press.

DuBois, W.E.B. 1899. *The Philadelphia Negro.* Philadelphia: University of Pennsylvania Press.

Dutton, T. 1989. "Cities, Cultures and Resistance: Beyond Leon Krier and the Postmodern Condition." *JAE* 42: 3–9.

The Economist. 1990, May 19. "Toronto and Detroit: Canadians Do It Better." Pp. 17–20.

Ehrenreich, B. 1990. *Fear of Falling.* New York: HarperCollins.

Eisenstadt, S. and A. Shachar. 1987. *Society, Culture and Urbanization.* Newbury Park, CA: Sage.

Engels, F. 1973. *The Condition of the Working Class in England: From Personal Observations and Authentic Sources.* Moscow: Progress Publishers.

Ernst, R. 1970. "Immigrants and Tenements in New York City: 1825–1863." Pp. 113–126 in R. Mohl and N. Betten, eds., *Urban America in Historical Perspective.* New York: W. and T. Publishers.

Espiritu, Y. and I. Light. 1991. "The Changing Ethnic Shape of Contemporary Urban America." Pp. 35–54 in M. Gottdiener and C.G. Pickvance, *Urban Life in Transition.* Newbury Park: SAGE.

Farley, R. and W. Allen. 1987. *The Color Line and the Quality of Life in America.* New York: Russell Sage.

Feagin, J. 1983. *The Urban Real Estate Game.* Englewood Cliffs, NJ: Prentice-Hall.

———. 1988. *Houston: The Free Enterprise City.* New Brunswick, NJ: Rutgers University Press.

———. 1992. "Why Not Study the American 'Overclass'?" *Contemporary Sociology.* 21, 4: 449–451.

Feagin, J. and M. Smith. 1987. "Cities and the New International Division of Labor: An Overview." Pp. 3–36 in M. Smith and J. Feagin, *The Capitalist City.* Oxford: Blackwell.

Fernandez-Kelly, M. 1991, December 6. "Labor Force Recomposition and Industrial Restructuring in Electronics." Paper presented at symposium: "Crossing National Borders: Invasions or Involvement." Columbia University.

Fischer, C. 1975. "Toward a Subcultural Theory of Urbanism." *American Journal of Sociology* 80: 1319–1341.

———. 1976. *The Urban Experience.* New York: Harcourt Brace.

———. 1982. *To Dwell Among Friends: Personal Networks in Town and City.* Chicago: University of Chicago Press.

Fishman, R. 1987. *Bourgeois Utopias: The Rise and Fall of Suburbia.* New York, Basic Books.

Flanagan, W. 1990. *Urban Sociology: Images and Structures.* Boston: Allyn and Bacon.

Fleischmann, A. 1991. "Atlanta: Urban Coalitions in a Suburban Sea." Pp. 97–114 in H. Savitch and J. Thomas, eds., *Big City Politics in Transition.* Newbury Park, CA: Sage.

Form, W. 1954. "The Place of Social Structure in the Determination of Land Use." *Social Forces* 32: 317–323.

Forrest, R. 1991. "The Privatization of Collective Consumption." Pp. 169–195 in M. Gottdiener and C. Pickvance *Urban Life in Transition.* Newbury Park, CA: Sage.

Frazier, E.F. 1932. *The Negro Family in Chicago.* Chicago: University of Chicago Press.

French, R. and F. Hamilton. 1979. Eds. *The Socialist City.* New York: J. Wiley and Sons.

Frey, W. 1979. "Population Movement and City-Suburban Redistribution: An Analytic Framework." *Demography* 15: 571–588.

Frey, W. and A. Speare. 1988. *Regional and Metropolitan Growth and Decline in the United States.* New York: Russell Sage.

Friedrichs, J. 1988. "Large Cities in Eastern Europe." Pp. 128–154 in M. Dogan and J. Kasarda, eds., *The Metropolis Era.* Newbury Park, CA: Sage.

Frobel, F., J. Heinrichs, and O. Krege. 1980. *The New International Division of Labor.* New York: Cambridge University Press.

Fuentes, A. and B. Ehrenreich. 1987. "Women in the Global Factory." Pp. 201–215 in R. Peet, ed., *International Capitalism and Industrial Restructuring.* Boston: Allen and Unwin.

Fujita, K. 1988. "The Technopolis: High Technology and Regional Development in Japan." *International Journal of Urban and Regional Research* 12: 573–581.

Fussell, P. 1983. *Class.* New York: Ballantine Books.

Gale, R. 1983. "The Environmental Movement and the Left: Antagonists or Allies?" *Sociological Inquiry* 53: 179–199.

Gallup, G. 1982. *The Gallup Poll: Public Opinion 1981.* Wilmington, DE: Scholarly Resources.

Gans, H. 1962. *The Urban Villagers.* New York: Free Press.

———. 1968. *People and Plans.* New York: Basic Books.

———. 1968. "Urbanism and Suburbanism as a Way of Life: A Reevaluation of Definitions." Pp. 34–52 in H. Gans, *People and Plans.* New York: Basic Books.

———. 1990. "Deconstructing the Underclass: The Term's Dangers as a Planning Concept." *American Planning Association Journal* (Summer): 271–277.

Geisse, G. and F. Sabatini. 1988. "Latin American Cities and Their Poor." Pp. 322–327 in M. Dogan and J. Kasarda, eds., *The Metropolis Era.* Newbury Park, CA: Sage.

Geruson, R. and D. McGrath. 1977. *Cities and Urbanization.* New York: Praeger.

Gibbs, L. 1982. *Love Canal: My Story.* Albany, NY: SUNY Press.

Glaab, C. and A.T. Brown. 1967. *A History of Urban America.* New York: Macmillan.

Glaberson, W. 1992. "Swaddling Shoppers: A Mall's Cocoon Effect." *New York Times* April 21, 1992: A10.

Glazer, N. and P. Moynihan. 1963. *Beyond the Melting Pot.* Cambridge, MA: MIT Press.

Goffman, E. 1963. *Behavior in Public Places.* New York: Free Press.

―――. 1971. *Relations in Public.* New York: Basic Books.

Golledge, R. and G. Ruston. 1976. Eds., *Spatial Choice and Spatial Behavior.* Columbus: Ohio State University Press.

Goodman, P. and P. Goodman. 1974. *Communitas.* New York: Vintage.

Gordon, D. 1977. "Class Struggle and the Stages of Urban Development." In A. Watkins and R. Perry, eds., *The Rise of the Sunbelt Cities.* Beverly Hills, CA: Sage.

―――. 1984. "Capitalist Development and the History of American Cities." Pp. 21–53 in W. Tabb and L. Sawers, eds., *Marxism and the Metropolis.* 2nd Ed. New York: Oxford University Press.

Gordon, M. 1964. *Assimilation in American Life: The Role of Race, Religion and National Origins.* New York: Oxford University Press.

Gore, A. 1992. *Earth in the Balance: Ecology and the Human Spirit.* Boston: Houghton-Mifflin.

Gottdiener, M. 1977. *Planned Sprawl: Public and Private Interests in Suburbia.* Beverly Hills, CA: Sage.

―――. 1982. "Suburban Crime: Testing the Police Hypothesis." *Journal of Police Science and Administration.* 10, 4: 425–434.

―――. 1985. *The Social Production of Urban Space.* Austin: University of Texas Press.

―――. 1987. *The Decline of Urban Politics: Political Theory and the Crisis of the Local State.* Newbury Park, CA: Sage.

―――. 1990. "Crisis Theory and State Financed Capital." *International Journal of Urban and Regional Research* 14: 383–403.

Gottdiener, M. and J. Feagin. 1988. "The Paradigm Shift in Urban Sociology." *Urban Affairs Quarterly* 24: 163–187.

Gottdiener, M. and G. Kephart. 1991. "The Multinucleated Metropolitan Region: A Comparative Analysis." Pp. 31–54 in R. Kling, S. Olin, and M. Poster, eds., *Postsuburban California.* Berkeley and Los Angeles: University of California Press.

Gottdiener, M. and N. Komninos. 1989. *Capitalist Development and Crisis Theory.* London: Macmillan.

Gottdiener, M. and A. Lagopoulos. 1986. *The City and the Sign: Introduction to Urban Semiotics.* New York: Columbia University Press.

Gottdiener, M. and M. Neiman. 1981. "Characteristics of Support for Local Growth Control." *Urban Affairs Quarterly* 17: 55–73.

Gottdiener, M. and C.G. Pickvance. 1991. Eds., *Urban Life in Transition.* Newbury Park, CA: Sage.

Green, C. and B. Wilson. 1992. *The Struggle for Black Empowerment in New York City.* New York: McGraw-Hill.

Greenberg, J. 1990. "All About Crime." *New York* (September): 20–32.

Grief, G. 1985. *Single Fathers.* Lexington, MA: Lexington Books.

Habermas, J. 1989. *The Structural Transformation of the Public Sphere: An Inquiry into a Category of Bourgeois Society.* Cambridge, MA: MIT Press.

Hacker, A. 1992. *Two Nations.* New York: Scribner's.

Hall, P. 1966. *The World Cities.* London: Weidenfeld and Nicolson.

―――. 1988. "Urban Growth and Decline in Western Europe." Pp. 111–127 in M. Dogan and J. Kasarda, eds., *The Metropolis Era.* Newbury Park, CA: Sage.

Handlin, O. 1951. *The Uprooted.* Boston: Little Brown.

Hannerz, U. 1969. *Soulside.* New York: Columbia University Press.

————. 1980. *Exploring the City.* New York: Columbia University Press.

Hareven, T. 1982. *Family Time and Industrial Time.* New York: Cambridge University Press.

Harrington, M. 1962. *The Other America.* New York: Macmillan.

Harris, C. and E. Ullman. 1945. "The Nature of Cities." *Annals of the Academy of Political and Social Science* 242: 7–17.

Harrison, R. and D. Weinberg. 1992. "Changes in Racial and Ethnic Residential Segregation, 1980–1990." Paper prepared for the American Statistical Association Meetings in Boston, MA, August, 1992.

Harvey, D. 1973. *Social Justice and the City.* Baltimore: Johns Hopkins University Press.

————. 1975. "Class-Monopoly Rent, France Capital and the Urban Revolution." In S. Gale and E. Moore, eds., *The Manipulated City.* Chicago: Maaroufa Press.

————. 1976. "Labor, Capital and Class Struggle Around the Built Environment." *Politics and Society* 6: 265–295.

————. 1982. "The Urban Process Under Capitalism: A Framework for Analysis." Pp. 91–122 in M. Dear and A. Scott, eds., *Urbanization and Urban Planning in Capitalist Society.* New York: Methuen.

————. 1985. *The Urbanization of Capital.* Baltimore: Johns Hopkins University Press.

Haussermann, H. and W. Siebel. 1990. "The Polarization of Urban Development in the Federal Republic of Germany and the Question of a New Municipal Policy." *International Journal of Urban and Regional Research* 14: 369–382.

Hawley, A. 1950. *Human Ecology.* New York: Ronald Press.

————. 1956. *The Changing Shape of Metropolitan America.* Glencoe, IL: Free Press.

————. 1981. *Urban Society: An Ecological Approach.* 2nd Ed. New York: J. Wiley and Sons.

Hayden, D. 1981. *The Grand Domestic Revolution.* Cambridge, MA: MIT Press.

Hayner, N. 1936. *Hotel Life.* Chicago: University of Chicago Press.

Henslin, J. 1972. "What Makes for Trust?" In J. Henslin, ed., *Down to Earth Sociology.* New York: Free Press.

Herbert, D. and R. Johnston. 1976. *Social Areas in Cities, Vol. II.* New York: John Wiley and Sons.

Hero, R. and R. Durand. 1985. "Explaining Citizen Evaluations of Urban Services." *Urban Affairs Quarterly* 20: 344–354.

Higham, J. 1977. *Strangers in the Land.* New York: Atheneum.

Hightower, J. 1975. *Eat Your Heart Out.* New York: Crown Publishers.

Hill, R.C. 1986. "Economic Crisis and Political Response in the Motor City." Pp. 313–338 in W. Tabb and L. Sawers, eds., *Sunbelt/Snowbelt.* New York: Oxford University Press.

Hochschild, A. and A. Machung. 1989. *The Second Shift.* New York: Viking.

Hoston, J. 1989. *The Modernist City: An Anthropological Critique of Brasília.* Chicago: University of Chicago Press.

Hoover, D. 1971. *A Teacher's Guide to American Urban History.* Chicago: Quadrangle.

Hoyt, H. 1933. *One Hundred Years of Land Values in Chicago.* Chicago: University of Chicago Press.

Hughes, E. 1928. "A Study of a Secular Institution: The Chicago Real Estate Board." Ph.D. Dissertation, University of Chicago.

Hummon, D. 1986. "Urban Views: Popular Perspectives on City Life." *Urban Life* 15: 3–37.

Hunter, A. 1979. "The Urban Neighborhood: Its Analytical and Social Contexts." *Urban Affairs Quarterly* 14: 267–288.

Hunter, F. 1953. *Community Power Structure*. Chapel Hill: University of North Carolina Press.

Hutchinson, R. 1988. "The Hispanic Population in Chicago: A Study in Population Growth and Assimilation." Pp. 193–229 in C. Marrett and C. Leggon, eds., *Research in Race and Ethnic Relations*. Greenwich, CT: JAI Press.

Jackson, K. 1985. *Crabgrass Frontier: The Suburbanization of the United States*. New York: Oxford University Press.

Jacob, J. 1984. *The Mall*. Prospect Heights, IL: Waveland Press.

Jacobs, J. 1961. *The Death and Life of Great American Cities*. New York: Random House.

Jefferson, T. 1977. *Notes on the State of Virginia*. B. Wishey and W.G. Leuchtenberg, eds. New York: Harper and Row.

Jencks, C. 1992. *Rethinking Social Policy: Race, Poverty and the Underclass*. Cambridge, MA: Harvard University Press.

Jencks, C. and P. Peterson. 1991. Eds., *The Urban Underclass*. Washington, DC: Brookings Institution.

Jezierski, L. 1988. "Political Limits to Development in Two Declining Cities: Cleveland and Pittsburgh." Pp. 173–189 in M. Wallace and J. Rothschild, eds., *Deindustrialization and the Restructuring of American Industry*. Greenwich, CT: JAI Press.

Josey, A. 1980. *Singapore*. London: Andre Deutsch LTD.

Kain, J. 1970. "The Distribution and Movement of Jobs and Industry." Pp. 1–44 in J.Q. Wilson, ed., *The Metropolitan Enigma*. Garden City, NY: Anchor.

Kanter, P. 1987. *The Dependent City: The Changing Political Economy of Urban America*. Glenview, IL: Scott, Foresman.

Karp, D., G. Stone, and W. Yoels. 1977. *Being Urban*. Lexington, MA: D.C. Heath.

Karp, D. and W. Yoels. 1986. *Sociology and Everyday Life*. Itasca, IL: Peacock Publishers.

Kasarda, J. 1988. "Economic Restructuring of America's Urban Dilemma." Pp. 30–55 in M. Dogan and J. Kasarda, eds., *The Metropolis Era*. Newbury Park, CA: Sage.

Kasarda, J. and E. Crenshaw. 1991. "Third World Urbanization: Dimensions, Theories, and Determinants." *Annual Review of Sociology*. 17: 467–501.

Kazis, R. and R. Grossman. 1983. *Fear at Work: Job Blackmail, Labor, and the Environment*. New York: Pilgram Press.

Keller, S. 1968. *The Urban Neighborhood*. New York: Random House.

Kephart, G. 1991. "Economic Restructuring, Population Redistribution, and Migration in the United States." Pp. 12–34 in M. Gottdiener and C.G. Pickvance *Urban Life in Transition*. Newbury Park, CA: Sage.

Kim, J. 1988. "China's Modernizations, Reforms and Mobile Population." *International Journal of Urban and Regional Research* 12: 595–608.

King, D. 1990. "Economic Activity and the Challenge to Local Government." Pp. 265–287 in D. King and J. Pierre, eds., *Challenges to Local Government*. London: Sage.

Kling, R., S. Olin, and M. Poster. 1991. *Postsuburban California*. Berkeley and Los Angeles: University of Califorina Press.

Komninos, N. 1989. "From National to Local: The Janus Face of Crisis." Pp. 348–365 in M. Gottdiener and N. Komninos, eds., *Capitalist Development and Crisis Theory*. New York and London: Macmillan.

Korff, R. 1990. "Social Creativity, Power and Trading Relations in Bangkok." Pp. 168–185 in S. Datta, ed., *Third World Urbanization: Reappraisals and New Perspectives.* Stockholm: HSFR.

Ladanyi, J. 1989. "Changing Patterns of Residential Segregation in Budapest." *International Journal of Urban and Regional Research* 13: 556–566.

Lagopoulos, A. 1986. "Semiotic Urban Models and Modes of Production: A Semiotic Approach." Pp. 176–201 in M. Gottdiener and A. Lagopoulos, eds., *The City and the Sign.* New York: Columbia University Press.

LaGory, M. and J. Pipkin. 1981. *Urban Social Space.* Belmont, CA: Wadsworth.

Lamarche, F. 1977. "Property Development and the Economic Foundations of the Urban Question." Pp. 85–119 in C. Pickvance, ed., *Urban Sociology: Critical Essays.* New York: St. Martin's Press.

Lamb, M. 1986 ed. *The Father's Role: Applied Perspectives.* New York: Wiley.

Landry, B. 1987. *The New Black Middle Class.* Berkeley: University of California Press.

Langdon, P. 1988. "A Good Place to Live." *The Atlantic* 261, 3: 39–60.

Larkin, R. 1979. *Suburban Youth in Cultural Crisis.* New York: Oxford University Press.

Lawson, C. 1991. "A Writer Reveals the 'Dark Underside of Suburbia': Car Pools," *The New York Times.* September 12, 1991: C-1.

Leborgne, D. and A. Lipietz. 1988. "Two Social Strategies in the Production of New Economic Spaces." *CEPREMAP Working Papers #8911.* Paris: CEPREMAP.

Lee, E. 1982. *Export-Led Industrialization and Development.* Geneva: ILO.

Lefebvre, H. 1991. *The Production of Space.* Oxford: Blackwell.

Leinsdorf, D., and D. Etra. 1973. *Citibank.* New York: Grossman.

Lemann, N. 1991a. "Four Generations in the Projects." *New York Times Magazine* January 13, 1991: 16–21, 36–38, 49.

———. 1991b. *The Promised Land: The Great Black Migration and How It Changed America.* New York: Alfred A. Knopf.

Leshner, A. 1992. *Outcasts on Main Street: Report of the Federal Task Force on Homelessness and Severe Mental Illness.* Washington DC: National Institute of Mental Health.

Lévi-Strauss, C. 1963. "Do Dual Organizations Exist." Pp. 128–160 in *Structural Anthropology.* New York: Basic Books.

Lieberson, S. 1962. "Suburbs of Ethnic Residential Patterns." *American Journal of Sociology* 67: 673–681.

———. 1980. *A Piece of the Pie: Black and White Immigrants since 1880.* Berkeley and Los Angeles: University of California Press.

Lieberson, S. and M.C. Walters. 1988. *From Many Strands: Ethnic and Racial Groups in Contemporary America.* New York: Russell Sage.

Lineberry, R. 1977. *Equality and Urban Policy.* Beverly Hills, CA: Sage.

Lineberry, R. and I. Sharkansky. 1978. *Urban Politics and Public Policy.* New York: Harper and Row.

Lipsky, M. 1976. "Toward a Theory of Street-Level Bureaucracy." In W. Hawley, et al., eds., *Theoretical Perspectives on Urban Politics.* Englewood Cliffs, NJ: Prentice Hall.

Logan, J. and H. Molotch. 1988. *Urban Fortunes: The Political Economy of Place.* Berkeley and Los Angeles: University of California Press.

Logan, J. and G. Rabrenovic. 1990. "Neighborhood Associations: Their Issues, Their Allies, and Their Opponents." *Urban Affairs Quarterly.* 26, 1: 68–94.

Long, J. 1981. *Population Deconcentration in the United States.* Washington, DC: Bureau of the Census.

Longstreet, S. 1973. *Chicago: 1860–1919.* New York: David McKay.

Los Angeles Times. 1982, April 25. P. A3.

Lynch, K. 1960. *The Image of the City.* Cambridge: MIT Press.

Mabogunje, A. 1990. "Organization of Urban Communities in Nigeria." *International Social Science Journal* 125: 355–366.

MacDonald, M. 1984. *America's Cities: A Report on the Myth of Urban Renaissance.* New York: Simon and Schuster.

Mandel, E. 1975. *Late Capitalism.* London: Verso.

Marples, D. 1988. *The Social Impact of the Chernobyl Disaster.* New York: St. Martin's Press.

Marshall, D. 1990. "Continuing Significance of Race: The Transformation of American Politics." *American Political Science Review* 84: 611–616.

Martinelli, F. 1985. "Public Policy and Industrial Development in Southern Italy." *International Journal of Urban and Regional Research* 9: 48–56.

Marx, K. 1967. *Capital.* New York: International Publishers.

Matrix Collective. 1984. *Making Space.* London: Pluto.

Matzer, J., Jr. 1986. "Local Control of Fiscal Stress." Pp. 63–80 in M. Gottdiener, ed., *Cities in Stress.* Newbury Park, CA: Sage.

Mayo, J. 1988. "Urban Design as Uneven Development." *Environment and Behavior* 20: 633–663.

McDowell, B. 1984. "Mexico City: An Alarming Giant." *National Geographic* 166: 139–144.

McDowell, L. 1991. "Restructuring Production and Reproduction: Some Theoretical and Empirical Issues Relating to Gender, or Women in Britain." Pp. 77–105 in M. Gottdiener and C.G. Pickvance, eds., *Urban Life in Transition.* Newbury Park: Sage.

McInerney, J. 1984. *Bright Lights, Big City.* New York: Vintage.

McKenzie, R. 1933. *The Metropolitan Community.* New York: McGraw-Hill.

McKeown, T. 1976. *The Modern Rise of Population.* London: Edward Arnold.

Mellor, R. 1989. "Transitions in Urbanization: Twentieth Century Britain." *International Journal of Urban and Regional Research* 13: 579–592.

Melman, S. 1983. *Profits Without Production.* New York: Knopf.

Mingione, E. 1988. "Urban Survival Strategies, Family Structure and Informal Practices." Pp. 297–322 in *The Capitalist City.* Oxford: Blackwell.

Minsky, H. 1989. "Financial Crises and the Evolution of Capitalism: The Crash of '87." Pp. 391–403 in M. Gottdiener and N. Komninos *Capitalist Development and Crisis Theory.* New York: Macmillan.

Misra, R. 1978. *Million Cities of India.* New Delhi: Vikas Publishing House.

Mollenkopf, J. 1975. "The Postwar Politics of Urban Development." *Politics and Society* 5: 247–296.

Mollenkopf, J. and M. Castells. 1991. *The Dual City: Restructuring New York.* New York: Russell Sage.

Monkkonen, E. 1986. "The Sense of Crisis: A Historian's Point of View." Pp. 20–38 in M. Gottdiener, *Cities in Stress.* Newbury Park, CA: Sage.

———. 1989. *American Becomes Urban.* Berkeley and Los Angeles: University of California Press.

Montgomery, R. and K. Bristol. 1987. *Pruitt-Igoe: An Annotated Bibliography.* Chicago, IL: Council of Planning Librarians.

Moore, J.W. 1976. *Mexican Americans.* Englewood Cliffs, NJ: Prentice-Hall.

————. 1978. *Homeboys: Gangs, Drugs and Prison in the Barrios of L.A.* Philadelphia: Temple University Press.

Morawska, B. 1990. "The Sociology and Historiography of Immigration." Pp. 187–238 in V. Yans-McLaughlin, ed., *Immigration Reconsidered: History, Sociology and Politics.* New York: Oxford University Press.

Muller, P. 1981. *Contemporary Suburban America.* Englewood Cliffs, NJ: Prentice-Hall.

Mumford, L. 1961. *The City in History.* New York: Harcourt, Brace and World.

Murphy, R. 1988. "Shanghai." Pp. 157–183 in M. Dogan and J. Kasarda, eds., *The Metropolis Era.* Vol. 2. Newbury Park, CA: Sage.

Naess, A. 1989. *Ecology, Community, and Lifestyle: Outline of an Ecosophy.* New York: Cambridge University Press.

Nagpaul, H. 1988. "India's Giant Cities." Pp. 252–290 in M. Dogan and J. Kasarda, eds., *The Metropolis Era,* Vol. 1. Newbury Park, CA: Sage.

Nakamura, H. and J. White. 1988. "Tokyo." Pp. 123–156 in M. Dogan and J. Kasarda, eds. *The Metropolis Era,* Vol. 2. Newbury Park, CA: Sage.

Nardulli, P. and J. Stonecash. 1981. *Politics, Professionalism and Urban Services: The Police.* Cambridge, MA: Oelgeschlager, Gunn, and Hain.

Nash, G. 1974. *Red, White and Black: The People of Early America.* Englewood Cliffs, NJ: Prentice-Hall.

Nash, N. 1992. "Latin America's Shantytowns Grow As People Flock to Cities." *The Press Enterprise* November 15, 1992: A18.

Nath, V. 1989. "Urbanization and Urban Development in India." *International Journal of Urban and Regional Research* 13: 258–269.

National Institute of Justice. 1990. *Drug Use Forecasting, Annual Report, 1988.* Washington, DC: U.S. Department of Justice.

New York Times. 1991, December 7. "Wider Mosaic: Suburbs' Jobs Lure Immigrants to Greater Opportunity." Metro Section: L–28.

New York Times. 1990, September 30. International Section: 17.

Noyelle, T. and T.M. Stanback, Jr. 1984. *The Economic Transformation of American Cities.* Totowa, NJ: Rowman and Allenheld.

Oakes, J. 1985. *Keeping Track: How Schools Structure Inequality.* New Haven, CT: Yale University Press.

O'Connor, A. 1978. *The Geography of Tropical African Development.* Oxford: Pergamon.

Olin, S. 1991. "Intraclass Conflict and the Politics of a Fragmented Region." Pp. 223–253 in R. Kling, S. Olin, and M. Poster, eds., *Postsuburban California.* Berkeley and Los Angeles: University of California Press.

Palen, J. 1990. "Singapore." Pp. 626–640 in W. Van Vliet, ed., *International Handbook of Housing Policies and Practices.* New York: Greenwood Press.

————. 1991. *The Urban World.* New York: McGraw-Hill.

Pallas, A., G. Natriello, and E. McDill. 1989. "The Changing Nature of the Disadvantaged

Population: Current Dimensions and Future Challenges." *Educational Researcher* 18: 16–22.

Park, R. 1925. "The City: Suggestions for the Investigations of Human Behavior in the Urban Environment." In R. Park, E. Burgess, and R. McKenzie, eds., *The City*. Chicago: University of Chicago Press.

Peet, R. 1987. *International Capitalism and Industrial Restructuring*. Boston: Allen and Unwin.

Perlman, J. 1976. *The Myth of Marginality*. Berkeley: University of California Press.

Peroff, A. 1987. "Who Are the Homeless and How Many Are There?" Pp. 33–45 in R. Bingham, R. Green, and S. White, eds., *The Homeless in Contemporary Society*. Beverly Hills, CA: Sage.

Pickvance, C. 1977. Ed., *Urban Sociology: Critical Essays*. New York: St. Martin's Press.

Piore, M. and C. Sabel. 1984. *The Second Industrial Divide: Possibilities for Prosperity*. New York: Basic Books.

Piven, F. and R. Cloward. 1977. *Poor People's Movements*. New York: Vintage.

Polsby, N. 1980. *Community Power and Political Theory*. New Haven, CT: Yale University Press.

Population Reference Bureau. 1990. *1990 World Population Sheet*. Washington, DC.

Portes, A. and R. Rumbant. 1990. *Immigrant America: A Portrait*. Berkeley: University of California Press.

Portes, A. and J. Walton. 1981. *Labor, Class, and the International System*. New York: Academic Press.

Pred, A. 1973. *Urban Growth and the Circulation of Information: The United States System of Cities, 1790–1840*. Cambridge, MA: Harvard University Press.

Press Enterprise. 1992, January 19. "School Integration into Revenge." Pp. A1, A7.

———. 1992. "Our Altered Planet." May 17, 1992: AA-1.

Pressman, J. and A. Wildavsky. 1973. *Implementation*. Berkeley: University of California Press.

Pye, R. 1977. "Office Location and the Cost of Maintaining Contact." *Environment and Planning* 9: 149–168.

Quante, W. 1976. *The Exodus of Corporate Headquarters from New York*. New York: Praeger.

Raban, J. 1974. *The Soft City*. New York: Dutton.

Ramirez, R. 1990. "Urbanization, Housing and the (Withdrawing) State: The Production-Reproduction Nexus." Pp. 204–234 in S. Datta, *Third World Urbanization: Reappraisals and New Perspective*. Stockholm: HSFR.

Reckless, W. 1933. *Vice in Chicago*. Chicago: University of Chicago Press.

Reff, T. 1982. *Manet and Modern Paris*. Washington, DC: National Gallery of Art.

Repplier, A. 1898. *Philadelphia: The Place and the People*. New York: Macmillan.

Reynolds. 1980. "Triana, Alabama: The Unhealthiest Town in America." *National Wildlife*. 18 (August).

Riposa, G. 1992. "Urban Empowerment: The Cambodian Struggle for Political Incorporation in California." Working Paper. Department of Political Science, Long Beach State College.

Roberts, B. 1978. *Cities and Peasants: The Political Economy of Peasants in the Third World*. Beverly Hills, CA: Sage.

Roberts, B. 1991. "Household Coping Strategies and Urban Poverty in a Comparative Perspective." Pp. 135–168 in M. Gottdiener and C. Pickvance, *Urban Life in Transition*. Newbury Park, CA: Sage.

Robertson, D. and D. Judd. 1989. *The Development of American Public Policy*. Glenview, IL: Scott, Foresman.

Robertson, I. 1987. *Sociology*. 3rd Ed. New York: Worth.

Rondinelli, D. 1988. "Giant and Secondary City Growth in Africa." Pp. 291–321 in M. Dogan and J. Kasarda, eds., *The Metropolis Era*. Newbury Park, CA: Sage.

Rubin, J. 1970. "Canals, Railroads and Urban Rivalries." Pp. 127–139 in Mohl and Betten, eds., *Urban America in Historical Perspective*. New York: W. and T. Publishers.

Safa, H. 1987. "Urbanization, the Informal Economy and State Policy in Latin America." Pp. 252–274 in M. Smith and J. Feagin, *The Capitalist City*. Oxford: Blackwell.

Sale, K. 1975. *Power Shift: The Rise of the Southern Rim and Its Challenge to the Eastern Establishment*. New York: Random House.

Sandburg, C. 1944. "Chicago." *Chicago Poems*. New York: Harcourt Brace Jovanovich.

Sassen, S. 1989. "New Trends in the Socio-Spatial Organization of the New York Economy." In R. Beauregard, ed., *Economic Restructuring and Political Response*. Newbury Park, CA: Sage.

———. 1991. *The Global City*. Princeton, NJ: Princeton University Press.

Sassen-Koob, S. 1984. "The New International Division of Labor in Global Cities." In M. Smith, ed., *Cities in Transformation*. Beverly Hills, CA: Sage.

Schlyter, A. 1990. "Housing and Gender: Important Aspects of Urbanization." Pp. 235–246 in S. Datta, ed., *Third World Urbanization: Reappraisals and New Perspectives*. Stockholm: HSFR.

Schneier, G. 1990. "Latin America: A Tale of Cities." *International Social Science Journal* 125: 337–354.

Schnore, L. 1957. "Metropolitan Growth and Decentralization." *American Journal of Sociology* 63: 171–180.

———. 1963. "The Socio-Economic Status of Cities and Suburbs." *American Sociological Review* 28: 76–85.

———. 1965. *The Urban Scene*. Glencoe, IL: The Free Press.

Schteingart, M. 1990. "Production and Reproduction Practices in the Informal Sector: The Case of Mexico." Pp. 105–117 in S. Datta, ed., *Third World Urbanization: Reappraisals and New Perspective*. Stockholm: HSFR.

Schwartz, D., P. Ferlauto, and D. Hoffman. 1988. *A New Housing Policy for America: Recapturing the American Dream*. Philadelphia: Temple University Press.

Scott, A. 1980. *The Urban Land Nexus and the State*. London: Pion.

———. 1988. *Metropolis*. Berkeley and Los Angeles: University of California Press.

Scott, J. 1972. *Comparative Political Corruption*. Englewood Cliffs, NJ: Prentice-Hall.

Seeley, J., R. Sim, and E. Looseley. 1956. *Crestwood Heights*. Toronto: University of Toronto Press.

Serrin, W. 1992. *Homestead: The Glory and Tragedy of an American Steel Town*. New York: Times Books.

Sexton, P. 1961. *Education and Income*. New York: Viking Press.

———. 1965. *Spanish Harlem*. New York: Harper and Row.

Shannon, T., N. Kleiniewski, and W. Cross. 1991. *Urban Problems in Sociological Perspective*. 2nd Ed. Prospect Heights, IL: Waveland Press.

Sharpe, W. and L. Wallock. 1987. *Visions of the Modern City.* Baltimore: Johns Hopkins University Press.

———. 1930. *The Jack Roller.* Chicago: University of Chicago Press.

Shover, J. 1976. *First Majority-Last Minority.* DeKalb: North Illinois University Press.

Simmel, G. 1950. "The Metropolis and Mental Life." Pp. 409–424 in K. Wolff, ed., *The Sociology of Georg Simmel.* New York: Free Press.

Simon, D. 1989. "Postcolonial Africa and the World Economy." *International Journal of Urban and Regional Research* 13: 68–92.

Sjoberg. 1960. *The Pre-Industrial City.* New York: Free Press.

Sleeper, J. 1990. *The Closest of Strangers: Liberalism and the Politics of Race in New York.* New York: W.W. Norton.

Smith, C. 1985. "Theories and Methods of Urban Primacy: A Critique." Pp. 87–120 in M. Timberlake, ed., *Urbanization in the World-Economy.* Orlando, FL: Academic Press.

Smith, D. 1992. "Valley of Gloom." *Press Enterprise* October 15, 1992: A1, A7.

Smith, D. and M. Timberlake. 1993. "World Cities: A Political Economy/Global Network Approach." In R. Hutchinson, ed., *Urban Theory in Transition.* Greenwich, CT: JAI.

Smith, M. and J. Feagin. 1987. *The Capitalist City.* Oxford: Blackwell.

Snell, B. 1979. "American Ground Transport." Pp. 239–266 in J. Feagin, ed., *The Urban Scene.* New York: Random House.

Snipp, C. 1989. *American Indians: The First of This Land.* New York: Russell Sage.

South, S. and D. Poston. 1982. "The United States Metropolitan System." *Urban Affairs Quarterly* 18: 187–206.

Sowell, T. 1981. *Ethnic America.* New York: Basic Books.

Spain, D. 1992. *Gendered Spaces.* Chapel Hill: University of North Carolina Press.

Speer, A. 1968. *Black Chicago: The Making of a Negro Ghetto: 1890–1920.* Chicago: University of Chicago Press.

Squires, G. 1991. "Partnership and the Pursuit of the Private City." Pp. 196–221 in M. Gottdiener and C.G. Pickvance, *Urban Life in Transition.* Newbury Park, CA: Sage.

———. 1992. "Economic Development Is Killing Education." *In These Times* December 28: 28–29.

Stack, C. 1974. *All Our Kin: Strategies for Survival in a Black Community.* New York: Harper and Row.

Stahura, J., K. Huff, and B. Smith. 1980. "Crime in the Suburbs." *Urban Affairs Quarterly.* 15 (March): 291–316.

Steele, S. 1990. *The Content of Our Character.* New York: St. Martin's Press.

Stone, C. 1989. *Regime Politics: Governing Atlanta, 1946–1988.* Lawrence, KS: University of Kansas Press.

Storper, M. 1984. "The Spatial Division of Labor: Labor and the Location of Industries." In L. Sawers and W. Tabb, eds., *Sunbelt/Snowbelt.* New York: Oxford University Press.

Storper, M. and R. Walker. 1983. "The Theory of Labor and the Theory of Location." *International Journal of Urban and Regional Research* 7: 1–41.

Strong, A. 1968. *Planned Urban Environments.* Baltimore: Johns Hopkins University Press.

Strong, J. 1891. *Our Country.* New York: Baker and Taylor.

Stubbing, R. and R. Model. 1986. *The Defense Game.* New York: Harper.

Susser, I. 1982. *Norman Street.* New York: Oxford University Press.

Suttles, G. 1972. *The Social Construction of Communities.* Chicago: University of Chicago Press.

———. 1989. *The Man Made City.* Chicago: University of Chicago Press.

Taeuber, K. and A. Taeuber. 1965. *Negroes in Cities: Residential Segregation and Neighborhood Change.* Chicago: Aldine.

Taylor, G. 1915. *Satellite Cities: A Study of Industrial Suburbs.* New York: Appleton.

Taylor, R. 1991. "Urban Communities and Crime." Pp. 106–134 in M. Gottdiener and C.G. Pickvance, *Urban Life in Transition.* Newbury Park, CA: Sage.

Thorne, B. 1993. "Girls and Boys Together . . . But Mostly Apart: Gender Arrangements in Elementary Schools." Pp. 115–126 in C. Richardson and V. Taylor, eds., *Feminist Frontiers III.* New York: McGraw-Hill.

Thrasher, F. 1927. *The Gang.* Chicago: University of Chicago Press.

Tobio, C. 1989. "Economic and Social Restructuring in the Metropolitan Area of Madrid: 1970–85." *International Journal of Urban and Regional Research* 13: 324–335.

United Nations, Department of International and Social Affairs. 1985. *Estimates and Projections of Urban, Rural, and City Populations, 1950–2025: The 1982 Assessment.* (ST/ESA/SER.R./58). New York.

United States Bureau of the Census. 1990. *Census of Population.* Washington, DC: U.S. Government.

USA Today. 1991, November 11. "Segregation: Walls Between Us." Pp. A1–3.

Vance, J. 1977. *This Scene of Man.* New York: Harpers College Press.

———. 1990. *The Continuing City.* Baltimore: Johns Hopkins University Press.

Veblen, T. 1899. *The Theory of the Leisure Class.* New York: Viking Press.

Vigil, J. 1988. *Barrio Gangs: Street Life and Identity in Southern California.* Austin: University of Texas Press.

Wagenknecht, E. 1964. *Chicago.* Norman: University of Oklahoma Press.

Wakefield, D. 1960. *Island in the City.* New York: Citadel Press.

Walloch, L. 1988. Ed., *New York: Culture Capital of the World.* New York: Rizzoli.

Walton, J. 1982. "The International Economy and Peripheral Urbanization." Pp. 119–135 in N. and S. Fainstein, eds., *Urban Policy Under Capitalism.* Beverly Hills: Sage.

———. 1987. "Urban Protest and the Global Political Economy: The IMF Riots." Pp. 364–386 in M. Smith and J. Feagin *The Capitalist City.* Oxford: Blackwell.

Warner, S.B., Jr. 1962. *Streetcar Suburbs.* Cambridge: Harvard University Press.

———. 1968. *The Private City: Philadelphia in Three Periods of Its Growth.* Philadelphia: University of Pennsylvania Press.

Warren, R. and D.I. Warren. 1977. *The Neighborhood Organizer's Handbook.* Notre Dame, IN: Notre Dame University Press.

Weber, A.F. 1899. *The Growth of Cities in the Nineteenth Century.* New York: Macmillan.

Weber, M. 1958. *The Protestant Ethic and The Spirit of Capitalism.* New York: Scribner's.

———. 1966. *The City.* New York: Free Press.

———. 1968. *Economy and Society.* New York: Bedminster Press.

Weiner, M. 1985. "On International Migration and International Relations." *Population and Development Review* 11: 441–455.

Weiss, M. 1987. *The Rise of Community Builders: The American Real Estate Industry and Urban Land Planning.* New York: Columbia University Press.

Weiss, Michael. 1988. *The Clustering of America.* New York: Harper and Row.

Wellman, B. 1979. "The Community Question." *American Journal of Sociology* 84: 1201–1231.

———. 1988. "The Community Question Re-evaluated." Pp. 81–107 in M. Smith, ed., *Power, Community and the City.* New Brunswick, NJ: Transaction.

Wellman, B. and B. Leighton. 1979. "Networks, Neighborhoods and Communities." *Urban Affairs Quarterly* 14: 363–390.

Whitt, J.A. 1982. *Urban Elites and Mass Transportation.* Princeton, NJ: Princeton University Press.

Whyte, M. and W. Parish. 1984. *Urban Life in Contemporary China.* Chicago: University of Chicago Press.

Whyte, W.F. 1955. *Street Corner Society: The Social Structure of an Italian Slum.* Chicago: University of Chicago Press.

Whyte, W.H. 1956. *The Organization Man.* Garden City, NJ: Anchor.

———. 1988. *City: Rediscovering the Center.* New York: Doubleday.

Wilkerson, I. 1991. "How Milwaukee Boomed but Left Blacks Behind." *New York Times* March 19, 1991: A1, D22.

———. 1992. "The Loop Is Still Dark." *Press Enterprise* April 15, 1992: A1, A8.

Williams, T. and W. Kornblum. 1985. *Growing Up Poor.* Lexington, MA: DC Heath.

Wilson, J. 1992. "Anarchy Spreads on Day 2." *Press Enterprise* May 1, 1992: A1.

Wilson, W.J. 1987. *The Truly Disadvantaged.* Chicago: University of Chicago Press.

Wirth, L. 1928. *The Ghetto.* Chicago: University of Chicago Press.

———. 1938. "Urbanism As a Way of Life." *American Journal of Sociology* 44: 3–24.

Wohl, R. and A. Strauss. 1958. "Symbolic Representation and the Urban Milieu." *American Journal of Sociology* 63: 523–532.

Yago, G. 1984. *The Decline of Transit: Urban Transportation in German and United States Cities: 1900–1970.* New York: Cambridge University Press.

Yago, G., H. Korman, S-Y Wu, M. Schwartz. 1984. "Investments and Disinvestment in New York, 1960–1990." *Annals of the American Academy of Political and Social Science.* 475 (September): 28–38.

Yeung, Y. 1988. "Great Cities of Eastern Asia." Pp. 155–186 in M. Dogan and J. Kasarda, eds., *The Metropolis Era.* Newbury Park, CA: Sage.

Zorbaugh, H. 1929. *The Gold Coast and the Slum.* Chicago: University of Chicago Press.

Zukin, S. 1985. "The Regional Challenge to French Industrial Policy." *International Journal of Urban & Regional Research.* 9, 3: 352–367.

ACKNOWLEDGMENTS

Photo Credits

4 Top, Courtesy Naval Research Laboratory; bottom, Julie O'Neil/Stock, Boston   **9** Top, David M. Grossman/Photo Researchers; bottom, Stock, Boston   **15** Peter Menzel/Stock, Boston   **20** Georg Gerster/Comstock   **23** Historical Pictures/Stock Montage   **24** Mary Evans Picture Library/Photo Researchers   **25** Historical Pictures/Stock Montage   **29** Top, Bettmann; bottom, Art Resource   **34** Bettmann   **40** Courtesy The Bostonian Society   **46** Photo Researchers   **52** Bettmann   **54** Bettmann   **58** Bettmann   **60** Bettmann   **71** UPI/Bettmann   **77** UPI/Bettmann   **87** Van Bucher/Photo Researchers   **88** Robert A. Isaacs/Photo Researchers   **91** Francois Gohier/Photo Researchers   **97** Georg Gerster/ Comstock   **102** Photoreporters   **107** Courtesy The University of Chicago Office of Press Relations   **111** Courtesy The University of Chicago Office of Press Relations   **123** Bettmann   **126** Pierre Verdy/AFP Photo   **130** AP/Wide World Photos   **139** Spencer Grant/Stock, Boston   **141** UPI/Bettmann   **149** Ray Ellis/Photo Researchers   **152** Margot Granitsas/ Image Works   **154** Sybil Shackman/Monkmeyer   **160** R.M. Collins III/Image Works   **163** P. Werner/Image Works   **170** Barbara Rios/Photo Researchers   **171** Spencer Grant/ Photo Researchers   **177** Collection of The Whitney Museum of American Art, NY   **188** Jerome Wexler/Photo Researchers   **190** Cary Wolinsky/Stock, Boston   **195** Michael Weisbrot/Stock, Boston   **209** Michael L. Kimble   **211** Reuters/Bettmann   **216** AP/Wide World Photos   **221** AP/Wide World Photos   **224** Rapho/Photo Researchers   **229** Bettmann   **236** AP/Wide World Photos   **242** R. Lord/Image Works   **244** Roberta Hershenson/Photo Researchers   **250** Georg Gerster/Comstock   **254** Arvind Garg/Photo Researchers   **257** Owen Franken/Stock, Boston   **272** Steve Conlan/Select   **277** Superstock   **279** Courtesy The German Information Center   **285** Reuters/Bettmann   **292** AP/Wide World Photos   **297** UPI/Bettmann   **303** Courtesy The Frank Lloyd Wright Foundation   **304** from La Ville Radieuse (1935)   **306** Courtesy The Frank Lloyd Wright Foundation   **321** John A. Jakle and David Wilson, *Derelict Landscapes: The Wasting of America's Built Environment* (Savage, MD: Rowman & Littlefield, 1992)   **328** AP/Wide World Photos   **335** Top, Courtesy The Frank Lloyd Wright Foundation; bottom, Photofest

Illustration and Text Credits

21 Excerpt from D. Fitts, 1966; *Greek Plays in Modern Translation*, p. 156. Reprinted with permission of Holt, Rinehart and Winston.   **35** Excerpt from "Chicago" from *Chicago Poems* by Carl Sandburg, reprinted by permission of Harcourt Brace & Company.
35 Excerpt from G. Keynes, 1977, "London," in William Blake, *Songs of Innocence and Experience.* NY: Oxford University Press.   **48** Excerpt from R. Ernst, 1970, "Immigrants and Tenements in New York City: 1825–1963," pp. 113–126 in R. Mohl and N. Betten, eds.,

357

Urban America in Historical Perspective. NY: W and T Publishers.   **69** Map of electrified trolley routes of Los Angeles © Spencer Crump.   **98** Excerpt from "The Valley of Gloom . . ." reprinted with the permission of *The Press Enterprise.*   **108** Figure 6.1 from Burgess, *The City,* reprinted by permission of the University of Chicago.   **117** Figure 6.4 from Thrasher, *The Gang,* reprinted by permission of the University of Chicago.   **133** David Harvey, *The Urbanization of Capital,* The Johns Hopkins University Press, Baltimore/London, 1983, pp. 72–78. Reprinted by permission of the publisher.   **150** Excerpt from E. Digby Baltzell, *Philadelphia Gentlemen,* reprinted by permission of E. Digby Baltzell.   **155** Excerpt from M. Weiss, 1988, *The Clustering of America.* Reprinted with permission from HarperCollins Publishers.   **155** Excerpt from Jay McInerney; 1984; *Bright Lights, Big City.* Reprinted with permission of Random House Publishers.   **157** Jerry Jacobs, *The Mall: An Attempted Escape from Everyday Life.* Copyright © 1984 by Waveland Press, Inc., Prospect Heights, Illinois.   **157–158** Peter O. Muller, *Contemporary Urban America,* © 1981, pp. 10, 72, 74–75. Adapted by permission of Prentice Hall, Englewood Cliffs, New Jersey.   **159** Excerpt from Whyte, *Street Corner Society,* reprinted by permission from the publisher, the University of Chicago Press.   **161** Excerpt in Box 8.5: Reprinted with the permission of Lexington Books, an imprint of Macmillan, Inc., from *Growing Up Poor* by Terry Williams and William Kornblum. Copyright © 1985 by Lexington Books.   **173** Excerpt from "Wider Mosaic . . ." by Lisa Fodermo, 12/7/91: L-28, copyright © 1991/92 by the New York Times Co. Reprinted by permission.   **179** Excerpt from Herbert J. Gans; 1962; *The Urban Villagers.* Reprinted by permission of The Free Press.   **181** Excerpt from p. 198 of *Social Areas in Cities: Vol II* by D. Herbert and R. Johnston, reprinted by permission of the publisher, David Fulton Publishers.   **185** Excerpt from p. 6 of "Urban Views: Popular Perspectives on City Life," from Urban Life by D. Hummon, reprinted by permission of SAGE Publications.   **225** Excerpt from p. 528 of "Homelessness in the Postindustrial City," from *Urban Affairs Quarterly* by C. Adams, reprinted by permission of SAGE Publications.   **204** Excerpt from the article "Segregation: Walls Between Us, USA at Home: Streets Still Isolate Races." Copyright 1991, USA TODAY. Reprinted with permission.   **207–208** Excerpt from "As Urban Blight Worsens, Victims Find Their Isolation Is Deepening," copyright © 1991/92 by The New York Times Company. Reprinted by permission.   **209** Excerpt from "How Milwaukee Boomed But Left Blacks Behind," copyright © 1991/92 by The New York Times Company. Reprinted by permission.   **211** Excerpt from the article "Anarchy Spreads on Day 2," reprinted by permission from the Associated Press.   **251** Excerpt from pages viii and 16 from Pauline Baker, *Urbanization and Political Change: The Politics of Lagos, 1917–1967.* Copyright © 1974 The Regents of the University of California.   **267** Excerpt from A. Josey, *Singapore,* reprinted by permission of the publisher, Andre Deutsch LTD.   **277** Excerpt from *Manet and Modern Paris,* by T. Reff, © 1992, Board of Trustees, National Gallery of Art, Washington, D.C. Reprinted with permission.   **287** Excerpt from P. Hall; 1966; *The World Cities.* Published by George Weidenfeld and Nicolson, LTD. Publishers.   **300** Excerpt from pp. 307–308 from *City: Rediscovering Its Center* by William Whyte. Copyright © 1989 by William H. Whyte. Used by permission of Doubleday, a division of Bantam Doubleday Dell Publishing Group, Inc.   **310** Excerpt from p. 52, "A Good Place to Live," copyright 1988 by Philip Langdon. Originally published in the March 1988 issue of *The Atlantic Monthly.*   **333** Excerpt from "Toronto and Detroit: Canadians Do It Better," © 1990 The Economist Newspaper Group, Inc. Reprinted with permission. Further reproduction prohibited.

INDEX

Abrams, Charles, 322–323
Abstract space, 127–128
Adams, Carolyn, 225
Addams, Jane, 52
Administration, apparatus of, 230
AFDC (Aid to Families with Dependent Children), 240–241
Africa, 268–269
African Americans, 64, 167–168
  racism and, 203–207
Agora, 23
Agriculture, 103
Agriculture industry, 95
Aid to Families with Dependent Children (AFDC), 240–241
American Dream, 169
Ancient urbanization, 26–28
Anderson, Elijah, 210
Anomic neighborhoods, 196
Antiurban bias in United States, 199–200
Arab cities, 269
Argentina, 261–263
Armour, Philip D., 52
Asia, 263–268
  cities in, 266
Asian immigrants, 235–236
Athens, ancient, 22–23
Auletta, Ken, 156
Auto era city, 68
Aztec cities, 30–31

Badillo, Herman, 238
Balanced urbanization, 62, 255
Baltimore housing market, 133–135
Baltzell, E. Digby, 149–151
Banfield, Edward, 332
Bangkok, 266
Bazaars, 269
Behavior:
  in public space, 188–191
  space and, 177–194
Beijing, 264, 266
  ancient, 25–26
Bellevue, Washington, case, 300–301
Berry, Brian, 118–119
Bible, 20–22
Bibliography, 341–356

Biotic level of urban life, 106
Black empowerment in New York City, 238–239
Blake, William, 35
Blue collar neighborhoods, 77
Bogardus, James, 54
Bombay, 264–265
Bookchin, Murray, 30
Boosterism, 43
Booth, Charles, 35
Borchert, John, 66
Boston, 62
  colonial, 40
Bradley, Tom, 235
Brasília, 305
Braudel, Fernand, 19
Brazil, 261–263
Broadacre City, 306
Budapest, 281–284
Burgess, Ernest W., 106–109
Bush, George, 148

Cairo, 269
Calcutta, 264
California, 96–97
Capital, internationalization of, 252
Capital accumulation, extended conditions of, 123
Capitalism:
  global, 11–12
  industrial cities and, 31–36
  monopoly, 59
  poverty and, 123
Capitalist industrialization, 33
Capitalist system, 12
Castells, Manuel, 131–132
Castelman, Richard, 45
Central Business District (CBD), 108
Central cities, 64
Centralization, 108
Chernobyl, 291–292
Chicago:
  activities in, 175–176
  case study in nineteenth century, 51–53
  Columbian Exhibition, 53
  fire, 52
  gangland, 116–117

Chicago: (*continued*)
  infrastructure crisis in, 221
Chicago School urbanists, 105–115
Childe, V. Gordon, 26–27
China, 263–265
Chinese empire, 28
Chisolm, Shirley, 238
Cities, 11
  Arab, 269
  in Asia, 266
  Aztec, 30–31
  central, 64
  changed, 76–82
  changes in demographic differentiation, 64–65
  changes in functional differentiation, 61–62
  changes in spatial differentiation, 59–60
  classical, 22–26
  concentric zone model, 107–108
  crime in largest, 213, 214
  dual, 82
  early, 22
  in Europe, 32–34
  growth rates by decade, 119
  industrial, capitalism and, 31–36
  Japanese, 287
  primate, 255–256
  satellite, 67
  sector theory of, 109
  service, 81
  social movement in, 236–237
  Sunbelt, 79
  system of, 61
  transnational corporate headquarters in, 273
  U.S. Colonial, 39–41
  U.S. (*see* United States cities)
  world's largest, 10
  (*See also* Urban *entries*)
City council hall, 23
City government, 227–247
City managers, 231
Class accumulation theories, 132–138
Class conflict theories, 128–132
Class differences, spatial location and, 147–156
Class stratification, in United States, 147–148
Classical cities, 22–26
Cleveland, 8
Clinton, Bill, 330–331
Cocaine, 216
Colonial Period in United States, 38–44

Colonialism, 254
Columbia, Maryland, 310
Columbian Exhibition, Chicago, 53
Commodity production, 32
Commons, tragedy of the, 316–317
Communism, fall of, 283
Community:
  field research on, 178–180
  neighboring and, 191–194
  search for, 177–182
Community benefits, lack of, from public investment, 328–329
Community interaction, types of, 194–197
Community power structure, 232
Competing commitments, 192
Competition:
  cutthroat, fostering of, 329–330
  global, support for, 325–327
Compositional approach, 201
Compositional factors, 180, 182
Concentric zone model for cities, 107–108
Congestion, traffic, 99
Conservative positions on urban problems, 331–332
Conspicuous consumption, 66, 149–151
Contemporary urban sociology, 121–146
Corporate headquarters, 89
  transnational, 273
Corporation, municipal, 227
Crime, 99, 211–217
  drugs and, 215–217
  in largest cities, 213, 214
  property, 212
  suburban, 217
  as urban problem, 215
  violent, 212
Crump, Spencer, 69
Cultural level of urban life, 106
Culture:
  metropolitan, sociospatial approach to, 182–184
  in metropolitan life, 14–16
  Paris and, 277
Cuomo, Mario, 238
Cutthroat competition, fostering of, 329–330
Czech Republic, 281–282

Damascus, 29
Das Silvas, Beneditas, 260
Decentralization, 108
Decline, cycles of growth and, 98
Deconcentration, 75
  economic, 86–89

Deconcentration: (*continued*)
  of industry, 67
  process of, 336
Defended neighborhoods, 196
Deindustrialization, 75, 76, 208
Delhi, 264–265
Demand-side view, 13
Democracy, decline of, in local politics,
  330–331
Demographic differentiation, city changes in,
  64–65
Demographic transition, 253
Demography, third world urbanization and,
  253–255
Depression, Great, 57, 70–71
Deterioration of urban infrastructure, 220–
  221
Detroit, 8, 59, 76, 79, 333
Development:
  economic, support for, 324
  land, 46–48
  uneven, 81–82, 124–125, 317–319
  urbanized, 3
Diffuse neighborhoods, 196
Dinkins, David, 235, 236, 239
Dinks, 152
Disintegration, vertical, 136–137
Disneyland, 97
Disorganization, social (*see* Social disorgani-
  zation *entries*)
Domestic labor, 161–162
Douglass, Frederick, 44
Drugs, crime and, 215–217
Dual cities, 82
Duany, Andres, 308
Durkheim, Emile, 27, 31, 101
Dystopia, 301

E/R (employment/residence) ratio, 85
Earnings, average hourly, 130
Eastern Europe:
  emergence of free markets in, 284
  housing shortage in, 283–284
  urbanization in, 281–284
Ecological approach, 11
Ecological perspective in urban sociology,
  115–119
Ecology, human, 105
Economic activity, 11
Economic deconcentration, 86–89
Economic development, support for, 324
Economic restructuring and problems of
  poor, 208

Economic return, lack of, on public invest-
  ment, 329
Economy:
  global, 144–145
  impersonal money, 104
  informal, 82, 257–259
  market, 258
Education, urban, crisis of, 219–220
El Capitan Hotel, 46
Elite theory of local politics, 232–233
Elitist/populist dilemma, 299
Employment/residence (E/R) ratio, 85
Empowerment:
  black, in New York City, 238–239
  ethnic and racial changes in, 235–236
Engels, Friedrich, 34–35, 101, 122–124
Environment, women and, 163–164
Environmental costs of rapid growth, 99
Environmental issues, 291–296
Environmental Protection Agency (EPA),
  294
Environmental quality, 293–296
EPA (Environmental Protection Agency), 294
Era of Expansion, U.S., 44–55
Erie Canal, 47
Ethnic changes in empowerment, 235–236
Ethnic groups, segregated metro areas by,
  204–206
Ethnic suburbs, 172–173
Ethnic urban village, 195
Ethnicity, 164–165
  immigration and, 164–174
  spatial segregation and, 167–169
Etruscans, 22
Euripides, 20–22
Europe:
  Eastern (*see* Eastern Europe)
  growth of cities in, 32–34
  Western, urbanization in, 271–281
Examples of everyday urban life, 1–3
Exclusionary zoning, 85, 222–223
Extended commodity production, 32
Extended conditions of capital accumulation,
  123

Factory towns, 59
Falling Water House, 305
Fannie Mae program, 72
Feagin, Joe R., 66, 95, 140, 233
Federal Housing Authority (FHA), 71
Federal National Mortgage Association (Fan-
  nie Mae), 72
Federal republic, power in, 227

FHA (Federal Housing Authority), 71
Field, Marshall, 51
Field research on community, 178–180
Financial conduits, 141
Fiscal crisis, 217–219
  public service problems and, 217–221
Fiscal discrimination, 219
Fischer, Claude, 180, 201
Forbidden City, 25–26
Ford, Henry, 166
Ford Motor Plant, 60
Fordism, 72, 251
Fortresses, 43
France, 276–278
Free markets, emergence in Eastern Europe
  of, 284
Frey, William, 72
Functional differentiation, city changes in,
  61–62
Future prospects:
  of metropolis, 334–338
  for urban sociology, 334–339

Gangland Chicago case study, 116–117
Gans, Herbert J., 178, 179, 201
Garden City, 302–303
Gasoline tax, 84
Gender roles, space and, 156, 158–164
Gentrification, 152–153
Germany, 278–280
Ghettoization, 210
Ghettoized poor, 156, 161
Ginnie Mae program, 72
Ginza district in Tokyo, 15
Global capitalism, 11–12
Global competition, support for, 325–327
Global economy, 144–145
Goffman, Erving, 189
Goodman, Paul and Percival, 309
Gordon, David, 128
Government:
  city, 227–247
  in space, 127
Government intervention, 319–327
  political agency and, 143–144
  real estate and, 139–144
Government National Mortgage Association
  (Ginnie Mae), 72
Grassroots mobilization, 295
Great Britain, 273–275
Great Depression, 57, 70–71
Growth:
  and decline, cycles of, 98

Growth: (continued)
  rapid, environmental costs of, 99
  real estate and, 13–14
  real estate investment and, 141–143
  urban (see Urban growth)
Growth control movements, 240–242
Growth machine, 138–139
Growth networks, 43, 143
Growth poles, high tech, 87–88

Habitat, term, 116
Hannerz, Ulf, 178, 181
Harvey, David, 132–136
Hawley, Amos, 66, 116–118
Headquarters, corporate, 89
  transnational, 273
Henslin, J., 190
Heterotopias, 301–302
High tech growth poles, 87–88
Highway fund, 84
Hinterland, 20
Home mortgage subsidy, 84
Home ownership, 66
Homelessness, 223–225
Homes, single-family, 65
Hong Kong, 9, 266
Horizontal integration, 136
Households, third world, 257–258
Housing, 222–225
  public, 322–323
  shortage in Eastern Europe, 283–284
  suburban, 222–223
  and Urban Development Department
    (HUD), 320
Houston, 94, 95–96
Howard, Ebenezer, 302–303
Hoyt, Homer, 109
HUD (Housing and Urban Development De-
  partment), 320
Human ecology, 105
Hummon, David, 185
Hungary, 281–284
Hunter, Albert, 194
Hunter, Floyd, 232

Illinois Central Railroad, 48
IMF (International Monetary Fund), 260
Immigrant adjustment, theories of, 166–170
Immigrants, Asian, 235–236
Immigration, 50, 54
  ethnicity and, 164–174
  waves of, 165–173
Impersonal money economy, 104

India, 30, 263–265
Indian Removal Act, 169
Indonesia, 266
Industrial cities, capitalism and, 31–36
Industrial parks, 87
Industrialization:
  capitalist, 33
  manufacturing and, 49–50
Industrialized world, urbanization in, 271–289
Industry:
  agriculture, 95
  deconcentration of, 67
Influence, phenomenon of, 232
Informal economy, 82, 257–259
Infrastructure, 227
  urban, deterioration of, 220–221
Institutional racism, 204
Integration, horizontal, 136
Interactionist perspective, 114
Interactive middle-class neighborhoods, 195–196
International division of labor, 129
International Monetary Fund (IMF), 260
International Style of design, 303–305
Internationalization of capital, 252
Intervention, government (*see* Government intervention)
Introversion technique, 187
Investment, public (*see* Public investment)
Islamic civilization, 269
Italy, 275–276

Jackson, Jesse, 239
Jackson, Kenneth, 65
Jackson, Maynard, 235
Jacobs, Jane, 307–308
Japan, 266
  urbanization in, 284–288
Japanese cities, 287
Jefferson, Thomas, 37
Jencks, Christopher, 318
Jenny, William L., 55
Jericho, 27
Job loss, 202
Justice, social, privatism and, 327–331

Kasarda, John, 118–119
Keller, Susanne, 192
Kenya, 268
King, Desmond, 326
King, Rodney, 211
Knossos, 19

Koch, Ed, 235, 238–239
Kornblum, William, 161
Krier, Leon, 308–309

La Guardia, Fiorello, 63
Labor:
  domestic, 161–162
  international division of, 129
Labor force participation of women, 159–160
Lagos, Nigeria, 249–251
Land development, 46–48
Land use planning, sociology of, 298–300
Latin America, 261–263
Lawrence, Massachusetts, 34
Le Corbusier, 303–305
Lefebvre, Henri, 125–128, 301
Leisure, symbols of, 150
Lemann, Nicholas, 64
Lenox Square Shopping Center, 87
Lévi-Strauss, Claude, 186–187
Levitt, Abraham, 70
Levitt, William J., 71
Levittown, Long Island, 70–71
Liberal positions on urban problems, 331
Local politics, 227–247
  decline of democracy in, 330–331
  declining power of, 244–246
  drama of, 235–243
  theories of, 231–235
Logan, John, 138
London, 29, 273–274
Long-term debt, 217
Los Angeles, 5–7
  trolley routes and auto highways in, 69
Love Canal, 291
Lowell, Massachusetts, 49
Lynch, Kevin, 184

Machines, political, 228–229
Madrid, 280
Malaysia, 266
Malls, shopping, 86
  suburban, 186–188
Managerialism, state, in local politics, 233–234
Managers, city, 231
Manet, Edouard, 277
Manhattan street behavior, 183
Manufacturing:
  decline of, 87–89
  industrialization and, 49–50

Manufacturing: (*continued*)
  shift from, to service industries, 77–81
Maquilladoras systems, 262
Market economy, 258
Marx, Karl, 27, 32, 103–105, 122
Mayhew, Henry, 35
Mayors, minority, 81
McCormick, Cyrus, 45, 51
McInerney, Jay, 155
McKenzie, Roderick, 106
Meaning, social, 183
Megacities, 8–10
Megamalls, 86
Melting pot theory, 167–170
Mental maps, 184, 186–187
Mercantilism, 38–39
Metropolis, future prospects of, 334–338
Metropolitan culture, sociospatial approach
  to, 182–184
Metropolitan life, culture in, 14–16
Metropolitan period in United States, 57–73
Metropolitan planning, 296–297
Metropolitan problems (*see* Urban problems)
Metropolitan regions, 3–5
  defining, 7–8
  multinucleated, 5
  twenty most populated, 6
Metropolitan Statistical Area (MSA), 7–8
Mexican Americans, 168–169
Mexico, 261–263
Mexico City, 261
Middle-class neighborhoods, interactive,
  195–196
Middle-class suburban living, 153, 157
Middle East, 28–30, 269
Military spending in Sunbelt, 96
Minority mayors, 81
Minority population, increasing, 81
Minority women, 160
Modernism, 304
Modernity, 103
Mohenjo-Daro, 19
Molotch, Harvey, 138
Money economy, impersonal, 104
Monkkonen, Eric, 38
Monopoly capitalism, 59
Mortgage, home, subsidy, 84
Moscow, 281–284
MSA (Metropolitan Statistical Area), 7–8
Muller, Peter, 5, 158
Multicentered approach, 109–110
Multinucleated metropolitan regions, 5
Multinucleated regions, 89–90
Mumford, Lewis, 3

Municipal corporation, 227

Nader, Ralph, 326–327
Nash, Gary, 44
Nassau-Suffolk Counties, New York, 90
National Welfare Rights Organization
  (NWRO), 241
Native Americans, 169
Neighborhoods:
  anomic, 196
  defended, 196
  diffuse, 196
  interactive middle-class, 195–196
  transitory, 196
  types of, 194–197
Neighboring, community and, 191–194
Network analysis, 180–182
New York City:
  black empowerment in, 238–239
  colonial, 41
  fiscal crisis in, 218
  Hong Kong and, 9
  lower East side, 54
  in metropolitan period, 63
  Park Avenue, 58
Nigeria, 268
Nodal services, 76
North Korea, 266
NWRO (National Welfare Rights Organization), 241

Oakland County, Michigan, 90
Orange County, California, 90
Osaka, 285
Otis, Elisha, 55
Overurbanization, 255
Ownership, home, 66

Pacific Rim, 268
Paris, culture and, 277
Park, Robert E., 101, 103, 105–107
Pendergast, Jim, 228–229
Penn, William, 40
Peripheral urbanization concept, 251
Philadelphia, 8, 83
  case study of colonial, 45
  colonial, 39
  wealthy in, 150–151
Philippines, 266
Phoenix, 8, 76, 90–91
Physicalist fallacy, 299
Pinkerton, Allan, 52

Pittsburgh, 78
Place, semiotics of, 186–188
Planning:
    land use, sociology of, 298–300
    metropolitan, 296–297
    politics of, 299
    trends in, 309–311
    in United States, 297–298
Planning critics, 307–309
Planning paradox, 297
Plater-Zyberk, Elizabeth, 308
Pluralist theory of local politics, 232
Poland, 281–284
Political agency, government intervention
    and, 143–144
Political debate on urban policy, 331–334
Political economy of real estate, 13–16
Political machines, 228–229
Political progressive reforms, 230–231
Politics:
    local (see Local politics)
    of planning, 299
    urban social movements and, 259–261
Poor:
    ghettoized, 156, 161
    problems of, economic restructiring and,
        208
Population, minority, increasing, 81
Population churning, 50
Population deconcentration, 75
Population growth, Sunbelt cities, 92
Population segregation, 203
Post-fordism, 275, 278, 280
Postmodern architecture, 308
Poverty, 207–208
    capitalism and, 123
    racism and, 208–211
Powell, Adam Clayton, 238
Power, declining, of local politics, 244–246
Power structure, community, 232
Prague, 281–282
"Primary" relations, 103
Primate cities, 255–256
Privatism, 42, 315
    dominance of, 245–246
    social justice and, 327–331
Profit, pursuit of, 12
Progressive reforms, political, 230–231
Property crime, 212
Pruitt-Igoe housing project, 296–297
Public housing, 322–323
Public investment:
    lack of community benefits from, 328–329
    lack of economic return on, 329

Public space, behavior in, 188–191

Quality, environmental, 293–296
Questionnaire and interview method, 185

Racial changes, 81
    in empowerment, 235–236
Racial groups, segregated metro areas by,
        204–206
Racial harmony demonstration, 242
Racism, 72–73, 203–207
    institutional, 204
    poverty and, 208–211
Radiant City, 304
Rail corridor city, 68
Railroads, 47–48
Real estate, 14
    government intervention and, 139–144
    growth and, 13–14
    political economy of, 13–16
    Sunbelt and, 144–145
Real estate investment, growth and, 141–143
Realms, 5
Redistributive programs, 317–319
Reductionism, technological, 118
Reformist efforts, 114
Reforms, progressive political, 230–231
Regional maturation, suburbanization and,
        65–73
Reisenbach, John, 211–212
Rentier class, 138
Representation, apparatus of, 230
Retailing, 86
Revolutionary War, 41
Ricardo, David, 136
Riposa, Gerry, 235–236
Roman Forum, 24
Rome, ancient, 19, 23–24
Rouse, James, 310
Rupert, Jacob, 63
Russia, 281–284
Ruth, Babe, 63

San Francisco, 48–49
    metropolitan region, 4
San Jose, 62
Sandburg, Carl, 35
Santa Clara County, California, 98
Sassen, Saskia, 274
Satellite cities, 67
Satellite image of United States, 4
Schnore, Leo, 64, 84–85, 118

Science parks, 87
Scott, Allen J., 136–137, 138
"Secondary" relations, 103
Sector theory of cities, 109
Segregated metro areas, 204–206
Segregation:
  population, 203
  spatial, and ethnicity, 167–169
  in suburbs, 206
Semiotics, 15
  of place, 186–188
Seoul, 266
Serfs, 32
Service cities, 81
Service industries, shift from manufacturing
    to, 77–81
SES (socioeconomic status), 148
Settlement spaces, 16–17
  multicentered mode of, 337
  restructuring of, 75–99
Shanghai, 264, 265–266
Shantytowns, 254
  development of, 256–257
Sharpton, Al, 238–239
Shelter life, 224
Shopping malls, 86
  suburban, 186–188
Short-term debt, 217–218
Silicon Valley, 87–88, 124–125
Simmel, Georg, 101–106
Sinclair, Upton, 52
Singapore, 266, 267
Single-family homes, 65
Skyscrapers, 55
Sleeper, Jim, 239
Slum removal, support for, 320–324
SMA (Standard Metropolitan Area), 7
Small, Albion, 101
SMCA (Standard Metropolitan Consolidated
    Area), 8
Smith, 99
SMSA (Standard Metropolitan Statistical
    Area), 7
  characteristics, suburban, 84–86
  disorganization, 200
  disorganization thesis of urban life,
    8
Social dumping, 281
Social justice, privatism and, 327–331
Social meaning, 183
Social movements:
  class, 236–237
  urban, 237, 240–243
  (see Urban social movements)

Social services:
  cutbacks in, 219–221
  suburban, crisis of, 243
Social space, 127–128
Socioeconomic status (SES), 148
Sociological perspectives, 138–144
Sociology of land use planning, 298–300
Sociospatial approach, 16–17, 121–122
  to metropolitan culture, 182–184
Sociospatial perspective (SSP), 139–144,
    182, 201–202
  future of, 338–339
Sociospatial terms, 114
Sons of Liberty, 41–42
South Korea, 266
Space:
  abstract, 127–128
  behavior and, 177–194
  gender roles and, 156, 158–164
  government in, 127
  public, behavior in, 188–191
  social, 127–128
  term, 116
Spain, 280
Spatial differentiation, city changes in, 59–
    60
Spatial location, class differences and, 147–
    156
Spatial segregation and ethnicity, 167–169
Spatial semiotics, 16
Spencer, Herbert, 106
Spies, August, 53
Squatting phenomenon, 224
Squires, Gregory, 245
SSP (see Sociospatial perspective)
Standard Metropolitan Area (SMA), 7
Standard Metropolitan Consolidated Area
    (SMCA), 8
Standard Metropolitan Statistical Area
    (SMSA), 7
Stanford, Leland, 46
State managerialism in local politics, 233–
    234
Steele, Shelby, 332
Steering mechanism, 204
Stein, Clarence, 302
Stone, Clarence, 232
Storper, Michael, 128–129
Stratification, 148
Street behavior, Manhattan, 183
Strikes, worker participation in, 128
Studio Colony, 311
Subcultural view, 201
Subcultures, 15

Suburban crime, 217
Suburban housing, 222–223
Suburban living, middle-class, 153, 157
Suburban shopping mall, 186–188
Suburban social characteristics, 84–86
Suburban social movements, 237, 240–243
Suburban social services, crisis of, 243
Suburbanization, 76
    push and pull factors in, 83–84
    regional maturation and, 65–73
    timing of, 118–119
Suburbs:
    changes in, 82–89
    ethnic, 172–173
    growth rates by decade, 119
    segregation in, 206
Subways, 55
Sunbelt:
    cities in, 79
    defined, 90
    metropolitan regional growth for, 93
    military spending in, 96
    population growth for cities in, 92
    push and pull factors in development of,
        94–97
    real estate and, 144–145
    recent trends in, 97–99
    shift to, 90–99
Supply-side view, 13
Susser, Ida, 192–193
Suttles, Gerald, 11, 196
Swift, Gustavas F., 52
System of cities, 61

Tax revolts, 242–243
Taylor, Graham, 67
Technological reductionism, 118
Technology, 293–294
Tenements, 49, 54
Territory, term, 116
Tesla, Nikola, 55
Texas, 94
Thailand, 266
Third world households, 257–258
Third world urban social movements, 259–
    261
Third world urbanization, 249–270
    changing perspectives on, 249–253
    demography and, 253–255
    patterns of, 261–269
Thrasher, Frederick M., 114–115, 116–117
Three Mile Island, 292
Tianjin, 264

Tokyo, 266, 284–288
    Ginza district, 15
Tonnies, Ferdinand, 31
Toronto, 333
Toscanini, Arturo, 63
Towns, factory, 59
Traffic congestion, 99
Traffic controls, struggle for, 237, 240
Tragedy of the commons, 316–317
Transitory neighborhoods, 196
Transnational corporate headquarters, 273
Transport, urban, 55
Transportation technology, 48
Turin, 276
Tweed, Boss, 228–229

Underclass, 156, 209–210
Uneven development, 124–125, 317–319
United Kingdom, 273–275
United States, 37
    anti-urban bias in, 199–200
    cities in (see United States cities)
    class stratification in, 147–148
    Colonial Period, 38–44
    Era of Expansion, 44–55
    metropolitan period in, 57–73
    planning in, 297–298
    satellite image of, 4
    stages of urban growth in, 37–38
    urbanization in, 37–55
United States cities:
    ten most populated, 5
    twenty-four most populated, 80
Up-zoning, 242
Upper classes, 148–152
Urban agglomerations (see Cities)
Urban education, crisis of, 219–220
Urban expansion, 57
Urban growth, stages of, in United States,
    37–38
Urban implosion, 33
Urban infrastructure, deterioration of, 220–
    221
Urban inquiry, future of, 338–339
Urban life:
    examples of everyday, 1–3
    social disorganization thesis of, 178
Urban policy, political debate on, 331–334
Urban political economy, women and, 158–
    163
Urban problems, 199–225
    conservative positions on, 331–332
    crime as, 215

Urban problems: (*continued*)
  liberal positions on, 331
  theories of, 200–203
Urban renewal program, 320
Urban revolution, 26
Urban social movements, 237
  and politics, 259–261
Urban sociology, 103
  contemporary, 121–146
  ecological perspective in, 115–119
  future of, 315–339
  future prospects for, 334–339
  new approach to, 11–16
  rise of, 101–119
Urban transport, 55
Urban village, ethnic, 195
Urbanism, 102, 106
  effects of, 182
  factors in, 111
  new theory of, 182–194
Urbanists, Chicago School, 105–115
Urbanization, 11, 19, 102
  after A.D. 1000, 28–33
  ancient, 26–28
  balanced, 62, 255
  early, 22–26
  in Eastern Europe, 281–284
  in industrialized world, 271–289
  in Japan, 284–288
  origins of, 19–22
  third world (*see* Third world urbanization)
  in United States, 37–55
  in Western Europe, 271–281
Urbanized development, 3
U.S. (*see* United States)
Utopia, 301
Utopian schemes, 301–307

Vance, James, 49
Veblen, Thorstein, 66, 149
Vertical disintegration, 136–137
Village, ethnic urban, 195
Violent crime, 212
Voter turnout, 244

Wade, Richard C., 44
Wagenknecht, Edward, 52
Walker, David, 128–129
War on Poverty, 207, 240
Warner, Sam Bass, Jr., 42
Warren, Donald and Rachelle, 194–195
Warsaw, 281–284
Washington, George, 43–44
Wealthy, 148–152
Webb, Wellington, 235
Weber, Max, 27, 31, 101–102, 122
Welfare rights, campaign for, 240–241
Wellman, Barry, 180
Western Europe, urbanization in, 271–281
Weusi, Jitu, 238
Whyte, William F., 158–159
Whyte, William H., 178
Williams, Terry, 161
Wilson, James Q., 212
Wilson, William J., 156, 207, 209
Wirth, Louis, 110–112, 114, 177, 201
Wirthian theory, 201
Women:
  environment and, 163–164
  gender roles and space and, 156, 158–164
  labor force participation of, 159–160
  minority, 160
  urban political economy and, 158–163
Worker participation in strikes, 128
Working class, 154, 156, 158–159
Working poor, 154, 156
World Trade Center, 326–327
Wright, Frank Lloyd, 305–306

Yew, Lee Kwan, 267
Young, Coleman, 235
Youngstown, Ohio, plant closures at, 77, 78–79
Yuppies, 152–153, 155

Zoning, 298
  exclusionary, 85, 222–223
  up-zoning, 242